ALL AMERICAN
MAFIOSO

DOUBLEDAY

NEW YORK   LONDON   TORONTO

SYDNEY   AUCKLAND

ALL AMERICAN MAFIOSO

The Johnny Rosselli Story

CHARLES RAPPLEYE
and ED BECKER

PUBLISHED BY DOUBLEDAY
a division of Bantam Doubleday Dell Publishing Group, Inc.
666 Fifth Avenue, New York, New York 10103

DOUBLEDAY and the portrayal of an anchor with a dolphin are
trademarks of Doubleday, a division of Bantam Doubleday Dell
Publishing Group, Inc.

DESIGNED BY ANNE LING

Library of Congress Cataloging-in-Publication Data

Rappleye, Charles.
　　All American mafioso: the Johnny Rosselli story / by Charles
Rappleye and Ed Becker.—1st ed.
　　　　p.　　cm.
　　Includes bibliographical references.
　　1. Rosselli, Johnny. 2. Criminals—United States—Biography.
3. Mafia—United States—History. I. Becker, Ed. II. Title.
HV6248.R685R36　1991
364.1′ 092—dc20
[B]　　　　　　　　　　　　　　　　　　　　　　　90-28417
　　　　　　　　　　　　　　　　　　　　　　　　　CIP

ISBN 0-385-26676-6

September 1991

1　3　5　7　9　10　8　6　4　2

First Edition

For Gale and Barbara

PREFACE

In my lifetime I have associated with presidents and kings, motion picture and television stars, religious leaders and mobsters, the rich and the poor, and the middle-class majority of which I am a part. And yet, of the hundreds of people I have met, vivid memories remain of a man who projected both good and evil and was murdered for one or the other.

I first met the man I knew as John Rosselli in the latter part of the 1950s in Las Vegas, where I handled both public relations and entertainment for the Riviera Hotel.

During that period a group of businessmen were developing plans for a major new hotel, to be called the Tropicana, and met routinely for dinner in our Embers Room. On occasion these investors were joined by a handsome, well-dressed man who favored dark glasses, even at dinner. His style and his manner gave the immediate impression that this man had power, and knew how to use it. The other members of the group treated him with deference, and I soon learned that he had contacts with organized crime figures across the country.

John and I eventually came to know each other on a first-name basis. Nothing important, nothing deep, and no questions about his business were ever asked by me. He was very knowledgeable about entertainers and indicated he personally knew many top stars. For about a year I would join him for drinks when I ran into him; we developed a passing acquaintance-ship.

My tenure at the hotel ended in December 1958, when my friend and boss, Gus Greenbaum, and his wife were brutally murdered in their Phoenix home. Along with the other executives of the hotel I submitted an immediate resignation. Ironically, the killing launched my career as an investigative researcher when I served as the source for the *Reader's Digest* exposé on Greenbaum and the mob in Las Vegas. It was almost six years later that I realized that Rosselli likely had a hand in the Greenbaum slaying, but when I foolishly put the question to him directly, he erupted angrily, denying his involvement and warning me, "I don't want to hear anything more about it."

Our paths crossed several times over the years following Greenbaum's death, while I pursued a number of ventures in business and entertainment, and developed a sideline as a private investigator. I bumped into Rosselli at the Friars Club in Los Angeles, where he used the sauna whenever he was in town. Then, in the early 1960s, I hooked up with Ed Reid, an award-winning reporter from the Brooklyn *Eagle,* who was working on a book about the mob in Las Vegas with Boston journalist Ovid Demaris. It was while working as a researcher and writer for Ed Reid on his book, *The Green Felt Jungle,* that I saw Rosselli's testimony before the Kefauver hearings on organized crime. I was shocked to learn how much I had underrated his position and connections. Publication of *The Green Felt Jungle* left Rosselli incensed at Reid, but he remained cordial in his relations with me, and several years later he surprised me by requesting my assistance in a criminal case.

Rosselli had been charged by the federal government for failure to obtain citizenship after his immigration from Italy. He said he knew that I had good newspaper contacts in Washington and asked me to speak with his attorney, Jimmy Cantillon, who in turn persuaded me to find out what I could about the government's case. By the time the case came to trial I had been drafted onto the defense team.

As the trial got under way, I asked John what he thought of his chances. His eyes narrowed and a flash of real anger crossed his face as he told me, "I shouldn't even be here, much less be on trial. I did some very heavy work for this country, and they owe me."

"When was that, Johnny?" I pressed. "Do you mean when you were in the Army?"

"No," he replied. "It was when I worked for the CIA." He then gave me the name of Bob Maheu, a mutual friend, and told me to check with him. A few weeks later I put the question to Maheu, and he quickly answered, in that booming voice of his, "I can't discuss that because it concerns my country." I knew instantly Rosselli had been telling me the truth.

The trial went badly for Rosselli, and I lost contact with him when he went off to prison. The next I heard he had turned up, murdered, in Miami. Truncated accounts of Rosselli's exploits were published here and there, but the story of his life never came to light. It wasn't until after Rosselli's murder, when I had opened up a political consulting office in Washington, D.C., that I became aware through Joe Shimon, a mutual friend, that there was more to Rosselli's association with the CIA and of his abiding patriotic fervor for his adopted country. I knew the awful things that Rosselli and his associates were capable of, but I also knew his charm, his grace and generosity, and that whatever else, the government that had recruited him had turned on him in the end. It came to haunt me, an amazing tale of crime and complicity, of punishment and betrayal.

It was in Los Angeles that an old friend, former FBI field investigator Julian Blodgett, introduced me to Charles Rappleye, a free-lance journalist who had just completed a Master's Degree in nonfiction writing at the University of Southern California. We opened an office together and soon he was as fascinated with the Rosselli story as I have been for the past twenty years. We determined to do all the research we could, to let the story tell itself, and to let the chips lay where they fell. After three years of digging, after scores of interviews and a hundred dead ends, this is the result.

ED BECKER
Las Vegas
January 1991

INTRODUCTION

John Rosselli worked most of his days to see that his occupation, his travels, his friendships, even his nationality, would remain obscure. Yet by the time of his death, the crimes and conspiracies he was party to, and for which he was investigated or prosecuted, had established him as a crucial figure in the annals of twentieth-century crime and politics. Rosselli's scheme to extort millions of dollars from the Hollywood film studios was exposed in a sensational federal trial, his involvement in the plots against Fidel Castro was the subject of intensive inquiry by the Church Committee and later the House Assassinations Committee, and his connections to Judith Campbell Exner and the Kennedy clan fascinated a generation of investigative journalists. Before we commenced our work on this project, Rosselli's name was recorded in the index of more than one hundred books, with titles ranging from *Crime Movies* to *Citizen Hughes*, and including most of the literature on the Bay of Pigs and the Kennedy assassination.

As a result, much of this story has been told before, in bits and pieces scattered across fifty years of publishing. Still, until now, Rosselli was usually mentioned as a footnote, a historical curio whose presence raised eyebrows but was quickly dismissed as anomalous to the course of events. What follows represents the first full examination of Rosselli's life and career, tracing his evolution from rough-mannered immigrant to a crime chieftain whose activities touched on the course of history.

The focus of our interest was always Rosselli himself, a man of charm and contradiction, a professional criminal who lived by a strict moral code, whose path crisscrossed the continent and spanned the heyday of organized crime. We were determined to expand on the published record, and our research bore fruit in various and often unexpected ways. We learned for the first time the depth of his involvement in the film industry; the key role he played in the political life of prewar Los Angeles; his clandestine work for American interests in Central America and the Caribbean; his close, personal relationship with Judy Campbell. We found that Rosselli's work as an intelligence operative in the campaign against Castro went far beyond the particulars laid out by the Church Committee, and that the Kennedys, Bobby in particular, took extraordinary steps to conceal their knowledge of those activities. Finally, we reached the conclusion that while Rosselli may not have had a hand in the shooting of John Kennedy, he carried out a concerted disinformation campaign designed to deflect the subsequent investigations into the assassination. All of this material is detailed in the pages that follow, and to that extent, this book is an exposé.

But it was clear to us early on that this work would comprise more than a compendium of facts about a well-traveled gangster. Rosselli's rise was inextricably intertwined with the creation of the American myth on the sound stages of Hollywood, and with the nation's emergence as a modern world power. Viewed through the lens of his life, the epoch that some have dubbed "the American Century" takes on a new cast, more disturbing and yet more coherent than the transient appellations of New Frontier, Great Society, and Morning in America. From Ellis Island to the halls of Congress, from the neon lights of Las Vegas to the shadowy intrigues of Miami, Rosselli was truly the All American Mafioso.

ACKNOWLEDGMENTS

The Johnny Rosselli story could not have been told without the generous and sometimes courageous assistance of those who knew him and the circles in which he traveled, and who agreed to be interviewed for this book. They included Jack Anderson, Bryn Armstrong, Bradley Earl Ayers, Vincent Barbi, Frederick Baron, Alfred Barrett, Ben Batchelder, Fred Black, George Bland, Patricia Breen, Nancy Bretzfield, David Bushong, Joaun Cantillon, Jeanne Carmen, Ralph Clare, Grant Cooper, Refugio Cruz, Harry Drucker, Father George Dunne, Harold and Carmel Fitzgerald, Irving Foy, Jimmy Fratianno, William P. Gray, Matt Gregory, Betsy Duncan Hammes, Gary Hart, Nieson Himmel, Jean Howard, Allen Jarlsen, Boris Kostelanetz, Charles Ed "The Hat" Krebs, Jean La Vell, Dorothy Lewin, Ed Lutes, David MacMichael, Robert Maheu, Ralph Manza, Ernest Marquez, Sam Marx, Johnny Maschio, Frank McCulloch, David Nissen, Madeline Foy O'Donnell, John Oldrate, Richard Olsen, Fred

Otash, Roger Otis, Rafael Pagan, Marion Phillips, Tom Pryor, Dick Richards, Felix Rodriguez, Sig Rogich, Gloria Romanoff, Leslie Scherr, Frederick A. O. Schwarz, Jr., Richard Schweiker, Budd Schulberg, Leon Schwab, Joe Seide, Robert Slatzer, Sheldon Sloan, Jimmy Starr, Herb Tobhman, Gerald Uelmen, Jimmy Ullo, Billy Dick Unland, Tom Wadden, David Walters, Joyce White, Les Whitten, and Susan Woods. Our thanks to each, and especially to Joe Shimon, who granted a series of interviews and served as a guide from the beginning of the project.

A number of other individuals, at risk to career, reputation, or personal safety, agreed to be interviewed on condition of remaining anonymous. Some journalistic puritans contend that such material should be discarded out of hand, but we believe it was essential to learning some of the crucial elements of the story, and are most grateful to the men and women who cooperated with us in secret.

A special word of thanks is due to Rosselli's sister Concetta, who agreed to speak with us despite the opposition of some members of her family. We hope she has been rewarded with a more accurate, and more insightful, account of her brother's life.

Beyond delving into the details of Rosselli's personal saga, this book required extensive archival research. Valuable assistance was provided by Bernard Fensterwald, Jr., and James H. Lesar, the president and vice-president of the privately operated Assassination Archives and Research Center in Washington, D.C.; by Melinda Maas in Jack Anderson's office; by Howard Schwartz at the Gambler's Book Club in Las Vegas; by Dale Mayer at the Herbert Hoover Library in West Branch, Iowa; by the staff of the Margaret Herrick Library of the Academy of Motion Picture Arts and Sciences; by Marie Boltz, assistant curator of special collections at Lehigh University; by Lloyd Hooker at the Bureau of Prisons Library in Washington, D.C.; by the staff of the Southern California Library for Social Studies and Research; by the research and photo staff in the Special Collections department at the University of California at Los Angeles; by librarian Dacey Taube at the Regional History Collections division of the University of Southern California; and by Don Bowd at the Wide World Photo archive in New York. Thanks also to Eliza Chavez Fraga, who assisted in the translation of Spanish-language source materials.

In addition, and especially in the sensitive areas of organized crime in general, the Kennedy assassination in particular, and the secret history of the CIA, a number of authors and journalists opened their files and racked their memories to help keep our work on track. They included: Bradley

Earl Ayers, John Babcock, James Bacon, Lowell Bergman, Chris Blatchford, Richard Bonin, John H. Davis, Bob Dorff, Alan Fitzgibbons, Gaeton Fonzi, Stephen Fox, Paul L. Hoch, Jim Hougan, Susan Jonas, Ron Kessler, William Knoedelseder, Joanna Lancaster, Fred Landis, William Scott Malone, Jonathan Marshall, Ken Mate, Thomas McCann, Frank McNeil, Dan Moldea, Virgil Peterson, Dave Robb, Bob Rosenhouse, Stephen Schlesinger, Peter Dale Scott, Carl Sifakis, John L. Smith, Lyle and Carole Stuart, and Bob Thomas. In a profession distinguished by petty jealousies, their generosity was refreshing and remarkable.

Government files and materials were fundamental to documenting Rosselli's life, and were obtained primarily through aggressive use of the Freedom of Information Act, an effort ably assisted by Washington, D.C., attorney Jerris Leonard. While most of the government employees we dealt with, especially those at the FBI, seemed to consider the denial of access their primary mandate, a few took an opposite tack, readily providing us with all the material they felt they could legally dispense. FOIA/PA specialist Margaret Snyder at the Immigration and Naturalization Service in Miami was especially helpful, as was James Baynham at the U.S. Army Personnel Center in St. Louis. In addition, independent researcher Bob Goe was tireless in tracking the paper trail of Rosselli's years in Las Vegas through the Nevada state repositories in Carson City.

The authors are indebted to Julian Blodgett for making the initial introductions that gave rise to our collaboration. From that point on, we received wonderful support to see the project through, and finally, in writing the book. For their advice, encouragement, and assistance we wish to thank Michael Bird, Lydia Brazon, Anne Crompton, A. W. Crompton, Herb Fox, Michael Fox, Wink Glennon, Sue Horton, Larry Leamer, Harry Parker, Bill and Tim Rappleye, Willard C. Rappleye, Jr., Mark Richman, John Seeley, Claude Steiner, and Kirtley Thiesmeyer. In Washington, D.C., Rudy Maxa shared his savvy and his apartment, and the troika of I. Irving Davidson, Tom Adams, and John Graves shared insights and tables at Duke Zeibert's.

Publication of this book would not have been possible without the unwavering friendship and superb editing of Donald Spoto, who helped edit the original book proposal and critiqued the early drafts. Larry Welsh was inspirational in his enthusiasm and confidence. Mary Jane Ryan ratified a long friendship with trenchant critiques of the manuscript at critical junctures, and she and Gale Holland provided a crucial final edit. Our agent, Geri Thoma, saw promise where others had seen only headaches.

Our copy editor, Carol Siegel, was careful and consistently cheerful. And our editor, Paul Bresnick, showed confidence and patience where none was due.

Finally, we must thank our families, particularly Barbara Becker and Gale Holland, who saw us through the highs and lows that this project entailed, both financial and emotional, with the unflagging faith born of love. To them we owe a debt of gratitude that words cannot express.

CHARLES RAPPLEYE, Los Angeles
EDWARD BECKER, Las Vegas

CONTENTS

ALL AMERICAN
MAFIOSO

Look at those who are in labor with wickedness,
     who conceive evil, and give birth to a lie.

They dig a pit and make it deep
     and fall into the hole that they have made.

Their malice turns back upon their own head;
     their violence falls on their own scalp.

—Psalm 7

1

THE ELDEST SON

The Barrel in the Bay

The cool of the morning had given way to a muggy, hot Miami Saturday, and the fish were losing interest in Jim Blundell's bait. His two buddies continued casting into the inland shallows of Dumfoundling Bay, but Blundell rested his pole for a moment to gaze along the shore of the canal that led to the sluggish waters of the Intracoastal Waterway. He spotted the rim of a rusting steel drum, barely breaking the surface near the water's edge, and wondered at the heavy chains he saw wrapped around the canister. Blundell put down his gear and headed over to take a closer look.

The top of the drum faced south, away from shore, toward Miami. Blundell pulled it around, the warm, muddy water swirling gently against his legs. He found a hole hacked through one side where a five-inch steel hook anchored the chains. Peering into the opening, Blundell saw a scrap of a pale pink sports shirt and what seemed to be the wasted remains of a

3

corpse. He recoiled from the shock of his discovery, and from the stench of death issuing from the canister. Blundell called to his friends, Bob Hoffman and Ken Walls, and after they had completed the same inspection, they agreed, there seemed to be a body in there. Walls ran off to call the police.

Officer R. S. Wilkins took the radio call while patrolling the nearby community of Golden Shores. He turned east from Biscayne Boulevard onto a gravel causeway, and then headed south to the canal, located in a remote area frequently used for illegal dumping. He was the first officer to arrive, reaching the embankment above the canal just after 11 A.M. After speaking with the three fishermen, all local residents in their early twenties, Wilkins checked the drum himself and then radioed for assistance in the investigation of a homicide. It was August 7, 1976, and a murder that was intended to remain secret was quickly coming unraveled.

By noon, more than a dozen investigators from the Dade County Public Safety Department were gathered on the mud flats by the canal. Lieutenant Gary Minium, chief of the homicide squad, directed the investigation; a helicopter circled overhead, a patrol boat idled its engine near the shoreline, and two scuba divers searched the murky, polluted waters of the canal. News of the discovery had been transmitted to other police agencies in the area, and word came back to Minium from neighboring Broward County of a missing person named Johnny Rosselli, 71, an aging gangster who lived in apparent retirement with his sister. Minium decided immediately, and correctly, that Rosselli was the man whose body had been dumped in the bay.

There was more—the Broward sheriffs informed him that Rosselli had recently testified before Senator Frank Church's intelligence committee in Washington, D.C., and had apparently conspired with the CIA to assassinate Fidel Castro. Intrigued, Minium made an immediate request for information to the FBI. The plots against Castro had excited enormous interest in Miami, where the Cuban Premier was the object of bitter hatred; more important, one of Rosselli's accomplices in the plots had been Santo Trafficante, Jr., the leading Mafia don in southern Florida. If indeed the body was Rosselli's, this case would be, as one of Minium's detectives described it, "awesome."

While forensics experts continued to work over the scene, the steel drum was hoisted from the shallows onto a tow truck and transported to the offices of the Dade County Medical Examiner. It would be several hours before positive identification could be made from fingerprints on file with the FBI, but in the meantime, the autopsy revealed the details of a grisly killing—Rosselli's mouth had been gagged by a Cannon washcloth, which in turn was strapped in place with white adhesive tape wrapped twice around the head. A white nylon rope was knotted loosely around the neck, possibly for use as a handle to manipulate the body. He'd been shot or stabbed in the stomach—the coroner speculated later that his killers shot him and then dug the bullet out with a knife. The torso had been slit open from chest to navel. And the legs had been hacked off at the thigh, probably with a handsaw, and stuffed into the steel drum alongside the body. Cause of death was listed as asphyxiation.

Precautions had been taken to be sure Rosselli would not be discovered. The drum was sliced with a series of gashes to let water in and air out, then wrapped in twenty feet of heavy two-inch-link chain for ballast, and sunk in twenty-eight feet of water. "These guys went to an incredible amount of trouble to make sure the body was never found," observed Dr. Ronald Wright, chief deputy examiner for Dade County. In addition, Wright speculated that the drum was chained to an anchor of some sort, but had broken loose.

Even so, it was by the barest chance that the corpus delicti of Rosselli's murder was eventually discovered. Gases trapped inside the decomposing body had floated the drum with just enough buoyancy to bring it to the surface. By the time Jim Blundell came across it, Wright calculated, most of the gases had dissipated. "It was four or five days past maximum buoyancy," Wright told reporters. "It was getting to the point where it would have sunk again—it never would have been found."

Having escaped the enigmatic obscurity of a disappearance, John Rosselli's mutilated corpse, its face contorted by the gag into a grotesque grin, presented the Dade County authorities with a riddle. Certainly an underworld killing was unexceptional in Miami, where mobsters from around the country had been operating illicit business and feuding for turf since the late 1920s. But why Rosselli, elderly, ill, and certainly past his prime? Why the elaborate efforts to conceal the crime? And what were the implications of Rosselli's recent testimony on the CIA and Fidel Castro? Clearly, Rosselli's murder was not an end, but a beginning, a lead, which his killers believed could be traced to expose secrets and connections that were worth at least one man's life to keep hidden.

That knowledge only whetted the appetites of the two detectives assigned to the case. Charles Zatrepalek and Julio Ojeda were both brash young investigators, both 28, rising quickly in the department on the basis of enterprising and relentless pursuit of their quarry. They took pride in a remarkable homicide resolution rate of close to 90 percent, but this case looked tough from the start. The one clue the two detectives had was Rosselli himself, a relatively unknown gangster whose arrival in Miami had been noted by law enforcement, but who from then on was largely ignored and never placed under surveillance. Of the myriad questions facing Zatrepalek and Ojeda that Saturday night at the coroner's office, they agreed to focus on the simplest: Who was John Rosselli?

Mob Ambassador

THE FIRST ANSWER TO the Rosselli riddle lay in a file of more than 20,000 pages amassed by the FBI. Rosselli's crime career had been obscure but long and active, lasting more than fifty years and spanning the heyday of organized crime in America. He was a street thug, a rumrunner, a gunman for Al Capone in Prohibition Chicago, and an organizer of mob interests in the cash-rich casinos of Las Vegas. Rosselli's underworld sponsors and associates included the top names in organized crime—Frank Costello, Meyer Lansky, Sam Giancana, Santo Trafficante—and some of the lowest, card sharps and union racketeers and outright killers.

But Rosselli was more than a hustling lieutenant to the czars of the underworld, and the file chronicled that as well. Intertwined with his criminal exploits was a parallel career as a charismatic mystery man in the glamour capital of Hollywood. Since the early 1930s, Rosselli had been prominent in the film industry, forming close friendships with studio moguls like Harry Cohn, and later with entertainers like Frank Sinatra and George Jessel. It was this incarnation, as a man of style and sophistication, that gained Rosselli entrance to select circles of power in Washington, and eventually placed him in a pivotal role at a critical juncture in the nation's history. As a friend to the powerful and as emissary from the underworld, Rosselli served as a bridge between the glamorous public image of American power and the hidden ruthlessness that fueled it.

What the cold print of the file could not reproduce was the character and human qualities that allowed Rosselli to cross strict social boundaries and forge forbidden alliances. John Rosselli was handsome, slim, with a strong hawk nose and a mirthful, infectious smile, but it was his eyes that people remembered best, cool and blue-gray, "dancing and delightful," as one friend recalled, or flashing and steely in anger. His confidence and presumption of power proved irresistible to many women.

Rosselli dressed impeccably, in modern but understated styles from the finest makers; he practiced precise, cultivated manners, and spoke carefully, never betraying the urban streets of his youth. He played golf and tennis, drank sparingly, and spent money freely but not garishly. And there were other qualities, more ethereal but more elemental: a sense of fun that attended all his doings and which found expression in a lifelong attachment to children, and which they reciprocated; and a buoyant enthusiasm "that made you feel like you were the most important person in the world to him," as a Hollywood friend remembered.

Finally, Rosselli was a survivor, a streetfighter in every sense, who honed and blended these separate attributes with the calculated skill of a con artist. The result was a charm and presence that flattered even rich and powerful men, and they gravitated to him. On one occasion in Washington, on the way to a cocktail party, one of his attorneys proposed a joke: he would introduce Rosselli around as a federal judge, and see who took the bait. The ruse lasted all night, as attorneys and government executives solicited thoughts and opinions from the gangster.

Rosselli's many facets were reflected in the various reactions of his friends and enemies when news of his murder hit the papers across the nation. In Los Angeles, the headlines sparked anguish and frustration in Jimmy Fratianno, Rosselli's friend and onetime hit man. To Fratianno, Rosselli had been the consummate mafioso, stern and immensely powerful, astute in the intricate treacheries of family rivalries, committed to the traditions of honor and loyalty that bound the secret society. Though he was a seasoned killer, this murder left Fratianno shaken, forcing him to question the basic foundations of their creed—if they would hit such a man as Rosselli, respect and honor had lost their meaning.

Across town, in a rambling San Fernando Valley ranch house, Bryan Foy learned of Rosselli's demise on the television news. A veteran film producer, the most prolific in the history of Hollywood, Foy counted Rosselli among his closest friends. The Rosselli he knew was smart and savvy, handsome and always dapper, an habitué of fine restaurants and chic parties, a devoted and knowledgeable fan of the film industry. Foy knew well enough that Rosselli was a gangster, but the savage nature of his murder shocked him nonetheless. "It hit him pretty hard," Foy's niece recalled later. "It was one thing to know someone's in the mob, to read about things like that, but when it happens to someone you know personally, it's a whole other thing."

Foy felt compelled that night to call Rosselli's sister Edith in Florida, to ask if he should come down to visit, to ask if he could help, but there was nothing for him to do. Rosselli had always seemed a sort of mythic figure, confident and fearless, the embodiment of manhood in a town of poseurs. But now the other side of Rosselli's life had caught up with him, leaving Foy feeling frail and terribly mortal.

At the Towne Hotel in Cicero, Illinois, the news of Rosselli's murder generated irritation, but no shock, certainly no dismay. Formerly the home base for Al Capone, the Towne was now the seat of power for Joseph Aiuppa, a gunman, union fixer, and, more recently, successor to Sam Giancana as the head of the Chicago Outfit. Aiuppa had been there when the contract for Rosselli's murder was assigned, he'd been informed when it was carried out, and now, he learned that it had been bungled. A dour thug with a reputation for hunting rabbits and ducks with a shotgun, Aiuppa was disappointed in the killers' lack of professionalism.

Aiuppa vented his frustration soon after in a meeting with Frank Bompensiero, a bald, bulky mob assassin working out of San Diego. "Trafficante had the job, and he messed it up," Aiuppa complained. It was the judgment of an expert. Aiuppa was a man who savored his power, and Rosselli's killing was a measure of it. Weeks later he would lord it over Rosselli's friend, Fratianno. During a meeting in Chicago, Aiuppa started musing: "You remember that guy, what the fuck's his name, you know, the guy they found in a barrel in Florida? What do you think of that?"

In time, Rosselli's death was folded into the lexicon of black humor that gangsters use to euphemize their grim trade. "Johnny in a drum," they laughed. Like a thousand other gangsters before him, Rosselli had gotten his.

In Washington, too, news of the murder was received not as an individual tragedy but in the context of the role Rosselli had played. The 1970s were a decade of scandal and revelation in the capital, with stunning secrets aired about Watergate, about the Kennedy assassination, and in large part through Rosselli, about the CIA. And on those grounds, even in a town inured to sensation, Rosselli's murder generated shock waves. Word of his disappearance had reached the nation's capital via a brief news report published in the Washington *Post* on Tuesday, August 4, and

Rosselli's contacts there didn't bother waiting for a body to turn up. Tom Wadden, one of the attorneys who represented Rosselli in his appearances before the Senate, called to discuss the news with Edward P. Morgan, an influential attorney with contacts in law enforcement and Republican political circles. Both were convinced that Rosselli was killed for information he'd shared with the Senate committee—a theory that Jack Kennedy was murdered by Cubans in retaliation for the CIA plots against Castro. Morgan had once helped broadcast Rosselli's scenario by laying it out for Earl Weaver, chairman of the Warren Commission, and then for columnist Drew Pearson. A series of inquiries had been percolating ever since.

After speaking with Wadden, Morgan in turn telephoned Senator Howard Baker, the ranking Republican on the Senate Select Committee on Intelligence, which had succeeded the committee investigating the Castro plots. Baker was immediately struck by the parallel between Rosselli's death and Giancana's. Not only was the Chicago don involved in the CIA assassination plots, but his killing occurred a week before he was scheduled to testify on those intrigues before Baker's committee. The last thing the senator wanted to see was a trail of dead bodies littering the path of the committee investigation. Baker called FBI Director Clarence Kelley to insist that his agency take a lead role in the case.

Far from the capital, another of Rosselli's sisters, Connie, learned of his disappearance by telephone, but the confirmation, the discovery of the body, had come to her via the evening news broadcast. Her reaction was simple and utter dismay. "Sure, he'd done a lot of wrong things, but he was family," she said later in an interview. "To end up like that . . ." Her voice trailed off, and her gray head bowed forward, shaking slowly back and forth. Through most of his career, Rosselli had left his family behind, but toward the end of his life, he'd returned, attempting to repair bonds eroded by neglect. His family responded with some caution—they were ashamed of his reputation, and fearful of what it might reflect on them—but also with some pride. The son of an immigrant shoemaker, Rosselli had overcome poverty and ignorance to become wealthy, powerful, and respected. He was an American success story, and he'd come home.

2

THE OLD AND THE NEW

Esperia

Equidistant from Rome and Naples, marked on some tourist maps for a medieval stone fort that still stands, Esperia is a tiny village in the heart of Campania, a rural province of low scrub and high, rocky hills, and among the poorest in all of Italy. Ten miles to the west lie the warm waters of the Tyrrhenian Sea, but in between stands Mount Petrella, soaring 5,000 feet above the coast, the highest point in the ancient Aurunci Mountains. To the north lies the River Sacco, a turbulent stream that feeds the Liri, and then the Garigliano, which flows past Mount Petrella to the sea. The largest town nearby is Cassino, a village that serves as a way station on the inland highway linking Rome to the south. Around the turn of the century, a visit from Esperia to Cassino would entail a full day's trek across steep and treacherous roads—Esperia was isolated and remote, a world unto itself.

John Rosselli was born in Esperia on July 4, 1905, the first son of

11

Maria Antoinette DiPascuale Sacco, then 19, and Vincenzo Sacco, 21 years old. Later in his life Rosselli loved the fact that his birthday coincided with that of his adoptive country, but in Esperia the date was as innocuous as the circumstances of the birth. Rosselli's given name, his true name, was Filippo Sacco, the same as his grandfather, who was born in the village as well. The Saccos and the DiPascuales had lived in Esperia for generations, but even as the younger Filippo was born, the old pattern was changing—Vincenzo had departed two months prior, joining the great steamship migration to the eastern seaboard of America.

Young Filippo grew up with the idea of America constantly in his mind, a place where money could be made, a place free from political oppression, a place he would someday go to join the father he had never seen. For his mother, and even for his grandfather, America was a beacon, glimmering and distant but always there and ever approaching. They planned their future around it, they saved the money that Vincenzo sent back to pay for the journey, and in 1911, the dream became reality when they boarded a steamship bound for New York and the dense-packed holding rooms of Ellis Island.

But for Filippo Sacco, for the first six years of his life, while America represented the future, the present was comprised of the village of Esperia, and the stony mountains around it, and the centuries-old culture and traditions of the *Mezzogiorno,* the heartland of southern Italy and known colloquially as "the land that time forgot." Men dressed in simple dark wool, and women wore black smocks and white embroidered headdresses; the main form of transport was the mule.

★

Since before the founding of Rome, Campania had been subject to uninterrupted foreign conquest, occupied in turn by Hirpini, Roman, Goth, Byzantine, Lombard, Norman, Hohenstaufen, Aragonese, Hapsburg, and Bourbon armies. The nineteenth century brought the promise of change when the nationalist *Risorgimento* swept all of Italy, and in 1861, the guerrilla fighter Giuseppe Garibaldi "liberated" the South in the name of Victor Emmanuel II, monarch of the Piedmont. But the political domination of the South continued, this time from the north, along with punitive taxes and tariffs.

The subjugated people of the *Mezzogiorno* identified more with their counterparts in Sicily than with their new King—the region had once been known as the Kingdom of the Two Sicilies—and sporadic but stubborn resistance to the national government was widespread. In 1862, a state of siege was declared in Sicily and Campania, and Emmanuel II's royal troops instituted systematic repression that rivaled that of the foreigners in its intensity. "There were so many rebels that the executions were very frequent," one occupying general noted blandly in his log. "In fact I received instructions from Turin to moderate the use of firing squads and to shoot only the leaders."

Virtually the entire rural population was considered a legitimate target for military operations. "Delinquency is the war of the poor against the rich: this is the special characteristic of the bandits we are dealing with," an occupying general explained to his troops. "The brigands must seek shelter from the inhabitants of the countryside. . . . Only when the people begin to see that they are being constantly molested by the troops will they begin to cooperate in destroying the criminals."

The repression succeeded in forcing an official unity between North and South, but the hostilities, and the occasional flare-ups of violence, persisted even into the Fascist era. Over the course of a millennium of poverty and occupation, the people of the *Mezzogiorno* had forged a deep and enduring culture, autonomous, conservative, and intensely inward-looking, based on concentric circles of loyalty. The institutions of state were regarded as hostile and usually corrupt; even the Church was alien, providing a colorful backdrop but assuming little significance in the lives of its people.

Paramount in the dynamic of daily life was *la famiglia*, the family, the calm and constant center in a world of change and strife. "It was not that they venerated family relationship as a social, legal or sentimental tie, but rather that they cherished an occult and sacred sense of communality," Carlo Levi wrote after he was exiled to the South by Mussolini. *La famiglia* in the *Mezzogiorno* was "a unifying web not only of family ties [a first cousin was often as close as a brother], but of the acquired and symbolic kinship called *comparaggio,* or godparenthood." The individual without family had no identity and no purpose; larger groups outside the family had no relevance. In other cultures the family might form the cornerstone of larger society, but in southern Italy, in the land that time forgot, the family *was* the society.

A second tier in southern Italian life was the village, which provided a sort of cultural matrix in which the family could function, and was expressed in the word *campanilismo,* meaning roughly, the unity of everyone living within the sound of the village church bell. That was the extent of the relevant world. Beyond *campanilismo* lay only treachery, and the fearful unknown. The surrounding world, even including nearby villages, was regarded as universally dangerous and imputable.

The glue that bound together the tiny worlds of family and village was *onore*, which translates as honor, respect, and dignity. *Onore* was intrinsically entwined with family—the disgrace from bearing a child out of wedlock reached as far as the mother's second cousins—and set the standards by which lives were measured. A man could live without money, a woman could live without children, but stripped of *onore*, they were nothing, and their shame encompassed the family as well.

Internally, the product of this strict and simple code was a culture that was utterly self-referential. *Onore* was in the eyes of *la famiglia* and *companilismo*. The law was the mechanism of oppression: justice was dispensed within the circles of family and village. In their dealings with the outside world, the southern Italians similarly took the law to themselves in a tradition of banditry that reached deep into history. Small groups of men, sometimes on horseback, raided along the highways, harried the succession of foreign armies, and, on occasion, led uprisings against the fortified estates of the landed gentry. Crucial to the functioning of the bandits and the families that supported them was the code of *omerta*, a sort of variant of *onore*. Translated literally as manliness, *omerta* was a code of silence that forbade any discourse with outside authority, even barring a dying man from naming his assailant.

Banditry was widespread in the countryside, with each village harboring its own daring and headstrong young men, but it became institutionalized in Naples, the capital of the *Mezzogiorno*, as the Camorra. Even more than the Mafia, its sister organization in Sicily, the Camorra developed a disciplined, hierarchical form of organization, with separate families whose chieftains met to allocate territories; and like the Mafia, it evolved into a purely criminal organization, leaving its Robin Hood roots behind. By the time of the *Risorgimento*, according to one historian, "The Camorra in Naples was more than ever formidable; they controlled such forces and were so strongly bound together that the ordinary laws were of little avail against them."

This was the culture that nurtured the young Filippo Sacco. While his counterparts in America played at cowboys and Indians, Filippo learned to look up to men of honor, taciturn rebels who lived and died by the code of *omerta*. After traveling through Italy in 1974, sociologist Richard Gambino found that, "Even today tales of [the bandits'] bold exploits are a favorite theme in the children's storybooks and marionette shows I've seen in the *Mezzogiorno.*" The Saccos were not roughnecks or brigands, they were craftsmen, and to some degree insulated from the harsh realities of the peasantry. But neither were they immune—*famiglia* and *onore* had been the law of their land for centuries, and would come in turn to dominate life in the immigrant neighborhoods of industrial America.

Coming Over

DEPARTING THE FAMILIAR TERRAIN of the hill country was a drastic step for Vincenzo Sacco, but the centuries of economic privation and civil war had forced an entire generation to the point of desperation, and when steamship fares began to fall around the turn of the century, tens of thousands of his companions in southern Italy took the opportunity to escape. Adolfo Rossi, the Italian supervisor of Emigration, commented at the time that his countrymen were leaving the South "in such numbers that, in certain parts, it amounts to a general exodus. In some places the village priest and the doctor, having lost their flock, have followed them to America. Certain municipalities have had to be consolidated and the parish church abandoned."

The initial stage of emigration peaked in 1893, when 70,000 Italians departed for the New World; after a brief lull, the migration resumed in earnest. In 1905, the year Vincenzo sailed, more than 300,000 Italians booked passage, and more than 80 percent of them from the South.

Vincenzo Sacco was a shoemaker, in Italy a craft that required years of training and which allowed him to rise above the lot of the landless peasants. In America, Vincenzo lost some of his dignity—shoes were not made by hand but manufactured in large, mechanized plants—but his skills found him employment in one of the half-dozen shoe factories in Boston's North End. Entering the United States in 1905 at the age of 21, he probably boarded in the immigrant tenements of the North End, a commercial district of docks and industry that was almost purely Irish in 1850 but which, by the turn of the century, had been inundated in a second wave of Italian immigration.

The North End was intensely crowded, with workers bunking four and six to a room; poor sanitation gave rise to cholera and dysentery, and during the gray, frozen winters, the tenements were routinely swept by deadly strains of influenza. Still, Vincenzo Sacco was tenacious enough that within a few years he could move to East Boston, an island in Boston Harbor that could be reached by the city's new subway. Like the North End, East Boston was an immigrant neighborhood, but the tenements were not so fetid, and it had parks and wide, tree-shaded streets, the sort of place a man might consider raising a family. In 1911, Vincenzo wrote to his father to tell him that everything was ready, that he should bring Vincenzo's wife and his son and they should join him in America.

In August, at the height of the long, dry summer, the Saccos collected their funds—the fare was $35 apiece, equivalent to one hundred days' average wages—packed what they could carry, and said good-bye to the town where they had been born. Grandfather Sacco, Maria, her son Filippo, and a friend, Caterina Palazzo, who signed the documents of passage as Vincenzo's sister, then boarded a carriage for the long ride into Naples.

The exodus from the *Mezzogiorno* had spawned a booming industry on the docks of Naples, where close to 10,000 people made a living as ticket agents, boardinghouse operators, porters, and stevedores, as well as pamphleteers, hustlers, and pickpockets. Once past those hazards, the trip began in earnest. First there was an inspection, where American doctors examined the prospective emigrés for contagious disease, for physical infirmities, and for senility and mental retardation. Then there were the forms, seemingly endless, both Italian and American, asking where they had come from and where they were going. If she harbored any trepidation at leaving behind the life of her ancestors, Maria Antoinette DiPascuale Sacco showed none: under the heading Length of Intended Stay, she wrote, simply, "Permanent."

Once the official routine was completed, the Saccos proceeded to the docks, and to the S.S. *Cretic*, one of the White Flag Line's fleet of commercial steamers that served as a steel sea bridge to the New World. Built in 1902, the *Cretic* measured 550 feet by 60, and could muster a speed of twelve knots. Though not so miserable as the old packets that had ferried the original immigrants, the steamships were crowded, dank, and uncomfortable. As often as weather permitted, passengers camped out on deck, but when conditions turned inclement, they were herded below, into the steerage, where families huddled together in gloomy, cramped cabins.

The passage took two weeks, until word finally came, on September 12, that New York was within a day's distance. Then the belongings were gathered up, the children scrubbed and admonished, and the hundreds of passengers climbed above deck to peer over the railings as the harbor slid into view—first the Hudson Narrows, then the Statue of Liberty, and finally Ellis Island, with its drab, blocky stone and brick buildings. Still, the voyage was not over; First Class passengers were ferried direct to shore, but the steerage passengers had to wait, and for three days the *Cretic* sat at anchor, awaiting permission to dock. The Saccos had all their papers in order, they had money for the tariff, and had a certain destination, but still those days in limbo had to be anxious, with their past an ocean away, and their future thoroughly uncertain.

The year 1911 marked the height of the European migration to the United States, and despite a recent expansion, Ellis Island was overwhelmed by the 637,003 immigrants who passed through its gates. The scene that greeted the Sacco family as they clambered down the gangplanks of the *Cretic* was pure chaos, with enormous crowds milling confusedly in the main yard, wrestling with duffel bags and steamer trunks, and seeking direction from a handful of impatient, uniformed guards.

Slowly, the hours dragging by, they made their way into the main hall of the processing facility, where the press of humanity grew intense. "It was the smell that I remember best," one traveler recalled later. "Worse than I have ever smelled before. You could almost taste it and feel it." But the crush lasted only a few hours, and most of the other immigrants were Italian as well, from the South, and equally bewildered. When at last the Saccos reached the front of the line, the processing began again; another physical exam, conducted in stages by a series of doctors posted along winding corridors; then a legal inspection, which was the toughest, because the questions were in English, but answers carefully rehearsed on ship got them through. All four in the Sacco party were cleared, registered, and issued rail tickets, with tags clamped to their clothing to instruct train conductors where to put them off, and on the afternoon of September 16, 1911, the Saccos of Esperia boarded the train for Boston.

There is no record of the meeting on the platform between Vincenzo Sacco and his newly arrived family, no family myth of the celebration between husband and wife, united after six years apart, no recollection of the hugs for a son and father who had never met before. Certainly it was joyous, and just as certainly there was some awkwardness, as each had their imaginings supplanted with the reality of their blood relations. However it passed, there was still more traveling to do, and Vincenzo Sacco trundled his brood to the subway. Rail trams carried them under the waters of Boston Harbor to Maverick Square, and from there they made their way to Vincenzo's flat at 229 Maverick Street, in the heart of the Italian section.

The routine of daily life quickly interrupted whatever festivities were under way. The next morning Vincenzo headed off to work; Caterina Palazzo went to live with her cousin, Antonio, who had already settled in East Boston; the senior Filippo sought work as a tailor; and Maria pursued the business of setting up a household. On September 26, 1911, ten days after his arrival, Filippo Sacco entered the first grade at Theodore Lyman School.

Growing Up Foreign

FILIPPO SACCO FOUND OUT quickly what a wide gulf separated life in East Boston from the traditions of the Italian hill country. Language was an immediate barrier, and it was a high one. Maria Sacco spoke little English when she came over, and Filippo was enrolled in school with no training in his new tongue. The result, as he recalled in a brief autobiography submitted in court proceedings toward the end of his life, was a crash course in assimilation. "I stopped talking Italian because of the beatings I received in school," he wrote.

Of course, he didn't have to speak a word to be recognized for his foreign heritage. His thick, black hair, a pronounced nose, and his rough clothes identified him immediately as a boy just off the boat. But young Filippo Sacco was not alone in the strangeness of his new world. Like the North End, East Boston had been transformed by thirty years of immigration from an Irish stronghold to a mixed neighborhood of Italians, Russian Jews, and the old Irish families. The Italians were concentrated around Jeffries Point, at the southern end of the island, a district of docks, rail spurs, and blacksmiths, low rents and small vegetable gardens. There was tension between the new and the old, and especially between the Irish and the Italians: both groups were Catholic, but the congregations were segregated, with the Irish attending services presided over by Pastor Joseph Fitzgerald at Our Lady of Assumption, a huge, gloomy church situated on the tallest hill in town, while the Italians took mass at Our Lady of Mount Carmel, a smaller building on the lowlands near Maverick Square, with the Reverend James Merighi.

It was at home that Filippo Sacco found real peace. Maria Sacco was the classic Italian mother, waking before dawn to start the morning meals, seeing to it that her son attended mass and got to bed on time. Vincenzo Sacco, too, made the home the center of his world. He never dallied on his way back from the factory, and upon his arrival, got down on hands and knees to play with the son he was just coming to know. If there was any dissension in the family, it stemmed from Vincenzo's doting. "Mama would get angry because he didn't want to hear about the kids being bad —he just wanted to play," one of the Sacco girls said later.

In the year Filippo arrived in America, the small flat on Maverick Street was home to three generations: the grandfather Filippo, Vincenzo and Maria, and their boy. One year later, in 1912, Maria Sacco gave birth to a second son, named after his father; a third, Albert, was born in 1914; and 1915 saw the arrival of the first Sacco daughter, Concetta. By that time the family had outgrown the small apartment; listings in the Boston city directory show that the family split up, Vincenzo and his family moving to Frankfort Street near the Mount Carmel church, and Filippo Senior taking an apartment three blocks away on Chelsea Street, a busy boulevard leading into Maverick Square. In 1917, Edith, the last of the Sacco children, was born. For six years, Vincenzo and Maria slept with a crib in their bedroom.

Filippo remained close to his father as the family grew, and became very fond of his brother Vincent, the oldest of the new children, but he never lost his identity as separate and different. He was six years older than Vincent, and while the youngsters grew up speaking two languages, Italian remained Filippo's native tongue, with English a foreign language he mastered only under duress. Nevertheless, he advanced on schedule at school, graduating with his class from first through sixth grades. He learned to defend himself from his classmates outside the classroom as well, and the beatings he endured early on ceased. "By the time I reached the fourth grade, the tables were turned a little," he commented dryly in his autobiography.

Despite the upheaval of immigration to an alien culture, Filippo Sacco's young life was marked by a remarkable level of stability, rooted in the insulated family world that Vincenzo and Maria Sacco had created. All that began to change in December 1917, with the death of his grandfather, Filippo. Diagnosed with tuberculosis and what doctors described as "senile dementia," the senior Sacco suffered a breakdown in November, was taken to Mayfield State Hospital, and on December 8, at the age of 60, he succumbed.

With the loss of the family patriarch, the Saccos left the Italian enclave of East Boston and moved across the harbor to Somerville, a bedroom community near Cambridge that was opened up to Boston commuters by the construction of the Fitchburg Railroad. Vincenzo Sacco continued to work at making shoes, but his family had moved up a notch, out of the din and smoke of the city to an apartment in a two-story house at 13 Belmont Street. Though close to the racket of the railroad line and a nearby fire station, the house was also situated just a block from a handsome Catholic church at the first rise of Spring Hill, a quiet neighborhood of large houses and large yards, dotted with schools and parks and a small convent. On a clear day Vincenzo Sacco could peer from his living-room window and find the skyline of downtown Boston and measure how far he and his brood had come.

Filippo continued in school, enrolling in the seventh grade in Somerville. No record of his performance survives, but there is no reason to believe that he excelled—education was given little importance by the Italian emigrés of the era, who were more concerned with making a living and, of paramount priority, maintaining *la famiglia,* the close and warm circle of the family. Perhaps, if events had not interceded, Filippo Sacco would have followed in the footsteps of his father, as did many of his contemporaries, becoming a shoemaker and spending his life in the shady suburbs of greater Boston. But in 1918, while the murderous battles of World War I dominated the headlines, a less spectacular but equally virulent killer, one that claimed 20 million lives, helped to shatter the world of the Saccos of Esperia.

The influenza epidemic reached Somerville in late September, and by October 10, had stricken 6,854, killing 223. Schools, churches, theaters, pool halls, and bowling alleys were closed, with residents hunkering down behind closed doors as if under siege. Horse-drawn ambulances went from house to house, hauling the dead to burial, sometimes taking entire families. "It has been a terrible experience," the Somerville *Journal* observed at the time.

On October 5, Vincenzo Sacco felt the first aches in his muscles and the first heat of the influenza fever. Two days later he was delirious, and confined to bed, his lungs choked with mucus. The children were barred from the bedroom, but Maria nursed him night and day, and while she managed to escape the grip of the highly contagious disease, Vincenzo's condition only worsened. At 2:30 on the afternoon of October 13, he was dead, and three days later he was buried, in the same grave as his father, at the Holy Cross Cemetery in nearby Malden.

There were several friends there for the ceremony, a couple of cousins who had emigrated like the Saccos, and the five Sacco children; the grave stood at the edge of the sprawling cemetery, with the Charles River to the east, and Italy 4,000 miles away. Now the Sacco men were gone, and Maria Sacco must have wondered what would become of her family.

Growing Up Tough

WITH THE DEATH OF Vincenzo Sacco, Maria returned with her children to the familiar neighborhood of East Boston. "Everybody knew her and everybody liked her," her daughter Concetta recalled. "It was always Ma Sacco, that's what they called her, never Mrs. Sacco or Marie."

Relying on public assistance and the little money she could make taking in sewing, Maria Sacco took a flat in a wooden, cold-water "three-decker" apartment on Haynes Street, a small winding alley a block from the wharfs. There was no heat in the building, and in the winters the family would huddle around the kitchen stove for warmth while Maria made pasta or soup. "Whatever food she had around, she'd stretch it," Concetta said with some pride. "We always had something to eat."

On Sundays, Maria made sure her children took communion, and when they got home, gave them a glass of water "to wash down the host. Then she'd give us something nice, like a meatball or some meat sauce on toast," Concetta recounted. "Sunday was a big day."

But while Maria worked hard to provide for her children, her oldest boy, Filippo, then 12 years old and twice the age of his eldest sibling, was fast moving out of the family orbit and into the swirl of the urban scene around them. It was a classic syndrome for immigrant Italian families, and without a father to enforce the rules, even more pronounced. Italian newsman Stefano Miele, writing in 1920, lamented that his countrymen "apply the same principle in bringing up children that had been applied in the little village or the farm in Italy. They let the children run loose. And in the streets of the crowded tenement districts the children see graft, pickpocketing, street walking, easy money; they see the chance to make money without working."

So it was with Filippo Sacco. Through with school, he took a job driving a horse-drawn milk wagon around Maverick Square, and frequently stayed out after hours. "He was away a lot," Concetta remembered. "It was getting crowded at home," Filippo recounted later. "I started helling around on Maverick Street, where all the wise guys were."

By all accounts, "helling around" meant hanging out with the street gangs that dominated the social life of the boys growing up in East Boston. Turf boundaries were strictly observed, and for a teen-ager, the simple act of walking from one side of town to the other was to court a beating. The gangs were not particularly organized, but they were plentiful. Maverick Square, Eagle Hill, Orient Heights, Day Square, Jeffries Point—each urban crossroad was claimed by its own squad of young toughs.

In the battle for territory, local gangs would square off with each other, but would band together in the face of hostiles from outside. Streetfights were common, and sometimes engulfed entire sections of town. Throngs of ragged teen-agers, hundreds at a time, would choke the streets, pulling apart banisters and tearing up paving stones for weapons. Housewives would join in, jeering from the safety of their windows and tossing pots and frying pans into the crowd.

Turf was more of an issue than race in East Boston, where different nationalities managed to get along with each other. "It was an American neighborhood," Concetta Sacco recalled. "The Italians always stuck to each other in the North End, but it was not like that for us."

Another function of the gangs, besides asserting domain, was criminal enterprise. Numbers rackets, protection rings, simple extortion, and narcotics peddling thrived in the immigrant ghettos, and the youngsters served as eyes, ears, and runners for the adult mobsters. "When I was a kid, we all knew what a big-time crook was, and most of us looked up to them," recalled Jimmy Costa, born in the North End in 1914, who grew to become an accomplished safecracker. "There was a lot of crime then, oh yeah. A lot of deaths, a lot of killings."

This was the milieu that embraced Filippo Sacco after the death of his father, and he fit in easily. Like most of his peers, he was affiliated with a street gang, but he also developed ties to the criminal underworld, the ruthless but still small-time East Boston Mafia. With his milk route as a cover, he began making deliveries of contraband, including narcotics. He became a well-known figure in the bustle of vegetable carts and open-air fish and meat markets that crowded the cobblestones of Maverick Square, and went by the nickname of "Milky."

In the meantime, the Saccos' home life deteriorated steadily. Exhausted by the job of raising her five children on her own, Maria had moved in with Liberato Cianciulli, a butcher who was, at age 56, twenty-two years her senior. Cianciulli was an experienced womanizer. He had been married twice before; the second marriage, to a woman living in Italy, was still in effect at the time he met Maria Sacco, and he had two children by a third liaison living under his charge. Maria moved to Cianciulli's cramped two-story house on Everett Street, two blocks from the apartment on Haynes, in 1920, and a year later, gave birth to a daughter, Camilla, known as Mona, out of wedlock. Filippo found himself sharing a bed with Salvatore, one of Cianciulli's sons.

Cianciulli was loud and harsh, especially with his stepchildren. "He yelled a lot—screamed—so that he scared the kids," Concetta recalled later. Filippo Sacco himself told a probation officer in 1969, "The family life was very good while his father was alive, but poor and marginal thereafter." In a statement to federal authorities, Maria Sacco said she later separated from Cianciulli "because of the way he treated my children."

Shunning the conflict at home for the life of the ruckus of the street, Sacco drifted deeper into the underworld, becoming a regular trafficker in narcotics, a vocation that led to his first confrontation with the law. Morphine was available legally at the time, but only through prescription, and sales of unregistered supplies violated tax statutes. Federal officials considered dope peddling a practice of the Italian street gangs, and made enforcement of the tax statutes a priority.

On September 14, 1922, when Filippo was 17 years old, he was observed by a federal agent delivering a quarter-ounce bag of morphine to a man named Fisher, an addict who was collaborating with the government. Five days later, at Fisher's request, Sacco procured a half-ounce bag, and once the sale was made, he was arrested along with his source, another youth named Sarro Vaccarro. Both were jailed until October 18, when a federal grand jury returned an indictment for sales of narcotics. Two days later, Sacco made bail.

Six months later, with trial on the drug charges still pending, Filippo was arrested again, this time for a robbery in Arlington, a suburb east of Cambridge. Sentenced June 14 to three months in prison, Maria Sacco somehow found an attorney to appeal the ruling, and Filippo was released on $300 bail. The legal representation and the large bond seem well beyond the resources of Sacco's family and imply that he may have had assistance from allies on the street, but whatever the circumstances, Sacco realized the law was closing in on him. He decided to skip town.

Before he could leave, however, there were details to attend to. The first was Fisher, who had fingered Sacco in the dope deal. According to a federal sentencing memo prepared in 1969, "The government narcotics informant disappeared about the same time [as Sacco] and government sources believe that he may have been killed to prevent him from testifying." It was the first time that young Sacco was suspected of involvement in murder, but there would be many more.

Sacco's second task was assigned by his stepfather, Liberato Cianciulli, who had by then split with Maria Sacco and planned to return to Italy to resume residence with his former wife. Hoping to finance the trip with insurance money, Cianciulli instructed Sacco to set fire to the Everett Street house by torching the laundry that hung by the stove to dry. "I followed the instructions and started the fire," Sacco wrote later.

"I went across the street and sat on the curbstone to watch it burn. I thought it took hold because smoke and fire was coming out of the roof, but to my surprise, the firemen were there in about three minutes to put it out." Liberato Cianciulli sailed for Italy soon after, and Filippo disappeared. "He just left," Concetta Sacco recalled. "Mother never mentioned him. That was all we knew—he left."

Thus did Filippo Sacco leave behind his youth, on the lam, with a series of criminal charges—including suspicion of murder—hanging over his head, and with his family life and his home literally up in smoke. For *la famiglia*, he turned to the next best thing, *campanilismo*, the community of the village, which on the streets of urban America meant the gangs. In return for unquestioning loyalty, the gangs offered identity and protection, and, as the era of Prohibition took hold, growing allotments of money and power.

On the Road

DEPARTING BOSTON HASTILY AND without a word to his family, Filippo Sacco adopted an alias, most likely using the name John Stewart, which he returned to at several points later in his life, and may have worked briefly as a telephone lineman, as he claimed in 1970. But any jobs he took were by their nature incidental—he was drifting, finding his feet, learning to live by his wits. And while his sharp, angular face and threadbare clothes would have drawn immediate attention from the police and the genteel classes, he blended easily into the teeming urban subculture whose vestiges survive today in the ethnic neighborhoods of the eastern cities.

★

Criminal gangs dominated immigrant neighborhoods of all nationalities in all the big cities. Boston's Irish hoodlums were led by the Gustin Gang, the Jews by Charles "King" Solomon, and the Italians by a savvy bespectacled Sicilian fight promoter named Phil Buccola. In Detroit, the Italian Giannola and Vitale crime families vied for turf with the Jewish Purple Gang. Cleveland boasted the mob run by Irish saloon operator Thomas Jefferson McGinty; the Cleveland Syndicate, dominated by Jewish gamblers Moe Dalitz and Louis Rothkopf; and the Italian Mayfield Road Mob, led by "Big Al" Polizzi and the Milano brothers. And in Chicago and New York, the combination of generations of civic corruption and heavily segregated neighborhoods spawned dozens of gangs—before 1920, New York's street gangs included the Shirt Tails, the Whyos, the Dead Rabbits, the Plug Uglies, the Bowery Boys, the Hudson Dusters, the Havemeyer Streeters, the Eastman Gang, the Gophers, and the Five Points Gang—some counting as many as 1,500 members.

These early mobs were murderous and hard-fisted, a step up from the youth gangs that sprang up on any urban street corner, and generated revenues from control of prostitution, running numbers lotteries, and from extortion and simple robbery. Some even made money farming out their services—foreshadowing the infamous Murder Inc. of the 1930s, the

Whyos distributed a price list for assaults ranging from $2 for punching to $10 for "Nose and jaw broke," and topping out at $100 for "Doing the big job." The mobs kept on friendly terms with city hall and the local police by delivering votes in large numbers, a service which earned them autonomy on their own turf.

The power of the street gangs was elemental—they dominated their neighborhoods through fear enforced by beatings and an occasional murder, and fought deadly battles with rival mobs that threatened their turf. But their operations were intrinsically small-scale, limited to their countrymen and their tenements, and collaboration with other gangs was rare and insignificant.

★

Already accustomed to the furtive moments and quick cash of the criminal life, a confident brawler at his ease on the streets, Filippo Sacco was a natural recruit for the Italian street gangs. And in the summer of 1923, young men of his talents were in particularly high demand, because Prohibition, made an amendment to the Constitution three years prior, had evolved from novelty to industry, and bootlegging had become the primary underworld occupation.

As the traffic in contraband grew, it produced dramatic changes in the structure of the criminal gangs. Measured in cash, the volume of illegal enterprise in the country had increased exponentially, and the gangs began to battle each other in earnest for domination. Murders increased, as did official corruption. And the Italians, formerly peers with the other nationalities in the underworld, began to emerge as more dangerous, more ruthless, and ultimately more powerful. Entire cities came under the domination of syndicated criminal organizations or, in the case of Chicago, a single man, and in most cases, the dominant players were Italian.

There were two reasons for this, both related to the long history of bandits and secret societies in Italy's *Mezzogiorno*. The first was that the Italians were more accustomed to playing for stakes of life and death. "The most vicious of all the gangs were easily the Italians," asserted Daniel Fuchs, former member of a Jewish street gang, writing in the *New Republic* in 1931. "They were severe in their methods, seldom willing to fight with their fists or with stones, but resorting unethically to knives and guns. . . . The Irish could be said to fight almost for the fun of it, while the Jews always fought in self-defense. But the Italians went out definitely to maim and kill."

The second aspect that distinguished the Italian gangs was their long experience in the operation of secret, organized criminal enterprise. The Irish and the Jews and even the blacks had their mobs and their crime bosses, but none had anything similar to Italian crime families. Known to its membership alternately as the Camorra, the Mafia, or simply as Cosa Nostra—Italian for "our thing"—the secret societies first surfaced publicly in America in New Orleans in 1891, but remained obscure until Senator Estes Kefauver popularized the term Mafia in a series of sensational televised crime hearings in 1950. Even among the mobsters, the existence of the Mafia was regarded as something of a myth, but it was real and it was active, a sinister force lurking in the slums of a dozen cities across the country.

Bound by the code of *omerta*, ruled through a paramilitary command hierarchy, steeped in the art of treachery, the classic Mafia crime family was at once more ruthless and more systematic than anything their rivals could muster. More important, the inward-looking nature of the secret societies left them immune from equivocation. Members accepted their code without question, and regarded outsiders with the contempt of the chosen. Honed over the centuries, transplanted to foreign soil, the Mafia represented a sort of distillate of evil, and presented with the boundless opportunity of Prohibition, it pursued its goals relentlessly.

Not all the Italian gangsters were full-fledged mafiosi—that status could take years to attain—but the Mafia was at the core of the Italian underworld, and as young hoodlums gained skill and experience, they were recruited into the fold. At the age of 18, already a fugitive from the law, Filippo Sacco began to climb the ladder, working on the shore and at sea with a bootlegging crew out of New York. There is no record of the period except the comments of police officials and the reputation he established, along with Sacco's own account of a brief stay in New York City. But he must have proven effective in his chosen occupation, for within months he was dispatched to Chicago, to serve as a hired gun for the growing criminal organization headed by a pudgy-faced young gangster named Al Capone.

Scarface

IN THE FALL OF 1923, Al Capone was still an unknown entity to the Chicago public. He had moved from New York three years before to serve as chief henchman to Johnny Torrio, a short, sober, moon-faced criminal strategist who served, in turn, as the brains behind the throne of "Big Jim" Colosimo, a restaurateur and mob boss who was Torrio's uncle by marriage.

Torrio had established a reputation as a tough street fighter with the Five Points Gang in New York, but by 1915, when he was 33, Torrio developed a flair for management, and Colosimo recruited him to run his dozen-odd whorehouses in the Levee, Chicago's notorious red-light district. Torrio proved adept, one of the pioneers of the modern crime syndicate, and Chicago was fertile ground for the exercise of his talents. "Chicago is unique," Charles E. Merriam, a professor of political science at the University of Chicago and a city alderman, noted at the time. "It is the only completely corrupt city in America."

Concerned that the concentration of vice in the Levee left it an easy target for law enforcement, Torrio proposed and then carried out a program of diversification, opening brothels in the suburban villages of Burnham, Posen, Blue Island, Stickney, and finally Cicero, and then expanding into gambling, hijacking, narcotics, and with the passage of Prohibition, bootlegging. Largely as a result of Torrio's initiative, Colosimo became the dominant gangster in a city thoroughly dominated by crime.

As Torrio's own power grew, he decided he needed muscle of his own, and he sent for Capone, then 18 and a bouncer at the Harvard Inn, the hangout of the notorious Five Pointers. Suspected in connection with three murders, his face bearing a four-inch scar sustained during a knife fight, Capone was volatile, brutal, and an expert shot with a pistol—the perfect complement to the deliberate, calculating Torrio.

By 1920, Torrio and his young henchman were convinced that the future of crime lay in bootlegging, but Colosimo could not be persuaded. In May, that obstacle was removed when Colosimo was murdered in the foyer of his café, and Torrio proceeded with his greatest project, the syndication of the Chicago underworld. He called a meeting of the various Italian gangs, representing neighborhoods like Little Sicily, Little Italy, and Little Hell; the Irish of the North Side and the South Side; and the Poles of the Southwest section, where he proposed a plan: Torrio would supply the beer, Dion O'Banion would run liquor from Canada, and distribution would be carried out according to the territories of the separate mobs. After Torrio detailed his profit projections, the leaders of the gangs agreed, and Capone was designated to enforce the treaty.

The peace yielded immediate and fantastic profits, with Torrio himself grossing an estimated $12 million in a year, but cooperation was a new trick for Chicago's hardened crime lords, and in 1923, war broke out. Several of the assenting parties, including the Sicilian Genna family and the South Side O'Donnells, revolted against the treaty by hijacking trucks, murdering drivers, assaulting tavern operators, and developing their own sources of supply. Capone busied himself with the job of retaliation, while Torrio, apparently deciding that street battles were a young man's game, set sail for a European vacation.

As the war deepened and the killings multiplied, both sides sent to New York for reinforcements. Among the youngbloods who migrated west to join Capone's band was Filippo Sacco. If his youth on the streets of Boston was an apprenticeship, Chicago served Sacco as a crash-course finishing school. No documented record of Sacco's stay survives—he was never arrested in Chicago, and never surfaced in contemporary newspaper accounts—but by his connections, his reputation, and the stories he shared with friends, it is clear that his brief stint on the shores of Lake Michigan was seminal. In a span of less than a year, he perfected an alias that would serve him through the next four decades, honed his skills with the weapons and tactics of the underworld, and forged personal alliances that would ensure him from that time forward a welcome reception at the highest echelons of organized crime.

Al Capone's early outfit was not strictly Mafia, but it was structured after the model of the old secret societies. Membership was clearly demarked, and gained only by hoodlums who had successfully perpetrated a murder at the direction of the organization. The aspiring gangster was then inducted at a formal assembly of the entire mob by taking an oath which Capone administered himself, wherein the initiate swore fealty with his hand resting on a parchment manuscript of excerpts from the Bible written in Greek. The ceremony mirrored the rites of the Camorra and the Mafia, and its solemnity and mystic trappings lent it a religious aura. Sacco later confided to friends that he had been "made" in Chicago —it was the closest he ever came to admitting actual participation in a murder.

It was a decision, certainly, for Sacco to join the secret order, but little choice was involved—to spurn Capone's invitation could likely have resulted in death, and would have contradicted all of Sacco's life experience, like a soldier refusing a medal. It was a bridge Sacco had crossed at some tiny Rubicon years before, perhaps when he first agreed to deliver a bag of contraband on his milk route, or even earlier, when as a small boy he absorbed the folklore of the *Mezzogiorno*. But with Sacco's induction into the select fraternity of the underworld, there was no turning back. Ever after, he would look at the world through the eyes of an outsider, a man with a secret, to whom terror and murder were tools of the trade. In the mind of the world around him, he and his ilk were evil incarnate, living testimony to the darkest potential of the human psyche.

Several accounts indicate that Sacco flourished in his new status, gaining favor from Capone himself. Criminal informants in the early 1960s told federal investigators that Sacco was well-known in Chicago crime circles, and some believed he was even related to Capone. Frank Hronek, an investigator with the district attorney's office in Los Angeles, also developed information that Sacco was a "cousin" of Capone's, and though no family connection was ever established, the implications were certainly flattering to Sacco. Jimmy Fratianno, an accomplished hit man in the Los Angeles crime family, added in an interview, "He was very close to Capone."

Besides making him an official member of his organization, Capone took a personal interest in Sacco, insisting that he drop the cover name of John Stewart for a more suitably Italian alias. As he retold the story later, Sacco sat down with an encyclopedia and leafed through to find the name of Cosimo Rosselli, a fifteenth-century painter who contributed frescoes of Moses on Mount Sinai and the Last Supper to the walls of the Sistine Chapel. Sacco retained the comfortable first name of John and was known from then on as Johnny Rosselli. Sixty years later, even his family called him Johnny.

The Boys

AL CAPONE WAS IRASCIBLE and emotional, bullheaded and vain. Few believe that he possessed the vision and tact to forge an alliance of the various and combative Chicago gangs—that was Torrio's accomplishment. But when Torrio was wounded by an assassin in 1925 and retired from the mobs, Capone continued to build on his base until, in 1929, he reached the zenith of his power, the most feared and celebrated criminal in America.

The secret to Capone's success was not innate genius but his organization, a crew of men intensely loyal to their boss but which, after Capone's conviction on tax evasion in 1931, continued the expansion of the crime syndicate to dimensions Capone never dreamed of. Capone himself was a bubbling font of aggression, a natural force that drew people to him like moths to a flame. It was the clique that formed around him that became the architects and strategists of the nation's most powerful criminal organization. From the beginning, that inner circle included his family, brothers Frank, who liked to opine that "You never get no back talk from no corpse," and Ralph; and cousins Rocco, Charles, and Joe Fischetti, more businesslike than the Capones but fully aware of the roots of their power. And in 1923, the year that Filippo Sacco the street hustler was transformed into John Rosselli, mafioso, Capone's personal clique was expanding.

The first prerequisites for entrance to Capone's organization were loyalty and an instinct for violence. There were scores of gangs in Chicago in the early 1920s, and thousands of thugs, pimps, and labor racketeers, safecrackers and extortionists, con artists and gamblers; Capone required henchmen who could dominate this unruly throng through sheer terror. And he found them.

Jack McGurn was born James DeMora in Chicago's Little Italy, and abandoned a career as a welterweight boxer when his father was murdered by the Genna Gang. Obsessed with revenge, McGurn signed on with Capone, the Gennas' top rival, and quickly established a mark as a merciless assassin. McGurn made the machine gun his personal trademark, and made himself Capone's personal hit man. He killed with disdain, sometimes pressing a nickel into the hand of a prostrate victim to show what he thought the life he'd taken was worth. By the time his legacy caught up with him, in 1936, when five men surrounded him in a bowling alley and began blasting away, "Machine Gun" Jack McGurn was credited by police with twenty-eight known kills.

Like McGurn, the stories behind Capone's other "button men" were summarized in their nicknames. Tony "Joe Batters" Accardo delivered discipline with a baseball bat. Sam "Golf Bag" Hunt's penchant for the links provided him a handy case for concealing his favorite murder weapon, a semiautomatic shotgun. And Frank "The Enforcer" Nitti, fifteen years older than Capone, a former barber and jewelry fence, became chief of the organization's muscle arm.

But Capone was not so rigid as his Sicilian brethren in the Mafia—he recruited lieutenants for guile as well as brawn, and he didn't care about their ancestry. Jake Guzik came to prominence as business manager for Torrio's brothels, a position he kept when power changed hands. He never carried a gun, and he never needed to. Short and fat, a Russian Jew and a childhood pimp, Guzik earned Capone's lasting trust when, in 1922, he tipped him off to an ambush being plotted by a rival mob.

Other henchmen combined craft and muscle. Llewellyn Murray "The Camel" Humphreys (so named for his fondness for camel-hair coats), a Welshman, joined Capone as a contract killer, but he rose quickly in recognition of his adroit management of the political fix.

Of all of Capone's motley band, none combined the various elements of subtle instinct and murderous will so naturally as Paul "The Waiter" Ricca. Born Felice DeLucia in Naples in 1895, Ricca was convicted of murder at age 17 and served two years in prison, where he was trained in the code of the Camorra. Upon his release, he tracked down and killed the chief witness against him in the murder trial, then fled to Chicago, where he found employment waiting tables at "Diamond Joe" Esposito's Bella Napoli Café.

Lean, urbane, always respectful and always carefully dressed, The Waiter became the chief strategist for the Capone organization. He never hesitated to apply violence—he ordered murders with the simple directive, "Make him go away,"—but he'd seen what payoffs and political power had achieved for the Camorra in Naples, and he put those lessons to work in Chicago. In 1927, Capone showed his gratitude, standing as best man at Ricca's wedding.

John Rosselli encountered all of these men in Chicago in 1923. In wintry evenings the gang hung out with gamblers, politicians, and labor leaders at Diamond Joe's Bella Napoli, trading stories in Italian dialect and taking in the floor show. They were young and ambitious, just beginning to sense their power and to cash in on the sky-high profits of bootlegging. Rosselli was in the second rank, one of hundreds of drivers and sluggers in the gang's employ, but as a native Italian with an easy, eager manner, he quickly impressed.

Capone apparently enjoyed Rosselli's company and paid him the compliment of his personal attention, but Rosselli was not so taken with the exuberant bravura and garish dress of his boss. He gravitated instead to Ricca, more sober, more elegant, less conspicuous than Capone. This was the old-country mien celebrated in the unwritten codes of *omerta* and *onore*. Even in his youth, Rosselli could see that Ricca's soft-spoken power would endure, and he took Ricca as a model. Ricca's closest associate in the Outfit was Charlie Fischetti, Capone's cousin, who was cast from Ricca's more circumspect mold, and Rosselli befriended him as well.

These were fundamental relationships, the kind that college kids form in fraternities, the kind that serve as a power base for business executives years after graduation. So it would be for Rosselli, who maintained his connection to Chicago for the balance of his life. But in the winter of 1923, with the heyday of the Capone mob still before it, Rosselli's career with the nation's most notorious criminal gang was cut short. The guns and knives of rival mobsters were not a problem, but he could not shake the delicate lungs that plagued the Sacco family. The icy wind off Lake Michigan proved debilitating, and toward the end of the year, a doctor discerned the early stages of tuberculosis. Rosselli shared the news with Capone and was dispatched once again to unknown territory, this time to the edge of the continent.

3

CITY OF ANGELS

Freelancing

Los Angeles in the middle 1920s must have seemed a desolate outpost to an ambitious young hoodlum raised in the urban crush of the eastern seaboard. Dry and dusty, construction of the city's famous freeways still decades away, Los Angeles was an urban island in a sea of orange groves, populated by Midwest retirees and stragglers who had run out of continent. Bereft of skyscrapers, its cultural life dominated by a stiff-collared old guard, visitors termed the city "an enormous village." Even before Prohibition, sales and consumption of alcohol were strictly controlled.

But if Los Angeles was a backwater, it was a beautiful one, with ocean breezes, tropical flora, and balmy Mediterranean nights in place of the slate-gray winters of the East. Besides, whatever was left of the thatch-roofed pueblo the Mexicans had founded in 1781 would soon be swamped in a ceaseless tide of immigration. In the twenties, mass production of automobiles opened new horizons of freedom and mobility to an entire generation of Americans. Day by day, hundreds took to the open highway and turned West. By the end of the decade, the city's population had doubled, reaching more than 1.2 million.

Tourism, agriculture, and oil formed the backbone of the economy, but even at that early stage, fantasy was the region's best-known export. Cameras first started rolling on the West Coast in 1907, when winter storms forced Chicago's Selig Studio to abandon filming of *The Count of Monte Cristo* and head for warmer climes. By 1920, Los Angeles had replaced New York as America's film capital. Charlie Chaplin, Mary Pickford, and D. W. Griffith were all based there, earning phenomenal sums and capturing the nation's imagination in scores of velvet-draped movie palaces.

The studios were scattered across suburban Los Angeles, from Culver City southwest of downtown to the Cahuenga Pass, a twenty-minute drive northeast, and then farther east, to the satellite cities of Glendale and Edendale. Still, it was Hollywood that occupied the yearnings of America's youth. Lured by the slim chance of a career on the silver screen, thousands of young men and women landed on the corner of Hollywood Boulevard and Vine Street, there to be set upon by con artists promising an audience with a casting director—for a fee. If they were lucky, they made it to Central Casting, where their names were entered in a card file that by 1923 counted more than 10,000 aspiring stars.

More than the promise of easy money, Hollywood offered the prospect that reality could be transformed by illusion, that a person could adopt an identity the way an actor picked through a costume closet. It was the furthest extension of the American dream, and for the young John Rosselli, it proved a powerful tonic.

Operating under an assumed name and several outstanding federal warrants, Rosselli was already playing a role when he joined in the burgeoning confusion of Los Angeles in 1924. He was deeply attracted to the film industry, hanging around the back lots and finding occasional work as an extra or a bit player. Nobody asked where he was from or what he did for a living—verve and attitude were the currency of the studios, and he had an ample supply of both. Within a few short years, Rosselli would penetrate the highest echelon of Hollywood's social circuit, befriended by studio moguls who shared his immigrant background and his vaulting aspirations.

But that would take time. Penniless and gaunt from tuberculosis, Rosselli's immediate priority was survival. He migrated to the city's east side, an immigrant ghetto that was home to tight-knit communities of Italians, Jews, Russians, and Mexicans. His first recorded contact in Los Angeles was Anthony D'Acunto, an old family friend from Boston who had moved west several years before. A native Italian, D'Acunto introduced Rosselli to a niece, Frances Broszmer, who recalled the meeting in an interview with the FBI in 1958. "D'Acunto was a well-mannered individual," Broszmer reported, "while Rosselli was rough in his actions and speech."

The Italians had become established in Los Angeles at the turn of the century, forging a niche as merchants in the downtown markets and, if they prospered, founding wineries in the rich farmland of the San Gabriel Valley. They were concentrated in the flatlands east of downtown, a fringe neighborhood of small wood-frame houses bordered on the west by the floodplain of the Los Angeles River, on the north by Lincoln Heights, and on the southeast by Boyle Heights, a stronghold of Jewish and, later, Mexican immigrants.

While life was never so grim as in the tenements Rosselli had known in the East, Los Angeles' Italians were still an immigrant community, hemmed in by poverty and isolated by language and culture. The police were considered outsiders, and the laws of the land largely irrelevant. The Italian Hall, a brick building in downtown Los Angeles that served as the headquarters for several Italian civic groups, concealed a speakeasy behind a false wall in the rear.

Ghetto life was dominated by hard labor and by the Black Hand, a secret society and forerunner of the Mafia whose members practiced the ancient Sicilian arts of extortion and blackmail. Family feuds reaching back to the old country were settled by gunfire, usually just after nightfall, on crowded boulevards or even on the doorstep at home. Police reports from the time record a series of Black Hand murders where men named Cuccio and Perlini and Bentivegna were found clutching extortion letters written in Sicilian. The victims included fruit merchants and pushcart peddlers, barbers and shopkeepers. They were uniformly poor, and while some were active in mob rivalries, more often they were just unlucky, the random targets of extortion and "protection" rackets. Sawed-off shotguns were the favored method of dispatch, popular to the point that Darwin Avenue, running through the heart of the Italian section, was dubbed "Shotgun Alley."

As an unknown player in a new city, the single commodity Rosselli could offer his associates was nerve. Rosselli was physically small, only five feet eight inches, and not broad either, his frame constricted by chronic illness. But what he gave away in size he made up for in a boundless determination that manifested itself in ruthlessness. An outsider even among his family, Rosselli learned early on to view the world in self-referential terms, accepting no limits and entertaining no mediation of conscience. He joked later that "when Christ died on the cross, the closest man to him was a thief, and that's good enough for me."

This internal framework was buttressed by the ethic of the Italian criminal gangs. Vicious and remorseless, the rank-and-file mafiosi called themselves *soldati*, soldiers, out to provide for their family, and in some cases they acted like an army, battling rival gangs with strategy and gun-fire. But the romantic hues in the portrait fade in light of the base nature of the gangster's stock in trade—the extortion, kidnap, and murder of small businessmen, of desperate gamblers, of women pimped from an early age, of the weak and the weak-willed. Rosselli brought an ethic bred of the meanest settings the country had to offer, and transplanted to Los Angeles, it flourished.

For most of his contemporaries, refugees from the crowded continent of Europe, the American dream was a promise that life was theirs for the making, free from the fetters of class and convention that bound life in the old country. For Rosselli and the other outlaws, the message was twisted. Life was theirs for the taking, a quest for cash and cars and miscreant amusements limited only by the forces of law or, more likely, the firepower of competing thugs. Theirs was also an American dream, but stripped down to a cold, Darwinist core.

The dream that guided Rosselli wasn't all that different from the one followed by the robber barons and money-trust industrialists who helped shape America around the turn of the century. Like the gangsters, they were avaricious, and they destroyed anything that stood in their way. The difference was circumstance. Starting with nothing, stripped of his family, Rosselli had no center to his life that might instill some sense of purpose or community. From his direct experience, power and success came to those who took it by force. Of necessity, his crimes could not involve stock swindles or market manipulation, but simpler plots—bribery, extortion, sales of contraband. His victims were more tangible, and there was no room for delusions about morals.

From the outset, as became a hallmark of his career, John Rosselli played the field, sometimes free-lancing, but more often serving as accomplice and ultimately confidant to the city's top criminals. Not yet 20 years old, he left his tracks in a police record that began almost immediately upon his arrival in 1924. On some occasions he was picked up in connection with a particular crime; on others, he was arrested on vague charges as part of a general roundup of known gangsters in the city. Almost always, Rosselli was found in possession of the tools of his trade—unlicensed handguns, some with the serial numbers filed off. He even tried his hand as a moonshiner, but the operation was broken up when police raided his rented house and discovered a still in the basement.

After one arrest, Rosselli listed an occupation of fruit peddler, and another, merchant, but there is no record that he sought work or held a job, even as a front. As he put it later, "I was a young fellow with very little education. I am trying to sell whiskey, trying to do anything I possibly can to make a living." Pressed to explain his reputation as an enforcer, Rosselli dissembled: "I got into a few minor scrapes, fistfights as a young fellow, and naturally those things go on, and if you stand on your toes and fight back, you soon get that kind of reputation. The man who is thrown out on the street, naturally, that is what happens." And naturally, Rosselli might have added, he learns to handle the knife and the gun.

Tony the Hat

ROSSELLI FORMED HIS EARLIEST criminal alliance with another native Italian, a reputed mafioso named Anthony Cornero Stralla. Flamboyant, given to white Stetson hats and pearl-colored gloves, Tony Cornero personified the colorful, almost comic popular image of the gangster. His record included a series of arrests on suspicion of murder, but few convictions. His brash manner and thick, unschooled diction made him a favorite with the press, which he used as a forum to challenge the merits of Prohibition and tout his service to the working man.

Known to the underworld as "Tony the Hat," Cornero earned the newspaper moniker "King of the Western Rumrunners" by transporting spirits from Canada and Mexico. His freighters easily avoided an undermanned Coast Guard by off-loading under cover of rugged islands twenty miles off the California coast to small, fast powerboats, which then made high-speed deliveries to hundreds of secluded landings between San Diego and Santa Barbara. Once ashore, the bootlegger's biggest hazard was not law enforcement but rival gangsters. Hijackings and kidnappings were commonplace, with confrontations frequently ending in gunfire. These turf wars required that top smugglers recruit small bands of tough, cool-headed gunmen, qualities Cornero found in the young John Rosselli.

Rosselli's eastern street ethic was important to Cornero, as was the simple fact of Rosselli's Italian heritage. Cornero's gang included men with Anglo names like Calvin Warren and Ernest Morgan—certainly Cornero was pleased to find one of his countrymen to join in the fray.

Beginning in the summer of 1925, Tony Cornero was engaged in a running gang war with Milton B. "Farmer" Page, another bootlegger who gained a high public profile with lavish displays of money. For years the pair had competed for customers onshore, but when pirates working for Page raided one of Cornero's ships at sea, Cornero determined to retaliate. After recruiting one of Page's girl friends, he planted a tantalizing slip of intelligence—the date and location of his next run. Page took the bait, dispatching his bodyguard, Jake Barrett, and two other gunmen to ambush the rumrunners. This time, however, Cornero's men would be waiting.

No accounts exist that detail Rosselli's activities from this period, but scraps of a record survive—his arrest with Cornero in 1926, an anecdote from LAPD intelligence files related by respected underworld chronicler Hank Messick, address notations from press reports, and an FBI intelligence summary—which together make it clear that he was working closely with the leading Italian rumrunner. That position would have afforded him a front-row seat when Cornero's trap was sprung on a balmy Monday near midnight on the outskirts of Wilmington, a marshy coastal community fifteen miles due south of Los Angeles.

Working off Cornero's bogus tip, Barrett and his men pulled their dark sedan into the path of their prey. They learned they'd been had when the darkness erupted in fire from tommy guns, shotguns, and revolvers. The would-be hijackers never got off a round in defense, and all three sustained multiple gunshot wounds. The car they were driving was ventilated by thirty-eight bullet holes.

Tony Cornero was brought to police headquarters for questioning on August 4, the day after the gun battle, and while he denied any role in the ambush, he admitted to the war with Page and intimated more to come. The sequel took place the following March, with the murder of Walter

Hesketh, 28, another of Page's henchmen. Hesketh was walking toward his downtown apartment with a friend at 3:45 in the morning when a black sedan drove past them and swerved suddenly into a U-turn. Moments later, three shots rang out, Hesketh dropped to the sidewalk, and the second man fled. Taken to a hospital, Hesketh vowed, "I'm going to get well, and when I do I'll get my own revenge," but he died of his wounds days after.

The following week saw Los Angeles drenched in a steady downpour, the rain gathering in the hills around the city, running down canyons and dry creekbeds to flood streets engineered for a desert climate. Rosselli and the rest of Cornero's gunmen laid low, ducking the weather and the law in places like Bernie's Delicatessen or the Maple Bar downtown, or more plain hangouts with a simple "Café" stenciled on the window, where a wink and a dollar could get a shot of watered-down whiskey.

The police got a break in the case five weeks later, a tip from an underworld source, and Cornero was arrested with his brother Frank on May 3, 1926, on charges of conspiracy to commit murder. Cornero made bail and was immediately released, but was arrested again four weeks later, this time with John Rosselli and three other men.

Cornero again made bail, but Rosselli spent the night in the Central Jail, near city hall on Spring Street downtown, a windowless brick holding tank three stories high, where prisoners slept on metal benches in group cells that held a dozen men. The charges against Cornero were dropped for lack of evidence, while those against Rosselli were reduced to misdemeanors for two unregistered handguns police discovered upon his arrest. Rosselli pleaded not guilty, and the counts were dropped without explanation the following August.

Rosselli enjoyed his role as henchman to Cornero, and he prospered by it. Cornero was making hundreds of thousands of dollars, with more than enough to spread around, and for the first time, Rosselli could afford to leave the crowded immigrant neighborhoods he had known since his arrival in America. From the flatlands east of the Los Angeles River Rosselli moved into a home across the street from his boss's apartment on Witmer, a quiet avenue of elaborate Victorian-style houses just north of the exclusive Bunker Hill district that bordered on the city center.

At the same time, Rosselli was picking up the finer points of life as a gangster. He learned always to carry a pocketful of dimes, for ready use of phone booths, and to live off a wad of currency in his pocket, the better to thwart tax audits. He learned to speak in veiled language, in half sentences, never mentioning individuals or locations except by obscure references that would be understood only in context, thereby confounding law enforcement eavesdroppers. And at night, in the privacy of his room, he practiced the "Mafia stare," a menacing scowl calculated to terrify his adversaries. "The secret is not to look in their eyes," Rosselli once explained to a friend. "You pick a spot on their forehead and zero in. That way you don't blink, you don't move. It intimidates the hell out of them."

Most important, Rosselli developed the quick wits and nose for money that meant success on the streets. He liked to tell the story of a time he'd been shot in the leg during a gun battle, and was laid up in a low-rent hotel. When he'd recuperated enough, he tested his leg on a walk through the neighborhood, and happened to notice a house with a tangle of phone lines leading to the eaves, the telltale sign of a bookmaking operation. He climbed the porch and stood there until a man opened the front door and thrust out an envelope stuffed with $3,000 in cash. Rosselli accepted the package, mumbled, "I'll be back in a week," and calmly strolled back to his hotel.

Rosselli's last job for Cornero took place on the high seas. Cornero and his band were off-loading whiskey from his yacht, the *Donnarsari*, when one of the Coast Guard's lumbering steamers appeared over the horizon. Rosselli was piloting one of the speedboats, and had just secured 2,000 cases of high-proof contraband. As Hank Messick told the story, Rosselli gunned the engine and headed for shore, leaving Cornero to deal with the authorities. Cornero was arrested, but soon after jumped bail on the smuggling charge and went underground. Rosselli made sure that the proceeds of the haul found their way to his boss.

Police captured Cornero again in April 1927, but a bribe loosened their grasp and he boarded a train heading north. Fearful he'd been recognized as he approached Tacoma, Washington, Cornero leaped from the observation deck, rolled down an embankment, and made his way to Canada. While there, Cornero commended Rosselli's services to Abner "Longy" Zwillman, boss of the rackets in New Jersey and the most successful rumrunner on the East Coast. It was a crucial connection, affording Rosselli a personal link to the Jewish gangsters who shared power with the Italians in the highest echelons of organized crime. Zwillman in turn came to rely on Rosselli as his primary contact west of the Rockies.

Cornero would resume his role as a leader in the Los Angeles gambling picture in the early 1930s. But his flight, and his voluntary return in 1929 to face prosecution and a brief prison term, meant an unplanned hiatus for John Rosselli, it meant a break in the action. Despite the sunny climate, and perhaps because of his escapades in the Pacific, Rosselli's hacking cough persisted and worsened, and in 1927, he checked into a sanitarium in Redwood City, in rural northern California, for six months of recuperation. Apparently he was pleased with the treatment he received, for he referred a close relative to the same facility several years later.

The Pinnacle of Power

IN JUST THREE YEARS since his arrival on the West Coast, John Rosselli had established himself as a top hand in the criminal underworld of Los Angeles. He was feared for his ready use of a gun and respected as a trustworthy ally. Upon his return from Redwood City in 1927, he was well positioned to head his own band, smuggling liquor and collecting whatever booty he might claim. Yet as he would from that point forward, Rosselli avoided the title of boss. He was never a leader, preferring to remain in the shadows, situated close to the seat of power but letting others take the heat that came with center stage. Accordingly, Rosselli took the opportunity in September 1927 to return to Chicago and renew his friendship with the nation's most notorious gangster.

The occasion was the world heavyweight title fight between Jack Dempsey and Gene Tunney, a rematch between the two most celebrated sports heroes of the time. Dubbed "The Greatest Show on Earth" on the front page of the New York *Times*, the fight became the largest single public spectacle ever staged in Chicago.

For Rosselli, the party began the week before, when he boarded one of the scores of special trains chartered to haul fans to the bout from all around the country. Rosselli traveled with friends, drinking and laying bets and flaunting his cash as the train labored over the Rockies and out across the plains. Arriving in Chicago, the revelers joined a tide of sports fans that threatened to swamp the city. On the eve of the fight, a reporter observed that, "In the Loop district, the crowds are so dense it is almost impossible to walk on the sidewalks." The city's hotels were "hopelessly jammed."

Nobody enjoyed the festivities more than Capone, who was 28 years old and perched at the pinnacle of his career. In April he had engineered an election that returned to office Mayor "Big Bill" Thompson and his folksy approach to the question of illegal alcohol. "I'm wetter than the middle of the Atlantic Ocean," Thompson declared during the campaign. On a second, more pressing front, Capone had triumphed over rival mafioso Joseph Aiello. Four times that summer Aiello had slipped seasoned, out-of-town mercenaries into the city to assassinate Capone, and each time the killers were slain by tommy gun within days of their arrival.

The title fight itself represented a financial bonanza for Capone. The contest generated a gambling frenzy that raised an unprecedented $10 million betting pool, most of it handled by Capone's bookmaking organization. And despite mobilization of "an army" of federal Prohibition officers, the city was awash in Capone's bootleg booze, as both victors and the vanquished drank their way through the bout and its aftermath.

As a colleague of Scarface Al's, as a guest from out of town, John Rosselli, then just 23, enjoyed the finest possible treatment, an experience that made a deep impression on a man who five years prior was steering a milk wagon through the alleys of East Boston.

Rosselli's momentous Thursday night began with the fight—prized, up-close tickets to an historic contest that saw Tunney retain his title with the help of the famous "long count" on a seventh-round knockdown by Dempsey. More than 150,000 fans swarmed the grounds of then-modern Soldiers Field—the largest crowd ever to witness a boxing match. Rosselli's prime ticket placed him in heady company—"governors and mayors and United States senators and millionaires."

After Tunney's ten-round decision, Rosselli left the stadium in the company of his good friend, Capone's cousin Charlie Fischetti, and headed for the Metropole Hotel, Capone's headquarters in downtown Chicago. Serviced by a private elevator and consisting of more than fifty rooms, the complex served by day as the seat of business operations, with cops, politicians, and gangsters all checking in to pay respects and collect cash payoffs, and doubled by night as Capone's personal speakeasy, from which he had easy access to basement liquor stocks valued at more than $100,000. Women were available in abundance, and several suites were reserved for gambling.

The night of the fight, Capone hosted a party featuring Al Jolson, whose performance that year in *The Jazz Singer* ensured his position as the leading entertainer of the day. "There must have been a thousand people in that place," Rosselli remembered later with a touch of pride. "I guess everybody clamored to get up there." Rosselli had no problem gaining entrance, however, and even managed an audience with Capone himself.

This was the height of criminal power, a display of might and unlimited wealth that would never be matched again. Rosselli reveled in the opulence—he would recall the event to friends and to government authorities years later—but soon afterward he was exposed to the vexations and vulnerability that also attend public notoriety. Mayor Thompson, Capone's erstwhile ally, decided toward the end of 1927 to make a bid for the Republican presidential nomination, and in an effort to clean up his image, launched police raids on Capone's brothels, breweries, and gambling dens all over Chicago. Announcing that "I'm sick of the job," Capone attempted to take a vacation, boarding a train for Los Angeles with his wife and son, his cousin Charlie Fischetti, and a bodyguard.

John Rosselli visited with the itinerant crime chief when he checked into a suite at the Biltmore, the finest hotel in Los Angeles. Constructed of brick and terra-cotta, its entrance a columned archway with carved friezes, the hotel featured a grand ballroom with tapestries hanging from the walls, and, in the basement, a sauna and pool done in aquamarine tile. It was the perfect setting for a gang leader to relax, but Capone's respite was short-lived. His arrival was reported on the front page of the tabloid *Daily News,* and by the time Rosselli reached the hotel, the police were there in force.

Rosselli attempted to mollify the officers present, some of whom he knew personally, but to no effect. The following day the management at the Biltmore ordered that Scarface Al check out. Rosselli offered to have Capone stay at his home, but the police would have none of it, and that day, December 13, Capone boarded a train back to Chicago. "Pretty hard on a fellow like me that didn't mean no harm and only wanted a rest from business," Capone lamented to reporters.

Rosselli took the brief episode to heart, and throughout his life shunned Capone's flamboyant manner and lust for the spotlight. Even with close friends, Rosselli avoided discussing his criminal exploits, dismissing his reputation as the fabrication of copy-hungry reporters. Still, the lessons of Chicago could not have escaped Rosselli—the boundless potential of concerted criminal enterprise. Returning to Los Angeles as the twenties drew to their roaring climax, Rosselli determined to put these lessons to work in the employ of Jack Dragna, suggested by Capone as a prospective partner on the West Coast.

The Al Capone of Los Angeles

JACK DRAGNA WAS THE dean of Los Angeles' Italian gangsters, whose rise to the position of don in the city's Mafia family was accomplished the old way—through the systematic murder of his rivals. Stocky, with a broad nose, thick lips, and a short temper, Dragna had none of Cornero's style and rascally charm, but had a primal instinct for power, which he exercised as a sort of unofficial mayor of the Italian ghetto, settling family disputes and enforcing discipline. Born Anthony Rizzotti in Corleone, Sicily, before the turn of the century, Dragna arrived in California with his brother Tom around 1908. A conviction for extortion in 1915 and a three-year stint in San Quentin only enhanced his reputation as a man to fear and respect.

Dragna employed as a front the offices of the Italian Protective League, located on the eleventh floor of the Law Building in downtown Los Angeles. Dragna was president of the organization, formed ostensibly to promote immigrant rights, but described in police documents as "strictly a muscle outfit, preying on various business activities," which "also had its fingers in gambling, bootlegging, and smuggling, and was suspected of many Black Hand killings."

In later years, Dragna came to be referred to in the press and in government documents as "the Al Capone of Los Angeles." But in the middle 1920s, while he maintained preeminence in the affairs of his countrymen, Dragna was still an outsider in the world of Los Angeles crime. Most of the city's vice, prostitution, and gambling in particular, was controlled through a well-established syndicate, a small group of businessmen who managed their rackets through payoffs to the police and city administration, generally avoiding the less seemly tactics of the street gangsters.

The ostensible boss was Charlie Crawford, a saloon keeper and whoremaster who earned the tag "Gray Wolf" more through his cunning than any tendency to violence. Crawford mastered the art of the political fix in

Seattle, where his partners in an illegal casino included the mayor and chief of police, and then headed south. In Los Angeles, the key to Crawford's influence was a backroom alliance with Kent Kane Parrot, an attorney and political fixer who controlled Mayor George Cryer, and through his offices, the city police.

Crawford's criminal associates included Cornero's old rival, bootlegger and casino operator "Farmer" Page; Bob Gans, who made millions of dollars as owner and distributor of slot machines; old-style slugger Marco Albori, better known as Al Marco; and gambling specialist Guy McAfee. A former cop, once head of the LAPD vice squad, McAfee was known affectionately among gamblers as "The Whistler" for his practice, while still on the force, of dialing the target of an impending vice raid and, rather than speaking into the receiver, whistling a few bars from "Listen to the Mockingbird," which his contacts knew as the signal to clear out.

With the city's more lucrative rackets so neatly tied up, Jack Dragna and John Rosselli concentrated their attention on prying graft and tribute from the Italian community, and on bootlegging, a trade that remained wide open to anyone with the guts and means to drag a case of whiskey ashore. Dragna's methods, however, were not so discrete as those of the downtown syndicate. Police records reflect an increase in violence in the mid-1920s, known at the time as the Bootleg Wars.

"With the advent of Prohibition, the Mafia element struck out into broader fields of activity," the LAPD reported in a summary of gangland killings in the city. "In the ensuing struggle for money, power, and control, there was much jealousy and many violent crimes committed. It was one faction of the original association against another, and dog eat dog, for the plunder and the spoils."

This wasn't the Los Angeles that was chronicled in the pages of Harry Chandler's *Times*, which crusaded only to keep the city clean of labor unions. Nor was it the city that elected teetotaling Mayor John Porter, exhorted to office by Bob Shuler, a crusading cleric who proselytized for clean living in a magazine and a nightly radio show. But this was a time when America believed in its myths, when mayors campaigned on Protestant virtues while police chiefs accepted tribute from gangsters battling for turf.

John Rosselli lived the shadow of the myth, making a living off the vice and corruption that it masked. His role in the gang wars was never spelled out in detail, but earned him a reputation that dogged him for the rest of his career. A federal sentencing memo prepared in 1968 asserted flatly, "Reliable sources relate that [Rosselli] was an executioner for the criminal organization" in Los Angeles. Rosselli was never charged in a killing, but as former U.S. Attorney Dave Nissen noted: "John had a career of narrow escapes from prosecution. He had many arrests, usually at the scene or quite close to the scene of serious crimes like murder, and maybe with an unmarked gun lying nearby, but nothing would hold up against him because there weren't any witnesses that would come forward." Added Rosselli's friend and occasional hit man Jimmy Fratianno, "Johnny did a lot of work when he was a kid. He did a lot of fuckin' work, don't worry." "Work" is Mafia parlance for murder.

Beyond Rosselli's easy hand with a gun, Dragna valued his growing savvy in the operation of criminal enterprise. As Fratianno noted later, "Jack never made a move without talking to Johnny about it first." Rosselli had a gangster's nose for money, but in addition, he was sensitive to the intricate web of power relations in the underworld, who might be offended and who should be consulted on a particular move. More important, Rosselli brought Dragna invaluable connections to Chicago. Capone had by then established an unprecedented reputation for glamour and power, one underscored in the secret councils of the emerging national crime syndicate. As his liaison to the Chicago Outfit, Rosselli afforded Dragna a degree of status that reached beyond the scope of a regional crime boss.

Recognition from the crime lords back East helped awaken Jack Dragna to the lucrative potential that lay outside the confines of the city's Italian community, and with John Rosselli serving as confidant and chief strong arm, Dragna moved to assert his power in the city at large. More ruthless than his competition, Dragna demanded from the other underworld leaders in Los Angeles a share of the bookmaking and gambling-house rackets citywide.

According to the LAPD gangland survey, Guy McAfee controlled most of the city's illegal gambling toward the end of the 1920s when "the Italians, led by Jack Dragna," demanded a piece of the take. McAfee, who relied on his old friends in the vice squad to ensure peaceful operations, railed against the threat to his network, asking, "Who the hell is Jack Dragna?" The answer came over a period of weeks, when "stick-up men robbed bookmakers, dozens of runners were roughed up, all of which cost the books thousands of dollars—soon the Italians were cut in."

At the same time, probably at Rosselli's urging, and certainly with his collaboration, Dragna began looking west, to the shimmering lights and the ringing cash registers of the gambling ships that plied the placid Pacific off the port cities of Santa Monica, Long Beach, and, farther south, Seal Beach. Gambling took place on dry land, to be sure, but the games were illegal, and the take limited by the need to keep the clubs itinerant and secret. The seagoing casinos represented a bonanza for area gambling impresarios, and Dragna and Rosselli determined to get a piece of the action.

The Bountiful Pacific

THE MAFIA MADE ITS move on a December night in 1928, one of those breezy, comfortable winter evenings that convince tourists to leave their homes back East. Dragna and Rosselli made the hour drive from Los Angeles south to Long Beach, a city built with revenues from the oil boom that sported a row of amusement parks and first-rate hotels along the broad stretch of sand that gave the city its name. Reaching Ocean Boulevard, the pair headed north, over the mouth of the Los Angeles River, to the commercial pier, a tarry dock serving fishing and excursion boats that lay just south of the naval shipyard and the Coast Guard station. Here a small crowd gathered to wait for small water taxis with wooden hulls and stretched canvas roofs to take them out to the gambling ships.

Dragna stayed at the dock while Rosselli boarded a taxi for the bouncy ride to the newest of the ships, the *Monfalcone*. The oily harbor slick gave way to ocean swells as the skiff motored past the rocky breakwater that sheltered Los Angeles Harbor two miles offshore. The lights of Long Beach slowly receded, there was blackness for a time, and then the hazy white neon of the *Monfalcone* drifted into view ahead.

Rosselli generally carried a gun, but tonight, words would suffice, and he checked his weapon with the stout bouncers that manned the gangway. From the pontoon boat landing at the water line, the *Monfalcone* looked like the obsolete wooden schooner that she was, with a useless bowsprit reaching into the night. But as he climbed to the main deck, what emerged to Rosselli's view was a spectacle that might have inspired Jules Verne. The sail masts had been sheared in favor of a 145-foot glass-roofed dance and dining hall. Light from the ballroom cast the ship in a milky glow, and strains from a seven-piece orchestra filtered through the night. Belowdecks, at the foot of a grand staircase, lay a carpeted gambling parlor reaching the length of the 282-foot ship, and boasting four roulette wheels, fifty slot machines, six chuck-a-luck wheels, eight craps tables, dozens of card tables, and a horse book.

Rosselli made his way through the low din of the gambling throng until he located Tutor Sherer, a member of the downtown gambling syndicate and a partner in the *Monfalcone*. Sherer steered him to a private room, and with the door closed, Rosselli quietly delivered an ultimatum. From that time forward, all profits from the *Monfalcone* would be split with Jack Dragna.

Rosselli didn't have to press the issue. Sherer was shaken by the news, and made an immediate phone call to Rasmus "Razz" Pendleton, another partner in the ship. Pendleton knew the violent reputation of the Italian mob, and saw little alternative but to settle with the mobsters. Rosselli returned to the gaming floor and then headed back to the docks, where Dragna awaited word of the confrontation.

The Mafia share in the gaming ship was confirmed by chance a few hours after midnight on July 28, 1930, when two police officers noticed a moving violation by a dark, late-model sedan. When the black-and-white signaled to pull over, the sedan sped off, prompting a high-speed chase through the streets of downtown Los Angeles.

The officers finally forced the sedan over and approached the car, only to be confronted by a swarthy man brandishing a sawed-off shotgun. Three other occupants of the vehicle grabbed the weapon, however, and submitted to arrest. Booked for suspicion of robbery were Jack Dragna, John Rosselli, James Russo, and John Canzoneri, the hothead with the shotgun. Investigation revealed no robbery; rather, that the four had been transporting a large quantity of cash, proceeds from the weekend take on the *Monfalcone,* and weapons enough to ward off a hijack, including four revolvers and the shotgun. Further inquiry showed that "James Russo" was in fact Capone's cousin Charlie Fischetti, apparently on loan from Chicago, whose presence in the car that night underscored the link between Dragna, Rosselli, and the Capone organization. Ironically, despite extensive criminal records, both Dragna and Canzoneri had gun permits from the Sheriff's department. Rosselli was booked for weapons violations, but the charges were later dropped.

How much cash the four men carried was never disclosed, but profits from the gaming ships were enormous. In testimony before a congressional committee, California attorney general Warren Olney III explained later, "These ships made so much money, so much hard cash, that bringing in the money became a problem." One operator, for example, "used to deposit all of his money with a small bank in Santa Monica, and after some months of experience with them, the bank wrote them a letter and told them that they would close out his account unless they had a truck to handle the money. So he bought a truck." Dragna and Rosselli had entered the big time.

The syndicate operators chafed under their shotgun partnership with the Mafia. The continuing profits from the seagoing games drew intense competition, and the same gangsters who had battled so fiercely for control of the liquor trade—Tony Cornero, Farmer Page, and Dragna—were at odds again. War naturally ensued.

The stake in the opening skirmish was control of the *Monfalcone*. With the arrival of Dragna and Rosselli, the original ownership group split, with Sherer and "Doc" Dougherty aligning with the Italians. Several attempts at peaceful partnership failed, and on a Tuesday night in May 1930, Dougherty, Rosselli, and three other men, armed with revolvers and machine guns, set out to take the ship by force.

Arriving at the *Monfalcone* landing dock, Dougherty was recognized by a watchman, and a party of six crewmen was assembled to meet the challengers at the gangplank. The two groups tangled in hand-to-hand fighting, but Rosselli and his party carried more firepower. When two shots rang out, the crewmen backed off, leaving the gangsters in control of the ship. The gunshots brought the gambling crowd rushing to the top deck, but assured by Dougherty that the fighting was over, the players returned to the card tables, unperturbed by the gunplay or the sudden shift in power.

Rosselli and his partners in the *Monfalcone* suffered a setback in August 1930 when the ship caught fire and burned to the water line. But the *Monfalcone* group, including Sherer, Dragna, and Rosselli, was back in business in the spring of 1931 with the launch of a new gambling barge, a wallowing, 336-foot converted Navy steamer dating from 1889 called the *Rose Isle*. By then, however, the waters were getting crowded.

Floating off the coast of Long Beach were the *Rose Isle;* the *Johanna Smith,* owned by downtown syndicate operators Guy McAfee and Farmer Page; and the latest entry in the seagoing sweepstakes, the *Monte Carlo,* run by Rosselli's old friend Tony Cornero. Together, the ships became known as Gambler's Row, all anchored within a few miles of each other, their running lights winking back and forth in the darkness. The men behind all three vessels employed the brothers Eugene and Clarence Blazier as ownership fronts, but the cooperation ended there, and in July 1932, the rivalry peaked with the murder of Charles Bozeman, a card-table croupier, on board Rosselli's *Rose Isle*.

Arrested for the shooting was James O'Keefe, a St. Louis gangster associated with Page. Federal officials convened a grand jury to look into the affair, which they attributed to a "gambling war." Police intervention did not halt the conflict, however, as three days after the Bozeman murder, a fire was set aboard the *Johanna Smith*. The blaze completely destroyed the ship and sent Page the clear message that the Mafia would not be intimidated. No arrests were made in connection with the blaze, but the newspaper headline "Gang Warfare Seen in Ship Fire, Slayings" drew a clear inference.

Years later, his business and film associates said they couldn't imagine Rosselli engaging in violence, but his brethren in the underworld knew better. A mafioso trades on raw fear, and Rosselli earned his reputation in the Los Angeles gang wars of the late twenties and early thirties.

Into Hollywood

WHILE ROSSELLI AND DRAGNA counted their gambling and bootlegging profits in truckloads of cash, the arrival of the Great Depression ended the booming growth of Los Angeles. Bread lines and soup kitchens became standard features downtown, and by 1934 more than 300,000 people, nearly half the working population, were jobless. Los Angeles was especially hard-hit because it lacked the manufacturing base that many other cities relied on. Even those lucky enough to hold jobs earned only mean wages in the union-free environment maintained under the watchful eye of Harry Chandler's *Times*.

Faced with deepening crisis, the city reacted with hard-fisted law and order. Mayor John Porter gave free rein to his chief of police, a former steelworker named Roy "Strongarm Dick" Steckel. Employing tactics he had honed as leader of the department's Chinatown Detail, Steckel lashed out at the problems of economic dislocation with the billy club and the paddy wagon.

"Vagrants" were a primary target for Steckel's forces. "Unemployment is a crime in Sunny California," writer Louis Adamic observed at the time. "Shabby-looking men are stopped in the street, dragged out of flophouses, asked if they have work, and if they answer in the negative, they are arrested for vagrancy." In 1932 alone, 15,000 arrests for vagrancy were recorded. Resident Mexicans were another target throughout the decade, with more than 200,000 rounded up and shipped south of the border. Efforts to organize unions or political opposition to the mayor and his conservative allies were met with mass arrests.

The hard times surrounding them seemed only to buoy the fortunes of Dragna and Rosselli. To the poor and the unemployed, games of chance seemed the only likely escape, and gambling proliferated, from nickel bingo, where bettors crowded under tents pitched on empty lots, to the pricey tables on the gambling ships—all of which meant a larger take for the operators. Another betting venue was the Olympic Auditorium, a modern boxing arena that seated 15,000 and became the center of the town's sporting life. Rosselli was a regular there, with his flashing smile and his inside knowledge. "Everybody knew him, and he got a lot of respect," recalled Johnny Lange, a songwriter who started, incongruously, as a boxing manager in the early thirties. In a town groaning under economic privation, Rosselli was immune.

As he gained stature, Rosselli worked to shed the Italian accent and rough manners of his youth. His model was Paul Ricca, the suave and wily immigrant who had chosen sophistication over flamboyance in his rise to power as Capone's top strategist. Rosselli began to dress in hand-tailored suits, and pushed himself to master the manners and speech that marked men of wealth and influence. A longtime friend recalled later that, "John was very observant, and obviously when he was quite young, he realized that good manners and grooming and knowing the right things to do and the right wines to order and the right food and everything was very important if you were going to be a gentleman. It was all through observation." This penchant for etiquette was unusual in a street thug, and would come to distinguish Rosselli from most of his underworld colleagues.

★

Besides crime, the other Los Angeles institution that flourished despite the Depression was Hollywood. Though frequently dismissed as a glitzy diversion, the film industry had in fact, by the middle 1920s, emerged as a major financial institution, boasting some of the highest profits, and highest salaries, in the nation. In 1927, the film industry ranked as the fourth largest business in the country, with capital assets in the form of theaters, studios, and offices valued at $1.5 billion. That same year, the industry took its greatest single leap forward with the introduction of sound technology, marked by Al Jolson's *The Jazz Singer*, which broke every previous box-office record. By 1928, more than a million people bought tickets every week at 20,000 movie houses across the nation. At the end of the decade, the film studios were valued in astronomical figures for the time: the holding company that owned Warner Brothers, for example, was worth $160 million, with more than half the corporate stock held by the Warners themselves.

The sudden and enormous success of the movies spawned an orgy of vice that threatened to shatter the industry. Drug use was widespread, including cocaine, heroin, and illegal alcohol. Sexual favors were demanded by casting directors and became a sort of alternative currency—Mack Sennett's Keystone Studios had to be tented and fumigated for infestations of venereal crabs.

Flush with style and cash, the film colony found diversion at lavish nightclubs like the Cocoanut Grove, the New Cotton Club in Culver City, and Fatty Arbuckle's famous Plantation Café. Less posh but closer to work was the Clover Club, located in a nondescript stucco building off Sunset Boulevard where a secret passageway led to a second-floor game room hung in heavy red velvet. Late-night hands of poker and bridge and chemin de fer saw the pot routinely accumulate a fortune in Depression-era dollars. "After work the studio heads would drop in on the way home and drop fifteen, twenty thousand dollars a night," recalled Budd Schulberg, whose father, B. P. Schulberg, was head of production at Paramount, and a high-stakes gambler. "They worked hard and they played hard. That was the spirit of the place."

On weekends, the stars and the moguls headed south to Tijuana's Agua Caliente resort, where the drinking was legal and the gambling ran from 10 A.M. to 5 A.M.—nineteen hours at a stretch. Director William Wellman recalled that on weekend nights, "The huge barroom was loaded and so was everyone in it. The bar six deep with actors, actresses, jockeys, doctors, lawyers, and an Indian Chief from Oklahoma." For the elite, there was the Gold Room, where high rollers were treated to gourmet meals and a table service wrought from gold, which soon became the exclusive domain of studio heads Carl Laemmle and Joe Schenck. More important, the resort sported the richest horse-racing track in North America. The film executives became fanatics for the ponies, and as they grew more savvy, they learned to seek out independent bookmakers who could offer them better odds than the track.

One bookmaker in particular gained a reputation for handling outsized bets by "laying off" part of the wager through a national syndicate that could absorb major losses. If you curried his favor, he would on occasion pass along a tip about races that had been rigged by the same betting syndicate, a tip that could yield a windfall of tens of thousands of dollars. Well-groomed and handsome, with dark features and pale blue eyes, the bookmaker was soft-spoken but certainly at home in the hard-edged world of gambling. He was John Rosselli, not yet 30 years old but learning quickly the ways and manners of power.

As Jack Dragna was branching out into the larger arena of Los Angeles vice, so Rosselli was beginning to look afield. Providing muscle in the recurrent gambling wars remained his primary occupation, but he never accepted the boundaries of the criminal world as the limit of his activities. He had long been impressed with the money and beautiful women of Hollywood, and as he rose to become one of the city's leading criminals, Rosselli found that the attraction was mutual.

The studio head who first came to rely on Rosselli's special talents was Harry Cohn, a voracious gambler "whose best friends were card sharks and bookmakers," as one colleague recalled. Cohn's Columbia Studios was just emerging as a force in the film industry, and Rosselli was to become instrumental in his success.

4

STARS AND SCOUNDRELS

White Fang

Hot-tempered, incurably profane, arrogant in his power and spiteful of his minions, Harry Cohn was the consensus choice as the most hated man in Hollywood. Screenwriter Ben Hecht dubbed him "White Fang," and the nickname stuck. Cohn's idol was Benito Mussolini. He visited the Italian dictator in 1933, and upon returning to Los Angeles, had his office remodeled after Il Duce's, with his desk situated on a raised dais from which he would peer down with contempt at writers, directors, and stars alike.

Born in 1891, Harry Cohn grew up on the streets of New York's Upper East Side, the son of an immigrant tailor. After dropping out of school at age 14, he made his way by holding down odd jobs and playing piano in movie houses. He also indulged in small-time crime, fencing stolen furs and hustling pool and even bowling. He and his brother Jack devised an elaborate routine to scam bowling dollars—traveling to lanes outside the city, they would pose as novices or drunks, only revealing their impressive skill once the stakes were raised.

Hard-nosed and ruthless, Cohn never lost the toughness of his early years, and he took an immediate liking to Rosselli. They were a curious match, a meeting of opposites. Wealthy and powerful, a king in a world of glamour, Cohn remained bombastic and vulgar. Rosselli, on the other hand, was fresh off the streets, learning to mask his rough trade with a seamless veneer of gracious manners. He avoided profanity, learned to savor fine wines and to dress with understated flair. They must have enjoyed the contrast of their styles, for the two became fast friends.

Producer and story editor Sam Marx, who worked at Columbia in the thirties, recalled that Rosselli was a regular visitor at the studio, and never had to wait for an audience with the boss. Rosselli was also a frequent guest at Cohn's home, where he played tennis and lounged around the backyard pool, and they took weekends together at the second home Cohn maintained in Palm Springs. When Cohn separated from his first wife, Rose, in the winter of 1936, it was Rosselli who found him a penthouse at the Sunset Plaza, a complex of luxury bungalows situated at the opposite end of Sunset Strip from Columbia Studios. Cohn resided there until his second marriage in 1941, and Rosselli took an apartment on the ground floor of his duplex. Cohn once even offered Rosselli a position as a producer at the studio, but Rosselli disdained the $500 weekly salary. "I get that much from waitresses who take bets from me," he laughed.

The close association between gangster and studio boss was confounding to the law enforcement agencies that intermittently trailed Rosselli. One FBI summary speculated that Rosselli served as Cohn's bodyguard. Local police, more accurately, described him as a personal betting advisor and bookmaker.

Gambling formed the core of the relationship between the two men. Cohn was obsessed with gambling, more driven even than Joe Schenck, and he learned to rely on Rosselli's inside information. In return, Rosselli arranged to have a wire installed to transmit horse-racing results directly to Cohn's office. The friendship escalated in 1934 with the opening of the Santa Anita Racetrack in the foothills of the San Gabriel Mountains east of Los Angeles, followed by Hollywood Park, a second track formed at the initiative of Harry Warner. Cohn became a track fixture during the racing season, with Rosselli his companion and advisor. And when the track gates were closed, the pair would head for the bouts at the Olympic Auditorium, a hangout that drew the reigning Hollywood stars of the era, Al

Jolson and Mae West, along with the not-yet-famous, people like Milton Berle, Jack Benny, and George Burns.

Cohn and Rosselli's relationship was one of peers more than one between mogul and sidekick. The two became betting partners one afternoon in Palm Springs when Cohn was hustling for larger stakes than he could cover out of pocket. Rosselli obligingly took the bet and when Cohn won, the two pooled their earnings in a sort of revolving fund. Over the years, this betting pool grew to a total of more than $15,000—twice the wage most skilled laborers could make in a year.

On another occasion, in March of 1937, Rosselli had an opportunity to buy an ownership interest in a racetrack for an investment of $20,000. Rosselli approached Cohn for a loan, and his powerful friend wrote a personal check on the spot. In June, Rosselli paid Cohn $200 to cover interest, and in September, Rosselli presented Cohn with a $20,000 check to cancel the debt. Cohn balked at the idea of profiting off a loan to such a close friend, and insisted that he rewrite the check to $19,800. Rosselli was deeply moved by the gesture, and sought to reciprocate. Harking back to an old Italian custom, Rosselli purchased two matching rings, star rubies set in gold, put one on his right hand and offered the other to Cohn. The producer wore it proudly.

But Cohn's greatest debt to Rosselli had nothing to do with gambling. In 1932, Harry Cohn was locked in a struggle for control of the studio with his brother Jack, a less temperamental, more conservative executive who controlled the studio's finances from the corporate headquarters in New York. Relations between the two were always strained—when Harry would visit the studios, neither would speak to the other on official business without a witness present. Each brother owned a third of the company, with the balance held by Joe Brandt, Jack's partner from an early stint in advertising.

Columbia's fortunes were rising, largely as a result of Harry's rigid production budgets, but the constant acrimony between the brothers had become too much for Brandt, and he announced his intention to sell out to the first man to offer $500,000. Jack Cohn shopped the deal around New York financial circles, but the Depression had drained even the largest banks of their entrepreneurial nerve. By nature more desperate and less scrupulous than his brother, Harry Cohn turned to John Rosselli, who relayed the request to New Jersey rackets boss "Longy" Zwillman, who forwarded the funds in cash.

Backing Harry Cohn's interest in Columbia represented a straight business transaction for Zwillman and Rosselli, who most likely earned a finder's fee, but the deal carried special significance for Hollywood. From that time forward, organized crime was considered a player in the film industry, a factor the major producers accepted with no more tribulation than the arrival of a new labor union or a government commission.

The Moguls and the Mob

JOHN ROSSELLI WAS NOT the only gangster to take part in the fast living in Hollywood in the early 1930s. Every studio had its own private bootlegger, and several among them became prominent in the film industry, usually on the strength of their friendships with one or another studio mogul.

Frank and Victor Orsatti rose to power as premier Hollywood agents through their long association with the grandiloquent Louis B. Mayer, the genius behind the success of Metro-Goldwyn-Mayer Studios and, for several years, the highest-salaried executive in the United States. Frank Orsatti was Mayer's closest friend, a golf and travel companion who procured for him liquor, women, and, on the business side, talent. The association has been portrayed as a simple friendship, but there is little doubt Mayer was aware that Orsatti started as a hoodlum in the San Francisco underworld.

According to an FBI summary compiled in 1939, the Orsatti brothers, including Frank, Victor, Albert, Ernest, and Jess, rose to prominence through bootlegging and other criminal activity throughout California. The report asserted: "In former years L. B. Mayer furnished money to the father of Frank Orsatti in the operation of some criminal activities, and the Orsattis therefore have a hold on Mayer which places them in a position to obtain the cream of the theatrical business in Los Angeles. . . . The Orsattis are generally considered to be the criminal type of individuals, and have the reputation of handling 'all of the dirty work' that is done for MGM."

Further, the summary said that Frank Orsatti was subject to an IRS lien to collect $506,000 in unpaid income taxes for the years 1922 to 1926.

The case was settled for a flat $100,000, apparently due to Mayer's influence, despite Orsatti's guilty plea to charges of perjury in the case. "Information in the possession of the Los Angeles office is to the effect that the settlement of this case was effected by Louis B. Mayer through contacts that he had in Washington, D.C., with someone in the Income Tax Division," the report stated.

Mayer once was confronted about his mob associations by Carter Barron, a well-connected Washington lobbyist for Loew's. Barron refused to join a dinner table where Mayer was eating with one of his underworld friends, announcing that he did not want to be seen with a gangster. "You're a damn Baptist," Mayer shot back. "Don't you know you've got to know all sorts of people? I use him to do things for me that you wouldn't do."

At the Warner Brothers studio, Jack Warner was the most flamboyant of the four siblings, the biggest gambler and the closest to the gangster element. He counted among his personal friends Moses Annenberg, who rose to national prominence by supplying track information to illegal bookmakers; Mark Hellinger, a popular columnist and producer who, according to his biographer, "worked closely with both the FBI and the California underworld"; and, later, celebrated killer and socialite Ben Siegel. These associations were not criminal in nature, but they demonstrate the easy acquaintance between the worlds of crime and film.

The gangster's biggest friend in Hollywood was Joseph Schenck, the president of United Artists who, in 1933, founded Twentieth Century Studios. Gregarious, generous, a large man of imperious bearing with a broad nose and sleepy eyes, Joe Schenck was a central figure in Hollywood, organizer of film companies and other business ventures, card games and legendary drinking bouts. It was Schenck who fielded press inquiries for industry response to political or economic strife, and it was Schenck who stood on the railroad platform in 1922 to greet Will Hays and install him as head of the new Motion Picture Producers and Distributors of America (MPPDA).

Joe and his brother Nicholas Schenck emigrated from Rybinsk, Russia, with their parents in the late 1880s, and broke into the entertainment world running amusement parks in Manhattan and New Jersey, a business that required continuing relationships with the local mobs. The film concessions at the parks were leased to Marcus Loew, then assembling his New York theater chain. In 1910, both Schencks signed on as executives under Loew, and as a favor to their new boss, provided an introduction to

Arnold Rothstein, the forerunner to Meyer Lansky as the financial wizard of the underworld. Known alternately as The Big Bankroll, The Fixer, or sometimes simply Mister Big, Rothstein became a major stockholder in Loew's Inc.

While Nick Schenck prospered at the company, rising to become president upon Loew's death in 1927, Joe Schenck left New York in 1917 to produce pictures in Hollywood. He married the beautiful actress Norma Talmadge, but his passion was for the horses. Schenck spent nearly every weekend in Tijuana, and in 1932, took a seat on the board of the Agua Caliente Jockey Club, which oversaw track operations. Here, again, Schenck worked closely with gangsters, enlisting Zeke Caress in 1933 to head betting operations at the Caliente racetrack. A prominent member of Guy McAfee's gambling combine, Caress won fame as the subject of a sensational kidnapping by rival gangsters in 1931.

Schenck's entourage also included Lew and Al Wertheimer, natives of Detroit who operated the Café Royale, hangout for the Motor City's notorious Purple Gang. Schenck invited the Wertheimers to migrate West, where they founded the Clover Club and presided over the illegal gambling there. And along the way, Schenck formed a close friendship with Rosselli, one that survived in spite of the hard times it would eventually bring to both men.

The alliance between studio bosses and the gangsters might be viewed as consequence of doing business in the rough-and-tumble entertainment industry, but the connections were too frequent and too cordial for that. There was a natural affinity—like the moguls, the gangsters had clawed their way off the streets by dint of nerve, and like the moguls, they traded in power and intimidation. Surrounded by the ethereal, sometimes effete world of actors and writers and painters, the studio executives looked to the gangsters to affirm their machismo. Their employees might act tough in front of the cameras, but when the lights went down, men like Cohn and Mayer and Warner reveled in the company of the real tough guys, the ones whose lives the scenarists could only attempt to capture.

The relationship permeated Hollywood social life, manifesting at gambling clubs, on golf courses, on studio lots, even in barber shops. Toward the end of the 1930s, Billy Wilkerson, publisher of the Hollywood *Reporter*, took a liking to a barber at the Waldorf-Astoria in New York and invited him to relocate to Beverly Hills. Gangster Ben Siegel provided start-up money, and Harry Drucker's Barber Shop quickly became a hangout—for the leaders of the film industry, and for the gangsters. Drucker recalled John Rosselli as a regular customer, respected and admired.

These film executives, who associated so freely with practiced criminals in their personal lives, were the same men who proselytized so fiercely the American ideals of clean living and "traditional values" in the films they produced. Beginning in 1934, the Hollywood studios hired former Chicago *Tribune* editor Joseph I. Breen to administer a Production Code requiring that "Correct standards of life shall be presented," and that "the sympathy of the audience shall never be thrown to the side of crime, wrong-doing, evil or sin." Their movies propagated a sanctimonious myth of American life, but the moguls never bought into it themselves, and in fact flaunted it in company of pals like John Rosselli. Even Breen himself partook of the farce—he was personal friends with Rosselli, having met him in Chicago in the twenties.

Hollywood's fascination with career criminals was reflected in its production. Gangster films were standard fare from the beginning of the industry—*Bandit's Roost* was filmed in 1895, the first year of American film. The modern gangster epic, with its basis in street-life realism, arrived in 1927 with *Underworld,* a box-office hit directed by Josef von Sternberg and written by Chicago native Ben Hecht. After the advent of Joe Breen's Production Code, the image of the tough-talking, gun-wielding mobster remained an industry staple—but the gangster always died in the end.

One small-time hoodlum even became a star. George Raft, who grew up running with Ben Siegel and Meyer Lansky on the Lower East Side of New York, gave up crime for vaudeville, and then found fame being typecast as a slick-haired slugger. But of all the gangsters hanging in and around the film colony, it was John Rosselli who became the most deeply enmeshed in the fortunes of the industry, due in large part to his high rank in the underworld. While the Orsattis and the others had criminal backgrounds, Rosselli was a mafioso, which put him on an altogether different plane. His illegal activities took place on a broad scale, backed by a criminal organization that spanned the country, and which could marshal large forces of raw muscle or, as Harry Cohn had learned, capital. Moreover, dealing with Rosselli was never unseemly. Handsome and suave, he managed affairs with discretion and dispatch. Years later, the producers would lament their association with Rosselli and the nation's top criminals, but at the time, it seemed smart, exciting, and good for business.

A Little Rough Play

HOLLYWOOD'S PARTNERSHIP WITH ROSSELLI intensified when the Depression finally caught up with the film industry. The genial and slightly risqué social alliance that had grown up at watering holes and racetracks evolved easily into a more functional relationship when economic pressure, and its attendant labor crunch, threatened the abundant luxury to which the studio bosses had become accustomed.

Toward the end of 1932, audiences and box-office receipts began to dwindle, and though they continued to produce movies, RKO, Fox, Universal, and Paramount went into receivership following multimillion-dollar losses. The studio heads protected their own enormous earnings—in the mid-1930s nineteen of the nation's twenty-five highest-paid executives worked in the movies, prompting President Franklin Roosevelt in 1933 to declare Hollywood salaries "unconscionable." Instead, the studios responded to hard times by slashing wages at the bottom of the pay ladder. In the spring of 1933, production employee paychecks were cut 50 percent across the board, precipitating a full-blown labor crisis.

The drastic cuts brought mixed results for the industry. In the case of the writers and actors, the producers found they had pushed too far when the stars and scribes deserted the in-house Academy of Motion Picture Arts and Sciences to form vigorously independent guilds. The studios fared much better in confrontation with the industry's largest existing union, the International Alliance of Theatrical Stage Employees (IATSE).

Union complaints were referred to Pat Casey, Nick Schenck's choice as labor liaison for the Association of Motion Pictures Producers (Producers Association). A huge, gruff Irishman who learned his trade running theater security under the Schenck brothers in New York City, Casey rebuffed the IATSE business agents, and on July 24, 1933, the union struck. The producers determined to resist, and Casey turned to John Rosselli to help break the strike.

Rosselli recalled his entry into the labor field under questioning by a congressional committee in 1950:

"They had a strike in the industry and the studios were in difficulty. There was a little rough play around and the studios naturally didn't want it. They needed some cameramen to go back to work, and they had been threatened through some people. They asked if I could help. I said the only way to help is to fight fire with fire."

Casey and the producers apparently appreciated the advice, because Rosselli was hired to recruit a crew of thugs to ensure that nonunion laborers, plentiful in the lean days of the Depression, moved efficiently across picket lines. The strike was short but bitter, punctuated by the suicide of Norman de Vol, an unemployed cameraman who killed himself rather than help break his union. The Screen Writers Guild, newly formed and timorous, voted to remain "neutral." The International Brotherhood of Electrical Workers, long jealous of the IATSE hold on the film industry, crossed the picket lines along with cameramen provided by magazines and newspapers, led by the antilabor *Times.* Production was slowed, but the presence of Rosselli's men kept the studio gates open.

By August 1 it was over, with the IATSE broken as a power in the film industry. The producers announced an open-shop labor policy and erased the basic wage agreement with IATSE. The trade press reported that "the major companies have declared open season on any organized groups in Hollywood which attempt to impose minimum salary scales or working conditions." Over the next two years, IATSE membership fell from more than 6,500 to fewer than 100.

The Depression was hurting the industry, certainly, but with the destruction of IATSE, the producers had never been stronger. The fact that they had gained the upper hand in collaboration with organized crime was never an issue.

John Rosselli profited handsomely by the strike. His smooth management of the studio goon squads won him a permanent, if sub rosa, spot on Pat Casey's payroll, but it wasn't the money that mattered. More important was Rosselli's enhanced status in the film industry. No longer dependent on Harry Cohn and Columbia Studios, he became a regular face around the Hays Office, as the MPPDA came to be known under the rule of the sternly Presbyterian Will Hays. "The girls at the office all seemed to know him," one labor leader recalled. "They called him Johnny, and he was quite popular with the ladies—they thought he was a perfect gentleman." The Hays Office shared space with Central Casting, where a well-placed word from a man in Rosselli's position could mean a crucial break for a girl looking for an edge in filmdom's rat race.

In keeping with his new role as industry insider, Rosselli moved into new lodgings at the Garden of Allah, a collection of twenty-five stucco bungalows clustered behind a mansion. Silent-screen star Alla Nazimova built the estate and had converted it to a hotel as her career faded. Flagstone paths wound through exotic gardens that perfumed the air with the scent of jasmine and fuchsia and jacaranda. A monument to fantasy—it boasted a sixty-foot swimming pool sculpted in the shape of Nazimova's native Black Sea.

Located at the corner of Crescent Heights and Sunset Boulevard, near the terminus of the red line trolley from downtown and across the street from the elegant Chateau Marmont, the Garden of Allah became famous as the "Fabulous Baghdad on the Sunset Strip." Stars like Greta Garbo, Marlene Dietrich, and Humphrey Bogart lived there between homes and marriages, as did writers F. Scott Fitzgerald, Ernest Hemingway, and Thomas Wolfe. Liquor was available at all hours, games of dice and cards hummed in a rear cabana, and resident writer Lucius Beebe recalled that "nothing interrupted the continual tumult" of high Hollywood living. Humorist Robert Benchley summed up the spirit of the place when, arriving at the festivities one rainy night, he paused to announce, "I think I'll get out of these wet clothes and into a dry martini."

Thus ensconced in a key office and an equally strategic apartment, John Rosselli set about establishing a reputation as one of the town's leading socialites. He cultivated friendships in the entertainment press— show biz columnists Louella Parsons and Florabel Muir, and Billy Wilkerson, a restaurateur who founded the daily Hollywood *Reporter*. He bought into a Sunset Strip nightclub, the Club New Yorker, a place with a long bar and low lights which drew gamblers, gangsters, and film stars with a "Parisian" floor show. And he served as an occasional escort to Jean Harlow, the platinum-blond bombshell who was emerging as the nation's leading female box-office draw. Harlow was carrying on an intermittent affair with New Jersey rackets boss Abner "Longy" Zwillman, and he asked Rosselli to keep an eye on her.

Rosselli's American dream was coming true. He had assimilated to a degree he could never have expected, lived in luxurious quarters, and was embraced as a peer by the nation's richest and most envied community. But he never lost track of his role, or his allegiances. And when shifting fortunes forced the Capone organization in Chicago to seek new fields for plunder, Rosselli was well positioned to orchestrate one of the richest and certainly the most brazen crime of the era.

A Union in Hand

WHEN AL CAPONE WAS convicted on tax charges in 1931, his downfall came as a stunning rebuke to gangsters who had believed their leader immune, but the repeal of Prohibition in 1933 had a more profound impact. Cut off from a seemingly bottomless well of cash, Scarface Al's successors scrambled to develop new sources of revenue. Legitimate business was one option, and the Outfit, as Capone's criminal organization was known, invested heavily in breweries and real estate. But the big money, the easy money, still lay in operations outside the law, and labor unions, with their large cash reserves and loose central controls, became a favorite target.

Over the course of the decade, the Chicago Outfit extorted payments from or simply took over local and international organizations representing truck drivers, laundry workers, retail clerks, municipal workers, and hotel staff. And in 1934, at a national convention in Kentucky chaperoned by some of Chicago's heaviest sluggers, the Outfit placed a second-rank labor leader named George Browne in the presidency of the IATSE, which despite the debacle in Hollywood in 1933, still represented thousands of stagehands and projectionists in theaters across the country. The head of one of the union's Chicago locals, Browne had failed miserably in a bid for the presidency in 1932, but this time won on a near-unanimous ballot. His first official act was to name as his assistant Willie Bioff, a beefy pimp and bar bouncer who answered directly to the mob.

The union takeover was planned at a series of meetings in suburban Riverside, Illinois, where Bioff and Browne were introduced to the men who would be giving the orders: Frank Rio, Capone's former bodyguard and confidant; Frank "The Enforcer" Nitti, the "official" successor to Capone, though in fact used as a front by his more subtle associates; Nick Circella, a club operator who used the alias Nick Dean, and who made the first approach to George Browne; Louis Campagna, a ruthless killer imported from New York to help wage street wars in 1927; Capone's cousin

Charlie Fischetti; and Rosselli's old mentor Paul Ricca, considered the real brains of the Outfit.

The initial scheme was simple: to place mob leaders and their relatives on the union payroll, to siphon off some of the membership dues, and to extort payments from theater operators with threats of strikes. Opposition within the union was quickly silenced—Tommy Malloy, head of the largest Chicago locals and himself an accomplished grifter, was murdered by shotgun blast within a year of the takeover.

However, unbeknownst to Browne and Bioff, the Outfit had an even greater agenda on how to mine the union. John Rosselli made a trip to Chicago on the eve of Browne's election to lay out a plan for wholesale extortion of the Hollywood studios for Nitti, Ricca, and the rest of the leadership—Browne and Bioff were not invited. Rosselli described the profit structure of the industry, which studios employed how many men, and what unions were involved—information gleaned from his friendships with Joe Schenck and Harry Cohn, and from his vantage point as a "labor consultant" on Pat Casey's payroll. Rosselli explained that most of the studios owned their own chains of theaters, a monopoly practice that made them especially vulnerable to strikes. In addition, Rosselli knew firsthand from his experience as a management strikebreaker that the rival studio unions were too weak to block an IATSE resurgence.

After a presentation that ran roughly an hour, the Outfit leadership decided to move gradually, rebuilding their strength in Los Angeles. In July 1934, soon after the shanghaied IATSE convention, Bioff got in contact with Pat Casey, the labor man for the producers. A meeting was arranged in New York, where most of the film industry's important financial decisions took place.

Browne, Bioff, and Dean took a suite together at the Warwick Hotel, but the morning of the meeting, Bioff found Dean dead drunk and unable to attend. Browne and Bioff proceeded alone, joining Casey at the Producers Association office on Broadway. The labor leaders explained their intent to restore IATSE's dominant position in Hollywood, and surprisingly, Casey was amenable. While the studios enjoyed the unchecked power they exercised over their work force, the dismantling of IATSE had also brought on a degree of chaos, with twenty-seven separate guilds jockeying for the allegiance of the skilled laborers. Casey promised to bring the question of IATSE jurisdiction before the producers.

When Bioff and Browne returned to the Warwick, Dean was furious at having been left behind, and accused Bioff of selling out the mob-controlled union. Bioff assured him no money had exchanged hands, but Dean remained suspicious, and announced that he would find out exactly what had transpired with Casey. Taking Bioff in tow, Dean headed directly for the Medical Arts Sanitarium on West Fifty-seventh Street. Without a word of explanation, Dean guided Bioff into the hospital, up a staircase, down a hall, and into a room where a lean-faced young man was sitting up in bed. "Hello, Johnny," Dean greeted the patient. "Hello, Nick, how are you?" John Rosselli was recuperating from another bout of tuberculosis, but there was always time for business.

Dean introduced Bioff and then began to address Rosselli in Italian. Gracious as ever, Rosselli turned to Bioff, apologized for excluding him, and then spoke for about five minutes in his native tongue. Finally, Rosselli turned back to Bioff and repeated, nearly word for word, Bioff's discussions with Pat Casey that morning. "Are those the correct, the exact words you spoke to Mr. Casey, and the exact words he spoke to you?" Rosselli asked. "Correct," Bioff replied simply. Rosselli turned to Dean, who smiled and addressed Bioff. "Johnny Rosselli here is our man. He handles the West Coast for us. He is Pat Casey's man there, too, he is on Casey's payroll, and Casey will go along with us with Johnny in there. If there is anything that goes on on the West Coast with any producing company, we will know. There is nothing you or George can do or say that we won't know."

Later that week, George Browne got the same treatment. Browne was drinking at a nightclub with Pat Casey, Frank Costello, and Charles "Lucky" Luciano when Costello suggested an unlikely side trip to visit a friend in the hospital. The friend was John Rosselli, and Browne received the same instructions as Bioff; that Rosselli would supervise the operations of the union in Los Angeles.

Thus was the national leadership of the IATSE introduced to John Rosselli. Bioff in particular always resented Rosselli for his power, his connections, and his easy style, and the feeling was mutual, Rosselli disdaining Bioff's broad, barroom manner. But like it or not, they were partners, and for the next several years, there was money enough to keep them both happy.

The Studios Ante Up

THE TALKS WITH PAT Casey dragged out more than a year, and by the fall of 1935 it was apparent the producers had decided to ignore George Browne's entreaties. The Chicago Outfit stepped in on November 30, 1935, when the IATSE struck more than 500 Paramount theaters from Chicago to St. Louis. It was a Saturday night, and at 8 P.M., with the movie houses full and the shows under way, everything came to a halt. The lights went out, customers had to be refunded their tickets, and the studio heads learned a costly lesson in exactly how powerful the IATSE had become.

An emergency meeting was called for the following week at the Union League Club in New York. Browne presented a settle-or-strike ultimatum, demanding the IATSE's reinstatement in Hollywood under a closed-shop agreement. Faced with the crippling prospect of theater strikes across the country, Pat Casey and the producers capitulated. By the end of the session, the IATSE had regained more than 12,000 studio workers and its old status as Hollywood's primary crafts union.

Flush with sudden success, the IATSE executive board convened the following month for their annual meeting at the Fleetwood Hotel in Miami. The talks were dominated by arrangements for administration of the revived Los Angeles chapter, and by the presence of John Rosselli and the Chicago gang leaders, there to make sure the unionists remembered who was actually in charge. Bioff was named as the head of the Hollywood local, and with business disposed of, the executives retired to their amusements. Bioff headed for the golf course with Rosselli and Nick Dean— Bioff didn't play the game himself, but tagged along for the stroll.

The highlight of the weekend was a dinner party thrown for Bioff and Browne at the beach house of Al Capone. Old Scarface was in prison, but his brother Ralph was there, along with Rosselli, Dean, and the rest of the mob entourage. There was another meeting that weekend in Miami, this one attended only by Rosselli, Bioff, and Frank Nitti, at the home Nitti had rented for the confab. Gruff and menacing as always, Nitti reminded

Bioff that Rosselli would oversee the operations in Los Angeles, and that he should be placed on the union payroll. Bioff objected, but Nitti was adamant. "I want you to put him on," he growled. "That is your problem."

Accompanied by his wife, Bioff celebrated his otherwise good fortune with a pleasure cruise that brought him, for the first time, into Los Angeles. Landing at the dock in San Pedro, he was met by Rosselli and Browne, and during the hour-long drive into Los Angeles, the three men agreed on tactics to be employed in running the Hollywood local. As the first order of business, Bioff was to revoke the charter of the IATSE local in favor of direct rule by the Chicago-based international.

George Dunne, a Jesuit priest who studied the history of the Hollywood unions, described Bioff's first visit to the IATSE hall. "Bioff walked into a meeting of the union offices on Santa Monica Boulevard with these two hit men from Chicago, one on either side. Each one had a violin case under his arm, just like they do in the movies. Bioff stood up and said we're taking over the union, the international is, and they dismissed the local officers right there." The local IATSE organization was dissolved, all meetings and votes were suspended, and from then on, all decisions were made unilaterally by George Browne and Willie Bioff.

Soon after, the film industry rank and file received another shock. From that day forward, workers would be assessed an extra 2 percent charge against their paychecks, ostensibly for strike insurance but in fact as another source of graft for Browne, Bioff, and the Outfit. The surcharge yielded more than $1 million over the next several years, and marked the beginning of the "real dough" Nitti and the boys from Chicago had been seeking from the start. But the best was yet to come.

The studio heads chafed at the resurrection of the IATSE, but fearful of another theater strike, they agreed to meet in April 1936 with Browne and the other craft union heads to iron out the details of the new basic agreement. Two days before the meeting, Bioff and Browne dropped by Nick Schenck's New York office and outlined a new proposition. Bioff explained that he had helped elect Browne and then declared, "I want you to know that I am the boss and that I want two million dollars out of the motion picture industry." Schenck was astounded. "At first I could not talk and when I did answer I told him I could not understand him. I thought he was out of his mind," he recalled later.

On the scheduled day, April 16, the studio heads and the union leaders met in the heavily paneled conference rooms of Pat Casey's executive offices. Bioff came up with a formula—the major studios would pay a tribute of $50,000 a year each, in cash, with the smaller companies contributing $25,000, in return for labor peace. Nick Schenck accepted, and with Loew's in line, Bioff went after Sidney Kent of Twentieth Century-Fox, then Albert Warner, then Leo Spitz of RKO, huddling with each in private offices separate from the official talks, until all the majors had acquiesced. Nick Dean was at the meeting and Bioff informed him on the spot; he contacted Rosselli that night in a phone call to the West Coast to break the good news.

There was another factor besides the Paramount strike that helped persuade the producers to accept Bioff's terms. The surviving Hollywood craft unions had grown increasingly militant after IATSE's 1933 collapse, and were asking for wage increases between 33 and 100 percent at the 1936 negotiations. Bioff promised that, if his demands for a cash payoff were met, the studio workers would settle for 10 percent and a no-strike guarantee—an easy out in a year of labor unrest across the country. As Bioff himself admitted later, "It was very costly to [the competing studio unions] to have us in there."

As it turned out, the years of the mob's domination of the IATSE were marked by static and declining wages, despite pay scales already eroded by the Depression. Weekly wages for projection-booth operators in Philadelphia dropped from $120 to $68; stagehands in Kansas City saw their paychecks shrink 15 percent; and in New York, projectionists' hourly wages dropped from $2.12 to $1.58. By 1938, Bioff's "extortion" had enough of a silver lining that Sidney Kent felt compelled to attend the IATSE annual convention and declare, "We have had less interruption of employment, less hard feeling, less recrimination, and have built more goodwill than any industry I know of in the country."

Still, the alliance with Bioff and his thugs was uncomfortable for the producers, especially at the start, and Nick Schenck, the first of the producers to pay, remembered the moment bitterly. It took three days to pull the cash together, and when it was ready, Schenck wrapped it neatly in brown paper and took a taxi to Bioff and Browne's suite at the Waldorf-Astoria, where he interrupted the racketeers at breakfast. "Count it," he said shortly, laying his package on the bed. While they did, Schenck crossed the room, lit a cigarette, and stared out over the city, musing in frustration. Mob money was mixed up in the studios, and mob muscle, supervised by John Rosselli, had helped the producers control the labor picture. But now the game was getting out of hand. As Bioff would recall years later, "I had Hollywood dancing to my tune."

Nationwide

THERE WAS A SECOND avenue by which the Chicago Outfit sought to replace its bootlegging revenues. That was organized gambling, and here as well, Rosselli profited handsomely. More important, the resulting betting monopoly gave Rosselli the lever by which to finally best the competing crime syndicate in Los Angeles, and to take over the graft network that controlled the police and city hall.

The key to organized gambling in Los Angeles and across the country was a racetrack news service operated by Moses Annenberg, the hardheaded businessman whose publishing empire, later run by his son Walter, came to include the Philadelphia *Enquirer* and *TV Guide*. The Annenberg connection was central in the first truly national operation staged by the syndicated families of organized crime.

Moses Annenberg rose to power waging a desperate battle for market share as the circulation director of William Hearst's Chicago *Examiner*. Newsboys were attacked on street corners, delivery trucks were hijacked, and newsstands were bombed in what one writer called "the bloodiest and most ruthless circulation war in the history of journalism anywhere." Annenberg's sluggers included Dion O'Banion, Walter Stevens, and Tommy Malloy, all vicious killers who would come to serve or rival Al Capone in the heyday of Chicago crime.

Determined to be his own boss, Annenberg left Hearst in 1910 to head a newspaper distribution franchise in Milwaukee, where his special brand of competition helped him dominate the trade. In 1922, he brought his monopolistic instincts to racetrack publishing, an industry he came to dominate through a combination of business acumen and sheer force. On the legitimate side, he purchased the *Racing Form*, the daily racetrack bible, along with sister publications the *Morning Telegraph* and the *American Racing Record*. More importantly, he bought the General News Bureau, a wire service that supplied last-minute track information to bookmakers around the Chicago area. The data was crucial to the bookies, who would otherwise be helpless prey to bettors armed with information on scratches or late race results, and they paid handsome fees for the service. Off-track bookmaking was strictly illegal, but the news service operated in a gray area that yielded enormous profits to Annenberg.

Working with bookies in Chicago in the 1920s meant working with Al Capone, a partnership that was sealed when Annenberg paid Capone $100,000 in cash to muscle his partner in General News, John Lynch, out of the business. Capone shared Annenberg's dream of building the racing wire into a national monopoly, but to do so would require the cooperation of the crime chieftains who controlled gambling in all of the country's great urban centers. Accordingly, in 1929 Capone invited Annenberg to join him in attending the first recorded gathering of the heads of organized crime in America, known now simply as the Atlantic City Conference.

Meeting for three days in May at the Ritz and Ambassador hotels on the beach city's famed boardwalk, top gangsters from Chicago, Boston, Philadelphia, New York, New Jersey, Detroit, Cleveland, and Kansas City aired grievances, designated territories, and laid plans for cooperative enterprises. Chief among them was Annenberg's racing wire, which would help normalize bookmaking operations across the country. "That's how the Annenberg family really made its fortune, out of muscle in Chicago and betting ties with us," Charles "Lucky" Luciano recalled later. With the newly syndicated criminal underworld signed up in support, Annenberg adopted the name Nationwide News Service, and proceeded to knock out more than two dozen competing wire services. By the middle 1930s, he counted more than 15,000 clients in 223 cities in 39 states.

John Rosselli was appointed Annenberg's primary business representative in Los Angeles, where an estimated $1 million was bet on horse races every day. Operating out of offices in the Bank of America Building downtown, Rosselli organized the collection and transmission of race results and information from tracks in Los Angeles and Tijuana, and on the revenue side, made sure that bookmakers in the city subscribed to the service and kept current on their payments to Nationwide. "I would see books open and close, and when they would open I would just try to get more customers," he said blandly in later testimony to a congressional committee. "How would you persuade people?" Rosselli was asked. "Just by discussing it with them," he replied. If words didn't suffice, muscle did. His partner in the collections end was Jack Dragna, whose gunmen made short work of recalcitrant bookies.

In return for his services, Rosselli was paid 5 percent of the news wire's gross receipts, yielding him roughly $2,000 a month. But as with his parallel job as labor enforcer for the film industry, the wire service position carried side benefits that far outweighed the salary. As Rosselli noted in his later testimony, "The wire service company never could get along without local corruption."

That corruption centered on Frank L. Shaw, a smirking, backslapping former grocer elected mayor of Los Angeles in 1933 on the platform, "Throw the Grafters Out." Amiable but essentially a bumbler, Shaw left the nitty gritty of city management to his brother Joe, a former Navy lieutenant whose office in city hall came to be known as "the corner pocket." Cynical and profoundly avaricious, Joe Shaw quickly turned administration of the city into a sort of rolling auction, with commission appointments and civil service promotions on sale to the highest bidder. Recalled Grant Cooper, a prominent Los Angeles attorney, "Frank Shaw was the figurehead, and his brother Joe did all the dirty work behind the scenes. Bribes were everyday affairs." An FBI report prepared in 1938 added that "Joe Shaw is reported to be the man who collects payoffs from the underworld."

Here again, John Rosselli played a central role, serving as the Mafia's bridge to the mayor's brother. The connection was never revealed publicly, but a background report compiled by a newspaper reporter in 1937 found, "Right now it is no secret that Rosselli has an 'in' with the Shaw people, mainly through establishing a friendship with Joe Shaw. Everyone expects that he will try to branch out because of this connection." A subsequent police intelligence report identified Rosselli as a "gunman" for Joe Shaw.

The crucial asset that Shaw was able to deliver was control of the police, a roughhouse department set up along the same lines as city hall. Chief James Edgar "Two Gun" Davis was a round, boisterous man who liked to impress reporters by shooting the ash off a cigarette clamped in the teeth of a "volunteer" officer at a hundred paces. Davis railed against criminals and communists, but left most of the department's operations to subordinates Red Hynes, whose "Red Squad" specialized in strike-breaking and espionage against leftist political groups, and Earle Kynette, head of the department's notorious "Intelligence Division."

A specialist in wiretaps and surveillance, Kynette operated out of his own building a block from city hall and served as a personal emissary and enforcer for Joe Shaw. Critics of the city administration were spied upon and threatened. If they persisted, their homes or offices were bombed, with at least five documented attacks beginning in 1935, including one on a Methodist minister. In addition to his political duties, Kynette managed vice enforcement in the city, harassing racketeers not connected with Shaw, and monitoring payments from those who were.

Along with the paid police protection, the Rosselli-Shaw connection meant the end of the city's domination by the older, more civilized gambling syndicate, the one headed by Guy McAfee and Farmer Page. Joe Shaw had always resented the syndicate's power and autonomy, and Rosselli presented him with an opportunity to circumvent the old guard and still siphon off large-scale kickbacks from vice operations. Coupled with the Mafia monopoly over Los Angeles bookmaking, the Shaw connection comprised the coup de grace in a rivalry that reached back to the days of bootlegging and gambling ships. McAfee and Page were forced out of organized gambling and, eventually, out of the city, leaving Dragna, with Rosselli providing the connections and the brains behind him, as the top criminal in Los Angeles.

With their emergence as the undisputed bosses of the local underworld, the criminal domain of the Los Angeles Mafia reached as far south as Tijuana and as far north as San Francisco. For killings in one city, they would import hit men from another—San Diego's Frank "The Bomp" Bompensiero regularly carried out slayings in Los Angeles. Rosselli was arrested twice in San Francisco, and one time during a roust in Los Angeles, he was discovered carrying a bill for the funeral expenses of Luigi Malvese, a young hoodlum murdered in San Francisco's North Beach. Local papers said the killing resembled "a Capone gang execution": the assailant fired once and, when Malvese fell to the pavement, calmly approached the body and fired four more rounds at point-blank range. Rosselli never explained to police what Malvese's funeral tab was doing in his pocket.

This period represented the zenith of Jack Dragna's criminal career. He never demonstrated the vision or the financial acumen of his counterparts back East, but his national standing was recognized in the fall of 1934, when he attended a Mafia conference in New York. Gathered around a dinner table on the balcony of the theater café Casino de Paris were the top Italian gangsters in the country, including Paul Ricca from Chicago and Frank Costello from New York. The meeting was chaired by

Charles "Lucky" Luciano, who toasted Dragna to the others as one of "our people."

Jack Dragna held the title of boss, but Rosselli was the hidden "capo" of the Los Angeles Mafia, the trusted lieutenant to whom Dragna turned for advice and strategy. The police could only guess his role—one intelligence report placed Rosselli as "the closest man to another Italian, Jack Dragna," while another described the two as "inseparable companions." Ricca in particular watched his rise with satisfaction—he knew he could count on Rosselli's allegiance, and in turn, invested him with the full confidence and authority of the Outfit.

Civic reformer Guy Finney described Rosselli's handiwork in a tract published in 1945:

> Glaringly incompetent, corrupt and wasteful government, crooked police administration, a politically-protected underworld, vice and gambling concessions in full blast, murder, robberies unpunished, open prostitution, gangster warfare waged in public places, flashy nightspots flaunting indecencies, known criminals enjoying the friendship of movie magnates, vice provocateurs and racketeers hobnobbing with public officials—these were some of the shocking aspects of the failure of law enforcement in Los Angeles County in the period between 1930 and 1938.

A Double Life

THE DEFEAT OF THE old syndicate was the final plank in a formidable framework of power. John Rosselli's government, crime, and movie contacts gave him enormous influence. His weekly paychecks as a labor "consultant" and proceeds from his share of the wire service gave him as much cash as he could use. But there was another asset that was even more important to Rosselli, a commodity fundamental to his success, and ultimately, to his identity. That commodity was anonymity, and in Depression-era Los Angeles, Rosselli had that as well.

To his friends on the straight side of the law, Rosselli only hinted at his illegal activities, presenting himself as a public relations man, or more simply, a "consultant." Most never learned otherwise, and those who did knew better than to press for explanations. Genial but always circumspect, Rosselli never let on where he'd been or where he was going. As one contemporary intelligence report noted, "He has a habit of working quietly." To the day of his death, police officials and experts on organized crime knew only dimly of Rosselli's years in Los Angeles, some placing his arrival on the West Coast as late as 1940.

Even among the gangsters and bookmakers who knew Rosselli as an underworld power, his true status was a mystery. Only the closest associates in his illegal affairs knew his position as a member in good standing in the Mafia, a criminal organization so secret its existence was considered a myth until its vast influence was exposed in 1950 by Senator Estes Kefauver's sensational organized crime hearings.

Within the close brotherhood of the Mafia family, Rosselli had another identity, parallel to his legitimate life, that of favored son, the bearer of aspirations and pride. "You see, Johnny wasn't like the rest of them," recalled Vince Barbi, a boxer and Hollywood character actor who for years was close to Lucky Luciano. "Johnny had class, he was smart and he knew how to act, and the boys all loved him. They respected him, and they loved him." In a culture devoted to nicknames, Rosselli was dubbed "The Hollywood Kid," and in honor of his prowess with women, "Don Giovanni," the Italian Don Juan.

Rosselli never voiced the emotional drain of maintaining separate lives and personalities, but the strain may have contributed to his several chronic ailments, which included bronchitis, arthritis, and later, diverticulitis. He was frequently in the hospital, a regular visitor to the Sansum Clinic in Santa Barbara, and even his friends sometimes derided him as a hypochondriac.

In addition, despite an outwardly cool, unflappable demeanor, Rosselli was subject to rare but furious outbreaks of temper. Ed Becker recalls one such occasion, when he met with Rosselli on the way to a dinner engagement. As Rosselli approached the car, a young woman emerged from a neighboring apartment and implored him to stop and speak with her. Rosselli shook her off, climbed into Becker's car, and exploded into a violent rage. "He was just going crazy," Becker recalls of the incident. "I would have expected him to laugh it off, but he was screaming and shaking, saying that he was certain the girl was a police informant, and that she wouldn't leave him alone. It took him about ten minutes to calm down."

The tension was always there, gnawing, sometimes debilitating, but it never consumed him. At his core, deep within the shell of his various fronts, Rosselli maintained a final, inner identity, one rooted in *la famiglia*. Though he had left suddenly, though separated by the breadth of the continent, Rosselli remained the effective head of his family, the don of the tiny Sacco clan.

★

Of necessity, to protect his secret identity, Rosselli kept his family ties cloaked in secrecy, but he never cut them off. Around 1930, his younger brother Vincent Sacco contracted tuberculosis and was advised by his doctors to leave Boston's freezing climate. He headed to Los Angeles, and brother John folded him into his routine, dubbing him Jimmy Rosselli, introducing him around town, and finally sending him to the sanitarium in Redwood City for treatment.

Vincent Sacco returned to Boston in 1932, but his health remained poor. He contracted pneumonia in the winter of 1936, and by late May, his death seemed certain. This was a crucial juncture in the life of the family, and Rosselli stepped to the fore, risking a trip back to Boston, his first in a decade. He arrived on May 30 to find Vincent delirious, clutching at a crucifix in his hand and pleading over and over, "I don't want to go, I don't want to go." At age 31, Rosselli had seen his share of death and, anguished but stolid, he closed the door behind him and sat, alone with his brother, until Vincent calmed, closed his eyes, and perished.

When the dawn finally arrived, sunny and beautiful, Rosselli emerged to break the news to his mother. He put his arms around her, and the two stood there a moment, both quietly crying. Then the other Sacco children came in, and the family huddled together in embrace. Rosselli attended to all the funeral arrangements, and stayed in Boston for the wake and the visiting hours at the Sacco home, his demeanor smiling and warm. In the years that followed, Rosselli adopted the custom of sending money to his mother, a stipend to help her through the hard times of old age.

Rosselli was clearly aware of the hazards involved in maintaining his bond with his past—as if to compensate for his break from cover, he stopped off in Chicago on his trip out to Boston to file a fraudulent entry with the city health department reporting the birth of a Giovanni Rosselli on July 4, 1904, with an accompanying, forged, affidavit of witness. But that awareness only underscored the importance to Rosselli of preserving a core identity, that inner sanctum where he was honored and honorable, a man of principle and dignity. To the society at large, he was a criminal and a dangerous man, but he never accepted that verdict. He never doubted himself.

Rosselli returned to Los Angeles in June 1936 with his secret intact and resumed a life that had reached a sort of equilibrium, playing the multiple roles of socialite, labor boss, and gangster, a delicate balance resting on the illusion of his carefully orchestrated persona. But the illusion was not his alone. Rosselli's access to drawing rooms and studio lots required the active participation of the elites who cultivated his friendship, and who ignored the obvious hazards in the belief they could harness Rosselli's dangerous resources to their own ends. In all his endeavors Rosselli gained his initial foothold at the invitation of inside players. By enlisting his unique services, Rosselli's allies sought a hidden edge that would overwhelm any obstacles.

But the men who courted Rosselli were courting disaster. The initial advantage they gained by their underworld connection was soon lost in the chaos that attended the entry of the gangsters. The film industry paid for its mob alliance in the bundles of cash delivered to a gloating Willie Bioff, and then distributed to Rosselli and his cohorts in Chicago. The Shaw administration would pay a higher price the following year, when investigations into its crime connections engendered wholesale collapse.

In a sense, and certainly unwittingly, Rosselli served as moral equalizer in the game of power. He represented the outside option, a final solution available to anyone ruthless enough to recruit him, but in the end, that decision opened the door to men more dangerous than Rosselli's sponsors could have anticipated, men who had prospered in a milieu of fear and murder.

5

THE FALL

Enter "Bugsy"

The catalyst in the destruction of the Shaw regime was the arrival from the East of another flashy gangster, an ally of Rosselli's whose life was one of reckless excess. The gangster was Benjamin Siegel—behind his back, his friends called him "Bugsy."

Ben Siegel grew up as one of the toughest and most dangerous criminals to plague the Lower East Side of New York City. Even among the gangsters, he was regarded as a "cowboy," a gunman who killed so easily and so recklessly that they doubted his sanity. By the age of 14, he had joined forces with the young Meyer Lansky in the Bug and Meyer mob, a Jewish murder-for-hire outfit that handled heavy assignments for Italian crime families that wanted their entanglements obscured.

In 1928, Siegel gained a seat on an East Coast criminal cartel known as the Big Seven, which controlled bootlegging from Boston to Philadelphia, and in 1931, he played a key role in boosting Lucky Luciano to the top of the New York underworld, serving on the gun squad that assassinated Luciano's rival, Joe "The Boss" Masseria. Three years later, Luciano and Lansky agreed with Frank Costello, Longy Zwillman, and Paul Ricca to build on their initial steps toward syndication by dividing the country into geographic regions whose leaders would report to a national committee. Bugsy asked for California.

Arriving in Los Angeles in early 1937, Siegel made contact with Jack Dragna and opened an uneasy alliance as partners at the top of the city's underworld. Dragna distrusted the Jewish gangsters and resented sharing his control of the city but felt bound by the directives of the national commission. In a telephone call from New York, Meyer Lansky assured Dragna that Luciano endorsed the move, and Dragna agreed to go along.

Rosselli was Siegel's primary contact with the Italians in Los Angeles, befriending him and providing introductions to Hollywood's inner circle, to studio bosses Jack Warner and Louis B. Mayer, and to Jean Harlow, who became Siegel's close friend and godmother to one of his two daughters. Siegel was handsome, dark and dapper, and his reputation as a notorious gangster earned him a spot on Hollywood's social roster.

Another plum proffered by Rosselli was a share in Agua Caliente, Joe Schenck's Tijuana racetrack that served as a sort of Hollywood annex during the dry days of Prohibition. The track was closed by government decree in 1935, costing Schenck a small fortune. Two years later, plans were announced to reopen the track, and sensing an opportunity, Rosselli plumbed his racing connections and struck a bargain with Mexican authorities. For a flat payment of $100,000 in cash, Rosselli and a small syndicate could operate the track for a two-month meet, keeping whatever profits they could raise. Rosselli raised his quarter share from Harry Cohn, invited Siegel and a partner from the racing wire service to ante up, and called on friends in the press for splashy features in the travel pages. Opening in July 1937, it was a classic mob operation, clean, quick, and lucrative, and helped cement Rosselli's relationship with Siegel and, through him, with the Jewish arm of the national syndicate.

Siegel's personal henchman in Los Angeles was another flamboyant Jewish gangster, a boxer and hit man named Mickey Cohen who grew up in Los Angeles but had migrated East. When he drew police attention in Chicago for a 1937 assault on a cab-company slugger, Cohen was sent back to Los Angeles with instructions to check in with Siegel. Within weeks of his arrival, Cohen was making waves, and Rosselli was calming them in characteristic fashion.

The trouble started when Cohen, a free-lancer by nature, held up a bookmaking shop run by Dragna associates Louie Merli (nee Salvatore Piscopo) and Morey Orloff. It was a major operation, with more than thirty phones and two sheriff's deputies standing guard, but Cohen's band made short work of it, brandishing revolvers and a sawed-off shotgun. They collected more than $30,000 in cash and all the jewelry worn by the bookmakers—Cohen called it a "goddamn top score."

The heist infuriated Dragna, who contacted Siegel and demanded that order be restored. Siegel called a meeting with Cohen and explained that the money belonged to Dragna's organization, but Cohen refused to return the loot. Two days later, Siegel called a second meeting at the office of Hollywood attorney Jerry Giesler. Cohen arrived to find Siegel sitting with John Rosselli, who watched in silence as Siegel did the talking. The money was not so important, at least not worth fighting over, Siegel explained, but Cohen's flagrant disrespect was another matter. There was a solution, he added, involving a jeweled stickpin taken in the holdup. The bauble belonged to Merli, a family heirloom that couldn't be replaced, and he wanted it back. "Naturally, he knows I got too much class," Cohen recalled later. He would return the stickpin. Rosselli observed the exchange with a nod, satisfied that he had made his point with both Cohen and Siegel.

The confrontation with Cohen illustrated an approach to conflict that set John Rosselli apart from his more bull-headed colleagues. While fully capable of violence, Rosselli always sought another means of settling a dispute, even if it cost money or perceived stature in the short run. Rather than assert authority, Rosselli forged alliances, easing tensions and building his own reputation. In the Mickey Cohen case, Rosselli's intervention saved face for Dragna, preserved a marriage of convenience between the Italians and Siegel, and enhanced his stature with the power brokers back East.

By the summer of 1937, Bugsy Siegel had branched out into a series of rackets—he gained control of the extras union, which he used as a lever to extort thousands of dollars in "loans" from stars and directors fearful of wildcat strikes, and he invested with Rosselli in a short-lived dog track—but his primary interest was gambling. This time, however, Siegel's rivals were not the Mafia, which had agreed to cooperate with their Jewish ally, but the old Los Angeles syndicate, already reeling from the loss of the bookmakers.

A meeting was called for the city's top game-room operators, and when Siegel announced that all proceeds would have to be split with his outfit, the lone dissent was voiced by Les Bruneman, a balding veteran of the Crawford-McAfee syndicate who operated gambling clubs in the beach cities south of Los Angeles and lived at the Clover Club off the Sunset Strip. Siegel decided to make an example of Bruneman, and assigned Dragna to administer a dose of East Coast discipline. With mediation out of the question, Rosselli accepted the role of accomplice, and the violence that ensued spelled the end of the era of easy, open crime in Los Angeles.

Blowing the Lid Off City Hall

ON THE EVENING OF July 20, 1937, Bruneman was enjoying the perquisites that accrued to a small-time crime czar, taking a stroll on the ocean-front esplanade in Redondo Beach, one of a series of sleepy vacation resorts lying south of Los Angeles. On his arm was a pretty young blonde, a hostess from one of his gambling arcades. She was pleased that her boss had singled her out for his attentions, but reconsidered when two men stepped up behind them, leveled automatic pistols and began shooting. His date was unharmed, but Bruneman caught three slugs in his back. He staggered 200 feet to the lobby of a local movie theater and was rushed to a local hospital.

John Rosselli was one of a score of underworld figures who easily ducked a half-hearted police search. Bruneman's own men weren't any help, standing guard in hospital corridors but refusing to speculate on the attack. And the blonde, sporting if scared, likewise kept mum. "It's like the old gangster times in Prohibition," a frustrated sheriff's captain told reporters. "When anything like this happened, gangland just sat back and let us try to figure out what happened." The same day of the shooting, Los Angeles Mayor Frank Shaw denounced as "discredited politicians and sensation hunters" a group formed to demand police action against vice and gangsters in the city.

Bruneman recovered from his wounds sufficiently that, by the following October, rumors surfaced that he would renew his gambling operations on the coast and in Palm Springs. On October 25, his assailants struck again. Following dinner at the Montmartre Grill, Bruneman retired for a nightcap with a girl friend to a small café called The Roost. As he was ordering drinks, two men entered the café while a third stood guard at the door. The gunmen shot Bruneman sixteen times, this time making certain of the kill. A bar employee who chased the shooters was also murdered.

Newspaper accounts the following day speculated that Bruneman was killed by "eastern gangsters" in a gambling turf war, and for the first time, John Rosselli was named publicly as a suspect. Rosselli met with police the following day, declared that he hadn't seen Bruneman in over three years and had known him only slightly, and was quietly turned loose. Rosselli also took the occasion to dispute news reports that he was a bodyguard to a studio boss, terming himself a producer at Cohn's Columbia Studios. When reporters called the studio, however, a spokesman commented wryly, "All anybody around here knows is that he hangs around Holly-wood and Vine a lot and talks out of the corner of his mouth."

An intensive investigation failed to turn up members of the actual hit team, but informants in San Francisco and in Reno, Nevada, provided information leading directly to Dragna and Rosselli. The pair had left town three days after the shooting, and turned up in Las Vegas, where an informant said he witnessed the gang leaders paying off three men for the crime. The account could not be corroborated, however, and no charges were filed. Years later, gangster Jimmy Fratianno filled in the gaps, asserting that Frank Bompensiero, the San Diego button man for the L.A. mob, had been the lead assassin.

While Dragna, Rosselli, and ultimately Siegel escaped prosecution, the Bruneman murder had dire consequences for local government in Los Angeles. The crime was sensational, brutal, and obviously rooted in a gang rivalry, elements that sparked outrage in the city and attention from state and federal law enforcement. State Attorney General U. S. Webb blasted the Shaw administration for allowing "gambling, gangsterism, and vice" to operate openly in Los Angeles. The same week, the federal IRS and FBI weighed in, announcing a joint investigation into a horse-betting racket, "operating on a well-organized scale," that generated more than $1 million in gross revenues daily. The head of the IRS intelligence office in Los Angeles added his concern that "notorious eastern gunmen and mob-sters" had moved in "to get control of the horse-racing setup." A local newspaper followed up with a story headlined "Eastern Gun Gang Threatens Reign of Terror in L.A."

More troubling to the portly mayor's administration was the reaction of the county grand jury. The investigative panel had for years been dominated by the old Crawford organization, but the attack on Bruneman spurred to action the Criminal Complaints committee, chaired by Clifford Clinton, an eccentric cafeteria operator whose downtown dining room operated under the optimistic slogan, "Dine Free Unless Delighted."

When the Bruneman shooting forced the gangsters into the public eye, Clinton called his committee into special session, issuing subpoenas to witnesses of the Redondo Beach attack and to more than forty prominent gambling figures around the city. All but one failed to show up, but Deputy District Attorney Thomas O'Brien promised "a thorough investigation of the causes behind such warfare between bookies." O'Brien added a vague but prescient theory that "Sicilian gangsters" had been working with "the brother of a high public official," and that "two of these gangsters were the assailants who shot Les Bruneman." It was as close as the prosecution would get to Rosselli.

The leadership of the grand jury moved to muffle the committee investigation, but Clinton published his findings himself as a "minority report" declaiming the "deplorably bad influence being exerted on local government by a powerful, greedy, cruel, ruthless underworld political machine." At the same time, Clinton went outside the machinery of local government to form CIVIC—the Citizens Independent Vice Investigating Committee—and launched a one-man crusade to clean up Los Angeles vice. He enlisted the local papers in publicizing the location of 1,800 bookmakers, 600 brothels, and 200 gambling halls in the city, and hired private investigator Harry Raymond to develop firm information connecting Joe Shaw and the city police to the underworld.

Clinton's noisy campaign generated broad public support and brought intense heat on vice operations and the mayor's office. The backlash came just after midnight on the morning of October 30, 1937, less than a week after the second, fatal attack on Bruneman, when a black-powder pipe bomb ripped a gaping hole in the front of Clinton's home in the quiet Los Feliz district of the city. Interviewed by reporters that night, Clinton suggested that, "The same bunch did this bombing that did the Bruneman killing. By that I don't necessarily mean the same persons, but the same mob. They think I possibly know more than I do about Bruneman's murder and they are trying to frighten me." Clinton's speculation was better than his facts, for the stated targets in his anti-vice campaign were Guy McAfee and Bob Gans, longtime Bruneman allies who at that time were losing their turf war to Siegel, Dragna, and Rosselli. That his crusade was abetting the goals of Bruneman's killers was an irony Clinton would probably not have appreciated.

Clinton pressed on with his campaign, and on the morning of January 14, 1938, his antagonists struck again, this time wiring a bomb into the starter of CIVIC investigator Harry Raymond's car. The explosion wrecked the car and a nearby garage, but incredibly, Raymond himself survived. This time, however, there was abundant evidence to implicate Raymond's assailants. It turned out that for months Raymond had been kept under surveillance by Captain Earle Kynette's LAPD Intelligence Division from a house across the street from Raymond's, and that his telephone was tapped. When it was learned that Kynette had personally purchased the materials for the bomb, he was indicted for attempted murder.

The Raymond bombing and the Bruneman murder gave CIVIC the mandate it had been seeking, and on September 16, 1938, Mayor Frank Shaw was defeated in a recall election by a two-to-one margin. In the subsequent housecleaning, the new mayor, Fletcher Bowron, fired Chief Davis and twenty-three of his officials. Kynette was convicted of the Raymond bombing and sentenced to ten years in San Quentin, and Joe Shaw was tried and convicted on sixty-three counts of altering public records to cover bribery in city appointments. The entire Civil Service Commission resigned.

The conviction of Joe Shaw satisfied the press and the public that justice had been done. But in all the rancor and the sensational headlines that attended the toppling of the city administration, the roots of the corruption remained obscure. It was John Rosselli who had conspired with Shaw and the police to rig the city's vice operations. And it was Rosselli who had arranged for the murder of Les Bruneman, the spark which ignited the political firestorm that followed. When Shaw's alliance with Rosselli spun out of control, it was Shaw, not Rosselli, who paid the price.

Just how Rosselli handled the collapse of the Shaw administration can only be surmised. He may have tried unsuccessfully to block Clinton's campaign against his allies in city hall, or he may have been satisfied to let the investigation proceed, so long as he himself did not become a target. At any rate, Rosselli had little time to spare in assisting beleaguered public officials. Because in the turbulent year of 1937, investigators and crime fighters caught their first glimpse of the IATSE labor racket and the continuing extortion in the film studios.

The Producers Collect Their Due

WILLIE BIOFF ENCOUNTERED LITTLE initial resistance when he invoked George Browne's authority in taking over the IATSE Hollywood local. After all, he had the cooperation of the studios, which posted notices ordering all their unaffiliated craft workers to sign on with the revitalized union, and he offered the additional incentive of an immediate 10 percent raise. The fact that Bioff had taken over the local with the aid of several intimidating thugs, and that he had summarily ousted the local leadership, was unsettling, but not wholly surprising, in the bare-fisted world of labor.

There were, however, several craft unions that predated IATSE on the studio lots, and which remained independent through the Bioff take-over. The carpenters, the set painters, the plumbers, and eight other small craft unions were shut out of the new basic agreement signed by IATSE and the producers in January 1936, and when the National Labor Relations Act was upheld by the Supreme Court in early April 1937, the independent craft organizations demanded recognition independent of the Alliance, and wage hikes of up to 20 percent. When Pat Casey turned them down, the various unions banned together as the Federated Motion Picture Crafts (FMPC), and on April 30, 1937, they struck.

The walkout presented a threat both to the studios and to the IATSE, which together sought to control the entire Hollywood labor scene. It also presented the studios the opportunity to collect on their end of the shotgun alliance forged with the Chicago mob. Who better to break a strike than a labor union? Working in constant coordination with the producers, the IATSE immediately swung into action, and John Rosselli once again found himself engaged to sway the outcome of a labor dispute.

Where in 1933 Rosselli brought in thugs to help break the IATSE, now, four years later, he was charged with helping the IATSE block a strike by a rival labor organization. But while the parties had switched, the tactics remained the same. Sheer force would decide who prevailed on the picket lines, and force was a Rosselli specialty. To assist the IATSE strike-breakers, Rosselli imported a squad of twenty seasoned gunmen from San Francisco and Chicago. After checking in with local police and obtaining gun permits on the orders of Joe Shaw, the thugs were dispatched to the studio gates. Herb Sorrell, a popular and colorful labor organizer who was head of the painters union, recalled the tenor of the strife. "There were roving goons who came and pushed our picket lines around. They were hired by the studios, and by the IATSE, which was run by the Capone gang. A number of people from Chicago came in, and they mixed with the boys they had hired at the gymnasiums and places like that."

A former boxer with a flattened nose to prove it, Sorrell had faced company thugs during organizing wars in the San Francisco area, and he was prepared to fight back. After he recruited labor radicals from the longshoreman's union at Los Angeles Harbor, "There were numerous fights, and it was a rough strike," Sorrell said later. "In the six weeks that it lasted, there were several killed and a lot of people injured. In fact, it was the roughest strike I ever participated in. At the shipyards in Oakland we had some violence, but nothing like this studio strike."

Hollywood columnist Florabel Muir covered the FMPC strike for the *Saturday Evening Post.* "It was a bitter war," Muir wrote. "There was free-for-all fighting. At the height of the trouble, a group of strange out-landers arrived in town. Some of these men told around that they came from Chicago." Actress Jean La Vell had just arrived in Hollywood at the time, and recalled the violence in an interview: "We were living on Monroe, a dead end near the Goldwyn studio. We could hear the fighting from the house, hear men screaming and crying. You'd go out in the street, and you'd see men lying there with blood running down their faces."

In the street fighting for control of the Hollywood unions, Rosselli operated like a field general, making strategy, ensuring security, and de-ploying gun-toting troops by the carload, their flashy, late-model Zephyrs becoming a hallmark of the strike. His contacts were Bioff at the union and Pat Casey at the Producers Association, but it was Rosselli who man-aged the muscle.

At the outbreak of hostilities, Willie Bioff was summoned back to Chicago to report on the action. While meeting at a restaurant with Frank Nitti and Charlie Fischetti, a radio broadcast was interrupted to report on a riot breaking out at the IATSE hiring hall in Los Angeles.

Sorrell's forces had seen an IATSE newspaper ad recruiting strike-breaking labor, and had turned on the rival union. Fischetti immediately called Rosselli, who promised to deal with the trouble. Heading to union headquarters, Rosselli found IATSE vice-president Harlan Holmden in a frantic state following calls from both Bioff and Browne. Holmden described the damage to the hiring-hall office—windows broken, desks overturned, furniture demolished—and asked Rosselli to intervene. Rosselli turned to Holmden and said evenly, "There is nothing to worry about." That evening, a cordon of eight men, including the bookmaker Louie Merli, was on guard at the union hall, with another group at the Taft Building offices.

The battle against the upstart unionists was also waged in the press. George Browne invoked the threat of communists lurking among the FMPC organizers, and denounced as a "red herring" charges that IATSE was a company union. The studio bosses were equally vitriolic. Rosselli's gambling friend Joe Schenck, speaking as chairman of the producers labor committee, attacked the strike leadership for "misleading and misinforming the studio workers." The facts of the producers' concurrent payoffs to the IATSE chiefs were, of course, never mentioned; nor were a series of meetings between Schenck and Bioff to coordinate tactics against the insurgents.

The combined efforts of the producers and the IATSE finally succeeded in breaking the strike, with the smaller crafts either disbanded or folded into the stagehands union, and the Federation of Motion Picture Crafts was destroyed. The turning point came when the Screen Actors Guild voted to ignore the FMPC picket lines after signing a no-strike contract with the producers. Only Sorrell's painters, more militant and more physical than the other craft unions, prevailed, holding out to win a 20 percent wage increase. "We had organized thugs going after us, but in many respects we out-thugged the thugs," Sorrell recalled with satisfaction.

John Rosselli celebrated IATSE's victory by adjourning to the secluded and exclusive colony of Malibu, where the union had rented a beach house for Louis Campagna and three other Capone henchmen out from Chicago on vacation. Under a cloudy June sky, accompanied by the murmuring roil of the nearby Pacific surf, the gangsters played cards and discussed the progress of the film and racetrack rackets. There were trips to the city's best nightclubs, and a jaunt to Tijuana for the opening of Rosselli's Caliente resort. An IATSE steward served as chauffeur, adding to the frolicksome mood. It was a pleasant hiatus that gave Rosselli a chance to show off his success in building a lucrative West Coast outpost for the mob.

Backfire

JUST AS THE BRUNEMAN murder solved a small problem only to generate a much larger one, Bioff and Rosselli's heavy-handed approach to the smaller craft unions' bid for autonomy, coupled with the arrogant takeover of the IATSE local, came back to haunt them. Disturbed at their role as strike-breakers, frustrated at their own loss of autonomy, the IATSE rank and file began to rebel against their autocratic hoodlum leadership.

The trouble began when a militant faction that dubbed itself "The White Rats of '37" approached Carey McWilliams, then an activist labor attorney, who later earned renown as editor of *The Nation*. McWilliams took the case, filing a class action suit to restore the IATSE local organization and lift the 2 percent dues surcharge. At the same time, McWilliams launched an investigation into Bioff's criminal past in Chicago, and learned that he'd once been convicted of pandering but had never served his sentence. Leaked to the press, the story made sensational headlines.

The presence of gangsters in the IATSE leadership gained further exposure as a result of a simmering feud between Bioff and Rosselli. Bioff had always chafed at having to submit to Rosselli looking over his shoulder, but his repeated complaints to the Outfit bosses in Chicago only confirmed Rosselli's good standing. The feud reached the boiling point in November 1937, over the handling of Harry Cohn and Columbia Studios. Always ferocious when it came to money, Cohn had rejected the IATSE extortion bid, reasoning that he was at least partially immune to retaliatory strikes because he owned no theaters. Besides, if there was any trouble with gangsters, he could always turn to his good friend John Rosselli.

Bioff took matters into his own hands on Monday, November 8, when without warning, all of Columbia's cameramen, makeup artists, electricians, and other craft workers walked out. Harry Cohn was in Palm Springs, and learned of the wildcat strike by telephone. There were no grounds given, no demands made by the workers.

Cohn's first call was to Producers Association president Louis B. Mayer, who made repeated efforts to reach Bioff but got no response. After several hours of frustration, Cohn called Rosselli, who asked him to return immediately to Los Angeles, and promised to look into the matter. Rosselli called Casey and then called Bioff, who was reported out of the office. Rosselli went over anyway.

Arriving at the IATSE headquarters in Hollywood, Rosselli found Bioff hunkered down behind his desk, his snap-brim hat on his head and a gun lying conspicuously before him. Ignoring the implied threat, Rosselli demanded an accounting from his sometime partner. "I just called you up. What is the idea of your not answering the telephone?"

"Well," Bioff said blandly, "I think I know what you want." Furious, Rosselli railed at Bioff for compromising his relationship with Harry Cohn by calling a strike without clearing it first. He ordered Bioff to send the workers back on the lot, but Bioff refused, citing vague contract violations by Cohn and telling Rosselli to check with Frank Nitti in Chicago. "To hell with you and Nitti," Rosselli raged, and he stormed out of the office. Rosselli knew the importance of contacts, but he also knew the importance of turf, and he was determined to demonstrate to Bioff that he held the power in Los Angeles.

That evening Rosselli played a trump card, asking Jack Dragna to accompany him on an unannounced visit to Bioff's eighty-acre San Fernando Valley estate. During his brief stay in Hollywood, Bioff had outfitted himself and his home in the lavish style of the people he was extorting —handmade mahogany furniture, a twenty-six-foot Persian rug on the floor—but Bioff lost his sheen when a Mexican maid ushered Rosselli in with the don of the Los Angeles Mafia. It was a show of force, and it worked: Dragna's presence meant that continued obstinance on Bioff's part would lead to mayhem. Bioff's attitude altered accordingly, and he agreed to meet with Cohn that night. The three men drove together to Rosselli's Sunset Plaza apartment, in the same building as Cohn's, where the producer was waiting on instructions from Rosselli. Dragna and Rosselli headed upstairs for drinks while Bioff made amends. "The strike is off," Bioff told Cohn, and then added, "You can thank Johnny—nobody but Johnny could have done this for you."

Bioff could not have picked a worse time to test his muscle. That same week, a committee of the state assembly was meeting in Los Angeles to investigate a strike at the Metropolitan Water District, but the Columbia walkout promised more sensational results, and the panel issued a surprise subpoena to Willie Bioff, announcing an inquiry into "conditions bordering on racketeering."

It was the first public intimation of mob infiltration in the union, and the press feasted on it, invoking the "sinister shadow of bloody gang history" in front-page coverage. Bioff was grilled on the 2 percent dues surcharge, and on his autocratic management style. Headlines from the trial vied for space with coverage of the Les Bruneman murder, which took place two weeks prior. A frustrated Rosselli could only watch the events unfold and be satisfied that the multiple investigations surrounding him had so far missed their mark.

The assembly investigations into Bioff and the IATSE peaked on November 17, when actor Robert Montgomery testified that the Screen Actors Guild had joined with the writers and directors to stave off a threatened take-over by the IATSE. Bioff was next on the stand, and after relating details of his salary and benefits, was challenged on the question of mob influence. "It has been alleged that the Alliance is a racket and that a Chicago gang has been brought in here to enforce the racket," a legislator asserted. Bioff rejected the charge as coming "from Communists," and the meeting suddenly erupted into what the papers termed "a vocal riot." Just as abruptly, the assembly committee announced that the hearings were adjourned.

A subsequent investigation in Sacramento revealed that Bioff had helped terminate the hearings by paying a $5,000 retainer to the law firm of Assembly Speaker William Mosley Jones, who controlled the labor committee budget. But despite the closure of the hearings, the damage had been done. In December, the IATSE dissidents issued a leaflet, illustrated with a police mug shot of Bioff, describing him as an "associate of gangsters and criminal elements" in Chicago. And in a crushing blow, the Sacramento County District Attorney turned up evidence of a $100,000 payment to Bioff from Joe Schenck. Federal tax agents launched inquiries into Schenck, Bioff, and all the major studios. The situation became untenable.

In February 1938, about the time the recall drive was launched against Los Angeles Mayor Frank Shaw, Bioff resigned from his official position with the union, though he kept his salary and continued to make key decisions for the organization. That same month, Bioff was approached by Sidney Kent and proffered the services of the tax attorneys for Twentieth Century-Fox. Joe Schenck followed by handing the heavyset gangster tickets for a cruise on the luxury liner *Normandie* to Rio de Janeiro. Bioff sailed within a week, departing in the company of his wife and a traveling companion, Mrs. L. B. Mayer, and buoyed by a bon voyage telegram courtesy Mr. and Mrs. Harry M. Warner. He might be a gangster, but he was their gangster.

Everybody Has Squawked

BIOFF'S DEPARTURE BROUGHT A brief period of calm to the Los Angeles crime scene. The IATSE maintained its tight grip on the studios, and the bookmaking racket, despite pressure from police investigations, remained secure, rooted in the unshakable monopoly of Annenberg's wire service. With his business interests well in hand, and with turf wars and official investigations at a lull, John Rosselli occupied himself with the pleasant routine of a Hollywood power broker.

It was as if, during the waning years of the 1930s, in the face of mounting pressure on his various criminal enterprises, Rosselli felt he could beat his problems by ignoring them. Never in a crime career already spanning more than twenty years had Rosselli spent more than a few weeks in prison; with his connections in law enforcement and politics, he must have felt immune.

Certainly, he acted like it. In late 1939, he gave up his Sunset Plaza duplex for a new and grand apartment in the Wilshire Palms, a luxury building situated across the street from the lush greens of the Los Angeles Country Club, just blocks from the exclusive shopping and night life of Beverly Hills. Owned by comedian Red Skelton, the Palms boasted some of the most illustrious tenants in the entertainment world, including actress Judy Garland, her husband Vincente Minnelli, and the Gabor sisters. Rosselli got to know his neighbors around the apartment pool, where banter and booze were readily available.

Rosselli's daily routine would begin at a civilized hour, closer to noon than to dawn, talking on the phone or eating breakfast at poolside. Once or twice a week he would start early with a plate of eggs at the famous filmland soda counter at Schwab's Pharmacy. Proprietor Leon Schwab recalled Rosselli as a regular customer, and "a real gentleman, the sweetest guy you'd ever want to meet." Rosselli's clothes and personal affairs were attended by a butler, a handsome young man with the dubious name Phillip Dare. When the time came to head out, Rosselli rarely drove, preferring to be chauffeured by a strong-arm assistant like Louie Merli. It was a neat way for Rosselli to maintain appearances and at the same time stay in close contact with his hidden interests in the underworld.

Lunchtime would find Rosselli at Hollywood's favorite eateries, places like Musso and Frank's or the Brown Derby, establishments known for the stars and film executives and gossip columnists that used the wood-and-leather booths as off-the-lot offices. Besides the studio chiefs, Rosselli cultivated the friendship of mid-level Hollywood players who in turn enjoyed his air of mystery and confidence. One such friend was Bryan Foy, a tough-talking producer who helped inaugurate sound technology at Warner Brothers and specialized in low-budget, high-grossing "B" films. Another was June Lang, blond with porcelain skin and sparkling eyes, a rising star with Twentieth Century-Fox described in the press as "the prettiest girl in Hollywood."

"Rosselli was impressed by the movie people, and he liked to hang around them," recalled boxer and character actor Vincent Barbi. He also liked to do them favors. On one occasion he was visiting with Billy Wilkerson, publisher of the Hollywood *Reporter,* at one of Wilkerson's several restaurants. A C.O.D. shipment arrived, $1,800 in furniture, and Wilkerson was strapped for cash. He began a heated argument with the delivery man when Rosselli interjected softly, "I can let you have the money if you want it," and proceeded to peel $2,000 in cash from a wad of bills in his pocket, enough to make a down payment on a house. The gesture left Wilkerson deeply impressed.

Another close friend was Allen Smehoff, known to his friends as Allen Smiley, one of a small circle who, like Rosselli, straddled the worlds of crime and film. A Russian immigrant who spent his youth on the streets of New York with the Bug and Meyer mob, Smiley served Rosselli as a conduit to Ben Siegel. Tall, thin, with silver hair and the easy grin that earned him his nickname, he also was a familiar face at Paramount and other studios, where he started as a grip, and later peddled story scenarios and took horse bets. After hours, Smiley was prominent on the social circuit, and opened several Sunset Strip nightclubs.

In the afternoons, business might take Rosselli to the IATSE or Pat Casey's offices at the Producers Association, but during the racing season, Rosselli would turn up at the track boxes where the real business of show business was conducted. "You'd find all the important people at Santa Anita, and Johnny spent a lot of time out there," recalled film columnist Jimmy Starr. "It got so the studio heads in New York threatened to start scheduling work on Saturdays, because so many people spent afternoons during the week at the track." Rosselli's other daytime haunt was the golf course—another aristocratic habit that he mastered. "Rosselli had a big, open swing," one friend recalled. "He wasn't great, but he was good." He played at the Hillcrest Country Club and the Bel-Air Country Club in town, and at Arrowhead Springs, Billy Wilkerson's beautiful mountain resort in San Bernardino County, and in Palm Springs, talking business and gossip with the top names in the film industry, including Joseph Kennedy, Sr., an occasional partner on the links when attending business affairs on the Coast.

Come nightfall, "Johnny was in all the night spots," Starr reported. "I'd see him at the Luau [in Beverly Hills], Ciros [on Sunset Strip], at the Clover Club; there was a whole crowd of people you'd see every night, and he was one of them." Rosselli earned a reputation for generosity by tipping lavishly and buying drinks in rounds, but he was best known for his women. "Johnny always had a girl on his arm," Starr said. Added Jonie Taps, producer and longtime confidant of Harry Cohn, "If there were ten girls at a table, Rosselli wanted all ten of them." And he frequently had his way. He was at once suave and tough, gracious and menacing, a macho presence that some women found enchanting. Besides, a word from Rosselli could mean entrée to a studio, a crucial break in a touch-and-go business. Lana Turner, Donna Reed, and a score of lesser-known screen women were friends and sometime dates of Rosselli's, all adding to his aura as a man who possessed that elusive asset so coveted by the screen set, "class."

But toward the end of the 1930s, Rosselli found himself attracted to one woman in particular, innocent in demeanor yet a stalwart of the "café society," the striking blonde June Lang. Born Winifred Vlasek to Norwegian parents in Minneapolis, Minnesota, Lang was a second-rank film star, a Fox contract player from the age of 14 whose screen career peaked when she played opposite Gloria Swanson in *Music in the Air* in 1934. On Hollywood's social circuit, however, Lang was rated a top catch. She was petite, pretty, and eminently available, and her suitors included Howard Hughes, George Jessel, and the millionaire financier A. C. Blumenthal. Her dating was interrupted in 1937 by her marriage to shady talent agent Victor Orsatti at a wedding that featured 300 of the top names in the industry—Jack Warner, Hal Roach, and Louis B. Mayer were there, and Joe Schenck gave the bride away. But the union was short-lived—Orsatti divorced her after just two months, complaining that Lang's mother refused to leave the house.

Three years later, in what gossip columns termed "one of Hollywood's most unusual romances," Rosselli and June Lang eloped. Late on a Sunday night in April 1940, the couple headed east from Rosselli's apartment to Yuma, Arizona, where at five in the morning, they rousted a justice of the peace from bed to perform a brief ceremony. Returning to Los Angeles a week later, the newlyweds stopped for a honeymoon respite at the Grand Canyon. Of the groom, the trades reported that "Rosselli, although well-known in film circles, is somewhat of a mystery man."

It was Rosselli's first and only attempt at matrimony, and it failed utterly. Lang was prepared for a conventional home life, telling reporters of plans for a ranch home in the San Fernando Valley, but she had not counted on Rosselli's narrow idea of a wife. Jealous of her time and her career, Rosselli forbade any new movie work and objected to visits from Lang's screen friends. Perhaps more troubling was Rosselli's determination that his own life would remain the same as before. The couple never moved to their prospective suburban home, but remained at Rosselli's Wilshire Palms apartment. He would disappear without notice, at times for as long as two weeks, and when she would demand explanations, Rosselli angrily refused. There were loud fights followed by more absences, and in December 1941, Rosselli and Lang were separated. Divorce proceedings were initiated by Lang the following month.

Rosselli always lamented the failure of his marriage to June Lang—he sought her qualities in other women and, in sentimental moods, remembered her to friends. But there was little likelihood that he could ever have maintained the sort of flexible, evolving relationship that a marriage requires. He was a man governed by stern, brittle ideas—any real intimacy would have threatened those tenets, forcing a degree of self-examination that a onetime contract killer and shrewd manipulator like Rosselli could not broach. Women to him were baubles, objects upon whom he could work techniques and test his skill; if things progressed beyond the initial conquest, he invoked the old, Catholic, Italian ideas of a woman's role. He was relentless in pursuit and voracious in appetite, but while Rosselli was charming, his relationships with women left him alone and hungry for more.

In a way, June Lang was a perfect match for him. Her beauty attracted strong but distant men who married her and then shunted her aside, but she never tired of that brand of affection. Even after the divorce, which was finally granted in 1943 on grounds of "mental cruelty," she told Louella Parsons that Rosselli was "very good" to her. She married a third time in 1944, to a soldier and salesman from Chicago, but was divorced again after a bitter court battle nine years later. Interviewed in 1977, eight years before her death at age 60, Lang said wistfully, "The most stupid thing I ever did was marry—three times."

★

Still, it would have taken an extraordinary marriage to survive the events that followed Lang's separation from Rosselli, for investigators from the IRS and the Justice Department were finally closing in on the film studio extortion. The key was the 1938 revelation of the $100,000 "loan" to Willie Bioff from Twentieth Century-Fox magnate Joe Schenck. Labor activists had latched on to the loan as evidence of collusion between the producers and the IATSE, and launched several separate investigations, feeding their findings to the government and the press. In November 1939, Schenck was called before a federal grand jury to explain the transaction. His contorted answers yielded a two-count indictment for income tax evasion, and in April 1941, Schenck was convicted of tax violations and conspiracy, and sentenced to three years in prison.

Schenck's prosecutors knew there was more to the case than the stock manipulations they had proved against him, and once the sentence was handed down, they used the jail time as a lever to extract details about Browne, Bioff, and the film studio shakedown. Schenck cooperated to a degree, and though he denied any knowledge of the Capone gang's involvement, the government had enough to press charges against the union heads. Searching for more information, they convened another grand jury in New York, and in May 1941, Rosselli was called to testify. When he emerged from the closed proceedings, he knew, finally, that the game was up. He placed a call to Bioff in Los Angeles, and a terse conversation ensued.

"Everybody is talking here, there is going to be a lot of trouble," Rosselli reported. Then he repeated for emphasis, "Everybody you have done business with has squawked."

End Games

THE COLLAPSE OF THE film studio racket forced Rosselli out of the familiar environs of Pat Casey's labor office and the IATSE hiring hall, but he continued to hustle the fringes of the film industry, playing on his contacts and serving as a bridge between the producers and the mob.

One of Rosselli's associates was George Burrows, a New York banker who specialized in film production loans for the Morgan Guaranty Trust Company. Burrows met Rosselli in 1939 during a production meeting on the United Artists lot, and the two struck up a friendship. A year later, while Rosselli was staying at the Sherry Netherland Hotel in New York, Burrows dropped by with a proposition: Rosselli could pick up a sizable commission if he could use his Hollywood contacts to promote Dupont film over Eastman Kodak, which had a virtual monopoly in the industry. Lew Wertheimer, the Detroit gambler and Clover Club impresario, was there as well, and emphasized that there was money to be made. While there is no record of how much film Rosselli sold, it is clear he took the assignment, and peddled Dupont film in Los Angeles for the firm of Smith & Aller.

Also in New York, Rosselli was retained as an agent for Talk-A-Vision, a small-screen technology developed to compete with the emerging television industry. Talk-A-Vision was headed by former Paramount Company head John Otterson, but its financing reportedly came from New York Mafia chief Frank Costello. Rosselli was retained to do "public relations" for the firm, and in at least one transaction, convinced his friend Harry Cohn to produce short subjects for the new medium.

Separately, in Los Angeles, Rosselli was hired on by insurance broker Herman Spitzel, who relied on Rosselli to promote business in the film colony. Spitzel specialized in insuring movie productions, and labor peace, which Rosselli could provide, was a crucial factor in bringing a film in under budget. In addition, Rosselli convinced his friend Billy Wilkerson to insure his restaurants through Spitzel. When Spitzel was drafted into the Navy in 1940, Rosselli ran the business for him. According to investigative files, Spitzel's office became a mob hangout under Rosselli's tenure, with Jack Dragna a frequent visitor.

In Los Angeles, in the meantime, another temblor was rattling the underworld that required Rosselli's immediate attention. The epicenter was located in a federal courthouse in Chicago, where Moses Annenberg and his son Walter were indicted for tax evasion charges stemming from their control of the racing wire service. In a deal designed to protect his son, who pled not guilty, father Moses accepted a three-year prison term and paid off $9.5 million in back taxes. The arrangement settled the Annenberg family account with the government, but left open the question of control of the nation's racing wires.

The immediate successor to Annenberg was James Ragen, a survivor of the old Hearst newspaper wars who had served as circulation director for Annenberg's Nationwide News Service. Ragen ignored the connections his former boss had forged with the national crime syndicate, and adopting the new name of Continental Press, continued to publish the racing news that the bookies across the country relied upon, keeping all the profits to himself.

Pressure from the old Capone gang came almost immediately. They offered to buy Ragen out, then suggested a partnership. But Ragen, battle-hardened at 59 years old, turned them down flat. His jut-jawed obstinance won him a stalemate in Chicago, but in Los Angeles, the cream off the betting pool was too valuable to lose, and the syndicate leadership of Dragna, Rosselli, and Bugsy Siegel set about wresting the racing racket from Ragen's grip.

The western syndicate's first move was to establish a competing racing wire, the Trans-America News Service, with headquarters in Phoenix. Backed by Siegel's explicit threats of violence, Trans-America soon dominated the dusty betting parlors of Las Vegas, then still a backwater even for bettors, but failed to make inroads among the 1,800 bookmaking outlets doing business in Los Angeles.

Jack Dragna decided to press the matter and in July 1942 approached Russell Brophy, Ragen's son-in-law and proprietor of the Southern California franchise. A meeting was slated at a deserted drive-in restaurant at the corner of Sunset Boulevard and Vermont Avenue on the fringes of Hollywood. Dragna appeared friendly, asking only for license to distribute Continental's racing sheets, but Brophy checked with Ragen and the offer was rejected.

A second meeting was held at the same drive-in, but this time with the mob leaders Dragna, Siegel, and henchmen Mickey Cohen and Joe Sica. Siegel announced that he and Dragna had conferred with John Rosselli, and together they had settled on a new order for Los Angeles: Cohen would take charge of gambling, Sica would run narcotics, and Brophy had best step aside. The reference to Rosselli was the key—at that point he was final arbiter of all mob business in the Southwest.

Brophy failed to take the hint. A week later, on July 21, Cohen and Sica arrived at Brophy's office on the ninth floor of a downtown building. Cohen described what happened next: "We tore that fucking office apart. In fact, we busted Brophy's head open pretty good because he got out of line a little bit. But actually, the instructions were to knock him in pretty good anyway." Continental was finished in Los Angeles.

★

These were sidelines, sources of occasional revenue that built upon Rosselli's extensive contacts in Hollywood and Los Angeles. But the labor racket was Rosselli's first order of business, and on May 23, 1941, the heat was turned up another notch when Willie Bioff and George Browne were indicted by a New York grand jury on charges of tax evasion and racketeering.

The following day, May 24, Rosselli drove to Bioff's ranch house to review the details of the indictment and lay out an initial defense strategy. Old animosities were set aside as the two lifelong gangsters huddled in the handsome, knotty-pine furniture of the den. Rosselli detailed for Bioff the best intelligence available on the grand jury proceedings in New York— who had testified and what they said. Then he agreed with Bioff on a plan to limit Rosselli's own exposure, based on Rosselli's false testimony to the grand jury: the two had met for the first time in 1936 in front of the Brown Derby restaurant; Rosselli was an old friend of Browne's but not Bioff's; Rosselli's only business with Bioff was insurance.

Two days later, Bioff had a second meeting, this with Sidney R. Korshak, a Chicago attorney who frequently handled business for the old Capone mob. Meeting at the Ambassador Hotel in Los Angeles, Korshak explained to Bioff that Joe Schenck would serve as the fall guy for the studios in the payoff scheme—that Schenck's tax trial had produced numerous transactions that he could not account for, which Bioff in turn could use to present himself as a "collector" for Schenck. The cash, according to Korshak's strategy, was to serve as a legislative slush fund for the film industry. Korshak later provided Bioff with $15,000 to fund his defense, though he did not appear to present Bioff's case himself.

Consigned to the infamous Bridewell prison to await trial, Bioff became slightly unnerved, and relayed word to his colleagues that he wanted to resign from the Outfit. The next day, Louis Campagna came calling. It was a short visit.

Campagna asked Bioff if the rumor were true, and Bioff cautiously nodded.

"Well, Willie," Campagna replied, "anybody who resigns resigns feet first. Do you understand what that means?" Bioff withdrew his resignation.

Willie Bioff and George Browne went to trial in October 1941, and were convicted in December, the sensational headlines vying for front-page space with the war that was rapidly spreading from Europe to the rest of the world. The next month Bioff and Browne were sentenced to ten and eight years in prison, respectively.

The secret of the Chicago mob's involvement in the film extortion remained intact, but seemed increasingly vulnerable when Nick Dean was named as well in the Bioff indictment. He took flight and was underground as the trial began, but was located by the FBI and arrested on December 1, 1941. The government, however, was unable to force him to talk: on March 8, 1942, Dean pleaded guilty and was sentenced to eight years in jail.

Again, Rosselli seemed determined to ignore the ominous signals from New York. When June Lang filed divorce papers in January 1942, he returned to the social life and nightclubs that were his natural environment. He started a romance with Beatrice Ann Frank, a beautiful young actress who went by the stage name of Ann Corcoran and who possessed the looks and bearing of the young Lauren Bacall. In April, the gossip columns reported Rosselli turning up with Betty Hutton, then one of Hollywood's top female stars, at a swank club called Slapsie Maxie's. And around the same time, Rosselli entertained his mentor, Paul Ricca, who paid a visit to the Coast from Chicago.

But however much Rosselli enjoyed his distractions, U.S. Attorney Mathias Correa was making steady progress. Aided by a vigorous young assistant named Boris Kostelanetz, trained as both an accountant and a litigator, Correa had focused his inquiry on the money that flowed through the books of Isadore Zevin, an accountant placed by the Chicago Outfit as the personal secretary to George Browne. Kostelanetz grilled

Zevin before the grand jury during the summer, but Zevin's answers failed to jibe with IATSE financial documents, and in October 1942, he was indicted for perjury. With Kostelanetz serving as point man, Correa was determined to make his mark by bringing down the nation's premier criminals, and with Zevin under indictment, the noose was drawing tight.

An All-American Alibi

ROSSELLI WATCHED THE DEVELOPMENTS in New York, and he watched America's deepening involvement in fighting around the globe, and he seized upon an angle. It might not solve his problems, it wouldn't erase his links to Bioff and the studio racket, but it couldn't hurt the image of a reputed gangster born to parents who migrated from an Axis power. Though 37 years of age at the time, well out of range of the draft, John Rosselli would join the Army.

On his first approach, Rosselli was rejected as physically unfit for military service. His medical examination revealed neuritis and arthritis in the left foot, knee, and the spine, but what disqualified him was the chronic pulmonary tuberculosis that lingered throughout his life. No evidence of the disease turned up on an X ray, but Rosselli's six months in a sanitarium twenty years before, and the early death of his father from tuberculosis, convinced the Army doctor to pass him over.

But with the nation at war and the armed services needing all the warm bodies it could lay its hands on, it was hard for the Army to deter a persistent volunteer. Rosselli made a second trip to the offices of the selective service board in Westwood, and this time was accepted. He listed his occupation as "insurance solicitor," and was issued a serial number. Rosselli was inducted on December 4, 1942, at Fort MacArthur, California, and dispatched to Camp Cooke, near Santa Barbara, there to join the Headquarters Company of the First Battalion, 81st Armored Regiment, at the rank of private. His monthly paycheck totaled $18.75.

John Rosselli wasn't the only gangster to enter the ranks of the military in the early years of World War II. In Los Angeles alone, Rosselli's sometime henchman Joe Sica signed up along with his brother Fred.

Mickey Cohen even tried; he was turned down in light of the results of a psychological test administered by a court early in his career.

Rosselli was a natural for the military life, and by all accounts he enjoyed it. Patriotism came easily to him, with its straightforward morality and built-in camaraderie. Equally important was the essential simplicity of daily life in the military. The subtle distinctions of the civilian world were canvased over in standard tones of desert tan and olive green. A man's station did not depend on ancestry or connections, but on the insignia on his sleeve. There were no secrets, no suspicions about a hidden past. Nobody raised an eyebrow when Rosselli declared his birthplace as Chicago; nobody checked his fingerprints against those on file with the chief of detectives in Los Angeles. Left with a blank slate, Rosselli took the opportunity to embellish—he told the story that he had started out in Los Angeles as a bit player on the film studio lots, working as an extra until he came into the employ of labor negotiator Pat Casey.

His assignment as an orderly in the battalion headquarters did not impose too much physical strain, and his assignment to Camp Cooke, located within easy driving distance of Los Angeles, allowed him to return home for weekend furloughs. While in the service, Rosselli kept in touch with his friends back in Hollywood. He exchanged correspondence with Billy Wilkerson, the restaurateur and newspaper publisher, proposing that Wilkerson arrange to bring a stage show up to the base.

But charming as he found life in the armed service, there was a war going on, and the efforts to prepare him for battle left Rosselli aching. He was a killer, but he would never be a fighting machine. His arthritic joints became swollen and painful after calisthenics. And after four weeks of basic training, Rosselli's tubercular lungs began to act up. On January 4, 1943, he checked into the Camp Cooke infirmary with a condition diagnosed as acute, severe bronchitis. He was released after treatment with sulfur salts and two weeks of bed rest.

In February, the 81st was transferred to Fort McPherson, Georgia, Rosselli traveling with his regiment. Over the course of the following year, the 81st Armored Regiment was renamed the 81st Tank Battalion and assigned to the Fifth Armored Division, in which form it finally saw battle in Europe, landing at Normandy and fighting its way through the Rhineland and into Central Europe. That Rosselli would have held up under the extremes of combat seems dubious, but he was never put to the test. On March 19, 1943, the New York grand jury investigating the film studio payoff scandal returned indictments against John Rosselli, Paul "The

Waiter" Ricca, Frank "The Enforcer" Nitti, and four other top Chicago hoodlums. Their influence and raw muscle notwithstanding, the government had finally caught up with the Capone mob.

★

The first notice that the ruse was up came on February 1, when Correa wrote the War Department seeking yet another appearance by Rosselli before the New York grand jury investigating the involvement of the Chicago mob in the film industry. Rosselli was dispatched from Georgia to New York, where he took up brief residence at the Waldorf-Astoria. Rosselli had been there several times before, but never wearing such distinctive dress as his private's uniform.

Rosselli was the last witness to be called before the grand jury, U.S. Attorney Mathias Correa using him as a foil to test the effectiveness of the mob's defense strategy. The testimony was taken in secret, but Correa could not have been too impressed: on Friday, March 19, he concluded the proceedings by announcing the indictment of Rosselli and his cohorts for violations of federal racketeering statutes. Separate from the indictments, Correa accused Rosselli of perjury.

Since he was already in New York, John Rosselli was the first of the gangsters to be arrested. Picked up at the Waldorf, he played out the farce of his enlistment, wearing his Army uniform to his arraignment. The judge ignored the patriotic pose, and heeding the prosecutor's concern for the safety of government witnesses, set bail for Rosselli at the extraordinary figure of $100,000. That afternoon, he was taken to the Tombs prison in New York to await trial.

It may have taken a while to sink in. Having begun a life of crime twenty years before, Rosselli had been arrested more than a dozen times, but had never spent more than a few weeks in jail. He had cultivated the reputation of a man with ties to the underworld, but had avoided the stigma of a criminal conviction, winning acceptance in Hollywood's highest echelon. His enemies knew him to be ruthless, but to his friends he appeared generous and easygoing, and Rosselli, smiling and dapper, enjoyed keeping them guessing. It all ended in the resounding clang of steel against steel as the cellblock at the Tombs shut down for the night.

Caging the Tiger

THE INDICTMENT OF THE Capone syndicate for its role in the Hollywood labor racket was a landmark in the history of American law enforcement. There had been aggressive lawmen before, and successful prosecutions, but always the targets had been individuals, men quickly replaced by their lieutenants, as Capone was by Frank Rio, Frank Nitti, and Paul Ricca. By contrast, the film-racketeering case was unique, landing in prison the leadership clique of the nation's most dangerous criminal syndicate, an organization so secret that crime experts in Chicago could only speculate as to its membership. It took an extraordinary effort to bring the case to court.

Ironically, the country's leading crimefighter had nothing to do with the prosecution. Here, as became a hallmark of his career, J. Edgar Hoover was loath to go after the mob. In April 1939, the Justice Department made a specific request that the FBI investigate "certain alleged shakedown tactics" by the IATSE leadership. But in May 1941, Hoover issued explicit instructions to forego an inquiry.

Some feel Hoover avoided prosecuting sophisticated gangsters in order to beef up his success ratio. Others contend his reluctance to take on organized crime may have been related to his penchant for gambling, which led to connections with known bookmakers in New York, Florida, and California. Some veterans of the Justice Department report that Hoover even held secret meetings in New York with mob leader Frank Costello. John Rosselli himself may have had a personal connection to the director: Herman Spitzel, Rosselli's sponsor in the insurance business, was a close friend of Hoover's. But whatever the reason, FBI foot-dragging failed to block the government's interest in IATSE racketeering. The exposure in the California state legislature of Joe Schenck's $100,000 payment to Bioff was too blatant to ignore.

The transaction drew the attention of Alf Oftedal, a bright young agent in the Intelligence Unit of the IRS. After conducting his own inquiry, Oftedal decided to bypass the payoff in favor of prosecuting

Schenck on tax evasion, with U.S. Attorney Correa and his assistant, Kostelanetz, handling the prosecution. The trial took place in 1940, and when Schenck was sentenced in April 1941, the dominoes began to fall.

In return for a reduction of sentence and, later, a full pardon, Schenck detailed for a grand jury his dealings with Bioff, Browne, and the studio unions. Correa and Kostelanetz made quick use of the material, returning indictments in May for Bioff, Browne, and Nick Dean, all of whom had appeared on the union payroll. But it was not until Harry Warner took the witness stand in October 1941 that the prosecution team realized the extent of the conspiracy. Testifying on his payments to the union, Warner said he was approached by Bioff just before Christmas, 1937, and pressed for an unscheduled $20,000 in cash because "the boys in Chicago are insisting on more money."

With Browne, Bioff, and Dean in prison, Kostelanetz focused on the Chicago connection, promising reduced sentences in return for cooperation. Progress was slow but steady, marked by the arrest and sentencing of Nick Dean, and by the October 1942 indictment of IATSE bookkeeper Isadore Zevin for perjury. By January 1943, sensing that he would serve a full eight years while his mob colleagues escaped prosecution, Nick Dean had started to waver. "He never agreed to spell everything out for us, but there was a measure of cooperation," Prosecutor Kostelanetz later explained in an interview. Within days, word of Dean's cooperation was leaked to Chicago, and the mob responded with a ferocity that shocked even a city inured to the machine-gun methods of the underworld.

At 3 P.M. on the afternoon of February 2, 1943, firemen were called to put out a small fire in a four-bedroom apartment located near the lake on Chicago's fashionable North Side. Upon entering, they discovered the body of Estelle Carey, 34, a beautiful blond card dealer and longtime mistress of Nick Dean. Lying on the dining-room floor with an overturned chair pinning her shoulders, Carey had been beaten with a blunt object, stabbed, and slashed around the face, and then set afire, the flames consuming much of the dining-room furniture and both of Carey's legs nearly to the knee. No suspect was ever arrested. An autopsy determined that it was the fire that had caused Carey's death.

The murder of Estelle Carey was more symbol than strategy. The pressure of the grand jury investigation had provoked an involuntary spasm within the violent core of the Mafia psyche. The grisly killing had its intended effect on Nick Dean—"As soon as she was killed that was the end of it," Kostelanetz recalled of Dean's halting cooperation. "He turned off, boom, just like an electric light." But the savagery of the murder ultimately backfired when Willie Bioff, a pimp and a lifetime thug, decided the mob had gone too far. "We sit around in jail for those bastards and they go around killing our families," Bioff told Kostelanetz. "To hell with them. Whataya want to know, Boris?" Kostelanetz took Bioff to the grand jury, and three weeks later, the indictments were handed down, generating front-page headlines across the country.

The indictments came as a body blow to the Chicago syndicate, "total demolition," as Hearst's *Herald American* termed it. Along with Rosselli, Nitti, and Ricca, those charged included Louis "Little New York" Campagna, formerly Capone's personal bodyguard; Charlie "Cherry Nose" Gioe, a bookmaker and the owner of the Don the Beachcomber restaurant in Chicago; Phil D'Andrea, Nitti's right-hand man, president of the Italo-American National Union and publisher of the newspaper *L'Italia;* Ralph Pierce, a shootist who was arrested for the murder of unionist Tommy Malloy but never tried; and Francis Maritote, aka Frank Diamond, Capone's brother-in-law, whose success in evading past indictments had earned him the nickname "The Immune." They were a hard crew, each dangerous in his own right, and used to living beyond the reach of the law.

Frank Nitti, The Enforcer, Capone's muscle chief and the titular head of the organization after Capone's demise, took the indictment as hard as a man can—the afternoon the charges were announced, Nitti was seen stumbling across the tracks of the Illinois Central Railroad, apparently drunk, waving a .32-caliber pistol and threatening rail workers. Then he turned the gun on himself, and after firing two faltering shots through the crown of his brown fedora hat, killed himself with a blast to the head.

Rosselli waited in jail while the rest of his accomplices were picked up in Chicago the following week. Despite the crippling blow of the indictments and the humiliating suicide of strongman Nitti, the syndicate roused itself to respond to the plight of its leadership. On June 8, at a court hearing to review the status of the jailed suspects in the case, the mobsters posted more than $500,000 in bail to secure their colleagues' freedom before trial. The way the money was raised said a lot about the roots of the crime organization: it came not through muscle but through allegiance, the old *campanilismo* of the village community.

The word went out among Chicago's close-knit Italians that the boys, as they were known, needed a favor. The answer came back within days, in the form of checks and money orders and bundles of cash, in amounts of $5,000, $11,000, and $25,000. Most of the donors were businessmen with no established link to crime—grocers and macaroni-factory executives, haberdashers and brewery operators, along with several bookmakers and a couple of established hoodlums. Some dipped into their life savings while others simply wrote checks on company accounts, but all were ready to be counted as friends of the crime bosses.

But neither deep-seated loyalty nor threats of violence could erode the determination of the U.S. Attorney's office in New York, or of their star witness, Willie Bioff. When the trial got under way on October 5, 1943, Bioff performed with the same brash arrogance that had served him so well in muscling into the stagehands union. For ten days on the stand, more than half of that in direct examination, Bioff entertained the jury and the press with a richly detailed account of the inner workings of the Capone Outfit in Chicago, and their dealings with the moguls in Hollywood.

Bioff was willing and candid, his streetwise manner as compelling as the facts of his testimony. Asked to describe his duties as a youthful bouncer in a Chicago brothel, Bioff explained blandly, "I kept order." Asked about his prior testimony during his initial trial, he declared, "I lied, and lied, and lied." Confronted with his perjury in regard to his transactions with Joe Schenck, Bioff said simply, "I am just a low uncouth person. I'm a low type sort of man. People of my caliber don't do nice things."

Like the rest of the defendants, Rosselli watched the proceedings in silence. Mathias Correa had obtained an order from the Army stripping Rosselli of his uniform, so he sat in the relative anonymity of a conservative business suit, his jaw set and his blue eyes cool as Bioff detailed their collaboration and their occasional animosities. Rosselli's attorney, Otto Christensen, of Los Angeles, sought to establish that the contacts with Bioff stemmed from Rosselli's job for Pat Casey, but that could not explain the meetings in Miami and New York, or Rosselli's position on the IATSE payroll.

The case was overwhelming. George Browne proved reluctant on the stand, but Bioff's account was buttressed by the testimony of studio heads Nicholas Schenck and Harry Cohn, of union officials and theater operators, and with evidence from the files of the union itself. None of the gangsters took the stand in his own defense, and toward the end, it was too much to even watch—Ricca and Rosselli each missed several days of trial due to undetermined infirmities.

The trial was dragged out by weeks of objections and cross-examination from the battery of mob attorneys, who sought to show that the crime at issue was not extortion but bribery—that the producers had enlisted Bioff in order to dominate the studio unions. The argument was not without basis—in a subsequent, related trial, a federal judge observed that, "The monies were extracted from [the studio heads] with full knowledge on their part as to Browne's and Bioff's activities and assurances; and no effort was made to secure the assistance of law enforcement authorities." But the jury in New York had little interest in fine distinctions after the show put on by Willie Bioff, and on December 30, 1943, a verdict was returned.

The case against Ralph Pierce was dismissed by the court—his involvement had ended after the initial contact with Bioff and Browne—but the rest were found guilty as charged, and sentenced forthwith to ten years in jail. Their appeals were heard and quickly rejected, and on April 4, 1944, Rosselli and his colleagues from the Chicago mob were committed to the federal penitentiary in Atlanta.

6

LIFE AS A CONVICT

Behind Bars

Atlanta prison warden Joseph W. Sanford was a brute of a man, thick-necked, head shaved in the military style, a member of the Ku Klux Klan. Belligerent and hostile, he resented the meddling of the attorneys and Congressmen that occasionally sought transfers or special treatment for his prisoners, and he dispensed liberally of the jailhouse disciplines of solitary confinement and loss of "good time."

The prison Sanford administered was a drab, four-story, red-brick building referred to within the federal Bureau of Prisons as one of the "old Bastilles." Built in 1902 for a population of 1,200, it housed more than 1,900 prisoners in 1944. The cells were dank and gloomy, and according to one report, "infested with vermin of various types." There was little open space, little recreation, limited bathing facilities, and virtually no entertainment. Time served in Atlanta was, almost by definition, hard time.

111

The arrival of six leading underworld characters recently convicted in a trial that received national attention caused something of a sensation at the prison, and Warden Sanford moved immediately to assert control over his jailhouse. According to a prison bureau official in Washington later interviewed by the FBI, "When the subjects entered the Atlanta penitentiary they were very definitely told by Warden Sanford that they would have to toe the mark."

Shortly thereafter Phil D'Andrea sought a change in his prison diet by claiming he was ill, and when a urine test was required to corroborate his condition, D'Andrea threatened the orderly to find positive results "or else." Word of the threat reached the warden and he seized on the opportunity to teach the Chicago mobsters a lesson: Sanford went to D'Andrea's cell and personally administered a beating. Rosselli and his colleagues "realized then that they could expect no assistance at Atlanta," the FBI report observed.

Faced with hostile surroundings and a hostile administration, Rosselli laid low, avoiding confrontation with the authorities. In particular, Rosselli hated the loss of control inherent in the inmate's life—he later told a friend he was terrified when a food fight broke out in the dining hall. "He said that with the guards there you didn't have the option of dashing out, so the safest place to go was under the table," the friend later recalled. "He said you've gotta be stupid to get up and start throwing food too— you hit the wrong inmate and the guy's liable to come and kill you the next day. What stuck in my mind was the image of Johnny Rosselli, who could call on all the henchmen in Chicago, crawling under the table. He said, 'Jesus, it's more dangerous being in prison than being out on the street.' "

Warden Sanford later reported to the FBI that Campagna and Ricca "threw their weight around, continually bragging about their exploits to the other prisoners," but he observed, "Rosselli never had very much to say." Rosselli attended Catholic church services, obtained a position as a clerk in the prison library, and, according to one prison report, spent much of his time reading. Joking with friends after his release, he referred to jail as "college."

The story of a convict turning to books and even earning recognition for writing is a jailhouse staple, but in Rosselli's case it certainly reflected a new aspect of character. To a grade-school dropout, accustomed to the fast life of Hollywood and the racetrack, the world of ideas might have seemed alien and intimidating. But it provided an escape from the strict physical limits of prison life, and Rosselli took to it with some relish. Not surprisingly, his taste in literature ran to adventure and crime novels, but he kept up with news from the outside by reading *Time* and *Newsweek,* and read the Bible carefully enough that he was able to quote it later. He also kept up a steady flow of correspondence—to Isadore A. Ruman, Rosselli's partner at the Spitzel insurance agency; to Daniel Winkler, a Hollywood agent who related the latest film gossip; and most important, to Beatrice Ann Frank, the actress he dated briefly before entering the Army, to whom he wrote 164 letters, and from whom he received more than 250. None of the letters survive, but Rosselli must have proved a warm and even romantic correspondent—by 1947, Frank had become Rosselli's fiancée.

Still, the conditions in Atlanta were uniformly unpleasant, and Rosselli and his fellow gangsters put an impressive network of political and legal connections to work obtaining transfers to more hospitable quarters. Their prison of choice was Leavenworth, a facility more susceptible to the influence of the mob. Warden Sanford resented the bid to escape his influence and recommended against moving the prisoners, but a team of high-priced attorneys in Washington prevailed, and in July 1945 the Chicago clique was transferred to Leavenworth. Sanford succeeded, however, in separating Rosselli from his fellow gangsters; he remained at Atlanta until October 2, 1946, when he was moved to Terre Haute, Indiana.

Compared to Atlanta, Terre Haute was a country club. Built in 1940 as a model institution, it had exterior fences instead of walls, showers on each floor, and the first entertainment technology to be installed in a federal prison—radio by earphone in each cell. It was designed for more than a thousand prisoners, but only 750 were incarcerated at the time of Rosselli's arrival. No doubt relieved at the change in his circumstances, Rosselli continued in the pattern he established in Atlanta, working quietly as a clerk in the pantry, learning to use a typewriter, and taking lessons in Spanish. His prison monitors reported that Rosselli was "exceptionally obedient and cooperative, and associates with the more desirable types of men."

A prison psychiatrist interviewed Rosselli at Terre Haute in 1947, and while he remarked on the same "good attitude," the doctor was less impressed with the polished manners and respectful approach of the model prisoner. It's hard to put stock in the results of a cursory exam conducted by a staff clinician in the restricted setting of a prison compound, but in this particular case, the analysis proved surprisingly apt. The doctor's written report pierced Rosselli's cool surface to find the sort of internal conflict that might be expected in a man who lived a life of fear, danger, and constant secrecy.

"Beneath the surface one detected underlying systematized paranoid ideas with a coloring of hysteria," the report observed, and Rosselli was categorized as a "moderately severe paranoid personality." The psychiatrist was pessimistic about Rosselli's chances for "reform." "No disciplinary problems are anticipated but no prognosis can be made for release adjustment because he is fixed and rigid in his ideas." The psychiatrist then added, "The prisoner is no doubt 'biding his time' until his release from incarceration."

That last observation was especially prescient, because though Rosselli still had seven years to serve on his sentence, he was confident by then that his stay in prison was nearing its close. The Chicago Outfit had been unable to block the prosecution of its leadership by the U.S. Attorney in New York, but it never accepted as final the ten-year sentence imposed by the judge. The organization had extensive political connections and enormous amounts of money. Besides, coconspirator-turned-informant Joe Schenck had received a full pardon from President Harry Truman in October 1945, and Bioff and Browne had been released from prison on December 22, 1944, their ten-year sentences reduced to three for their cooperation with the government. The mob was determined that its faithful loyalists should receive equal justice.

Getting Sprung

THE FIRST LINE OF defense for the Mafia has always been fear. Not from any vague or implied threat but from direct application of violence—maiming and murder, slow torture, or the sudden, window-rattling explosion of a bomb wired to an automobile ignition. But when the strategy of violence failed, as in the case of the movie studio rackets, the Mafia turned to more subtle strategies of bribery and political influence. And with Ricca, Campagna, Rosselli, and the other mob leaders in jail, the Chicago

Outfit played a trump card, pulling strings that led directly to the White House.

The payoff came on August 13, 1947, at which point the coconspirators in the film case had served exactly one third of their full ten-year sentences. Despite their individual and collective reputation as dangerous career criminals, and despite appeals by the prosecutor and judge in the case for stiff punishment, the three members of the federal parole board voted unanimously to release each of the gangsters after they had served the bare minimum of time required under law. The decision was taken so quickly that the parole office in Chicago did not have time to submit its standard analysis of the cases, nor was the parole board furnished with complete inmate records.

The decision generated a howl from the Chicago press, and the *Daily Tribune*, the *Herald American*, and the *Chicago Sun* launched competing investigations into the paroles. The following month, in September 1947, the Congress followed suit when the House Committee on Expenditures in the Executive Departments convened a series of hearings on the paroles in Chicago and Washington. Finally, after public prodding by the committee, the FBI joined in the hunt.

There were enough leads to keep all the reporters and all the investigators busy chasing separate tips. Word came from New York City that Frank Costello had promised $250,000 to Postmaster General Robert Hannegan, a member of Harry Truman's cabinet, if he would use his influence to bring about the paroles. In Chicago, Jake Guzik, finance minister for the old Capone mob, was said to have channeled $300,000 into a special fund to spring his partners. Other rumors, relayed to authorities and reporters by underworld informants, placed the payoffs at such far-flung outposts as Dallas and Mississippi.

The newspapers gave banner headlines to the sensational but often meandering congressional investigation, but produced little independent evidence of a mob payoff. And the committee itself reported in June 1948, "While the hearings have disclosed the use of considerable money and the employment of individuals in a position to exert influence with those in authority, the committee has been unable to discover any violation of federal law."

That was as far as the story went. Attorney General Tom Clark ordered the FBI not to release the details of its investigation, and provided only a brief summary, which was dismissed by the chairman of the congressional committee as "a dud." Indeed, internal FBI documents reflect

J. Edgar Hoover's overriding concern with the image of his agency, rather than producing results in the parole inquiry. On October 23, 1947, project supervisor E. M. Gurnea noted, "Most of the additional work to be done is primarily for the purpose of clearing the record and protecting the Bureau." And the following week, at the end of a memo advising against disclosure of the investigative files, Hoover himself added the following handwritten passage: "I agree. We have had so many blunders and failures to properly review and supervise investigative cases in past months that I don't want to chance this."

In fact, while much of the FBI file was taken up with pointless interviews—asking Jake Guzik if he had created a slush fund for political payoffs, for example—the agents investigating the case did produce a convincing trail of political activity and influence by powerful attorneys representing the Chicago mob.

As detailed in the investigative reports, the key player in the Mafia scheme to release its imprisoned leadership was a St. Louis attorney named Paul Dillon, then 68 years old. Dillon had strong connections to the underworld organization that ran politics and crime throughout Missouri. His clients included Italian mob leader Johnny Lazia, a Kansas City gambling operator who was murdered in 1934; John F. Doherty, a political fixer, judge, and later sheriff in St. Louis; and Tom Pendergast, the massive, humorless crime chief who once declared, "I'm not bragging when I say I run the show in Kansas City. I am boss."

It was through Pendergast that Dillon met Harry Truman. In 1934, after spending ten years as a county judge for the Pendergast machine, Truman decided on a bid for a seat in the U.S. Senate. As Dillon testified to the committee investigating the mob paroles, "Tom [Pendergast] asked me if I would take charge of the Truman campaign in St. Louis." Truman was elected Vice-President in 1944, and became President with the death of Franklin D. Roosevelt in April 1945, but he never forgot his friends in St. Louis, and Dillon became a frequent visitor to the White House.

About the same time that Truman became President, Dillon had his first contact with the parole board—to seek a reduction in sentence for Frank Boehm, a St. Louis utility executive convicted of perjury in connection with political payoffs. Dillon became friendly with T. Webber Wilson, chairman of the parole board, and the two became regular dinner partners. They were a natural match—Dillon peddled influence, and Wilson, a corpulent, small-time judge from Mississippi, was known around Washington as a grafter. Columnist Drew Pearson reported to the FBI (but not in his column) that he personally knew Wilson "was crooked," and that on two separate occasions that Pearson knew of, "money changed hands in connection with the granting of paroles." Boehm, in the meantime, was released when Truman commuted his sentence.

Dillon put the word out in mob circles about his friends in high places, and the Chicago mob responded by proffering a "price list" with a bounty for each gangster he could get released. The courier was Edward "Putty Nose" Brady, a saloon operator and Missouri state legislator with strong ties to Chicago. In October 1945, Dillon met with Brady and James Testa, a prizefighter and business partner of Brady's, to discuss an upcoming trip to Washington. According to Testa, Brady handed Dillon the price list, which included the names "Little New York [Campagna], Charles Gioe, and Phil D'Andrea."

Dillon subsequently admitted to two meetings with Wilson over the fate of the Chicago gangsters, one in May 1945, prior to the transfer of the prisoners from Atlanta, and another in August 1947, a week before the paroles. He denied receiving any fee for his efforts. Testa's report of the meeting between Dillon and Brady, and of the price list, was recorded by the FBI but never investigated, and was not forwarded to the congressional investigating committee.

A second attorney who traveled to Washington on behalf of the Chicago mob leaders was Maury Hughes, a Dallas resident and a neighbor and boyhood friend of Attorney General Clark. Hughes denied exerting any influence on his old chum, but it was apparent that Clark had at least once taken a direct interest in the status of the gangsters—Bureau of Prison files from 1945 note that "Tom Clark would like to have the subjects transferred to Leavenworth." Moreover, Clark was in charge of selecting members of the parole board, and it was Clark who barred Hoover from releasing the contents of the FBI investigation.

But it was parole board chairman T. Webber Wilson, along with board member Fred Rogers, who made the decision to release the leadership of the Capone mob. Rogers said later he relied on Wilson's advice "that the Al Capone gang was not functioning in Chicago," and that he had personally examined John Rosselli, whom he believed "will never be arrested again for anything on this earth." For his part, Wilson resigned from the parole board a month after the release of Rosselli and his colleagues, and died soon thereafter at his home in Coldwater, Mississippi.

An Ex-Con in L.A.

JOHNNY ROSSELLI LOST LITTLE time getting back on the fast track after his release from prison. He was greeted at the prison gates by Jack Kearns, a fight promoter who gained national prominence by managing Jack Dempsey at the height of his career. The two had met in Los Angeles in the early thirties, when Kearns was staging fights at the American Legion Stadium and Rosselli was operating the Club New Yorker. Kearns had a record—he was arrested for assault in 1932, and indicted in New York in 1945 in connection with a stock swindle—but despite his notoriety, he persuaded Illinois Congressman Tom O'Brien in 1947 to obtain permission for him to visit Rosselli. On May 21, Kearns made the trip to Indiana to see Rosselli in jail, and that August, he returned to Terre Haute to chauffeur Rosselli back to Chicago.

Rosselli spent the traditional first night of freedom touring the North Shore nightspots, and the following day, August 14, Kearns supplied him with a ticket for a flight to Los Angeles, where several friends had worked to ensure a smooth transition back into civil life. James Steinberg, a doctor and a friend of insurance man Herman Spitzel, had agreed to serve as Rosselli's parole advisor. Isadore Ruman, Spitzel's office manager during the war, had secured Rosselli a small apartment on Catalina Street, within view of the grand Ambassador Hotel. And Joe Schenck, apparently not embittered by his stint in federal prison, had arranged for a job at Eagle Lion Studios, where Rosselli's old friend Bryan Foy was vice-president in charge of production. Weakened by the years of incarceration, Rosselli checked himself in for a week at the Sansum Clinic, and then returned to reclaim his position as the mob's lead man in Los Angeles.

He had to work carefully. The trial and jail sentence had stripped Rosselli of the cloak of secrecy he had fashioned during fifteen years as a mystery man in the film industry. Now he was a convict on probation, a gangster publicly connected to the Chicago mob, whose every move would invite gossip and government scrutiny. Still, the film business was his milieu. He savored the style and the glamour of life in the studios and on the Sunset Strip. And Hollywood welcomed him back.

It seems strange that the film colony would accept without recrimination the return of a key player in the wholesale extortion of the industry, but there were a number of mitigating factors at work. First, there was the incestuous nature of the plot itself. Despite the government's assertion that outsiders had brazenly hijacked the studio unions and shaken down the studios, the denizens of the film industry knew full well the chummy relations Pat Casey and the studio heads had maintained with Rosselli and Willie Bioff. It was not hard, and not too far from the truth, for Rosselli to float the story that he had simply taken the fall for the studios in a scheme to keep a lid on labor unrest.

Moreover, Hollywood has always been an open society, where style and personal contacts counted more than the skeletons that might be rattling around a person's closet. "This is a town that always had a lot of shifting sand, and especially after the war," observed Gloria Romanoff, widow of the restaurateur Mike Romanoff. "This was not a town where people checked your pedigree, because they were all out here looking for an opportunity. You couldn't probe anyone too much."

Finally, Rosselli's rehabilitation was supported by his continuing friendships—with Harry Cohn, who still wore the star ruby ring Rosselli had given him; with Billy Wilkerson, who remained a publishing and social power in the film industry despite well-publicized gambling investments with Bugsy Siegel; with Mike Romanoff, who provided Rosselli credit and social standing at his celebrated Rodeo Drive eatery; and with Joe Schenck, who had resumed his position as head of production at Twentieth Century-Fox after being paroled from his income tax conviction. One character was missing from the picture—Rosselli's jailhouse fiancée. Beatrice Ann Frank never again surfaced in the record, and none of his friends recall meeting her.

Rosselli's most important friendship was with Bryan Foy. A veteran producer who moved to Los Angeles in 1922 and grew up with the film industry, Foy was the eldest son of vaudeville comedian Eddie Foy, whose seven children became a traveling troupe under the tag line "The Seven Little Foys." Featured in a 1941 profile by Damon Runyon, Foy was tall, slim, and acerbic, rarely missing an opportunity to rail against high-salaried writers and stars. Foy was popular with the studios for producing low-budget pictures, sometimes at a clip of more than thirty a year, sometimes cutting costs by shooting his B films on abandoned A-film sets. He specialized in the gritty, realistic genre of film noir, but would shoot anything, from *Hamlet* to *Elysia, the Valley of the Nude.*

Growing up in Chicago and New York, and on the road with the family troupe, Foy learned to enjoy the company of the fighters, promoters, and politicians who dominated public life in the thirties, a group that mixed easily with the underworld. Said one friend in an interview, "Brynie [his universal nickname] was always close to people who lived on the edge of right and wrong." Over the years, his houseguests in Beverly Hills and later Encino included Chicago mayor and political-machine boss Ed Kelly; his counterpart from New Jersey, Newark Mayor Frank Hague; the notorious international con artist Jake "The Barber" Factor; and Rosselli's old pal Allen Smiley. As an informant confided to the FBI in 1947, "Bryan Foy has a reputation for hiring any ex-convicts or hoodlums who come out to Hollywood in search of a job."

In 1947, Foy left Twentieth Century-Fox to take an executive position at Eagle Lion, a small, short-lived studio with offices and a sound stage on Santa Monica Boulevard, just west of the Sam Goldwyn lot. It was there that Rosselli took the only legitimate job he ever held, starting as an assistant purchasing agent at $50 a month, and rising quickly to the position of associate producer.

With Foy at the helm, and a support crew that included producers Robert T. Cain and Joe Schenck's nephew Aubrey Schenck, and veteran screenwriter and director Crane Wilbur, Eagle Lion turned out a series of fast-paced, low-budget, semidocumentary thrillers. Based on true stories that Foy culled from the tabloid press, they were popular with critics and fans, and became a major influence on early radio and television shows such as "Dragnet." What the audiences didn't realize was that three of the hit movies, *T-Men, Canon City,* and *He Walked by Night,* were produced in part by an actual gangster.

The exact nature of Rosselli's contribution to the production of the motion pictures he took part in was never clear—Foy once described him as an "artistic consultant," but screenwriter John Higgins said he never encountered Rosselli on an Eagle Lion set. Still, the movies are faithful to the life Rosselli had encountered since his youth in East Boston. Taken together, they paint an honest and unsettling picture of a grim, hard-edged world, a fitting contribution from Hollywood's top true-life gangster.

Each of Rosselli's films were crime stories where the bad guys got caught in the end. They showed little sympathy for the criminals, but little for the police, either: characters adapted to circumstance, with betrayal and blackmail part of the territory. The tension in the films derives from the hunt, the police net inexorably closing on its prey, and in all three, most of the lead characters, cops and crooks alike, die by gunfire. Ironically, considering Rosselli's background, the desperados are all loners; if the stories have a moral, it may be that lawbreakers should always be sure to have a gang to back them up.

Whatever Rosselli's artistic role, his financial involvement is well established. While he was never listed in the screen credits, he later testified under oath that he was an associate producer of the three films, and court documents reflected a 10 percent interest in the pictures. Rosselli's stake is further described in the confidential files of a private intelligence agency. A report from 1951 noted that "John Rosselli recently obtained some $400,000 in cash from a safe deposit box in a bank in New Jersey and turned it over to Eagle Lion Productions." Once again, as with Harry Cohn in 1932, Rosselli was providing fresh cash to the moguls in Hollywood, and nobody stopped to ask where it came from.

Rosselli may have been making money at Eagle Lion (he reported a total of $16,171 to the IRS), but his real purpose was to establish a cover story, both social and legal. "It was very important to Johnny to prove to the Hollywood community that he was back," recalled Betsy Duncan, a onetime girl friend of Rosselli's who met him in the latter part of the 1950s. "That Bioff story followed him everywhere when I first met him, and that was ten years later."

At the same time, Rosselli was under close scrutiny from the parole authorities in Los Angeles. Seeking to present the image of a reformed man, he had to limit his expenditures and scrupulously avoid public contacts with known gangsters. "He drove a beat-up old Ford, which looked pretty funny on him," recalled Patricia Breen, widow of Joe Breen, Jr., who was son of the Production Code administrator and worked with Rosselli at Eagle Lion. Rosselli was even careful to avoid traffic tickets while on probation. "Johnny said, 'I won't drive over 20 mph in the city,'" recalled another Eagle Lion colleague. "'I don't care what the speed limit, I don't want a cop pulling me over.' He wouldn't even go by the [private guard] in uniform at the studio gates without stopping."

Yet despite Rosselli's precautions, the congressional committee investigating his early release from prison brought intense public and press attention to bear on the federal parole board. Rosselli managed to keep a clean record in Los Angeles, and had a Catholic priest, Father Joe Thompson, appointed to replace Dr. Steinberg as his parole advisor, but the pressure continued to mount, and on July 25, 1948, the parole office in Washington issued a warrant for his arrest on charges of associating with "unsavory characters." Three days later, eleven months after he left Terre Haute, Rosselli turned himself in.

The Battle for Los Angeles

THE GOVERNMENT CASE AGAINST Rosselli was trumped up. A series of pleadings filed by attorney Otto Christensen were rejected out of hand but no particulars against Rosselli were proffered by the parole authorities. A hearing before a federal judge was finally set for November 15 in Los Angeles, and Rosselli's most influential Hollywood friends, including Harry Cohn, Billy Wilkerson, and Monogram Pictures president George Burrows, were scheduled as character witnesses. None needed appear, because the government presented no evidence. Rosselli was summarily released, and all charges were dropped.

Yet if the government failed to make a case against Rosselli for engaging in criminal activity while out on parole, its instincts were correct. From the very first day of his return to Los Angeles, Rosselli had resumed his position as a leader in Jack Dragna's Mafia family, deliberating strategy and giving orders in a battle for dominance over the underworld.

The government even knew when the first contact was made. But then, in 1947, they didn't know the players. On the eve of his first night back in Los Angeles, Rosselli and his parole advisor, Dr. Steinberg, were met for dinner by a third man, an attorney by the name of Frank DeSimone. The successful son of one of the oldest and best known Italian families in Los Angeles, Frank DeSimone was also Jack Dragna's chief lieutenant, a ruthless power broker who used the confidentiality of his legal offices to protect the secret proceedings of mob conferences. DeSimone's affiliations were revealed with his arrest in November 14, 1957, along with more than fifty bona fide Mafia leaders from across the country at the Apalachin crime conference in upstate New York.

★

As DeSimone likely informed Rosselli the night they met in August 1947, and in a series of subsequent dinner meetings recorded by the FBI, a lot had changed in the mob during Rosselli's stay in prison. Dragna was still the don, but his alliance with Bugsy Siegel and their lucrative monopoly over Los Angeles bookmaking had ended with a bang two months prior. Seated on a sofa with Allen Smiley in the Beverly Hills mansion of his girl friend, Virginia Hill, Siegel had been perusing the day's paper when his face was shattered by two slugs from an Army carbine. Smiley was uninjured.

There were plenty of reasons for the mob to cut short Siegel's career. Ambitious and reckless, Siegel had spent the past few years pouring syndicate money into a lavish new hotel and casino in Las Vegas, the Flamingo, which would eclipse in style and earnings the folksy, western-style gaming halls then crowding the gambling capital. At the same time, in part to finance fantastic cost overruns at the Flamingo, Siegel had bucked the lead of the Chicago mob in the operation of the racing wire service. The old Capone gang's feud with Continental Press owner James Ragen had ended with his murder in Chicago in 1946, but when they called on Siegel to then fold up his competing Trans-America wire, he held out for a payoff of $2 million.

Bugsy had lost contact with his roots. His death warrant was signed at a syndicate confab in Havana in February 1947, attended by Tony Accardo and Charlie and Joe Fischetti of Chicago; Frank Costello, Albert Anastasia, Vito Genovese, and Carlo Gambino of New York; "Dandy" Phil Kastel of New Orleans; and Santo Trafficante and Meyer Lansky of Miami. All were there to honor Charles "Lucky" Luciano, the Mafia leader exiled to Italy during the war. Frank Sinatra flew in to add an element of levity to the proceedings, but when the mobsters retired to discuss business, the question of Bugsy Siegel dominated the agenda, and the decision was reached to have Jack Dragna's organization eliminate the problem.

Dragna never liked his Jewish counterpart. He waited long enough for Siegel to complete construction at the Flamingo, and then dispatched a crew of five men in two cars to carry out the hit. The murder was never solved by police, but Eddie Cannizzaro, a Dragna driver and gambling operator, later claimed credit. "It was a clean hit," he declared shortly before his death in 1987 in an interview with reporter John Babcock. "I was picked because I knew Siegel and wouldn't make a mistake."

Eliminating Bugsy Siegel may have bolstered Dragna's ego, but it left the Los Angeles underworld in a state of chaos. Siegel's mercurial lieutenant Mickey Cohen had been assigned control of bookmaking in 1942 with Dragna and Rosselli's consent, but with Siegel gone, Cohen renounced any ties to the Italians. Moreover, the shock waves generated by Siegel's assassination piqued the state's interest in the racing wire services, and in April 1948, the state Public Utilities Commission dealt the bookmaking monopoly a crippling blow by barring the transmission of racing information. With revenues from gambling suddenly sharply diminished, Dragna and Mickey Cohen embarked on a deadly, protracted battle for power.

Before engaging in open hostilities, Dragna moved to beef up the forces of the L.A. organization. In the late fall of 1947, in a basement storeroom of a small winery on the south side of town, Dragna initiated five new men into his crime family, incanting in Sicilian with a dagger and a revolver lying crossed on the table before him. John Rosselli greeted the initiates at the door and led them to Dragna: they were Jimmy Regace, Charley Dippolito, Salvatore Piscopo (aka Louie Merli), Dragna's nephew Louis Tom Dragna, and Jimmy "The Weasel" Fratianno, recently released from eight years in an Ohio prison on an assault charge, a hotheaded killer who was then serving as a gofer to Mickey Cohen.

The war with Mickey Cohen might have ended the day it began if it hadn't been for a personal neurosis of Cohen's reminiscent of Lady Macbeth. On the evening of August 18, 1948, Cohen was holding court at his Sunset Boulevard haberdashery shop with henchmen "Hooky" Rothman, Albert "Slick" Snyder, Jimmy Rist, and Fratianno, along with Fratianno's wife and daughter. Fratianno departed, ostensibly to take his family to see a play, but as he left the shop, he flashed a signal to Frank DeSimone, who was stationed across the street.

Moments later, a car roared up to the curb and out jumped Frank Bompensiero, Dragna's longtime henchman from San Diego. Wearing dark glasses and a white Panama hat, and followed by three other gunmen, Bompensiero confronted Hooky Rothman with a sawed-off shotgun as the other men entered the building. When Rothman moved to knock the gun away, The Bomp blasted him point-blank. Inside the shop, the gunfire was deafening but the damage was limited: Al Snyder was shot in the arm, Jimmy Rist lost part of an ear to a stray bullet, and Mickey Cohen escaped injury altogether. It seems when the shooting began, Cohen was in a rear bathroom washing his hands, a curious and increasing obsession of his. He ducked into a toilet stall until it was over.

Rosselli was in jail at the time fighting the parole violation charges, and missed the police roundup that followed the attack. But over the course of the next five years, Dragna and Rosselli made Cohen's elimination a top priority. Twice bombs were set under his house, and three times he was ambushed by a fusillade of small-arms fire, but each time he escaped harm. In his frustration, Rosselli compared Cohen to Bugs Moran, a Capone rival who survived a dozen hits. All the while, Cohen made the most of the press attention that came with the attacks, posing for photographs and declaring himself the king of the rackets. An embarrassed Rosselli grumbled to a girl friend, "That Mickey Cohen. He's a disgrace to the underworld."

Rosselli didn't take part in the gunplay—he was well past 40 years old, and had *soldati* like The Weasel and The Bomp to handle the dirty work. But according to Fratianno, Rosselli was integral to planning the hits on Cohen, and the murders of several of Cohen's henchmen. During an interview in November 1987, Fratianno described Rosselli as the brains behind the operation of the L.A. Mafia family. "See, Jack [Dragna] respected Johnny. He was in on everything. Johnny, you know, he gave the orders because he was smarter than all them guys."

Careful not to violate the conditions of his parole, Rosselli attended mob conferences at the offices of attorneys DeSimone or Otto Christensen, where conversations were protected under attorney-client privilege. For one-on-one contacts with Fratianno and other front-line thugs, he arranged for meetings in restaurants near the studios in Hollywood. "Twice a week we'd meet, just to keep everything straight," Fratianno said. "Usually at Napoli's, a place across the street from Columbia Studios. Johnny couldn't be seen with me, so we didn't sit at the same table. But I'd see him get up and go into the toilet, and I'd follow him in, and we'd bullshit about what was going on. If I had any problems, he'd take it to Jack and straighten it out."

Sobered by his experience in prison, Rosselli had learned well. He had resumed his double life, but paid better attention to the details. No longer a mystery man, he held a legitimate position in the movie business. And he left behind the tools of his youth, the guns and knives of his trade. But in the killing season, Rosselli was there, passing sentence while leaning over a washroom sink.

The Spotlight

JOHN ROSSELLI'S SCRUPULOUS EFFORTS to conceal his criminal activities were an unmitigated success. Chief William Parker had been appointed to clean up the corruption-tainted Los Angeles Police Department, and declared early on that organized crime had been driven from the city. Officials with Parker's organized crime division knew better, but spent much of their time tracking the antics of Mickey Cohen and his men. The more savvy of the cops kept tabs on Jack Dragna's Mafia family, but even the best of them knew little of Rosselli's role in the underworld's battle for gambling turf.

"We knew who Rosselli was, but we never knew what he was up to," recalled Marion Phillips, the police lieutenant in charge of Parker's intelligence division. Billy Dick Unland, one of Phillips's front-line investigators, added that efforts were made to track Rosselli, but with little success. "We knew him from the Bioff thing, so we kept an eye on him at his apartment on Crescent Heights. One time we rousted him and he went into a long thing about how he was friends with L. B. Mayer. But we never got anything on him. We'd see the others meeting places, but Rosselli didn't seem to be part of that."

The FBI also attempted to keep an eye on Rosselli's activities, with the same results. A brief memo in 1947 points out that agents in Los Angeles attempted to tap Rosselli's phone lines, but failed because his office phone at Eagle Lion ran through a studio switchboard, making a tap exceedingly difficult to monitor, and he maintained no telephone at home.

But circumspect as he was, Rosselli could not escape the notoriety of his conviction in the Hollywood labor rackets. Where the papers once referred to him as a "mystery man," they now tagged him, "a figure in the Willie Bioff 'film shakedown' case." And in 1950, soon after Rosselli's release from jail on the trumped-up parole violation case, he was called to testify before an unprecedented congressional inquiry into the national operations of organized crime.

★

Spanning more than ten months, convened in thirteen cities, the hearings were chaired by Estes Kefauver, the lanky, Yale-educated grandson of a Baptist preacher, and then the junior senator from Tennessee. In later years, the spectacle of a congressional committee grilling reluctant gangsters became a newsreel staple, but in 1950 the hearings were the first of their kind, and more ambitious than any that had gone before. The existence of a national crime syndicate, and behind it, of the secret criminal society of the Mafia, had until then been regarded as a myth even by leading law enforcement authorities, and was virtually unknown to the general public. Kefauver was determined to change that.

Besides the broad scope of his investigation—the Kefauver Committee called more than 600 witnesses and compiled 11,500 pages of testimony—the hearings were brought home to the public in a way that until then had been impossible—via television. The image of Frank Costello, dubbed "the Prime Minister of Organized Crime," nervously kneading his fingers during two days of intensive interrogation was broadcast to a national audience estimated at 20 to 30 million viewers. From that time forward, the Mafia was on the map.

It was public exposure, and not the prying questions of the committee counsel, that most concerned John Rosselli. Negotiating through attorney Otto Christensen, Rosselli agreed to testify and not to invoke the protection of the Fifth Amendment, but on condition that he appear in Chicago, not California, and in closed session. Bryan Foy helped lay the groundwork by phoning Kefauver's chief counsel, Rudolph Halley, to report that Rosselli had "gone straight" and was eager to cooperate with the committee. The hearing was scheduled for Saturday October 7, 1950.

The pressure on Rosselli was enormous. By agreeing to testify, he was putting to the test his Mafia oath of secrecy. At the same time, any false answer could result in a charge of perjury and a violation of parole, landing him in federal prison to serve the balance of his ten-year sentence. But under questioning by committee counsel Halley, Rosselli proved calm and confident, offering vague and carefully framed recollections.

"Were you in the liquor business during Prohibition?" Halley asked.

"Well, in some manner, yes," came the reply.

"Would you state in what manner?"

"Very, very, very small."

"What was the nature of your operation in the liquor business?"

"Other than just buying and selling a little liquor here and there."

Eventually Rosselli eased up, though not much. "Let's put it this way, Mr. Halley: I was a young fellow with very little education. I am trying to sell whiskey, trying to do anything I possibly can to make a living."

Halley went on with the same limited success to cover Rosselli's relationship with Al Capone, his role in operating the racing wire service, his involvement in the film industry. Finally, while asking about Ben Siegel's activities in Hollywood, Halley vented his frustration. "I can just see the wheels working in there, Mr. Rosselli, trying to think 'Who can I mention that I won't hurt. . . .' "

"Not at all," Rosselli parried. "I would really like to mention the names, but I can't truthfully say that I saw him with such and such and so and so at certain times because I can't truthfully answer that."

"I am going to ask you to think this over," Halley retorted. "This investigation is far from finished. It is practically just started. I think that you are trying to give this testimony of yours a quick brush over. If you are on our side of the fence, and by our side I mean out of the problem . . ."

Rosselli cut him off. "I am on the truth's side, Mr. Halley."

Later, Senator Kefauver tried his hand. "Mr. Rosselli," Kefauver said, "I think you could be very helpful to us."

"I would like to be," Rosselli agreed.

"You look like a man who would like to be helpful, but I don't think you are telling us as much about it as you could tell us."

"I wish I could," Rosselli answered.

Perhaps the most surprising revelations to come from the testimony were Rosselli's responses to names thrown out by the committee with the simple preamble, "Do you know . . . ?"

In rapid succession, Rosselli conceded a network of contacts with the highest echelons of the national syndicate. Capone cousin Charlie Fischetti was a close friend, as were Moe Sedway, Ben Siegel's top man in Nevada and Arizona, and San Francisco gambling boss "Bones" Remmer. In Los Angeles, Rosselli acknowledged "a nodding acquaintance" with Mickey Cohen, and friendships with certified gangsters Joe Sica, Al Marco, Farmer Page, Jimmy Utley, and Rosselli's old bootlegging partner, Tony Cornero. On a national level, he admitted knowing Frank Costello and Willie Moretti of New York, Paul Ricca and Louis Campagna of Chicago, Meyer Lansky of Miami, Texas Mafia chieftain Sam Maceo, Frank Milano and Al Polizzi of Cleveland, and the exiled kingpin of the national syndicate, Charlie "Lucky" Luciano. It was a roster of top-flight contacts that guaranteed Rosselli the close attention of law enforcement officials for the balance of his life.

Despite Rosselli's precautions, despite the closed session and his banter with the committee, the hearings proved deeply damaging. Rosselli had successfully walked the line between contempt and perjury, and managed to avoid revealing new details of syndicate business, but Senator Kefauver saw to the destruction of his public reputation. In a press conference immediately following the session, Kefauver declared that he had elicited "strong evidence" that the Capone syndicate was tied in "closely" with the underworld of New York, Cleveland, St. Louis, and Los Angeles. He went on to detail Rosselli's "wide acquaintance" with gangsters in cities across the country, and his past involvement in the racing wires. The press conference made headlines in Los Angeles.

★

In early 1953, Rosselli was broadsided again, this time by a state commission on organized crime. Denouncing the criminal infiltration of "legitimate society," the commission cited prominently the "amazing example of John Rosselli." After noting his conviction in the film industry "shakedown," the commission reported:

> This professional blackmailer and thug has been tolerated socially and in business in California just as [Benjamin] Siegel and many another racketeer. Upon his parole, he immediately returned to California and has had no trouble securing a lucrative position in the very industry from which he and his associates extorted millions of dollars, and was received again into the same social circles just as though nothing had happened. Certainly a community which takes a leper to a bosom need not be surprised if it becomes infected.

Out of Hollywood

GRADUALLY, BUT IN DISCERNIBLE stages, the exposure of John Rosselli's criminal life forced him out of the legitimate position he attempted to forge in Hollywood. It was one thing to engage in the social life of the film capital, to frequent the nightclubs and date the starlets and do favors for insiders and old friends like Billy Wilkerson and L. B. Mayer, but it was another to land a spot on the payroll, tying a studio directly to an ex-con recently involved in a sensational industry scandal.

Certainly, Rosselli was not shunned. Bryan Foy remained a close friend, joining Rosselli for evenings at Charlie Foy's popular nightclub in the San Fernando Valley or traveling to Brynie's Palm Springs home on the weekends. "They were like the Rover Boys," recalled Foy's niece, Madeline O'Donnell. "They went everywhere together." Another frequent companion at the time was Cora Sue Collins, then in her early twenties, a child star who appeared in movies such as *Tom Sawyer, Detective* in 1938 and *Get Hep to Love* in 1944. At the age of 16, Collins quit the movies to marry the former manager of the Clover Club; she divorced him in 1946 and, when Rosselli was released from prison the following year, became a regular date. Other friends of both Rosselli and Collins included James McKay, heir to a Virginia fortune and owner of a gambling house in Reno, Nevada; Ben Siegel's former attorney Jerry Giesler; and actor Pat O'Brien. Their haunts were Ciro's, the posh dinner club on the Sunset Strip, and Mocambo's which featured nightly entertainment and a tropical birdcage that ran the length of the bar.

But Rosselli's business prospects began to dim when Bryan Foy left Eagle Lion Studios in the early part of 1950. Despite Foy's substantial financial success, the owners of the studio had never enjoyed his brash, brusque demeanor, and when he reached the end of his three-year contract, they released him forthwith. Foy caught on quickly with Warner Brothers, but there was no room on the payroll for shady associates.

Rosselli cast about for several months, checking in for a brief stay at the Scripps Hospital in La Jolla, California, and entering into negotiations for purchase of the screen rights to a religious story, *The End of the Santa Fe Trail*. But following the appearance before the Kefauver Committee, his parole advisor pressed him to come up with a steady occupation, and Rosselli played what he figured to be a trump card—he called on Harry Cohn.

Initially Cohn was friendly, and he invited Rosselli to drop by the studio. Cohn greeted him warmly from atop the dais at the end of his office, still wearing the ruby ring Rosselli had presented him over a decade before. Cohn biographer Bob Thomas, who interviewed Rosselli in Las Vegas in the middle 1960s, detailed the scene (Rosselli was given a pseudonym in the book). After small talk about Cohn's family and Columbia's recent releases, Rosselli got down to business asking Cohn for a position at the studio. "Cohn looked pained. 'Johnny, how could I give you a job? The stockholders would scalp me.'"

Rosselli responded angrily to Cohn's flat refusal. "You're a rotten shit. Did the stockholders complain when I got ten years of prison because of you?" Cohn tried to placate Rosselli by offering to set him up as an agent along the lines of Mayer's friend Frank Orsatti, but Rosselli wasn't interested. "I don't want any tricky business. All I wanted was a job."

As Rosselli turned to leave the office, Cohn called after him, "Don't go away mad." But Rosselli didn't forget Cohn's betrayal. He disparaged the mogul to friends, and when the opportunity came to exact a little retribution two years later, Rosselli jumped at the chance.

Rosselli suffered similar indignities at Hollywood Park, the racetrack founded by producer Mervyn LeRoy that served as a sort of studio lounge for the film industry. Rosselli appeared regularly at the exclusive turf club there until June of 1951, when track security officials sent a warning through several friends of Rosselli's that he was no longer welcome at any of the tracks around Southern California, and would be escorted off the premises if he insisted on showing. Through an intermediary, Rosselli sent word that he was "extremely disappointed" to learn of his non grata status, and asked if intervention by Harry Cohn, Joe Schenck, or L. B. Mayer might alter the decision. The answer was a flat no.

The message from the film industry was clear, but Rosselli could not simply walk away—he needed to maintain a legitimate job to meet the requirements of his parole, and jumping into some new line of work without falling back on his mob ties simply wasn't feasible. As if to prove the point, he launched a venture called the Tom Thumb Doughnut Distributing Co., which he abandoned after eighteen months of inactivity.

The man who bailed Rosselli out was George Burrows, the former banker who was then a director of Monogram Pictures. Burrows certainly had less stature than Harry Cohn but proved more loyal, putting Rosselli on the staff roster briefly as an "associate producer." Rosselli also caught on as a "coproducer," though more likely as a cover than as a true staff worker, with Mutual Pictures, whose president, Jack Dietz, formerly operated Harlem's Cotton Club. The staff positions proved short-lived, but both men continued their sponsorship of Rosselli when they formed, in 1952, the Diburro Film Company, with Burrows, Dietz, and Rosselli as equal partners, ostensibly to produce a movie entitled *Invasion U.S.A.* The picture was never made, but the various assignments looked substantial enough on the surface that Rosselli's parole advisor never intervened.

Though exiled from the major studios, Rosselli remained the film industry contact for the national crime syndicate. He was 47 years old, but the leadership in the Chicago Outfit still called him The Hollywood Kid. And in 1952, according to several accounts published and broadcast over the years, the syndicate assigned Rosselli to call on Harry Cohn. This time the visit wasn't personal, but as an emissary for powerful friends, a role that Rosselli found more comfortable than that of supplicant for a salary position.

★

As the story goes, the assignment was to secure the part of Angelo Maggio in the film *From Here to Eternity* for Frank Sinatra, the longtime mob hanger-on whose failing voice and caustic personality had put his career into a tailspin. The problem was Harry Cohn, who was producing the film. Cohn hated Sinatra, and felt he was wrong for the part to boot. Sinatra felt that playing the part of Maggio could reverse his fortunes, and he was right: he won an Academy Award for his work, and once again was in demand as an entertainer.

It wasn't the first time that mobsters were attributed a role in Sinatra's career. In August 1943, as his singing career took off, he broke free of a long-term contract with band leader Tommy Dorsey. Ever after, Sinatra was dogged by the allegation that Willie Moretti, a lieutenant to New York mob leader Frank Costello and a friend of Sinatra's, scared Dorsey into dropping the contract by shoving the barrel of a gun into the band-leader's mouth. Tommy Dorsey's attorney denied any implication of mob intimidation, but Dorsey himself gave the story some credence in 1951, when he told *American Mercury* magazine that, in the midst of the contract dispute, he received a visit from three men who grimly told him to "sign or else."

That the Mafia played a role in obtaining the Maggio part has been emphatically denied by Sinatra; by Harry Cohn's widow; by Dan Taradash, who scripted the film; and by Abe Lastfogel, Sinatra's agent. But the event was popularized in dramatic, fictional fashion in Mario Puzo's bestselling 1969 novel, *The Godfather*, wherein Italian singer "Johnny Fontaine" seeks to revive a flagging career with a certain film role, and when he is rebuffed by movie mogul "Jack Woltz," he turns to friends in the Mafia, who make Woltz "an offer he can't refuse"—leaving the severed head of a prized racehorse on the mogul's bed as a warning. Fontaine gets the part.

In her book on Sinatra, tell-all biographer Kitty Kelley posits, among other scenarios, that Rosselli was the messenger who delivered Sinatra's appeal to Harry Cohn. And toward the end of his life, when Rosselli's niece asked him if he'd done such a service, Rosselli allowed that he had once played an instrumental role in Sinatra's career.

A more detailed account was published in 1976 by former New York *Post* reporter Tony Sciacca, who alleged that Frank Costello told dinner friends at the Copacabana that "he was asked to intercede for Sinatra, . . . and while he and Frank weren't close friends they had met on many occasions over the years. Costello then called several West Coast Mafia men who control film industry unions and asked them to intercede." The syndicate man in the film industry unions was, of course, Rosselli.

Author Leonard Katz suggests a slightly different scenario, asserting that Frank Costello got the part for Sinatra, but that he used talent-agency connections in Hollywood. But John Rosselli had long served Costello as a contact on the West Coast, and would be a natural emissary, especially to Harry Cohn. If such a meeting transpired there would have been no witnesses, but one longtime Hollywood player contends it actually took place, and that he learned of it back in 1952.

Joe Seide, a onetime publicist and an associate of Rosselli's who later served jail time for income tax evasion, said he was told about Rosselli's role by Jack Farrell, a childhood friend of Seide's who was connected to Costello's mob in New York. According to Seide, Farrell made a trip to Los Angeles on Sinatra's behalf and met with Rosselli, who in turn met with Cohn to insist that Sinatra receive the part he coveted.

"The Maggio role, Sinatra wasn't going to get it. There was no two ways about it," Seide recalled. "He got it through New York friends, and John Rosselli was the go-between. Johnny was the one who talked to Harry—he was the one who laid it out. That was serious business. It was in the form of look, you do this for me and maybe we won't do this to you. There was none of that stuff about a horse's head, but a lot of 'juice' was directed. When Jackie came by to see me, that's what he told me. It wasn't even a secret in the business."

The story may be apocryphal, but the characters fit, and if indeed the meeting took place, then Rosselli may have considered his score with Cohn even. At least he got a chance to see the imperious producer squirm.

By that point, Rosselli didn't mind burning a few bridges. On March

7, 1954, his parole expired, and he was free to travel and associate as he pleased, subject only to the annual scrutiny of the IRS. Rosselli would maintain the contacts and friendships he had developed in the film industry for the rest of his life, but his official role as a labor "consultant," and his curious career as movie producer and artistic consultant, were over.

7

BACK IN ACTION

Into the Desert

John Rosselli celebrated the expiration of his parole with a party that reflected both the life he was leaving behind and the one he was entering. "Johnny called it his coming out party," recalled Patricia Breen, who attended with her husband, Joe Breen, Jr. Rosselli marked the occasion with a display of disposable cash that was impossible under the watchful eye of his parole officer—he arrived in a new, deep blue vicuna suit, and a matching deep blue convertible Cadillac coupe. His hair by that time had gone completely gray, a silver mane brushed straight back, and his pale blue eyes glistened in the company of his friends.

The party was held at Perino's, an elegant and very expensive Italian restaurant on Wilshire Boulevard just east of the Ambassador Hotel. The guest list was short but revealing: as recounted by Patricia Breen, his Hollywood friends were represented by the Breens, columnist Florabel Muir ("She loved Johnny"), and actress Donna Reed and her husband. In addition, there were two guests from Chicago—Charlie Baron and Louis Lederer. The celebrants from Hollywood represented sentiment and a dash of glamour, but those from Chicago represented the future, for Rosselli and for organized crime.

Charlie "Babe" Baron was a classic Chicago insider. A confidant of political machine boss Jacob Arvey, Baron was a credit enforcer who earned notoriety as a primary suspect in two murders, the first in 1929 and the second, a gambling-related machine-gun execution, in 1934. Despite his reputation, he was accepted into the Illinois National Guard, where he rose to the position of brigadier general, earning his second nickname, "Major." At the time of Rosselli's party, Baron was working with the organizers of several new casinos in Las Vegas. Lou Lederer had a less violent history than Baron, but was skilled in every aspect of managing gambling operations and later became affiliated with Bally, the manufacturer of pinball and slot machines. Lederer and his unique talents were considered wholly owned property of the Chicago Outfit.

Baron and Lederer were both close friends of Rosselli's and both proved pleasant guests at the "coming out" party, but of course there was more to it than that. Rosselli was preparing to move back into the gambling operations of the national crime syndicate.

★

The war of attrition between Jack Dragna and Mickey Cohen, combined with the collapse of the California division of the racing wire service, had left the Los Angeles Mafia family weak, with no immediate prospects for revival. Dragna was old and tired, content to maintain his control over the garment industry and to run his fruit business, shipping bananas from Central America aboard rusting government surplus freighters. In 1954, Dragna made a halfhearted attempt to break into Las Vegas, sending slugger Jimmy Fratianno to assault Meyer Lansky operatives Moe Sedway and Joseph "Doc" Stacher in an effort to assert his prerogatives. But rather than a piece of the action, Dragna accepted a cash payoff, and according to veteran mob investigator Ed Reid, "made very few dents in the behind-the-scenes Las Vegas economy."

At the same time, Rosselli's stock in the eyes of gangsters across the country had never been higher. His new status was indicated by Moe Sedway, Ben Siegel's former lieutenant in the racing wire service and a successor in interest at the Flamingo Hotel and casino in Las Vegas after his boss's murder. In a statement relayed to the FBI by an informant in

February 1951, Sedway declared, "John Rosselli was the chief representative of the 'syndicate' on the West Coast. Jack Dragna was formerly the leader of the mob, but Rosselli is now on top because Rosselli took a penitentiary sentence and did not complain."

John Rosselli was never an empire builder, as Sedway's statement might imply. He never moved to assert control over Dragna's Mafia family in Los Angeles. But like many of his brethren in the mob, he was an opportunist, and he did not allow his new degree of power and status to go to seed. Stripped of his legitimate cover as a show business entrepreneur, and with the Los Angeles family virtually moribund, Rosselli headed east, into the desert.

★

Rosselli laid the foundation for his new incarnation as a gambling executive in Reno, the site of the first large casinos in Nevada, where he showed up, unbeknownst to his parole officer, almost immediately upon his release from Terre Haute. According to Bryn Armstrong, then a reporter in Reno and later chair of the Nevada State Parole Board, Rosselli represented hidden financial interests in the Bank Club, the biggest casino in the country at the time, owned by Rosselli's socialite friend James McKay and by Bill Graham, a forty-year veteran of the Nevada gaming scene. The contact with Graham was crucial—he knew every politician in the state, and could obtain licenses and government concessions when other men could not.

More important, however, were the hidden interests that Rosselli spoke for. McKay and Graham had obtained financial backing for their casino operations from an underworld consortium led by Charlie Fischetti of Chicago and Lansky emissary Doc Stacher, a former enforcer for Rosselli's old friend from New Jersey, Longy Zwillman. Fischetti, Stacher, and Lansky were all friends with Rosselli, their trust underscored when they asked him to monitor their interests in the Bank. And when Las Vegas began to supplant Reno as the gaming capital of the Silver State, Rosselli naturally followed, bringing his connections in tow.

Las Vegas in the early 1950s was just beginning to take shape as the infernal canyon of light and sound and action that now stands along the sun-baked blacktop of Highway 91. Gambling had been legal since 1931, but it was not until 1947 that the visionary but profligate Bugsy Siegel had ushered in the era of the plush gaming palace with the construction of the "Fabulous" Flamingo. Its first few months had proved disastrous, especially for Siegel, as the gambling crowd stayed away, and the untested gaming-room crew pocketed what winnings there were. The losses ensured Siegel's execution.

Yet as the syndicate operators hustled to recoup the millions Siegel had poured into the place, and when the money began to roll in, they realized that in spite of his tendency to hyperbole, Bugsy had been on to something. Over the next seven years, mobsters from across the country joined the scramble, opening a series of neon-lit casinos that offered the cash-rich adventurers of post-war America a whole new way to part with their money. Meyer Lansky led the way, launching the Thunderbird Hotel in 1948; Moe Dalitz, entrepreneurial leader of Cleveland's Mayfield Road Gang, opened the Desert Inn in 1950; the Sahara opened in 1952, backed by a gambling cartel from Portland, as did the Sands, run by Doc Stacher. The year 1955 saw four new entries on the suddenly booming Las Vegas strip—the Hacienda, the Riviera, the Dunes, and the Royal Nevada.

Los Angeles had its own presence in the gambling mecca, but it was from a prior generation, and it wasn't Dragna's Mafia family. In the late 1930s, when Dragna and Rosselli locked up the racetrack gambling racket under the administration of Mayor Frank Shaw, the leaders of the old L.A. syndicate, gamblers Farmer Page, Tutor Sherer, and Guy McAfee, headed for Las Vegas. They opened casinos such as the Golden Nugget and the Pioneer, folksy places with sawdust on the floor, crowded side by side at a downtown crossroads dubbed "glitter gulch." They were jealous when the fancy new hotels began opening down the road, but didn't dare attempt to thwart the invasion of their desert money machine.

Rosselli's old bootlegging boss Tony Cornero was the only West Coast gambler to make the jump to the big time, financing the $6 million Stardust, which boasted 1,032 hotel rooms and, when it opened for business in 1955, the desert's biggest casino. But Cornero would never see a nickel in profit. On July 31, 1955, two weeks before the scheduled opening of the Stardust, Cornero suffered a heart attack while shooting craps at the Desert Inn and died on the spot. A year later, the Stardust was reporting heavy profits under the tutelage of John "Jake the Barber" Factor, a stock swindler fronting for the Chicago syndicate.

John Rosselli's activity in the days of heady growth was as a West Coast contact, a facilitator, a man who could put people together. As early as 1951, he was reported in the files of the LAPD holding "interests" in Las Vegas, but the intelligence officers could only speculate as to their nature. The record was augmented by observations of the "airport squad," the consistently effective surveillance team established by the police to monitor the travels of known criminals, which noted in 1952 the arrival of Charlie Baron, who stopped en route to Las Vegas on behalf of the Chicago mob, to confer with Rosselli in Los Angeles. In 1955, Rosselli was spotted meeting with Jake and Beldon Katleman, owners of El Rancho Vegas, and then joining them on a flight to Nevada; the same year he was seen returning on a flight from Vegas with "Dandy" Phil Kastel, a much-traveled Jewish mobster who embodied the link between gangland heavies Frank Costello, Meyer Lansky, and Carlos Marcello, don of the New Orleans Mafia.

Rosselli's work in Las Vegas was nebulous, but crucial. He served as oil on waters easily roiled by the long-toothed fish gliding beneath the surface. He maintained open channels to all the different out-of-town factions, as well as to the California-based operators downtown, and served as a conduit to political fixers like Bill Graham in Reno, and Artie Samish, known in California political circles as "the Governor of the Legislature." Rosselli also provided muscle.

The case of Louis "Russian Louis" Strauss serves as an example. An itinerant card sharp, Strauss was also a hit man, and carried out a contract murder for Benny Binion, a Dallas crime lord and owner of the Horseshoe Club in Vegas's glitter gulch. Always looking for an angle, Strauss used the incriminating scheme to extort cash from Binion, but the blackmail scheme didn't last long. Binion took his problem to Dragna henchman Nick Licata, offering a piece of a new casino he was planning to build in return for the murder of Russian Louis.

Licata let the matter lay fallow for eighteen months, at which point the business was referred to Rosselli. According to Jimmy Fratianno, Rosselli enlisted Fratianno along with the notorious Chicago hoodlum Felix "Milwaukee Phil" Alderisio, then on assignment in Las Vegas. Rosselli made the contact with Strauss at the Desert Inn and introduced him to Fratianno, who enlisted him in a purported rip-off scheme in Palm Springs. Strauss took the bait, and joined Fratianno and Alderisio in a late-model Cadillac convertible for a ride across the desert.

The crew made a detour through Upland, California, where Fratianno said he could pick up some ready cash, but where in fact the ubiquitous Frank Bompensiero and half a dozen thugs awaited their arrival. Strauss was thoroughly taken in. Pulling up before a suburban tract house, the three men headed inside. The execution took about two minutes. One man grabbed Strauss while Bompensiero threw a garrote around his neck.

The Bomp pulled from one side, Fratianno from the other, and Russian Louis was done for.

The share of the casino Binion had promised never materialized, but years later, Fratianno picked up a $60,000 fee for his labors. He split it four ways: an even split between himself, Alderisio, The Bomp, and Rosselli. "Johnny was, you know, more or less the engineer," Fratianno explained in an interview. For years after, there was an "in" joke around Las Vegas: if a gambler owed some money that he knew he wouldn't repay, he'd slap his lender on the back and insist, "Sure, you'll get your money, soon as Russian Louis gets back to town."

On the Road Again

THE EXPIRATION OF HIS parole left Rosselli one final score to settle, one loose end from the film extortion rackets that had to be tied down. That loose end was Willie Bioff, and in 1955, Bioff had the temerity to show his face in Las Vegas.

After gaining his release from prison on the strength of his testimony against his fellow mobsters, Bioff had changed his name to William Nelson and moved with his wife to Phoenix, Arizona. Bioff never acclimated to obscurity, however, and soon befriended Arizona Senator Barry Goldwater, who liked to consult with "Nelson" on the thorny question of labor racketeering.

Enjoying his return to public life, Bioff took a position as entertainment consultant at the Riviera Hotel in Las Vegas. He continued to use his alias, but the Nevada gambling halls were thick with Chicago gangsters, and Bioff was soon spotted. His new life ended along with his old one on November 4, 1955. Planning to spend the day fishing, he kissed his wife good-bye, climbed into his pickup truck, and switched on the ignition. The blast demolished Willie and his truck, scattering bits of metal a hundred feet in all directions.

John Rosselli never let on how much he knew of Bioff's demise, but his reaction to the event was speedy and precise. He first placed a phone call to a Los Angeles reporter, and stated for the record that he "hadn't

seen Bioff in years," and that, "I thought he was in South America somewhere." Rosselli then called his friend Patricia Breen, and asked if he
might stay in the Breens' guest room until the excitement died down.
"They're going to be on my back instantly," Rosselli explained. "I'm
going to need to lie low for a few days." Of course he could stay—Rosselli
was a close friend of the family. It was a perfect sanctuary, and it worked.
By the time he surfaced again in public, the sensation of the bombing had
blown over. The police never did question John Rosselli about the murder
of Willie Bioff.

★

Bioff's demise marked the beginning of a period of constant travel and
activity that would take Rosselli from coast to coast. Rosselli showed in
Las Vegas and Los Angeles on occasion in the middle 1950s, but they
were brief stops, layovers on his itinerary. It may have been that Rosselli
was simply restless, taking full measure of his freedom after ten years of
incarceration and strict parole supervision. More important, Rosselli was
renewing and expanding the singular array of underworld contacts that he
had cultivated over a criminal career that already reached back thirty-five
years, and which he had detailed in part under questioning by the
Kefauver Committee. Or it may have been, as one source put it, that the
mob leadership was "grooming" Rosselli.

Between 1954 and 1957, Rosselli crisscrossed the country, traveling
the seams of the national syndicate, offering "juice" and protection in the
nether regions where no single crime family had established hegemony.
There were perhaps a dozen such hot spots around the nation, places that,
like Las Vegas, had been declared open territory by the national commission. Gambling wasn't legal, as it was in Vegas, but these were outposts
where local authorities tactfully overlooked backroom gambling operations, and club owners and casino managers operated independent of the
major crime families. Here Rosselli gave free rein to the dark side of his
character, purveying the wares of free-lance muscle, getting what he
wanted through intimidation.

According to a source with long experience in the entertainment industry and extensive contacts in the underworld, Rosselli was at different
times a silent partner in gambling halls in Newport, Kentucky; in Hot
Springs, Arkansas; and in a string of clubs reaching from Florida to Washington, D.C., and up the eastern seaboard to Boston. "They had illegal
gambling and burlesque shows," said the source, who spoke only on condi-

tion of anonymity. "The money wasn't so important, but it was a constant source of girls for John whenever he was in town."

The city and outskirts of Miami was in many ways the capital of these open territories. Santo Trafficante had for years held sway on the west coast of the Florida peninsula, making his headquarters in Tampa, where he was succeeded in 1952 by his son, Santo Trafficante, Jr. But Miami was a special case, a favorite vacation spot of leading East Coast mobsters, and a gambling and horse-racing hub. Al Capone had an estate there, as did syndicate financier Meyer Lansky, his Italian henchman Vincent "Jimmy Blue Eyes" Alo, Joe Adonis and Charlie "The Blade" Tourine of New York, Morris Kleinman of Cleveland, Murray Humphreys of Chicago, and Rosselli's old friend Charlie Fischetti, who died of a heart attack in 1951 after he was taken into custody on a warrant issued by the Kefauver Committee. Gangsters held controlling interest in more than two dozen hotels and nearly that many restaurants in and around Miami, and ran a variety of gaming halls, some mobile but some well entrenched, with others ensconced in the hotels themselves.

"Miami was pretty wide open then, all around there," observed the entertainment-business informant. "John Rosselli was in and out, and he became something of a force."

The source recalled a particular incident that he said he knew first-hand, and which was typical of Rosselli's modus operandi at the time: "There was a place called the Crossroads near the city, it was a big place with big-name acts, but they weren't connected, and they were getting a rough time, especially from a couple of customers who were causing problems on a regular basis.

"So the partners in the club sit down with Rosselli and tell him they've got a problem, and John says, 'Sell me a piece of the joint and I'll take care of it.' They said, 'Oh, well, that would be very expensive,' and John laughed and said, 'No, you don't get it, I'll give you the $20,000 it will cost for my services, and you'll give me a percentage.' In other words, no money. So they think it over and decide to go along.

"So John goes ahead and meets with these two characters at the club, and says he hears that they've been getting out of line. They're jerking him around and say they're sorry, but they're prizefighters and sometimes they get a little out of control. So John leans forward and gives them one of his looks and says, real slow, 'You don't understand. Around here, we fuck fighters.' That straightened them up a little, and they did a little checking about John and they stopped coming around after that. John could be very tough, but only with the wise guys."

Throughout more than a decade of managing nightclubs and booking acts, this source said Rosselli was unique to his experience. "He was like the Henry Kissinger of the mob. He was in the amazing position of being independent—Chicago was obviously behind him, but he didn't represent any one faction. Nobody knew where the power came from, but they all knew it was there."

A second source recounted a similar anecdote involving an altercation between Rosselli and a booking agent for several major nightclubs. "This guy had ties to the old Mayfield Road Gang, and things got to a point where he threatened Rosselli. He said, 'If we got a problem here, I'll make a call to Cleveland,' and Rosselli cut him off. He said, 'If we have a problem, you're dead.' " The informant laughed as he recounted the story. "Johnny didn't fuck around."

Heaven in Havana

JUST A SHORT HOP south from Miami lay Cuba, the gateway to the Caribbean, fragrant and deep green in a tempestuous sea, its whitewashed cities gleaming in the tropical heat. Exhausted by its legacy of slavery and colonialism, Cuba served as an easy testing ground for a succession of American presidents who imposed the Monroe Doctrine by threat and force, and in the process, rendered the government there pliable. In Havana as in other Caribbean capitals, American intelligence planners, arms dealers, and business interests like United Fruit vied for influence with rulers who realized that their tenure was transient and negotiable.

It was a condition that the mob found to its liking. Graft was centralized, with only the national government to pay off. There were no crime busters, congressional probes, or federal strike forces. Operations were limited only by the volume of tourist traffic. As Meyer Lansky observed when he temporarily folded up his offshore operations during World War II, "You can't live off the Cuban people." But the setting was ideal. Gambling, sometimes legal and sometimes not, depending on the whim of the current government, was a national pastime. Prostitution was well entrenched. White tourists with green dollars could live like royalty, waited on by brown and black servants in a land of poverty and exotica.

It was beautiful, it was profitable, and while Havana remained the centerpiece of mob activity south of the border, it also became a model that some of the more ambitious of the American gangsters sought to re-create in other republics around the Caribbean. From Puerto Rico to Panama, presidents and dictators received visits from sleek representatives of American "gambling interests" seeking a foothold on their shores. In a world of veiled alliances and raw power plays, the gangsters fit right in.

The mob came to Cuba in the 1930s under the auspices of Meyer Lansky, who briefly took over the operations of the Casino Nacional, a stately complex including bars, restaurants, ballrooms and two separate gaming halls set around a white marble fountain carved by the Italian sculptor Aldo Gamba. Lansky forged a close alliance with once-and-future dictator Fulgencio Batista y Zaldivar, a former Army sergeant who ran the country from 1933 to 1944, but abdicated under pressure from Washington, which feared his "soft line" on the Cuban communists.

The connection with Batista represented a new and intriguing position for the mob. In the United States, they were always on the outside of power, gaining temporary footholds in legislatures or courts through bribes but always falling back in the face of reform movements or federal inter-vention. In Cuba, however, they enjoyed equal if not better standing than the administration in Washington. The mob's special status in the Carib-bean was certified in 1944 when Franklin D. Roosevelt decided Batista had become a liability. According to Hank Messick's biography of Lansky, Roosevelt instructed Navy Intelligence to obtain Lansky's assistance in persuading Batista to step down.

Six years later, Batista, campaigning from exile in Miami, won a seat in the Cuban Senate and determined to return to the presidency. He plotted strategy with Lansky, and by the time he seized power in 1952, Lansky had approval for a novel proposal: the mob and the government would become partners. Batista or his agencies would match syndicate invest-ments, dollar for dollar, in a string of new high-rise hotel-casinos similar to those then sprouting in the Nevada desert. License fees, corporate taxes, and import duties on construction materials would all be suspended. Lansky and his designates would retain full management authority.

The mob had struck pay dirt and Lansky, always a believer in organiza-tion, was careful to spread the wealth around. Families from around the country lined up to receive their shares. As on the mainland, the threads of interest and influence were carefully hidden, but reports issued at the time by the American consulate, and later by officials in Fidel Castro's revolutionary government, provided names that helped draw the puzzle into focus. Moe Dalitz and his Cleveland mob were assigned the old Nacional, with Meyer's brother Jake Lansky serving as pit boss in charge of handling the gambling proceeds; the new Capri was operated by Lansky associate Charlie "The Blade" Tourine, with George Raft serving as official host; the Havana Hilton, built at a cost of $24 million, was run by a syndicate that included Las Vegas front man Eddie Levinson and Cliff Jones, former lieutenant governor of Nevada.

As the strongest "local" power, Santo Trafficante, Jr., was assigned the largest share of the spoils, with direct control of the Sans Souci, and shares of the Capri, the Hilton, and the old Hotel Commodoro. Near the end of his life, Charles "Lucky" Luciano said that Trafficante had established a mutual understanding with Lansky in Florida and Cuba. Luciano termed Trafficante, "A guy who always managed to hug the background, but he is rough and reliable. In fact, he's one of the few guys in the whole country that Meyer Lansky would never tangle with." For his own part, Lansky built the plush $14 million Riviera, listing himself on official documents as "kitchen manager." Rosselli's good friend Charlie Baron did a stint in charge of gambling operations there.

★

John Rosselli was another key operator in Batista's Havana. His presence in Havana was mentioned only once in papers released to the authors by the FBI or CIA, in part because the FBI had stopped tailing Rosselli during that period. But half a dozen different sources and crime experts place Rosselli in Havana's high-rise gambling district, performing various functions—as a contact for hidden investments, as an organizer of junkets that brought "big spenders" down from the States, and operating for a time in a management capacity at Trafficante's Sans Souci. Most striking, but not surprisingly, Rosselli became a friend to Batista, one of the few gangsters besides Lansky to establish a personal relationship with the dictator.

The published source closest to the story is Antoinette Giancana, daughter of Chicago mob leader Sam Giancana, who said in her book *Mafia Princess* that Rosselli accompanied her father on trips to Havana and "other Caribbean areas" in the middle 1950s. And years before that account was printed, Notre Dame law professor G. Robert Blakey, a former government prosecutor who headed the investigative staff of the House Select Committee on Assassinations in 1977, cited government sources in asserting that Rosselli "had a management role" at Trafficante's Sans Souci. In 1978, Trafficante himself testified that in 1960 he had known Rosselli "about fifteen years," though he did not describe the nature of their relationship.

By 1957, Rosselli was receiving white-glove treatment at the Cuban casinos. Refugio Cruz, a former casino floor manager at the Hotel Nacional who later moved to Miami, said in an interview that he saw Rosselli at the casino "several times" in 1957 and twice in early 1958. "It was as if royalty was visiting," the elderly Cuban recalled. Rosselli was usually in the company of Charlie Baron, but once appeared with Las Vegas casino operator Moe Dalitz and, on another occasion, sat down to dinner with Meyer Lansky. Always, Rosselli had "a very beautiful girl" in tow, Cruz remembered.

Another source, this one anonymous, said he was hired by Rosselli in 1957 to handle publicity for special events at several casinos. "I saw him in Havana twice. I'm not sure of the dates, but it was in the middle fifties. He was indirectly representing some people—George Raft was one. The second trip I made just to see John. It was a beautiful paradise down there, it truly was."

The sojourn to Havana marked Rosselli's elevation to a new level in the hierarchy of organized crime. No longer the lead man in the distant albeit glitzy outpost of Hollywood, he was now troubleshooting and orchestrating investments in an international arena. The new position brought new status and a new degree of authority and respect. It also brought him into contact with a new element in the old hierarchy of cops and government officials that were the mafioso's stock in trade. In Havana in the late 1950s, Rosselli came in contact with the CIA.

John Rosselli's parallel in the intelligence community, a man who played the same clandestine role for the American government that Rosselli did for the mob, was David Sanchez Morales, a barrel-chested Mexican-American from Phoenix, Arizona, who went by the nickname "El Indio." Within the CIA, Morales was considered a dangerous but effective agent, a trained assassin who honed his skills in the bloody repression of the Tupemaro guerrillas in Montevideo, Uruguay. He was a heavy block of a man, six feet two inches tall, with a square jaw and high forehead, a heavy drinker with a violent temper. "He was outrageous," one of his colleagues recalled. "He would fly off the handle and throw things around and slam doors and kick ass. He intimidated the hell out of people."

In accord with Agency policy, the CIA declines to confirm or deny any official relationship with Morales. But his career can be traced through his cover assignments, which turn up in the registers of the various private and public entities to which he was assigned. In 1953, he was listed as a "purchasing agent for a lumber company." In 1954, he was reported as a political officer with the Department of State in Caracas, Venezuela. Morales also turns up in Guatemala in 1954, referred to as El Indio in a book by CIA political officer David Atlee Phillips. From 1958 to 1960, Morales was listed as a "political attaché to the American consulate in Havana."

Besides his temper and his propensity for killing, Morales distinguished himself from his fellow CIA agents by cultivating relationships with the Mafia. A close friend of Morales's from Arizona contends that he frequently associated with Capone cousin Joe Fischetti. Later, Morales made regular trips to the gambling casinos in Las Vegas. It seems likely that he put those connections to work for him during his years in Havana, and that John Rosselli was his primary contact. There is no record of their association on the island, but an associate of both men said that in Miami in the early 1960s, Rosselli and Morales were good friends, regular drinking partners who seemed to enjoy a well-established relationship. "Rosselli was the only man who could make Morales laugh," their colleague reported.

To Lansky and the various mob interests active in Havana, Rosselli's presence assured a degree of stability in volatile circumstances. His connection to Batista demonstrated Rosselli's deft handling of the vicissitudes of politics. And his connection to Morales allowed easy access to the other hidden power interest on the island. Moreover, given his experience running Tijuana's Agua Caliente track in 1937, shepherding mob interests in the Caribbean was a natural progression for Rosselli.

Equally important, the gangsters knew they could trust Rosselli. He was known to most of the different parties on the scene, if not to their sponsors in the States: ringleader Lansky had been impressed with Rosselli's work in Reno; George Raft was a Hollywood pal; and Babe Baron was a close friend, Rosselli's guest at the "coming out party" in 1954. He was not tied to any particular crime family, but was trusted by all of them, serving as a sort of ambassador-at-large for the syndicate. As Havana represented a new plateau for the mob, so it did for Rosselli, and as the mob branched out into the Caribbean, Rosselli did as well.

Guatemala

WHILE FULGENCIO BATISTA WAS learning to play the angles as a client and partner of both the American government and the mob, Guatemalan President Jacobo Arbenz Guzman discovered the cost of bucking the prevailing powers. A liberal who initiated a sweeping land-reform program, Arbenz was deposed in June 1954, in a coup orchestrated by the CIA, the State Department, and the United Fruit Company. Arbenz's replacement was Carlos Castillo Armas, a slight, malleable Army colonel who was, as one of his CIA contacts recalled, "in way over his head."

The tenure of Castillo Armas was a dark period of scheming and sporadic violence involving Guatemalan security forces, American intelligence agents, and the foreign fruit companies. More ominously, the collapse of the Arbenz government opened the door to the Mafia, represented by John Rosselli, the mob's man from Havana.

Lacking a strong man in the center, the relationships of power in Guatemala were more fluid than in Cuba, and more deadly. Castillo Armas himself was murdered in 1957, shot by a member of the palace guard. The official explanation, promulgated by the Guatemalan Army the day of the shooting, was that the killer was a lone communist fanatic, guided by orders from Moscow. But that scenario was quickly dismissed by observers on the scene as a fabrication, and the assassination endures as one of the persistent mysteries of Guatemala's unhappy history.

A more plausible explanation, one that gained currency in Guatemala City at the time of the shooting, was that Castillo Armas had run afoul of an illicit alliance between corrupt factions of the Army and the Mafia. After the fall of the Arbenz government, American gangsters reportedly enlisted Army officers in the operation of a plush new gambling hall which drew its clientele from the cream of the government and international community. "They took over a large house in Zone 10 [on the northwest side of the city]," recalled Alfred Barrett, a cultural attaché in the government and a personal advisor to Castillo Armas. "The restaurant served wonderful food, and people were very excited to go there," Barrett said in an interview.

Most contemporary observers assumed the gambling was being run by New Orleans mafioso Carlos Marcello, who claimed birth in Guatemala and maintained business and legal contacts there. But in fact, the owner of the casino was Ted Lewin, a globe-trotting gaming operator whose roots ran to Los Angeles. A veteran of the old gambling ships, Lewin ran in the same circles as John Rosselli in the thirties, and turned up in association with Rosselli again in Las Vegas in the middle 1960s. Lewin ran casinos and contraband in the Philippines until World War II, when he was captured and held for two years by the Japanese, earning the Medal of Freedom for smuggling food into the prison camps. After the war, Lewin spent time in Guatemala and then returned to the Philippines, reportedly forging a dual alliance with dictator Ferdinand Marcos and the CIA.

To Barrett and to the President, the arrival of American gambling promoters boded danger. "We thought it was a shame to see the gambling come in—after what had happened in Cuba. I was disgusted by it, and I know that Armas was very, very angry about it." Castillo Armas was installed by the CIA in the coup against Arbenz, but he was, as one observer recalled, "a man of great probity," and he moved to close the gambling casino in Zone 10, jailing Ted Lewin. Four days later, Castillo Armas was murdered. Whether the CIA knew of the plot or abetted it is unknown, but they had no objection to the outcome: Castillo Armas was replaced by Miguel Ydigoras Fuentes, a corrupt right-wing politician and another accomplice in the CIA coup against Arbenz.

One of Ted Lewin's top hands in Guatemala denied that the closing of the casino had anything to do with the murder of the President, but did say that the gambling operation was run under the tutelage of corrupt government officials, in particular, the chief of police in Guatemala City. Gus Nichols traveled as Lewin's sidekick to Las Vegas, the Philippines, and Africa, as well as Guatemala. Nichols said in an interview that Lewin was no gangster, but kept on good terms with the Mafia—a prerequisite in his business. "They liked Ted, he did favors for them. But they knew not to push him. He could take care of himself."

Nichols also said that Lewin knew John Rosselli, and that he and Lewin had seen Rosselli in Guatemala, "around 1956." But he said Rosselli had nothing to do with the casino. "I'm not sure what he was doing down there," Nichols said.

Again, as in Cuba, Rosselli's presence is not reflected in the government documents obtained by the authors. In this case his activity was detailed by two sources who said they worked with Rosselli on frequent occasions in Guatemala. Both sources insisted on anonymity, but both were able to give details to corroborate their accounts. The first source was the same underworld operator who described trips to Havana with Rosselli. He said he joined Rosselli in Guatemala City and Mexico City on half a dozen separate trips beginning in 1956. Mexico City served at the time as a nerve center for plots in Guatemala, which borders on Mexico to the south, and as the base for all CIA operations in Central America. This source said he sometimes traveled alone and sometimes in the company of two young union sluggers, "righteous killers," as he described them, brought in by Rosselli from Los Angeles to provide protection and muscle when diplomacy proved inadequate.

The second source was a longtime government field worker assigned to Guatemala with the International Cooperation Administration (ICA), a forerunner to the Agency for International Development. As with its successor agency, the ICA served as thin cover for wholesale meddling in business and politics, to the point that in 1959, Agriculture Minister Clemente Marroquin Rojas accused the agency of "direct intervention in Guatemalan affairs," and called for an end to all American aid programs, then running at more than $45 million per annum. Marroquin Rojas was soon removed from his post.

The ICA source was extremely reluctant to talk, but confirmed that he had become acquainted with the underworld source in Guatemala, and that Rosselli had been "a major force" beneath the surface of events in Guatemala City and in other states in Central America. "John had access to everyone and everything that was going on there," the government source asserted. That included the fruit companies, the Guatemalan Army, and the American delegation. "He had an open door at the embassy in Guatemala, and in Costa Rica. He was in there plenty of times. I know because I saw him. He supplied information to the government, and had a hand in a lot of the intrigues that were going on."

According to both sources, Rosselli's primary concern in Guatemala was to protect and advance the interests of Standard Fruit and Steamship Company, a relatively small competitor to the better-known United Fruit, but still one of the largest foreign corporations operating in Central America. Rosselli was a solid candidate for the job of free-lance work in Guatemala—he had proved himself in Cuba, and he could rely on independent contacts established throughout Central America through Jack Dragna's banana shipping business.

The informants could not provide a name for Rosselli's contact with Standard Fruit, but the allegation of collaboration with the Mafia is consistent with the company's history. Founded around the turn of the century by Sicilian fruit vendors in the old Mafia stronghold of New Orleans, the company grew in tandem with the machine assembled by Louisiana political strongman Huey Long and Mafia don Carlos Marcello.

Standard Fruit's initial consortium with the mob developed, of necessity, on the waterfront. Loading and off-loading of ships was controlled by the International Longshoreman's Union, which in early New Orleans was beset by Black Hand extortionists, and later was dominated from New York by Murder Inc. founder Albert Anastasia. The docks of New Orleans were presided over by a three-member, state-appointed board that included, at different times, Standard Fruit founder and vice-president Lucca Vaccaro, and Seymour Weiss, a member of the company's board of directors. In 1940, Vaccaro was indicted along with the rest of the dock board and former Lousiana Governor Earl Long on charges of embezzlement and extortion. Thirty years later, a *Wall Street Journal* exposé on mob control of the docks in New Jersey linked Standard Fruit to a trucking firm controlled by the Genovese family in New York, successors in interest to Anastasia's crime family.

But it was Standard Fruit board member Seymour Weiss who comprised the strongest tie between the company and the mob. A power broker for Huey Long and onetime president of the dock board, an habitué of Frank Costello's Hot Springs, Arkansas, gambling resort, Weiss was subject to a string of indictments for tax evasion and bribery, and was finally convicted in 1940. After his release from jail, according to writer Hank Messick, Weiss was assigned with Marcello "to run New Orleans" for the national crime syndicate.

While Rosselli was connected to Standard Fruit in Guatemala, the company was not his sole interest. Both informants contend that Rosselli was also active in labor and government affairs, and possibly in helping Ted Lewin launch his casino. "Johnny was a flywheel, everything spun off from him," said the underworld informant. In a world of dangerous plots and secret alliances, Rosselli was a master, combining subtlety and iron will to keep money moving and dependable allies in power. "John had an incredible knack for keeping the most hostile factions happy, both with him and even with each other," his accomplice recalled. "That was his greatest talent."

Intelligence and the Mob

A CENTRAL THEME IN both informants' account of Rosselli's activities in Guatemala is that he was working in concert with representatives of the American government, including both the ICA, which administered U.S. aid to the country, and the CIA. Indeed, the CIA played a central role in Guatemalan affairs almost from the inception of the Agency in 1947. The CIA engineered the Arbenz coup, and remained closely involved thereafter; when it recruited an army of anti-Castro exiles in southern Florida in 1960, the CIA trained them at secret bases located inside Guatemala.

According to Frank McNeil, the junior political officer in the Guatemalan Embassy in 1960, the CIA was a constant presence, and a constant irritant, in U.S. diplomacy south of the border. "Throughout Latin America there were two American governments—one intelligence and one official," and frequently one did not know the activities of the other, McNeil said. As an example, he said that John Muccio, the ambassador he served in Guatemala, only learned that the CIA had trained the Bay of Pigs invasion troops in Guatemala when he read it in the New York *Times.*

Central America wasn't the only theater of CIA operations in the middle 1950s. At the same time it was deposing the government in Guatemala, it was launching its first round of covert activities around the globe —in Iran, Italy, Greece, and the Philippines, where popular, elected governments were undermined or deposed in the name of John Foster Dulles's campaign to "roll back" communism. But Guatemala was a special case. It was close to home, it served as an anchor in the neocolonial enterprise of the United Fruit Company, and, after the Arbenz coup, it was regarded as a major success, a model for covert operations in the decade to follow.

Another thread that runs to the inception of the CIA is their ongoing secret relationship with the Mafia. The connection was first established in 1942, when officials of Navy Intelligence and the Office of Strategic Ser-

vices, forerunner to the CIA, arranged a deal with New York Mafia boss
Lucky Luciano, then serving the tenth year of a thirty-to-fifty-year prison
sentence. In return for his assistance in patrolling American ports to prevent wartime sabotage, and later for intelligence in the invasion of Sicily,
Luciano was deported to relative freedom in Italy, with the single condition that he not return to the United States.

Ensuring the security of the American waterfront was an enormous
undertaking, and required prison visits to Luciano by most of the leadership of the national crime syndicate, including Rosselli's associates Frank
Costello, Meyer Lansky, and Ben Siegel. The operation remained an official secret until it was detailed in 1977 in Rodney Campbell's book, *The
Luciano Project*, based on a series of closed hearings conducted by New
York Governor Thomas E. Dewey. But while the American public remained in the dark, both the intelligence agencies and the mob knew of
their extensive and successful wartime collaboration.

Initially the relationship was based on the wartime premise of "Victory at Any Cost." With Hitler ascendant, any alliance, even with the
Mafia, with its unchallenged control of the waterfront unions, might be
considered expedient. But once breached, the channel remained tempting
to intelligence planners driven by their perception of the national interest.
It was utilized again in 1944 when Navy Intelligence turned to Lansky to
help precipitate the ouster of Batista in Cuba. And it was revived in
Guatemala, where John Rosselli was playing all sides in the interest of the
mob and of his corporate sponsor, Standard Fruit.

That Rosselli had an easy affinity with American intelligence agents
was understandable. Like the spies he worked with, Rosselli was accustomed to a world of secrecy and intrigue, where a wrong move could result
in exposure or sudden death. Through a lifetime of experience, Rosselli
had mastered the tricks of the spy trade. He was discreet with information
and secretive by nature. He could spot surveillance and lose a tail as soon
as he realized he was being followed. He was cautious with phone lines,
always conducting business in person. And he was tough. That was never
in question.

There was also an apparent connection between Standard Fruit and
the CIA. It was never so highly evolved as that of its counterpart in the
banana trade, United Fruit. But the CIA and Standard Fruit were both
instrumental in the operation of the Information Council on the Americas, or INCA, a right-wing propaganda institute based in New Orleans.
INCA was founded by Ed Butler, who testified that in 1963 he'd received

inspiration for some of his propaganda projects while serving in a special U.S. Army unit "in the quiet little town of Alexandria, Virginia." INCA's president was Dr. Alton Ochsner, a consultant to the Air Force "on the medical side of subversive matters," who also sponsored the *Latin America Report*, edited by United Fruit PR man and admitted CIA agent William Gaudet. Standard Fruit was represented at INCA by several employees, including Standard's security chief, former FBI agent William I. Monaghan, and the company's general counsel, Eberhard Deutsch. Another Standard Fruit employee, Cuban refugee Manuel Gil, served at both the INCA and the CIA-sponsored Cuban Revolutionary Council. And Seymour Weiss was a charter member of INCA.

Later, Standard Fruit was implicated with the CIA in the same brand of subterfuge pioneered by its rivals at United Fruit. In 1974, the fruit company was accused by Panama's ambassador to Costa Rica of plotting to overthrow the governments of Costa Rica and Honduras, and to assassinate General Omar Torrijos of Panama. And in 1975, Standard Fruit admitted to the Securities and Exchange Commission that it had made payments "for years" to government officials in Latin America. But its involvement in Guatemala in the 1950s was never disclosed.

John Rosselli assisted Standard Fruit, according to the two sources who said they worked with him, by providing the company leverage in its rivalry with United Fruit. Through its payments to the Guatemalan government and its conspiracies with the CIA, United Fruit had achieved a virtual monopoly over political influence, which complemented its more concrete monopoly over the rail lines and shipping facilities that Standard Fruit needed to ship its product to market. Effectively boxed out, the smaller company turned to the mob to help break the logjam.

Rosselli's strategy was twofold. Within the government he cultivated relationships with the Army faction that was tempted by the potential financial rewards of casino gambling. His primary contact was Lieutenant Colonel Enrique Trinidad Oliva, half-brother to the minister of defense and coordinator of all foreign aid under Castillo Armas; after the 1957 assassination, Oliva was elevated to chief of the secret police. A slim, smiling opportunist who dressed in cream suits and silk ties, Oliva was described in one account as a "liaison between the government and the ICA; he was involved in all sorts of scandals and intrigues, and was reportedly linked to international gambling interests."

Rosselli's second channel was muscle, which consisted of contacts with some of the rebel bands, often led by renegade Army officers, whom he supplied with munitions and cash in return for occasional raids on United Fruit facilities when talks over rail access and freight rates stalled. Hints of that strategy surfaced at the time—former United Fruit executive Thomas McCann said in an interview the company received reports at its Boston headquarters that Standard Fruit had sponsored attacks on its rail lines and plantations, but had discounted them. And scattered press accounts in 1958 reflect a series of more than thirty bombings, including one on United Fruit's central rail office, that left police "mystified." In October 1959, President Ydigoras charged that unnamed "North Americans," not related to the U.S. government, had "directed" the attacks.

The two channels complemented each other, placing Rosselli at the center of the intrigues in Guatemala City. He could supply Oliva with information on the activities of the rebels and the fruit companies, and separately, with mob backing for gambling ventures. Using Oliva as a source, he served a similar "intelligence" function for the American agents on the scene. In addition, he served the purposes of the U.S. government by helping preserve the viability of Standard Fruit as a competitor to United Fruit, whose monopoly status was the subject of an antitrust action filed by the Justice Department the week after the Arbenz coup.

Rosselli's role as power broker and informant for business and government flowed from his personal history of bootlegging, managing payoffs to the Los Angeles police, and playing both sides in the Hollywood labor scene. But for the American government, the liaison to the mob represented a crucial step, a decision at the highest levels that in the crucible of the banana republics, where great corporations battled for hegemony over tiny, unstable governments and fertile jungle plantations, the traditional concepts of friend and foe were no longer relevant. Following the guidelines set down in the Luciano Project, friends included whomever could be of assistance, be they gangsters or corrupt colonels. Life was cheap in Guatemala, where torture was commonplace and opponents of the government were routinely shot. Maintaining an edge required alliances with people who could play on that level—people like John Rosselli.

Family Man

BUSINESS AFFAIRS DREW JOHN Rosselli to the Caribbean in the middle and late 1950s, but always as a visitor, a resident of hotels, staying for three days or a week and then moving on. Through it all, Southern California remained his base, the place he came home to and where he maintained lasting friendships.

Rosselli kept an apartment on 1259 Crescent Heights Avenue, just below the Sunset Strip, and while he was in town he lived in the swinging Hollywood style he established before the war and his stint in prison. The apartment was a corner suite in a two-story complex painted in desert tones of beige and pale blue, and built around a pool with a terrace of terra-cotta flagstone. The other residents included some of the hot young names in show business, producer Jack Gilardi and pop idols Fabian, Frankie Avalon, and Annette Funicello. On sunny afternoons Rosselli would lounge on the pool deck with the other residents, an elder statesman in the industry, a celebrity for the stars.

Yet while Rosselli enjoyed his proximity to the fast-living crowd, the life he lived was actually more mature and more grounded, and he cultivated strong, lasting relationships with a select circle of friends. For despite his ongoing criminal career and his high status in the secret society of the Mafia, Rosselli maintained at his core a strict sense of personal morality. He attended church, gave to charity, and on some weekends brought boys from a Catholic orphanage to swim at the Crescent Heights pool. His donations to the Jesuit Seminary Association in Los Angeles brought him into regular contact with Joseph M. Clark, a Catholic priest —the resulting friendship lasted the rest of Rosselli's life. Later, in 1958, he prevailed on columnist Walter Winchell to obtain a $10,000 grant from the Damon Runyon Foundation for cancer research at the Sansum Medical Clinic in Santa Barbara.

On a personal level, Rosselli was loyal, he was gracious, and he impressed those close to him by acts of kindness and consideration that they treasured. To a number of individuals, including film executive George

Burrows, producer Brynie Foy, and Joe Breen, Jr., Rosselli was remembered as their best and sometimes only friend, a man they regarded, in the words of their surviving spouses, as a brother.

Rosselli's women friends also relate warm reminiscences, stories of gallantry and conscientious manners all the more notable for the craven circumstances in which they cropped up. Betsy Duncan, a onetime lover and long-time friend of Rosselli's, was a nightclub singer who broke out of television when she landed bookings at the Las Vegas casinos. She recalls meeting Rosselli at El Rancho Vegas, one of the leading hotels in the city, owned by Beldon Katleman. "Katleman was awful," Duncan said. "I called him Bedlam Katleman. He was decadent and depraved. The things that went on in the steam room there I won't even talk about.

"That's how I met John—Katleman was after me, chasing me and sending men after me, and I went up to a friend to ask for help getting him off my back, and he told me to talk to Rosselli. John said, 'Don't worry, I'll take care of it,' and he did."

"You treat people the way they treat you, and John treated people like a saint," commented Joaun Cantillon, widow of Rosselli's attorney at the time. "There was a real sense of concern. You knew that he would do anything for you."

One man who benefited by Rosselli's generosity was Harold Fitzgerald, an insurance executive who studied theology at Loyola Marymount University in 1949, but left because of encroaching blindness in one eye. Seeking employment for the first time, he was referred by a priest to Bryan Foy, who invited him to lunch. Foy brought along Rosselli, and while Fitzgerald said Foy gave him a cordial brush-off, Rosselli took him on as a personal project. Fitzgerald said Rosselli secured him a rewrite job at Eagle Lion, and insisted that Fitzgerald share his Crescent Heights apartment rather than pay rent. Later, when Fitzgerald's wife was pregnant and he was called out of town on business, he asked Rosselli to look after her, which he did "as if she were his own sister."

At the center of Rosselli's code of ethics was the family—the fundamental building block of the old Italian culture. Rosselli emphasized to his friends the paramount position he afforded to parents and siblings and children, and he demonstrated his convictions in the most concrete fashion. Madeline Foy O'Donnell recalled that when Bryan Foy's wife Vivian was ill with cancer in 1949, Rosselli made sure he was at the Foy home almost around the clock. One night in December, "Brynie happened to be out of the house for a while, and I guess the kids were somewhere else in the house, but Johnny was sitting with Vivian when she died. He closed her eyes." Five years later, O'Donnell said, Rosselli learned of some transgression Bryan Foy had committed against one of his brothers. He confronted his friend, and when Foy did not back down, "Johnny slugged him, he knocked Brynie down. It was ten years before they patched it up. That's how strongly Johnny felt about family."

Betsy Duncan remembered that she was dating Rosselli on Mother's Day in 1958, and that "John insisted that we take my mother out to dinner, and he took us to Perino's. Now my mother mentioned that she had some sores on her leg that weren't healing, and John insisted that she get them looked at. So he called a doctor he knew and booked her into the Sansum Clinic in Santa Barbara. She found out that she was diabetic. She never knew that before. I think John really saved her life. He'd go out of his way to do things for people like that. That's what made him such a good friend."

Children are sometimes considered a true test of character, whose affections cannot be bought by flattery or false attention, and Rosselli always made a deep impression on them. "All my children fell in love with him," said Bob Maheu, a private investigator and CIA operative who met Rosselli in the middle 1950s. "He had that ability to make children feel important." "He was always wonderful with the kids," added Joaun Cantillon. "It wasn't that he sat and played with them on his lap, but he listened to them, he paid attention."

More than simply enjoying his time with children, Rosselli "took a sort of proprietary interest" in their development. Patricia Breen recalled: "One time his goddaughter [one of the Breen children] had a date with a young Italian boy. Joe wasn't very strict with things like that, but Johnny was. The boy came to the door and Johnny brought him in and sat him down and grilled him, practically, 'What are your intentions, young man,' and he was just going to take her to a movie or something. That was very typical of John."

Close friends speculated that Rosselli was borrowing their home life, in a sense, to replace the one he did not have. Unknown to them at the time, Rosselli did have a family, and he remained in touch with them, but only secretly, and only through intermediaries. Beginning early on, and continuing without interruption, Rosselli sent couriers to Boston with packets of money for his mother, who by then was living with one of her daughters in a suburb outside Boston. With his true identity a secret, he could not make the trip in person, but despite substantial risk, he always paid homage to his past.

Rosselli's warm nature didn't necessarily contradict his criminal side. Like a lot of the Italian gangsters (though by no means all), Rosselli was a believer. Styling himself after his mentor, Paul Ricca, Rosselli was committed to the ideal of the mafioso as a sort of gentleman soldier, a man of honor and dignity, who commanded respect as well as fear. To his friends he was loyal, charming, and generous. That he was a dangerous and formidable enemy was another facet of the same framework.

Like his "straight" friends, Rosselli's colleagues in the mob recognized his virtues. His own men, killers like Jimmy Fratianno and operators like Allen Smiley, obeyed him without question. And the leaders of the underworld, dons of national stature like Ricca and Murray Humphreys in Chicago, Meyer Lansky in Miami, and Frank Costello in New York, were impressed with his values, his honesty, and above all, his loyalty. Taken together, they combined to make Rosselli a rare asset.

8

LIFE AT THE TOP

A New Assignment

The year 1957 marked a critical juncture in John Rosselli's career as a mafioso. He severed his ties to the family in Los Angeles, already weak in the years since his parole from federal prison. He arranged for the transfer of his official affiliation back to the old Capone organization in Chicago, which was itself undergoing something of a metamorphosis. And almost immediately upon his transfer, he was assigned to Las Vegas, where he would oversee the distribution of proceeds from the mob's biggest cash bonanza since Prohibition. No longer a roving free-lancer, Rosselli became an executive, in charge of development and security over a multimillion-dollar enterprise.

Rosselli's sponsor, the man who assigned him to Las Vegas, was Sam Giancana, the former leader of an adolescent street gang whose rise to power marked a changing of the guard in the Chicago syndicate. Following the custom of the underworld, the transition was marked by death:

Jake Guzik, Sam "Golf Bag" Hunt, Louis Campagna, and Phil D'Andrea all died of old age in the middle 1950s, and Charles Gioe and Frank "Diamond" Maritote, coconspirators with Rosselli in the film labor rackets, were murdered when they proved inflexible. Longtime leaders Paul "The Waiter" Ricca and Tony Accardo continued as the final arbiters of mob power well into the 1960s, but both were preoccupied with fending off persistent federal prosecutors. Political fixer Murray "The Camel" Humphreys remained the Outfit's chief strategist, but muscle was never his forte, and muscle remained the bedrock of the mob. Besides, Humphreys was a Welshman, and organized crime in Chicago was predominantly, if not exclusively, Italian.

The consensus choice for succession was Giancana, balding and homely with a sloping forehead and a jutting chin, weighing just 150 pounds, but with a dominating will and a talent for making money. Murderous and hot-tempered, he demonstrated entrepreneurial verve in taking over the numbers rackets on Chicago's South Side, the coup punctuated by the shotgun murder of black crime kingpin Teddy Roe in 1952. Giancana was a close personal friend of Ricca, and he spent several years in apprenticeship to Accardo, attending gang conferences in Miami and Mexico City, and at the steak houses on the Loop in Chicago. A full-blooded Sicilian, Giancana assumed the mantle of leadership around 1956.

Immediately upon his elevation, Giancana turned his attention West, to the fast-growing gambling halls of Las Vegas, where he and Humphreys agreed that the Chicago Outfit was missing their chance for a share in a major economic opportunity. The Chicago mob had maintained a presence in Las Vegas as far back as 1947, when they held an interest in Ben Siegel's Flamingo, but they had slipped into the role of bystander during the recent spurt of growth along the desert highway. Giancana and Humphreys were determined to reassert their primacy in the "open city" of Las Vegas.

Their first official emissary to Nevada was John "Marshall" Caifano, a scowling, dangerous man with a nose flattened in the boxing ring and a hair-trigger temper. Suspected in some of the mob's most grisly killings, including the arson murder of Nick Circella's girl friend Estelle Carey, Caifano asserted Chicago's interest in Las Vegas through sheer intimidation, and while the tactic brought results in spots, it alienated as many as it won over. Terror might succeed in union rackets or simple extortion, but in Las Vegas, where the hoodlums relied on the cooperation of front men who carried hidden ownership interests, a more sophisticated approach was required. At the suggestion of Ricca and Humphreys, Giancana assigned John Rosselli to step in for Caifano.

Once again, Rosselli's combination of tact and muscle made him perfect for the job. As he had demonstrated in Hollywood and later in the Caribbean, he could be relied on to finesse delicate negotiations without driving prospective partners from the table. He had impeccable credentials with the other powerful crime families around the country. Yet at the same time, he carried the cudgel of fear wielded by the traditional mafioso. He could be crossed only at the risk of execution.

Rosselli's first deal in Las Vegas drew upon all those talents—the construction of the $50 million Tropicana, the last and most luxurious of the high-rise "carpet joints" on the strip. The hidden ownerships represented the peaceable combination of the most powerful mob chieftains in the country, including Rosselli's backers in Chicago, Frank Costello of New York, Meyer Lansky in Miami, and Carlos Marcello, the don of the New Orleans Mafia. The ownerships were hidden through an elaborate front involving Ben Jaffe, an Indiana insurance executive who also fronted for mob interests at the Fontainebleau Hotel in Miami, and Las Vegas resident J. Kell Houssels, Sr.

To oversee the genesis of this ultimate underworld collaboration, the mob leaders selected Rosselli and "Dandy" Phil Kastel, then based in New Orleans. Kastel was a roving gambling operator, a onetime runner for Arnold Rothstein in New York who became a partner in Costello's slot-machine empire. In 1935, when Fiorello La Guardia's campaign to "drive the bums out of town" retired hundreds of slot machines, Kastel helped engineer Costello's entry into Louisiana—they shipped their merchandise South, installed the slots with assistance from Meyer Lansky and Carlos Marcello, and shipped the profits back North. The relationship with Marcello blossomed, and in 1947 the same consortium opened the Beverly Club in Jefferson Parish near New Orleans, the most lavish illegal casino in the nation, with huge crystal chandeliers, fine china for diners, and name entertainers like Sophie Tucker and Tony Martin.

Ten years later, the Costello-Marcello-Lansky combination joined forces again in the construction of the Tropicana, this time with the Chicago Outfit as a fourth partner, and with Rosselli and Kastel providing direct supervision. The two men got on easily, Rosselli suave and stylish, and Kastel living up to his moniker, sporting silk suits and a gold-tipped walking stick. Kastel supervised the decor, contributing silverware, glasses, and china from the then-shuttered Beverly, and assigning his wife Helen to select carpeting and wallpaper. Rosselli assembled the personnel to run the operation. He appointed Chicago gambling experts Lou Lederer to run the casino and Babe Baron to dispense credit to the "high rollers"; he brought his friends Harry Drucker from Beverly Hills to set up a barber shop and restaurateur Alex Perino to oversee gourmet service in the hotel dining room. Power was carefully divided: Mike Tanico, husband of Kastel's niece and cashier at the Beverly Club, was installed in the cashier's cage at the Tropicana. In addition, Rosselli ran the concessions, one of the main sources of funds apart from the casino itself; he owned the parking franchise, owned the hotel gift shop, and was in charge of entertainment, which yielded him 10 percent of the fees paid the headline acts, the stage shows, and the band. In all, he could anticipate income of more than $1 million a year.

Elegant, almost stately, the Tropicana's spacious dining room overlooked an elaborate, tulip-shaped fountain whose pattern of spray changed continuously, and played at night under vibrant red spotlights. The highline hotel was an immediate hit in an era wedded to the old ideas of glamour, when tuxedoes, gowns, and furs were de rigueur after dark on the strip.

Rosselli suffered a minor personal setback when the Tropicana came up for licensing before the Nevada Gaming Control Board—in light of his Browne-Bioff conviction, he could not be associated directly with the hotel, and so had to sell his interest in the gift shop. But he remained intimately involved with the operation of the Tropicana, and on the day the casino opened its doors, he was on the scene, occupying room 312 at the hotel.

Despite the meticulous care taken to hide the mob interests in the Tropicana, they were exposed within three weeks of the opening, but it was only by a stroke of luck, dumb luck, underworld luck. On the evening of May 2, 1957, a stocky, half-witted gunman, a "button" for rising Mafia underboss Vito Genovese, waited nervously in the foyer of the Majestic Apartments on Central Park West in Manhattan, home of Frank Costello. When Costello entered at around 11:30 P.M., the nervous thug stepped from behind a marble pillar, called out, "This is for you, Frank," and delivered a single blast from a .32-caliber pistol at point-blank range. The bullet creased Costello's skull just above the right ear and, seeing the blood spurt, the gunman bolted to a waiting Cadillac.

He left too soon. The wound was only superficial, and Costello was released from the hospital later that night. But while doctors attended to the furrow carved by the gunshot, police detectives rummaged through the gang leader's pockets, and discovered an extraordinary document, a slip of paper bearing some handwritten notations:

Gross casino wins as of 4/27/57	$651,284
Casino wins less markers	434,695
Slot wins	62,844
Markers	153,745

Mike $150 a week, totaling $600; Jake $100 a week, totaling $400; L.-$30,000; H.-$9,000.

Costello refused to answer questions about the roughly scrawled ledger, but within weeks, their source became apparent. The $651,284 figure matched perfectly the casino profits for the first twenty-four days of operation at the Tropicana, and handwriting analysis showed that Lou Lederer had penned the figures.

The Nevada Gaming Control Board responded quickly. Lederer was immediately ejected from the casino, and the interests of Costello and Kastel were exposed and retired. The episode generated intense publicity that made skimming of excess profits difficult for years after. Yet while the mob interests were damaged, they were not eradicated—Ben Jaffe continued to hold a lien of close to $3 million against the casino. In 1961, the Tropicana was the biggest money-maker in Las Vegas.

Despite the collapse of Costello's interest in the casino, Rosselli gained renown as the genius behind the success of the Tropicana. His status as an expert in real estate development and finance was unparalleled, and his position of trust within the leadership of the Chicago syndicate, and as a connection to the other top gangsters around the country, was secure. As Costello commented to a friend years later, "We were always lucky to have Johnny in Las Vegas."

The Silver Fox

SHEPHERDING THE HIDDEN INVESTMENTS of the national crime syndicate in Las Vegas wasn't always so pleasant or so businesslike as the launching of the Tropicana. As the final arbiter of disputes and personnel assignments, John Rosselli was occasionally required to invoke the old forms of mob persuasion and discipline. The story of Gus Greenbaum is a case in point.

A former bootlegger with lifelong ties to the Capone gang, Greenbaum moved from Chicago to Phoenix in 1928 to manage the Southwest division of the Trans-America wire service. Tall and articulate, his long face divided by deep-set, brooding eyes, Greenbaum proved a master at the intricacies of gambling, and was called upon in 1947 to step in and run the Flamingo after the murder of Bugsy Siegel. Employing razor-sharp accounting and strict discipline—dealers caught cheating had their fingers crushed with leaded bats—Greenbaum turned the operation around, covering Siegel's initial losses and reporting a first-year profit of $4 million.

Greenbaum was ferocious in anger—once during an argument with Mickey Cohen, he reached across a card table, grabbed the belligerent gangster by the necktie, and commenced shouting and cursing at him while under the table kicking him in the shins until they bled. Yet Gus Greenbaum could also be warm and sensitive, a softer side that expressed itself in a fatherly manner with his younger executives, but also in compulsive gambling, whoring, and drinking. He realized that he could not handle the ubiquitous vices of Las Vegas, and in early 1955, he retired, moving back to Phoenix.

Soon after, however, a group of Miami investors with ties to the Chicago mob opened the $10 million Riviera Hotel, and promptly lost money. A call was put in to Greenbaum. When he declined the new assignment, Tony Accardo and Jake Guzik flew to Phoenix in an effort to persuade Greenbaum to change his mind, but he was adamant. A week later, the wife of Greenbaum's brother was found murdered in her Phoenix bedroom. Devastated, he returned to Las Vegas, assuming a 27 percent interest in the Riviera.

Once again, Greenbaum's talents turned a loser into a money-maker. And once again, his weakness for gambling, liquor, and women, complemented this time by heroin prescribed by a feel-good doctor, consumed him. By the summer of 1958, when Rosselli had moved into the top position in Las Vegas, Greenbaum was ordered to sell out of the Riviera. But he was too far gone. "This goddamn town is in my blood," he told his partners. Marshall Caifano was dispatched to deliver an ultimatum. Greenbaum refused, and then flew to Phoenix for a vacation.

On December 3, 1958, Gus Greenbaum's body was discovered in his bedroom, nearly decapitated, with two pillows pressed against either side of his head to sop up the blood. His wife Bess lay on a sofa in the den, hands bound behind her back, her throat slashed with a butcher knife. Nothing in the house was stolen. When asked by a friend of Greenbaum's if he had anything to do with the murders, John Rosselli protested vehemently. "I would never be involved in something like that!" he shouted, leaping up from the restaurant booth he was seated in. But Las Vegas was Rosselli's territory, and mob protocol required all moves in the gambling city to be cleared through him. More to the point, a confidential informant told the FBI in December 1958 that Rosselli had "set up protection for the Sands, the Tropicana, and the Riviera hotels." Clearly, Gus Greenbaum fell outside that "protection."

★

Few of the scores of businessmen, legitimate and otherwise, who invested in the hotels and casinos of Las Vegas ever learned of the danger that lurked in their dealings with John Rosselli. More common were the impressions of Michael Hellerman, a New York stock manipulator who sought in 1961 to build a hotel in Nevada, and who was introduced to Rosselli simply as "the man you went to see to get things done."

"Of all the people I got to know in Nevada, John Rosselli was the most impressive," Hellerman wrote later. "He was the last man you'd think of as being a mobster. From the first time I met him to the last time I saw him, . . . he was always a gentleman. That was the role he played to the hilt, whether he was talking to chorus girls, who he loved, a casino owner's wife, a crime boss, or a politician. His hair was always carefully groomed. His clothes were always expensive and immaculate. And his mannerisms together with the silver gray of his hair gave him a distinguished, almost classical look." The hair, and the smart, cunning eyes that it framed, gave rise to a new nickname that went along with his new prestige. Rosselli came to be known around the casinos and the hotel lounges as the Silver Fox, the power behind the scenes in the gambling capital.

There was another element to Rosselli's makeup, besides the dealmaker's tact and the killer's will, that helped him guide the fortunes of the desert boomtown. "John Rosselli had incredible vision," recalled Fred Black, an influence peddler who gained national notoriety as an accomplice to Capitol Hill dealmaker Bobby Baker, and a close friend of Rosselli's. "He understood before anybody else the potential of Las Vegas, how big it could be, and how rich. Everything you see in Las Vegas today, the new hotels, even the satellite gambling centers like Laughlin, Johnny saw all that back then."

It wasn't just the future of Las Vegas that Rosselli divined in his conversations with Fred Black, but the lure of it, that element deep in the American consciousness that felt drawn irresistibly to the towers of glass and neon pulsating above the Nevada desert. According to its own mythology, America was a sober place, built by the work ethic and enduring through the practice of law-abiding thrift. But the experience of Rosselli's life had taught him otherwise, of a people beset by an unnamed hunger, ready to lay down their last dollar on a chance to break free from the mundane routine of everyday life. Vice—gambling, liquor, prostitution— was a shadow that haunted the American dream, and Rosselli was convinced that the spring it welled from was bottomless.

★

The decade that followed Rosselli's assignment to Las Vegas would bear out his highest ambitions. The room capacity of the city's hotels doubled and doubled again, and still there was no limit to the boom. The growth of California, and of Los Angeles especially, provided a steady stream of traffic over the desert highway, and airlines competed for the right to land at the cavernous, federally funded McCarran Field.

This was the golden era for Las Vegas, the years that veteran gamblers would look back on decades later as the good old days. The entertainment was bright and young and smart, the styles were more glamorous than casual, and the town was still small enough that regulars were called by their first names. The casinos made money, but they reciprocated, with generous drinks and free hotel rooms, and floor captains cheerfully handed out house scrip to timid patrons. On New Year's Eve at the Sands, the management poured it on—guests entered the show room to find waist-high barrels filled with silver dollars to be grabbed by the handful, and at midnight, uniformed ushers circulated through the cocktail tables, distributing Italian silk purses to the women and English leather wallets to the men, each containing a crisp, hundred dollar bill.

Living variously at the Tropicana, the Desert Inn, or an apartment on Paradise Road, holding court from a table overlooking the eighteenth green at the Desert Inn golf course, conducting business in the secure settings of the Desert Inn steam room or behind the wheel of his late-model Cadillac Coupe de Ville, Rosselli came to preside over every facet of business in the gambling capital. As was his custom, Rosselli was careful to keep his role hidden. A five-part, front-page series on Las Vegas gambling published in the New York *Times* in November 1963 never mentioned his name. But his power was universal.

Rosselli dominated the booking of high-priced entertainment that the hotels used to attract gamblers and became a hallmark of the Las Vegas casinos. His vehicle was hidden control of Monte Prosser Productions, which booked talent for several of the large casinos and, in 1958, landed world production rights to entertainment at the Hilton chain, termed "the biggest deal in club entertainment history" by the Hollywood *Reporter.* Rosselli's name never appeared on the company roster, but as informants told the FBI in 1958, Rosselli "owned Monte Prosser Productions lock, stock, and barrel." A friend of Prosser's indicated the degree of Rosselli's control: at the request of Prosser's wife, who lived with four children in New York City, Rosselli arranged for Prosser's paychecks to be sent directly to his family back East, leaving Prosser just enough cash to get by.

Rosselli was also instrumental in arranging financing for construction of new hotels and expansion of existing ones, often through the offices of the Teamsters Central States Pension Fund, which was controlled by Chicago mob figure Paul Dorfman and his son Allen. As Fred Black graphically explained in an interview, "If John Rosselli told Allen Dorfman to go shit on the courthouse steps in Carson City, he would shit on the courthouse steps."

The local police were normally docile, but in case they started getting nosy, Rosselli had recruited a paid informant within the Las Vegas Sheriff's Department, an officer with access to sensitive files. It was a minor coup, considered standard practice for the Mafia, but troubling to the

FBI, which feared leaks of their most important organized crime investigations.

Rosselli even controlled the placement of ice machines in the restaurants and hotels in Las Vegas, collecting commissions on each and using the proceeds as one of the few sources of income he declared to the IRS.

While always capable of invoking a threat or carrying one out, Rosselli was loath to use force in administering his reign in the desert. He was convinced that the way to keep the peace was to keep everyone happy, and that there was enough money around for everyone. If a businessman or a crime family sought a piece of the action, there was always a new project just around the corner, and Rosselli could arrange their participation. If there were a dispute over dispersals, Rosselli would see that everyone collected their due.

The aversion to violence was more than a personal code. Rosselli insisted that there would be no crime in Las Vegas, no headlines to mar a vacationer's image of the city. Robberies and holdups, and even smaller crimes like pickpocketing, were virtually unknown. If "official" business required that someone be eliminated, as in the case of Russian Louis or Gus Greenbaum, the job had to take place outside the county line. Las Vegas might come to be known as Sin City, but under the Pax Rosselli, the sins would be those of Bacchus.

The Money Mill

ALL THE AMENITIES THAT Las Vegas had to offer, the high-priced entertainment, the cheap booze, the legal prostitution, all were window dressing. The heart and soul of Vegas, its reason for being, was gambling. This was the font from which the money flowed, in small trickles from the nickel slots, in larger streams from the card tables and roulette wheels and keno rooms, until it gathered, a sea of cold currency, in the casino counting rooms. It was here that investors recouped millions of dollars sunk into swank hotels and cut-rate air fares.

In the simplistic analysis of an actuary, gambling would seem a cut-and-dry proposition, with earnings based on carefully honed percentages, and dividends distributed by shares of ownership. But calculations on a ledger fail to account for the human factor, the inevitable awakening of raw greed in the face of piles of cash. It began at the tables and continued into the cashier's cage; dealers could pocket chips or lose hands to a partner at the table; runners taking money in from the tables might write down their totals on accounting receipts; and in the counting rooms, a steady skim off the gross, especially if committed in cahoots with the management, was nearly impossible to detect. Veterans of the rackets know that this is the crucial element in the success of a gambling enterprise, and it was here that the mob asserted its full authority in Las Vegas.

Mob discipline, as demonstrated by Greenbaum, was the most efficient method of policing the employees in a gambling hall. But that was only the first step. More important was control of the counting room, the staff and equipment that tallied the daily take. And, still another step removed, there was the question of which of the dozens of liens against a given casino would be paid off first, and from which source of revenue. These issues were frequently nebulous, and usually resolved in favor of sheer power.

Beyond the staffing of the casinos and the operation of the skim, the Mafia was especially efficient in collection of delinquent debts. The travails of Denver attorney Robert Sunshine serve as a case in point. In early 1960, Sunshine, a high-rolling patron of the Desert Inn, offered to sell shares in an oil venture to Ruby Kolod, a close friend of Rosselli's and a partner with Moe Dalitz in the hotel. Kolod agreed, and proceeded to the cashier's cage, where he swiftly withdrew $68,000 in currency. Soon after, Kolod sold half his interest to Israel Alderman, a pit boss at the Flamingo and later the Riviera.

About a year later, Sunshine called Kolod to inform him that the drilling project had gone bust in dry wells. Kolod frostily told Sunshine to expect a visit from his "lawyers," and promptly dispatched Milwaukee Phil Alderisio and Americo DePietto, two accomplished Chicago enforcers, to explain to Sunshine the gravity of his mistake. Arriving in Denver in July 1961, Alderisio came directly to the point. "We're here to kill you," he said.

Sunshine averted his doom by promising to repay Kolod at a rate of $2,000 a month, funds he raised by embezzling from his law clients. When his clumsy thefts were discovered, Sunshine explained his straits to the FBI, and Kolod, Alderisio, and Alderman were indicted for extortion.

These were the affairs that most concerned John Rosselli in his tenure as the ranking mafioso in Las Vegas. Since the confrontation with the state gaming board over the Tropicana, Rosselli never appeared on a single gaming license or hotel deed, but his position was reflected frequently in the file compiled by the FBI. One confidential informant provided the following detailed account, recorded in 1961:

> The source stated that through his experience and through current sources that he declined to identify, every major casino in Las Vegas is currently under domination of "hoodlums." He said he would divide the "hoodlums" having interest in Las Vegas into three major groups as follows: the "eastern mob" including New York, Boston and Miami; the Chicago mob and the Cleveland mob. Source stated that, in his opinion, there is an overall control of these groups and close coordination of the groups. He cited that John Rosselli acts in a capacity of coordinator of the groups on the scene in Las Vegas. The source stated that this was a fact but he did not know how it could be proven.

Another informant, this time quoted in 1964, was more succinct. "Source stated that Rosselli was the 'power' of Las Vegas, and that Rosselli must give the 'OK' for the use of Las Vegas people in gambling casinos in or outside of Las Vegas."

The key to control of the casinos were the appointment of the personnel who staffed them, veteran gamblers like Carl Cohen and Yale Cohen, Nicholas "Peanuts" Danolfo, and Rosselli's old friend Babe Baron, a small group of men who had grown up in the sunless world of dealer's slots and cashier's cages, and who knew the odds of the various games of chance the way a teen-ager knows the batting averages of his favorite baseball team. They were a strange assortment, their charm honed by decades of contact with the gambling public, but they were ruthless in the application of game-room discipline.

An example was Israel Alderman, Kolod's accomplice in the Sunshine affair, who went by the nickname "Icepick Willie." A short man with a broad face and a daffy, Rodney Dangerfield demeanor, Alderman was recalled by entertainer Betsy Duncan as "a sweet little man, really cute." Not so cute was the genesis of his nickname—while operating a Minneapolis, Minnesota, speakeasy during Prohibition, Alderman used to dispose of troublesome customers by playfully draping an arm around their shoulders and then quietly pressing the tip of an icepick into one ear, piercing the victim's brain so quickly that other customers at the bar failed to notice. The dead man would slump over the bar as if drunk, and Alderman would haul him to a back room to "sleep it off."

The declared earnings garnered by the casinos were astronomical for their time—in 1963, Nevada's gaming halls posted profits of $248 million—but that was a fraction of the total take. More important to the gangsters controlling the casino operations was the skim, the daily rake-off in the casino counting rooms that was shipped directly to the mob centers in Chicago, Buffalo, Detroit, and Miami, bypassing the stockholders and IRS. Estimates of the skim vary, but a large casino like the Desert Inn could be expected to yield as much as $5 million a year in untraceable cash.

The proceeds of the skim were divided according to prearranged agreement among the mob interests controlling the casino, and then shipped by courier to destinations around the country. The exact breakdown was always a carefully guarded secret, but an illegal microphone placed by the FBI in the offices of the Desert Inn in 1962 provided a rare glimpse of the actual operation, revealing a twelve-way split. According to George Bland, a retired agent interviewed by the authors, the recipients included Sam Giancana, Meyer Lansky, Brooklyn mafioso Joseph Bonanno, and John Rosselli.

As the arbiter of mob interests in Las Vegas, collecting revenue from half a dozen different sources, a direct recipient of the skim from at least one major casino and probably several others, John Rosselli was at the pinnacle of his criminal career, relaxed and confident. "Everything's nice and cool," he told a friend over dinner one night late in 1960. "There's money pouring in like there's no tomorrow. I've never seen so much money."

9

CASTRO

The Enemy

John Rosselli might well have been satisfied to spend the rest of his days in Las Vegas, his life playing out to the accompaniment of churning cash registers and crooning Rat-Packers. But his desert reverie was interrupted by a sudden swerve of history on New Year's Day, 1959, when Fidel Castro swept into Havana.

The success of Castro's grass-roots revolution portended the end of the gambling empire that flourished under Batista, and a shuddering blow to the finances of the national crime syndicate. It was as if the American auto industry lost Detroit to popular rebellion. Cuba was one of two poles on the mob's post-war map, the second being Las Vegas, an engine that pumped hundreds of millions of dollars in legal cash profits to racket bosses and crime families across the country. And money was a life and death issue for the syndicate, more than pride, more even than *omerta*.

The crisis in Havana dominated the attention of the top criminal minds in the country. Meyer Lansky and Santo Trafficante had the most direct interest, as did Sam Giancana—along with casino interests, the Chicago don had separate investments, as in the Cuban shrimp trade. John Rosselli, the mob's roving ambassador in Las Vegas and throughout the Caribbean, also was on the scene. His initial moves were unseen, but when the mob swung into action, Rosselli emerged as a lead player, taking the role of point man in a series of seagoing adventures that very nearly cost him his life.

Castro became an obsession, too, with the United States government, which regarded his arrival as a breach in the anti-communist strategy of "containment" and, perhaps more important, as a threat to American hegemony in the hemisphere. The State Department initially sought grounds for accommodation with Castro, but the CIA took a hard line from the outset, following the lead of Eisenhower's top foreign-policy hit man, Vice-President Richard Nixon.

Fidel Castro met with Nixon in Washington in April 1959, and the Vice-President decided then that the United States should move "vigorously," as he wrote in 1962, "to eradicate this cancer on our own hemisphere and to prevent further Soviet penetration." Once again, as happened in Guatemala and earlier in Cuba, the mob and the government found themselves closely aligned in their efforts to manage the turbulent politics of the Caribbean. Not surprisingly, perhaps, it was the mob that first responded to the threat.

Fulgencio Batista seemed at the height of his powers in 1957, when Castro and his ragtag band gained their foothold in the Sierra Maestra Mountains. But already, despite the millions they were reaping from their gambling syndicate in Havana, the American gangsters in Cuba sensed the intrinsic weakness of Batista's corrupt regime. Always ready to hedge a bet, the gangsters opened a channel to Castro, offering to supply weapons in return for assurances that casinos would have a place in revolutionary Cuba.

The mob collaboration with Castro lasted for the duration of the insurgency. According to FBI and court records and interviews compiled by investigator William Scott Malone and several others, Castro received a steady supply of arms from Santo Trafficante and gambling boss Norman "Roughhouse" Rothman, whose gunrunning network included a Dallas nightclub operator and onetime mob slugger named Jack Ruby. Another weapons trafficker was soldier of fortune Frank Sturgis, aka Frank Fiorini, who later gained fame as one of the Watergate burglars. Sturgis maintained intermittent contacts with both the CIA and Santo Trafficante, and proved valuable enough to become an aide to Castro. Jimmy Hoffa also reportedly ferried arms to Castro.

Despite their assistance, Castro never felt beholden to the mob. Upon entering Havana he placed Sturgis in charge of the casinos, and though he left them open temporarily, Castro had clear plans for the future. "I'm going to run all these fascist mobsters, all these American gangsters, out of Cuba," Sturgis quoted him later. "I'm going to nationalize everything."

In April 1959, Castro made good his vow, jailing Trafficante, Jake Lansky, and a number of other top gambling figures. Still, the mob wasn't ready to abandon its Cuban gold mine. Prison wasn't too trying an ordeal —Trafficante testified later, "We had it pretty good. It was like a big camp." He was able to plot strategy, receiving visits from both Cuban and American associates, including John Rosselli, Sam Giancana, and Jack Ruby, and upon his release in August, Trafficante remained in Havana, at one point arranging a meeting with Fidel Castro's brother Raoul.

By early 1960, despite his lingering hopes, Trafficante could not escape the conclusion that he could never make money in Castro's Cuba. "I could see that I had to leave there, there was nothing there for me, there was going to be trouble," he said. "Everybody was getting arrested and nobody was safe, so I made out I was coming to the States for just a visit and I never went back."

Castro had betrayed the gangsters, had accepted their weapons and then shuttered their casinos, and once his duplicity was clear, the mob responded in violent fashion. They began plotting Castro's murder.

The genesis of the mob plots against Castro is murky. Several sources cite anonymous leaks from the FBI reporting that Lansky placed a $1 million bounty on the head of the Cuban Premier. Separately, Frank Sturgis claimed in 1975 that he had given Castro's mistress poison to murder him, apparently in collaboration with the gambling interests. Finally, the FBI learned in October 1960 that Sam Giancana boasted to several friends that Castro was to be assassinated. He went into some detail, describing a plot similar to Sturgis's, where "a girl" would drop "a pill" into Castro's food or drink.

An early partner in the syndicate plots against Castro was a Cuban exile faction led by Carlos Prio Socarras, Batista's predecessor as Premier. Prio's cadre had learned to enjoy the fruits of power in wartime Cuba, and were ready to pay the price to win it back. Like the gangsters, Prio helped arrange arms shipments to Castro before the revolution, but when he proved ungrateful, Prio turned to the mob. In a meeting at Meyer Lansky's home in the summer of 1960, one of Prio's close lieutenants negotiated with Lansky for assistance in assassinating Castro and overthrowing his government.

Another connection ran from Prio to Sam Giancana through a shady Chicago cop named Richard Scalzetti Cain. A wiretap specialist on Giancana's dole while employed by the Chicago police and later the Cook County Sheriff's Office, Cain volunteered to the CIA in 1960 that he was requested by an agent for Prio to install wiretaps inside Castro's Cuba. Whether all these plots proceeded independently, or were all part of the same conspiracy, has not been determined. But it seems clear that the mob was planning Castro's murder in the summer and fall of 1960.

There was another party out for blood in the wake of the Cuban revolution, and that was the CIA. Again, as with the mob plots, the genesis of the conspiracy is subject to debate, but the uncertainty is understandable. Assassination of foreign leaders was new terrain, even for the Agency, and it was handled as the most sensitive of all the black deeds, hidden deep within the fold of a bureaucracy devoted to secrecy. The actual word "assassination" was never committed to paper.

Still, plots there were, efforts that left enough of a trail that the Church Committee was able to document them fifteen years later. The project began on a strange note, with the CIA hoping to undermine Castro's charismatic appeal by steps short of assassination. One scheme called for spraying Castro's broadcasting studio with a powerful hallucinogen to embarrass him during a speech; another proposed dusting the Premier's shoes with a depilatory, causing his famous beard to fall out. By comparison, murder must have looked like a simpler option, because in July 1960, top Agency officials authorized a $10,000 payment to a Cuban who said he could arrange for Raoul Castro to die in an "accident." And in August 1960, the CIA Office of Medical Services was given a box of Fidel Castro's favorite cigars with orders to treat them with a lethal dose of poison.

The first explicit reference to assassination came from Colonel J. C. King, chief of the CIA's Western Hemisphere division, who served as the Agency's CIA liaison to United Fruit in the Guatemala coup and later helped organize the Cuba task force. Late in 1959, King drew up an "action plan" for Cuba that included the recommendation: "Thorough consideration be given to the elimination of Fidel Castro." King's action plan was submitted to CIA Director Allen Dulles on December 11, 1959, and Dulles, in a handwritten note, concurred.

These assassination plots did not take place in a vacuum, but were one element of a broad CIA project that called for creation of a government-in-exile, raising an army of anti-Castro Cuban exiles, training them at secret base camps in Guatemala, and launching "a powerful propaganda offensive." Assassination was considered a trump card: Agency strategists believed that if Castro could be eliminated on the eve of the expedition, the fighting could be over in a matter of days. Given the ominous code name "Operation Pluto," the plan came to be known to the world as the Bay of Pigs.

The driving force behind Operation Pluto was Richard Nixon. His primary interest was a deeply felt anti-communism, but Nixon had personal roots in Cuba as well. He first visited the island before World War II, and was close to Florida Senator George Smathers, Batista's champion in Washington, and to Charles "Bebe" Rebozo, a Miami businessman whose partners on several occasions included organized crime figures, and who later handled a series of illegal political payoffs for the Nixon White House. Smathers, Rebozo, and Nixon reportedly invested in Batista's Cuba, and in 1955, the Vice-President traveled to Havana to present the dictator with a medal.

Nixon was well situated to implement a "vigorous" response to the downfall of Batista. He maintained close ties to CIA boss Dulles and sat as chairman of the 54/12 Group, a National Security Council subcommittee in charge of covert actions. As Nixon recalled in his book *Six Crises:* "Early in 1960 the position I had been advocating for nine months prevailed, and the CIA was given instructions to provide arms, ammunition and training for [exile] Cubans. . . . The program was covert." According to CIA agent E. Howard Hunt, "The vice-president was the project's action officer within the White House." Then-ambassador to Cuba Philip Bonsal called Nixon "the father of the operation."

Nixon made no mention of assassination in his book, of course, but Hunt said his own support for the murder of the Cuban leader received "high-level interest and good will" from the Vice-President. A decade later, Nixon's role in assassination planning came to haunt his own presidency.

Operation Pluto was officially authorized by President Dwight Eisenhower March 17, 1960; the assassination element was not spelled out, but in meetings of the National Security Council earlier that week, the President had been party to extended discussions concerning "removal of Cuban leaders." Richard Bissell, Jr., another Guatemala hand and a protégé of Dulles', was placed in charge.

The deputy director in charge of covert operations at the CIA, Richard Bissell seems an unlikely candidate to have organized a hit squad. He was a graduate of Groton and holder of a Yale Ph.D., universally regarded as a brilliant, creative thinker. In his youth Bissell was infatuated with railroads, with timetables and schedules and mileage charts, and later he applied that rigorous logic as a Ford Foundation economist.

Joining the CIA in 1954, Bissell emerged as a consummate planner, a "human computer" whose energy and vision could drive the entire federal bureaucracy. Devoted to secrecy, Bissell never questioned his assignments, but took Dulles' orders and made things happen: the U-2 spy plane program, a failed 1957 campaign to overthrow Indonesian President Sukarno, the successful coup in Guatemala. Cuba would be his most difficult task yet, but it was all a matter of planning, and Castro's elimination was simply part of the formula.

It soon became clear, however, that the CIA was spinning its wheels. Castro not only survived, but continued to consolidate his power. Frustrated, and pressured by Nixon to produce results, King and Bissell had a series of conversations on the need to develop "a capability to eliminate Castro." By August, Bissell decided to go outside the inner channels of the Agency. He turned to Colonel Sheffield Edwards, the director of the CIA Office of Security, and together they agreed to approach the Mafia.

Choosing to collaborate with the top criminals in America has been portrayed as a stunning and reckless decision by critics of the CIA, but at the time, to the officials running the Cuban invasion project, it made perfect sense: the Agency knew of the crime syndicate plots through their contacts with Richard Cain and with the Cuban exile community in Miami. An internal analysis conducted years later put it this way: "[The CIA] may have been piggybacking on the syndicate and in addition to its material contribution was also supplying an aura of official sanction."

Moreover, to Bissell's calculating mind, the mob had a special allure. After interviewing him for a book on the Bay of Pigs, author Peter Wyden wrote, "Bissell attributed high standards of efficiency to the Mafia. Its experience with successful 'hits' was unquestioned." Never mind the moral implications of a government conspiracy with a band of hoodlums targeted as public enemies by the Justice Department. Never mind the obvious violations of the neutrality act. Never mind the clear potential for corruption in whatever government might succeed Castro. Faced with another dirty job, unable to handle it on their own, the CIA called upon their partners in crime.

Bissell and Edwards handed the mission to Jim O'Connell, the operations chief of the security division. "Big Jim" was a former FBI agent who brought a hands-on approach to the business of dirty tricks, but in this case, another layer of "insulation" for the government was in order: O'Connell needed someone familiar enough with organized crime that he could propose such a highly sensitive assignment with the confidence that, even if he were turned down, the nature of the operation would remain secret. O'Connell knew such a man, someone who had served under him at the FBI and who, in later years, handled covert "black bag" jobs for the Agency. That man was Bob Maheu.

Contact

ROBERT AIMEE MAHEU'S CAREER as a private detective mirrored the rise of covert operations at the CIA. A deft undercover operator who distinguished himself as an FBI counterintelligence agent during World War II, Maheu resented his post-war assignment to a remote post in Waterville, Maine, and left the Bureau in 1947. He cropped up in government service again five years later as a security consultant to the Small Defense Plant Administration (forerunner to the Small Business Administration), but left in February 1954 to launch a detective agency in Washington, D.C.

Maheu had excellent connections in the capital, including power-broker attorney Ed Bennett Williams, and former FBI accountant and later Kennedy family confidant Carmen Bellino; from the beginning, Robert A. Maheu Associates' client list was strictly blue chip. Billionaire industrialist Howard Hughes, the Teamsters, the Senate Banking and Currency Committee, and the New York Central Railroad were all early customers, but Maheu's most important and most enduring client was the CIA.

From the moment he opened his doors in "private" business, the CIA paid Maheu a retainer of $500 a month—more than some contract agents received in salary at the time. Maheu later explained vaguely that he handled "delicate matters" for the Agency, but in testimony before the Church Committee, Jim O'Connell described them in more detail. He used Maheu, O'Connell said, "in several sensitive covert operations in which he didn't want to have an agency or government person get caught."

In the campaign to bring down Indonesian President Sukarno, Maheu was tabbed to produce a porno film in Hollywood, which was made but never released, purporting to show the upstart nonaligned leader in bed with a Soviet agent. And when the CIA in 1954 joined with competitors of Aristotle Onassis in an effort to break his monopoly over Arabian shipping, RAMA got the contract. Installing wiretaps and snapping photographs in Rome, Paris, New York, reporting the details to Richard Nixon and the CIA, Maheu successfully smeared Onassis's reputation to the point that the Saudi monarchs turned their backs on the Greek. Ever resourceful, Onassis survived and prospered, but so did Maheu.

RAMA was an organization custom-designed for such exotic operations as the Onassis sabotage. Assignments were handled by a cadre of former FBI, CIA, and Secret Service agents who worked on a contract or part-time basis, some moonlighting for Maheu while maintaining their own client lists. The RAMA office was strictly compartmentalized, with the various gumshoes, wiretap experts, and intelligence specialists sharing information on a need-to-know basis. Adding another layer of complexity, RAMA was used occasionally to provide cover for actual CIA agents in their field operations.

Presiding over this carefully ordered confusion was Maheu himself, balding and round-eyed, his booming voice and loquacious manner incongruous in a career spook. Never much concerned with bookkeeping, Maheu ran his office on the strength of personal whim, dishing assignments almost randomly, and always ready to disavow knowledge of those who got caught. RAMA was a masterpiece of "deniability," a framework that proved essential in the aftermath of the kidnap and murder of a leftist Basque scholar and Columbia University lecturer named Jesus de Galindez.

A survivor of several years' service in Generalissimo Rafael Trujillo's government in the Dominican Republic, Galindez in the spring of 1956 presented a dissertation on Trujillo's penchant for political murder. Thirteen days later, on March 12, Galindez disappeared. After more than a year's investigation, the FBI turned up disturbing evidence of RAMA complicity: the men who engineered the kidnap were Arturo Espaillat, a Dominican military man known to his fellow officers as The Yellow Cat, and John Joseph Frank, formerly of the CIA and the FBI and, in 1956, a friend of Maheu and part-time contract RAMA employee.

Operating out of offices maintained by Maheu at the National Republican Club in New York, Frank had monitored Galindez' movements, and hired a pilot to transport him to the Dominican. The preparations required a series of trips by Frank to Miami and the Dominican, most of which were charged on Frank's RAMA credit card. Further, the FBI learned that Frank and Maheu had contracted with Trujillo to provide electronic surveillance equipment to the dictator, activities which Maheu had reported to his friends at the CIA. They also discovered that Maheu had obtained tickets for himself, Frank, and Espaillat to attend the Republican National Convention in San Francisco in August 1956.

These various connections led the FBI to interview Maheu, but he claimed to have no knowledge of the Galindez affair, and while he acknowledged that Frank "always dropped by the office to say hello," Maheu said Frank did only limited work for RAMA. Frank's airline credit card, Maheu explained, was one of the routine services RAMA provided its contract sleuths. No charges were ever filed against Maheu or RAMA in connection with Galindez; Frank was eventually indicted for failure to register as a Dominican agent, and after being convicted at trial in federal court, fined $500. The possible complicity of the CIA was never at issue, despite the assertion by Trujillo allies in Washington that "the Galindez operation, the Galindez money and the Galindez disappearance . . . were directly tied to the CIA."

A final element in the saga came to light in 1967, when Sandy Smith, a crack crime reporter with excellent sources in the Justice Department, related that Galindez' abduction from a street corner in New York City was carried out by gangsters operating on orders from New Jersey mob boss Joseph Zicarelli, who had sold more than $1 million in black-market munitions to Trujillo. If indeed the CIA was party to the kidnapping, Smith's revelation marks the Galindez case as the earliest instance of the Agency enlisting the mob in illegal domestic operations.

Bob Maheu thrived in the four years following Galindez' disappearance, earning a reputation for accomplishing tasks no other private eye could perform. Maheu became something of a Georgetown celebrity, described in the press as "one of the fastest movers ever to sprint through Washington." He spent money lavishly, dressed in the latest European styles, and cultivated a reputation for notoriety. Journalist Les Whitten recalled that "Maheu was always impressed with the gangsters, and liked to let on that he knew them."

Maheu did, in fact, have connections to the mob. One was through Jimmy Hoffa, who hired Maheu to do electronics work in 1957. Another was through his close friend Edward Bennett Williams, the powerhouse Washington attorney who represented Hoffa before the McClellan Committee and, before that, Frank Costello. But his closest contact to the mob, his friendship with a true mafioso, was John Rosselli.

Maheu likes to tell the story that he met Rosselli "very casually at first," in 1958, referred by Ed Williams to help obtain Las Vegas hotel rooms "on a very busy weekend." "I had no idea who John Rosselli was." Later, Maheu said he was dispatched by attorney Greg Bautzer to serve a subpoena on El Rancho Vegas owner Beldon Katleman. Again, "It was a very busy weekend," Maheu recalled, "and I needed to get a hotel reservation, and Williams suggested I contact John Rosselli." Sure enough, Rosselli came through with a gratis room at the El Rancho and a friendly introduction to Katleman. Maheu explains that he never served the subpoena for fear of alienating his new friend Rosselli.

In his testimony to the Church Committee in 1975, Maheu also said he had known Rosselli only since the "late 1950s." The committee reported that "Maheu claims not to have been aware of the extent of Rosselli's underworld connections and activities." Here, too, Maheu said his knowledge of Rosselli stemmed from his experience in Nevada. "It was certainly evident to me that he was able to accomplish things in Las Vegas when nobody else seemed to get the same kind of attention."

In fact, Maheu knew John Rosselli better than he admits, and earlier. Joe Shimon, an electronics expert who free-lanced frequently for Maheu, contends that Maheu met Rosselli "in the middle fifties," that Maheu employed Rosselli's advice and services at least twice before 1960, and that the two were already good friends by the time Maheu made the trips to Las Vegas. "Bob introduced me to Rosselli back then, and he knew all about him," Shimon recalled in an interview. "That's how I met Johnny."

Rosselli himself corroborated Shimon's story. Accosted by the FBI at Drucker's Barber Shop in the fall of 1961, Rosselli admitted knowing Maheu "about five years," twice as long as by Maheu's account. Rosselli then declined to speak further with the federal agents. There are other indications of a deeper relationship than Maheu admits. In the spring of 1960, Rosselli was a frequent guest at Maheu's home in Arlington, Virginia, including a clambake where he was introduced to "Big Jim" O'Connell and CIA security chief Sheffield Edwards. After Maheu moved to Los Angeles, Rosselli joined the Maheu family for Thanksgiving dinner.

Confronted during a telephone interview with various incidents contradicting his account, Maheu grew obscure. Asked, "How did you meet John Rosselli?" he responded simply, "I can't tell you that," leaving open to speculation the apparently close relationship between a prominent mafioso and a Washington private eye with connections to the CIA. It may be that Maheu knew Rosselli through his work for Hoffa. Or it could be that Rosselli had served Maheu as an underworld contact in handling "dirty work" for the CIA, jobs like the Galindez affair.

Considering the course of subsequent events, the latter scenario seems more likely, because in September 1960, Maheu asked Rosselli to help the CIA assassinate Fidel Castro. The simple fact of a government agency approaching the mob to assist in a secret project seems strange enough. But it is inconceivable that the CIA, with its cult of secrecy, would reveal its most dangerous and explosive secret to a bona fide gangster, a career criminal listed on the FBI top hoodlum hit list, unless the Agency had enough working experience with the individual involved to believe their secret was in good hands.

In the telephone interview Maheu was pressed to explain his confidence in Rosselli. "Did Rosselli ever work for you?" "He made reservations for me in Las Vegas," Maheu replied flatly. "Why did you feel you could trust him?" Here the answer was slightly more expansive. "I considered him a good friend and a reliable person. I would never have gone to him with that assignment unless I felt that way." Maheu's voice then assumed a note of frustration. "If you took on that assignment and you didn't know where else to go, what would you do? This was not my idea." And so it was that the CIA engaged the Mafia in a plot that would later consume some of the mightiest powers in Washington, Presidents Kennedy and Richard Nixon, Attorneys General Robert Kennedy and John Mitchell, and successive directors of the CIA, in their efforts to keep it secret.

Jim O'Connell, the CIA security chief, told the Church Committee that he asked Maheu to arrange an initial contact with the Mafia in "late August or early September" of 1960, and Maheu proposed John Rosselli as the man to call. O'Connell suggested that Maheu not name the CIA, but represent himself as "the representative of businessmen with interests in Cuba who saw the elimination of Castro as the first essential step to the recovery of their investments." O'Connell then authorized Maheu to offer Rosselli $150,000 for a successful hit.

Maheu called Rosselli immediately and arranged for a meeting at the Brown Derby in Beverly Hills. Built to resemble a giant, round bowler hat, the restaurant is hard to envision as the site for international intrigue. But it was a film-industry hangout and one of Rosselli's favorite haunts for thirty years, the place where he had introduced Willie Bioff to Harry Cohn, a spawning ground for deals large and small. But for all the dreamers and gossips and screenwriters who made the bar at the Brown Derby a second home, none had conceived of a plot so implausible as the one Maheu presented to Rosselli that afternoon.

The meeting took the better part of two hours. Maheu broached the project carefully, waiting until Rosselli had enjoyed his meal. "After lunch I hit him with it," Maheu later told a television interviewer. Maheu shucked O'Connell's cover story about Cuban business interests early on, telling him flat out that "high government officials" needed his help to "get rid of Castro." By the accounts of both men present at the meeting, Rosselli was highly reluctant to tackle what would inevitably be a difficult and complex assignment.

Killing was never a topic that would give Rosselli pause. But here the purported client was the American government, and the target was an enormously popular leader, his face familiar to anyone within sight of a newsmagazine, a lion on the world stage. "He was flabbergasted," Maheu recalled. "He was in awe."

Rosselli was also suspicious. He insisted on meeting an official representative of the government before making a decision. Accordingly, Maheu arranged for a second meeting, in late September, between himself, Rosselli, and CIA division chief Jim O'Connell at the Plaza Hotel in New York. Ironically, at the same time the conspirators huddled at the Plaza, their quarry, Fidel Castro, was entertaining a tumultuous crowd across town as a guest of the United Nations.

During this parley Maheu resurrected for his boss the fiction of Caribbean business interests, introducing Big Jim as a "business associate," one of a group "pooling money to pay for the assassination of Castro." The face-to-face meeting was enough for Rosselli; he agreed to go along.

There are two schools of thought as to why John Rosselli decided to join the government in its effort to destroy Fidel Castro. The more obvious is that, by collaborating, Rosselli gained a valuable edge over the law enforcement agencies that had trailed him all his life. It makes perfect sense; the logic could not have escaped Rosselli at the time. Yet later, when he was faced with federal prosecution on two fronts, Rosselli played his CIA trump card very late in the game, and then only haltingly.

Rosselli's friends and the CIA officers he worked with offer an alternative explanation, the one Rosselli himself gave to anyone who asked. "He said it was his patriotic duty," said Betsy Duncan, Rosselli's longtime friend. "I think he would do it for his own behalf, sure, but he said he did it for his country. And he did hate the communists." By his own testimony to the Church Committee, Rosselli said he accepted the CIA assignment out of "honor and dedication."

That explanation may ring a bit hollow to ears conditioned by the aftershocks of Vietnam and the sixties generation, but at that time, to the generation whose politics was galvanized in the crucible of World War II, patriotism was a potent political idea. And like his thinking about women, about family, about personal ethics, Rosselli's approach to his country was bedrock conservative. "Johnny was always a great patriot," said Joe Shimon, Maheu's legman and later a close friend of Rosselli's. "Sam [Giancana] used to think it was funny. He always used to say, 'Give Johnny a flag and he'll follow you all around the yard.'"

Bob Maheu said he invoked patriotism when Rosselli first balked at the idea of assassinating Castro, and that the argument proved persuasive. "He finally said he felt that he had an obligation to his government, and he finally agreed to participate," Maheu testified. Later, Maheu and other CIA officials found it significant that Rosselli never accepted any funds in the course of his work for the Agency. "He paid his way, he paid his own hotel fees, he paid his own travel," Jim O'Connell testified to the Church Committee. "And he never took a nickel. He said no, as long as it is for the government of the United States, this is the least I can do, because I owe it a lot."

Finally, there is another factor, mentioned by Bissell when he first moved to recruit the mob, that Rosselli must have considered. That is, simply, the convergence of interests between the mob and the U.S. government. Both wanted Castro out of Cuba. If the CIA wanted to form a partnership to that end, how could the Mafia turn them down?

After the meeting at the Plaza in September, John Rosselli traveled to Miami Beach under the alias John Rawlston, where Bob Maheu joined him in a suite at the stately Kenilworth Hotel to begin making arrangements for a move against Castro. The location was significant. Rosselli's usual residence in Miami was the Fontainebleau Hotel; for the moment, he was keeping his presence in Florida secret even from his underworld colleagues.

In the meantime, Jim O'Connell reported to Sheffield Edwards at the CIA that the operation had commenced, and word of the contact with the mob was transmitted to the highest authorities in the Agency. Within a week of the meeting in New York with Rosselli, Edwards met with Bissell, Deputy Director Charles P. Cabell, and CIA Director Allen Dulles. The discussion was "circumlocutious," the term CIA officials apply to the vague language they use even inside the Agency to "deliberately blur" involvement in explosive covert operations. "Edwards deliberately avoided the use of any ' bad words,' " Bissell recalled. But the message got through: "That contact had been made with [the underworld], that a plan had been prepared for their use, and I think he either said in as many words or strongly inferred that the plan would be put into effect unless at that time or subsequently he was told by Mr. Dulles that it should not be."

Working for the G

FROM THE SEA, MIAMI in 1960 presented a front of glistening prosperity, its fine sand beaches anchored by a stately cordon of first-class hotels —the Eden Roc, the Fontainebleau, the Americana—that catered to jeweled and manicured sun-seekers from the sooty cities of the eastern seaboard. Surrounding the hotels were homes of matching opulence, insulated by carefully tended gardens, many with power yachts tethered at the waterfront.

But inland, along the sweltering avenues of Miami, among the fruit stands and the palm trees of Little Havana, and to the south, in communities like Coral Gables, Dade County was experiencing the first of a series of the great waves of migration that would transform it into a multiethnic polyglot, a dumping ground for refugees from the Caribbean and Central America. Tens of thousands of Cubans had fled Fidel Castro's revolution, many of them middle class, many of them former officials of the Batista and Carlos Prio regimes.

Operating from their suite of rooms at the Kenilworth, working separately and together, John Rosselli and Bob Maheu made their first, tentative forays into the itinerant world of the refugees, seeking out Castro's bitterest enemies, people who would assist in plotting his murder, and who had the contacts inside Cuba necessary to do the job.

They worked in part with the CIA, which had already gathered a force of several hundred men and were training them on secret bases in southern Florida and in Guatemala. And they utilized Rosselli's contacts in the gambling rackets, a trail that led Rosselli to Rafael "Macho" Gener, a Cuban native who had been instrumental in obtaining Castro's release of several leading gambling figures. Gener had solid contacts inside the revolutionary government, several of whom were ready to move against the Premier.

Jim O'Connell flew in from Washington on September 24, 1960, for an initial strategy session with the two conspirators. It was agreed Rosselli would stick with the alias John Rawlston, and would represent himself to his Cuban contacts as "an agent of some business interests in Wall Street that had nickel interests and properties around in Cuba," which were financing the assassination project. The cover story seemed simple enough to stand up, and it was a familiar one to Rosselli, corresponding closely to the one he employed a few years prior in Guatemala.

Once the basic groundwork was laid, Rosselli decided to introduce two new players into the picture. One was Rosselli's Chicago boss, Sam Giancana, and the other was Santo Trafficante, Meyer Lansky's colleague in the Havana casinos. Trafficante's connections could prove helpful in moving the plots along, and besides, Mafia tradition required that as the local don, he be informed of any activity taking place in his domain.

Rosselli approached Trafficante on his own and laid out his amazing story deadpan. "He told me that the CIA and the United States government was involved in eliminating Castro," Trafficante recalled later in sworn testimony. "And [he asked] if I would happen, and if Mr. Gener, if Mr. Macho Gener, if I knew about him, knew what kind of man he was. I told him I thought he was a good man, he was against Castro anyhow, and that is about it."

In early October 1960, Rosselli set up a meeting at the Fontainebleau Hotel to put the assassination plot against Fidel Castro into motion. Present were Santo Trafficante, Sam Giancana, and John Rosselli, and from the government, Jim O'Connell and Bob Maheu. Both sides were cautious: Giancana used the alias "Sam Gold," Trafficante was introduced as, simply, "Joe," and O'Connell called himself "Jim Olds." The secret identities were flimsy from the start—Rosselli took Big Jim aside and told him pointedly, "I'm not kidding, I know who you work for"—but they maintained the ruse anyway. "Joe" was described as a man with connections inside the new Cuban government.

O'Connell got right to the point. He wanted a "gangland-style killing," a Capone-era attack in which Castro would be gunned down, a scenario that might have included tommy guns and fedoras. But the real-life gangsters demurred. Rosselli suggested something "nice and clean, without getting into any kind of out and out ambushing." Giancana agreed, noting the difficulty in recruiting someone who would, in the case of an ambush, face almost certain execution.

The method they agreed upon followed the design of the earlier plot Giancana had alluded to in the conversation picked up by FBI microphones. They would poison the Cuban leader, using some slow-acting bane that would allow the culprit time to escape. O'Connell liked the idea, and turned the job over to the CIA's Technical Services Division, which developed a batch of pills containing botulismus toxin that "did the job expected of them" when tested on lab monkeys.

Once broached, the collaboration between the CIA and the mob took on an almost playful air. Both sides seemed to enjoy the cloak-and-dagger atmosphere, and the growing affinity between men who usually lived their lives on opposite sides of the law enforcement fence. It got to the point where the line that divided the two camps began to blur—at least in the eyes of the gangsters. One wintry night in Chicago in 1961, when the usual coterie of FBI agents was shadowing Sam Giancana and several of his mob enforcers as they left a swank nightspot, Giancana's close associate Chuckie English stepped off the curb and called out to the surveillance team. "What's wrong," English shouted, only half in jest. "Why don't you guys stop all this? We're all part of the same team."

As the lead player in the Mafia end of the conspiracy, Rosselli in particular enjoyed his friendships with the "G-men," first with Maheu and then with O'Connell and others at the CIA. In testimony before the House Committee on Assassinations, O'Connell recalled one incident where Rosselli was apparently ribbing him about his drab taste in clothes, and then offered Big Jim a glimpse into the hidden world occupied by his new partners.

One time, one afternoon, Rosselli and I were just whiling away the time. We were staying at a motel in Miami Beach and he suggested that we go downtown—not downtown Miami Beach—to just look around the sights. And we went down to a shopping mall and he suggested that we stop by a haberdashery store. For some reason or other he took a dislike to my shirt that I was wearing and he suggested that he'd buy me a real fancy shirt which I wasn't particularly keen on —his choice of it—but to humor him I went along.

We went in and he bought a very fancy silk shirt for me. And while we were in there it became obvious that he knew quite a few of the employees and it ended up by our going to the back of the store where, instead of it being a stockroom as I envisioned it would be, it was a rather lavish layout which looked like a club of some sort. And there were individuals there and he introduced me to some people. And then after we left the store, when we were walking away, he said, "Remember that fellow that was sitting in the back of the room?" He says, "That's 'Joe,' he's our courier."

O'Connell may be the only government man ever to have seen Santo Trafficante in his secret lair in downtown Miami.

The sense of fun persisted even on the occasion of the first concrete step in the attempt to murder Castro, the delivery of poison pills to a high-ranking Cuban official who had received kickbacks from the gambling syndicate. Miami night life was in high gear, featuring the third Patterson-Johansson World Heavyweight Title Fight, and Frank Sinatra was opening at the Fontainebleau. Combining business with pleasure, the gangsters made a weekend of it. Trafficante was there, and Giancana and Rosselli, along with Bob Maheu and his sometime associate, Joe Shimon.

The night following the fight, the conspirators gathered in a Fontainebleau suite. There was talk of how Patterson had overwhelmed Johansson, some disparaging jokes about Sinatra, and talk about "the contract," the Castro hit. The Cuban agent would receive $10,000 up front for the job; Maheu had brought the cash and the poison. Maheu then "opened up his briefcase and dumped a whole lot of money on his lap," Rosselli testified later. Maheu "also came up with the capsules and he explained how they were going to be used."

Rosselli collected the money and the pills, and the men headed downstairs to the Boom Boom Room, the Fontainebleau's dimly lit bar. After a few minutes, a small, brown-skinned man with reddish hair appeared in the doorway, and Rosselli got up to meet him. The contact may have been "Macho" Gener—the record is unclear—but the Cuban had recruited a cook in a restaurant frequented by Castro who was willing to poison the Premier's meal. As Rosselli and the Cuban left the bar, Maheu turned to Shimon and explained, "Johnny's going to handle everything. This is Johnny's contract."

A few days later, after he returned to Washington, Shimon got a telephone call from Maheu. "Did you see the paper?" Maheu asked, apparently excited, referring to a report that Castro had come down with the flu. "Castro's ill. He's going to be sick two, three days. Wow, we got him."

The timing of the murder attempt was crucial—the meeting at the Fontainebleau took place March 14, 1961, when the preparations for the Cuba invasion had reached a critical stage. But Maheu's reading of the press reports proved too optimistic. As Sheffield Edwards stated later, "Castro stopped visiting the restaurant where the 'asset' was employed."

With time drawing short, Rosselli and his CIA handlers scrambled to stage a second attempt. This time the contact was a prominent Cuban exile, a member of the "Revolutionary Democratic Front" put together by CIA political officer E. Howard Hunt. Bald, with broad shoulders and a barrel chest, Manuel Antonio de Varona was a former president of the Cuban Senate under President Carlos Prio, Batista's World War II replacement, who had been scheming his return to power ever since.

The CIA was one path de Varona hoped would lead him back to Cuba; a second was the mob. It was de Varona who had met with Meyer Lansky to secure financing for his nascent Frente; de Varona was also receiving funds through the Washington, D.C., public relations firm of Edward K. Moss & Associates, which represented the interests of Lansky gambling executives Dino and Eddie Cellini. Trafficante got wind of de Varona's organizing activities, and initiated a series of meetings between himself, Rosselli, Maheu, and de Varona at the exile leader's home.

De Varona was always seeking independent sources of money and equipment to buttress his position within the Frente—he maintained his own small fleet of powerboats, and frequently ran unauthorized raids on the Cuban coastline. Accordingly, he struck a deal with the Mafia conspirators: he would pass poison to a "disaffected official with access to Castro" in return for a truckload of modern communications equipment. If the plot succeeded, de Varona would collect the $150,000 reward, an additional bonus for his private army.

Rosselli relayed the news to O'Connell, who cleared the release of communications equipment with Bissell. They had little confidence in the second plot, but time was running short. The poison was passed in April, days before the scheduled invasion. But again, the plot failed: the Cuban official, later identified by Rosselli as Juan Orta, Castro's personal secretary, had been exposed as a counterrevolutionary and jailed. The plots had come close—excruciatingly close—but the invasion of Cuba would have to proceed with Castro and his government intact.

The Kennedy Vendetta

WHEN THE EXILE ARMY landed at the Bay of Pigs around midnight on April 17, 1961, Fidel Castro personally directed a crushing counterattack that humiliated the American government, and especially the CIA. More than a thousand invaders were rounded up and jailed. Secure on his rebel island, Castro laughed in contempt at "the imperialists" through a four-hour television monologue.

In the White House, the disaster in Cuba represented the first major crisis for a new and untested administration. John F. Kennedy had been elected by the narrowest of margins with a vow to redouble the war on communism. Upon taking office, he accepted the advice of Dulles and Bissell, and allowed the invasion plan to run its course. Now, three months later, he had to stand with his brother Robert in the White House Cabinet Room, seething with frustration as the dismal, fragmented reports of the fighting trickled in. Almost immediately, their thoughts turned to revenge.

Even before he took office, Castro and Cuba had been a focus of Jack Kennedy's world view. Castro's swaggering style and authentic, jut-chinned charisma galled him on a personal level: Kennedy's close advisor Ted Sorensen observed later that his boss harbored a "deep feeling against Castro (unusual for him)," that Castro caused Kennedy to "lose his cool." A month before his election, in the heat of the race against Nixon, Kennedy drew sharp criticism from the press for endorsing "the non-Batista democratic anti-Castro forces in exile, and in Cuba itself, who offer eventual hope of overthrowing Castro." But the speech was encouraging to the

CIA officials planning the Bay of Pigs invasion, who had chafed under the lukewarm support they endured under Dwight Eisenhower. Richard Nixon was their first choice to succeed Ike, but Kennedy looked more and more like a viable alternative.

Allen Dulles and Richard Bissell went out of their way to win the endorsement of Nixon's challenger. On July 23, 1960, with the presidential campaign well under way, Dulles traveled to Hyannis Port and met with the candidate for more than two hours, reviewing intelligence operations in general and the Cuba invasion in particular. The Kennedy White House later denied that such a briefing had taken place, and Dulles confirmed the denial. But Dulles had already reported his meeting with Kennedy to one of the last sessions of Eisenhower's National Security Council, a report that prompted Vice-President Richard Nixon to "explode" in anger, according to a CIA official who attended the meeting.

Four months later, on November 27, after the election but well before he took office, Kennedy received Dulles and Bissell at the Kennedy compound in Palm Beach for another briefing, this time covering "the most important details with respect to the operations of the Bay of Pigs." "Kennedy did not seem surprised" at their description of the invasion plan, Bissell recalled. The topic of assassination was not raised in Bissell's presence, but may have come up later: the conference concluded with Dulles and Kennedy taking a private stroll in the garden, deep in conversation.

Whether Kennedy knew of the crucial assassination element in the invasion plans has never been established. All the ranking administration officials outside the CIA said later they had never heard of any assassination plots, and Bissell testified to the Church Committee that he personally did not breathe a word of the conspiracy. Yet under questioning, Bissell conceded, "It is quite possible that Mr. Dulles did say something about an attempt to or the possibility of making use of syndicate characters for this purpose." In its summary, the committee noted, "Although Bissell testified that Allen Dulles never told him that Dulles had informed President Kennedy about the underworld plot, Bissell told the committee that he believed Dulles had so informed President Kennedy and that the plot had accordingly been approved by the highest authority." Dulles was not alive to share his version of events and authorization with the Church Committee.

Jack Kennedy himself made a guarded reference to the Castro plots in a March 1961 conversation with George Smathers, the Florida senator who was at the time rallying support in Congress for a move against

Castro. By the time of his meeting with the President on the White House lawn, the news media had made numerous references to the "secret" invasion plans, but Smathers had no idea that assassination might be part of the program. According to an oral history interview Smathers recorded in 1964, it was Kennedy who raised the subject, because someone else "had apparently discussed this and other possibilities with respect to Cuba."

As Smathers recalled, "He asked me what reaction I thought there would be throughout South America were Fidel Castro to be assassinated. I told the President that even as much as I disliked Fidel Castro that I did not think it would be a good idea for there to even be considered an assassination of Fidel Castro, and the President of the United States completely agreed with me. . . ."

Perhaps so. But Jack Kennedy was well-known for listening quietly, nodding in assent, and then adopting whatever plan he felt was right. He was headstrong, confident in his powers, and enamored of the potential of covert action. James Bond movies were a staple in the White House, and Ian Fleming was an honored dinner guest. Those within the administration who opposed the invasion were cut off from the planning, and mocked by the President for "grabbing their nuts" in fear.

If the Kennedy brothers were unwitting of the assassination plots before the failure at the Bay of Pigs, they had to work hard to remain unaware in its aftermath. Rather than retire the Cuba operations, the Kennedy administration expanded them. And rather than eliminate the assassination option, it was institutionalized and given a title. Moreover, its scope was enlarged to include, in addition to Fidel Castro, fellow insurgent leader Patrice Lumumba in Africa, and, ironically, the Dominican dictator Trujillo, formerly a U.S. client but, after the fall of Batista, an embarrassing reminder of the American legacy in the Caribbean.

Still, Fidel Castro remained the primary target. Robert Kennedy voiced an almost biblical fury, asserting that he wanted to bring "the terrors of the earth" to bear against Castro. Recalled Robert McNamara, "We were hysterical about Castro, at the time of the Bay of Pigs, and thereafter." It was a killing season at the White House.

On April 22, 1961, Bobby Kennedy selected Allen Dulles, General Maxwell Taylor, and Admiral Arleigh Burke to conduct a secret review of the entire Cuba operation. Taylor, the group chairman, was an Eisenhower-administration hawk who had argued in his book *The Uncertain Trumpet* (1960) that the U.S. should adopt a new doctrine of "flexible response" to counter "wars of liberation" in various hot spots around the globe. After six weeks of closed hearings, Taylor and RFK delivered a grim verdict. "We have been struck with the general feeling that there can be no long-term living with Castro as a neighbor. It is recommended that the Cuban situation be reappraised . . . and new guidance be provided for political, military, economic and propaganda action against Castro."

The Kennedys moved swiftly over the summer of 1961 to implement the recommendations of the Taylor Board of Inquiry, giving the new Cuba project the code name Mongoose. Bobby Kennedy took personal charge of the operation. While remaining in the post of attorney general, he added to his dossier the activities of the Special Group Augmented, a panel including representatives of the Pentagon, the CIA, and the Department of State; Cuba was its sole concern, and initial meetings were held in Robert Kennedy's office at the Department of Justice.

Mongoose was never expected to foster a Bay of Pigs–type invasion; instead, it was designed, as Bobby Kennedy described it, "to stir things up on the island with espionage, sabotage, general disorder, in an operation run essentially by the Cubans themselves." In addition, but off the record, Mongoose included the assassination element. And John Rosselli would spearhead that effort.

The Magic Button

THE CIA TEAM THAT had conceived the Bay of Pigs invasion was quickly replaced on the new Cuba project, Allen Dulles first, and then Richard Bissell. In their place, John McCone was named CIA director, Richard Helms took over as Deputy Director for Plans, and Brigadier General Edward Lansdale, a former CIA agent who made his reputation stamping out popular insurrection in Southeast Asia, was named the executive officer in charge of the Special Group Augmented. Within the CIA, veteran spy William King Harvey was assigned to run Task Force W, the Agency component of Mongoose. The new administration had installed a new team to implement its own Cuba projects, and at the end of the transition, only two elements remained continuous—the Kennedy brothers at the top, and John Rosselli at the action end.

Bill Harvey was the most accomplished spy in the brief history of the cold war. His first big break had come with the FBI in 1951, when dogged review of intelligence files had helped him crack the identity of the notorious Soviet double-agent Kim Philby. Picked up by the CIA and assigned to the espionage hotbed of West Berlin, Harvey headed a team that tunneled into the trunk line of the East German telephone system, allowing unhindered access to Soviet military and intelligence communications. Dubbed "Operation GOLD," it was hailed by Allen Dulles as "one of the most daring and valuable projects ever undertaken." The CIA learned later that the Soviets had known of the East Berlin leak all along, but by then, Harvey's reputation was made.

Revered as one of the few agents who could match wits with the KGB, Harvey rose quickly at the CIA, but he never fit the popular profile of the chic cold-war spy. He drank heavily, was pigeon-toed and physically ungainly, and unlike the careerists of the CIA brass, always packed a gun. Still, when Edward Lansdale recommended Harvey to run Task Force W, he described him to Jack Kennedy as the American answer to James Bond.

Jack Kennedy was already familiar with Harvey's reputation. Two weeks after his inauguration, Harvey had been assigned to launch a new, top-secret program from a small suite of offices protected by round-the-clock Marine guard within the CIA headquarters compound in Langley, Virginia. The official title was "Staff D," a section devoted to communications intercepts, but that was a cover. The true mission was the assassination of foreign leaders, something beyond even James Bond's 007 "license to kill" authorization, beyond Ian Fleming's most brazen cold-war imaginings. "Maximum security" and "nonattributability" were fundamental guidelines, and the mission would "require most professional proven operationally competent, ruthless, stable, counter-espionage experienced officers." The project was dubbed by Bissell "Executive Action," and code-named ZR/RIFLE. Harvey called it "the Magic Button."

In the beginning, Executive Action was sequestered within the CIA, a secret "capability" that was being studied but held in reserve. That bureaucratic division withered, however, under the pressure brought by the Kennedys on the question of Cuba. In early November 1961, near the end of his tenure at the Agency, Bissell was summoned to deliver an update on the progress of Operation Mongoose. According to the testimony of a CIA official present at the meeting, Bissell was "chewed out in the Cabinet Room of the White House by both the president and the attorney general for, as he put it, sitting on his ass and not doing anything to get rid of Castro and the Castro regime." Thereafter, RFK pressed constantly and in person for results from Mongoose. "The attorney general was on the phone to me, he was on the phone to Mr. Harvey . . . he was on the phone even to people on Harvey's staff, as I recall it," Richard Helms testified.

Roughly a week after the dressing-down at the White House, on November 15, 1961, Bissell ordered Harvey to implement the "application of ZR/RIFLE program to Cuba." Harvey's two tracks at the CIA, Mongoose and murder, had come together. The project remained in the planning stage for several months, but in April 1962, Harvey flew to Miami to confer with Jim O'Connell, and Big Jim introduced him to John Rosselli. Within the CIA, the new round of plots would be dubbed, simply, "Phase II."

Not surprisingly, there is scant record of presidential knowledge of Executive Action, or of the second round of assassination attempts against Fidel Castro. Administration officials summoned before the Church Committee in 1975 suffered broad and frequent lapses of memory. Yet an elaborate, multilayered killing apparatus was created during the Kennedy tenure, by career government officers who believed they were following orders. Richard Helms, Bissell's successor as director of CIA covert action under the Kennedys, testified that while he received no direct orders to "kill Castro," he felt fully authorized in pursuing assassinations. "It was made abundantly clear that the desire was to get rid of the Castro regime and to get rid of Castro . . . the point was that no limit was put on this injunction."

Jack Kennedy came close to declaring his complicity in November 1961, when he posed another of his famous queries during a conversation with journalist Tad Szulc. After an hour's discussion of the Cuba invasion, Kennedy asked him point-blank, "What would you think if I ordered Castro to be assassinated?" Szulc replied that the United States should not be party to murder, and the President heartily agreed, adding, according to Szulc's notes, that "he was under terrific pressure from advisors (think he said intelligence people, but not positive) to OK a Castro murder. sed (sic) he is resisting such pressures." In fact, of course, Harvey was directed "to apply ZR/RIFLE to Cuba" that same month.

Still, the record shows a number of tears in the carefully woven fabric of deniability. After a meeting of the Special Group on August 10, 1962,

General Lansdale asked Harvey in a memo to submit plans for "liquidation of foreign leaders;" Harvey responded angrily, pointing out "the inadmissibility and stupidity of putting this type of comment into writing." On another occasion, Harvey committed the same gaffe himself. In his personal notes he wrote that when Bissell ordered the creation of the Executive Action project in early 1961, Bissell told him, "The White House had twice urged me to create such a capability."

There was, in addition, one concrete instance in which one of the Kennedys was told of the use of the mob in the get-Castro project. As Sheffield Edwards later reported to J. Edgar Hoover, "Mr. Bissell, in his recent briefings of General Taylor and the attorney general and in connection with their inquiries into CIA relating to the Cuban situation told the attorney general that some of the associated planning included the use of Giancana and the underworld against Castro."

The Church Committee in 1975 pressed Bissell to explain Edwards's memo:

Q   Did you tell them that this use [of underworld figures] included actual attempts to assassinate Mr. Castro?

BISSELL   I have no idea whether I did. I think it might possibly have been left in the more general terms of using the underworld against the Castro regime, or the leadership of the Castro regime.

Q   Mr. Bissell, given the state of your knowledge at that time, wouldn't that have been deliberately misleading information?

BISSELL   I don't think it would have been. We were indeed doing precisely that. We were trying to use elements of the underworld against Castro and the Cuban leadership.

Q   But you had information, didn't you, that you were, in fact, trying to kill him?

BISSELL   I thought it signaled just exactly that to the attorney general, I'm sure.

The last was as forthright a statement as the committee was able to elicit from Bissell, who remained a strict adherent to the doctrine of "plausible deniability."

The strongest argument against the Kennedy brothers' knowledge of the Castro plots was that, as Secretary of Defense Robert McNamara testified, approval of an assassination would have been "totally inconsistent with everything I know about the two men." In reference to Jack Kennedy, Theodore Sorensen was even more eloquent. "Such an act was totally foreign to his character and conscience, foreign to his fundamental respect for human life and his respect for his adversaries, foreign to his insistence upon a moral dimension to U.S. foreign policy. . . ." Those assessments would presumably apply with double weight to murderous plots abetted by leaders of the national crime syndicate. But as history would reveal, there was much that McNamara and Sorensen, and the public at large, did not know of the Kennedys, of their character, of their fascination with the ruthless application and the rewards of raw power.

On November 16, 1961, the day after Harvey was directed to plan a new attempt on Castro's life, President John F. Kennedy delivered one of his classic speeches at the University of Washington commencement. The tone was righteous, uplifting: "We cannot, as a free nation, compete with our adversaries in tactics of terror, assassination, false promises, counterfeit mobs and crises."

If John Rosselli happened to come across news accounts of the speech from his haunts in Miami, they probably gave him little pause. Better than anyone else, Rosselli knew its bald hypocrisy. But, too, Rosselli knew the man behind the rhetoric.

10

THE KENNEDYS

The Kennedy Campaign

Beginning with their first positions of national prominence as member of and chief counsel to the racket-busting McClellan Committee, John and especially Robert Kennedy used the mob as a foil to project their image as tireless, fearless defenders of the public interest. Exhorting public vigilance with a dire warning, Bobby Kennedy wrote in 1960, "If we do not on a national scale attack organized criminals with weapons and techniques as effective as their own, they will destroy us."

More than any other issue, the war on organized crime helped to define the Kennedy brothers in the public mind. They were strongly anticommunist, but no more so than any other red-blooded American politician at the time. And their commitment to civil rights, considered a basic element in the Kennedy legacy, came later, and gradually. As Arthur Schlesinger, Jr. observed of Jack Kennedy, "He saw civil rights in 1961 as an issue in the middle distance, morally invincible but filled for the moment with operational difficulty." Organized crime, however, provided the opportunity for the kind of bold speeches and televised hearings that had made Estes Kefauver a national figure at the beginning of the decade.

There was irony in the Kennedy campaign against the mob, evident only to select intimates to the Kennedy family and to the gangsters they were hounding. That irony was embodied in Joseph P. Kennedy, the engine behind the boys' political careers. For in his own rise to wealth and influence decades before, and continuing even into the 1950s, Joe Kennedy had always maintained personal and financial ties to the underworld. He competed with the gangsters as a Prohibition rumrunner, and forged an alliance with Frank Costello in New York. Costello boasted of his connection to Kennedy to several of his friends, including columnist John Miller. "Frank said that he had helped Kennedy become wealthy," Miller reported.

In 1944, when the senior Kennedy sought to introduce his Haig & Haig whiskey to the Chicago market, his agent was Tom Cassara, a Miami Beach gangster who was shot dead in front of a Chicago restaurant soon after arranging a distribution deal with Joe Fusco, a Capone syndicate operative. Kennedy frequented mob restaurants in Miami and New York, and the Chicago Outfit's Cal-Neva Lodge in Lake Tahoe. John Rosselli knew Joe Kennedy directly—according to police files, and as Rosselli separately confided to an old friend, he and Kennedy Sr. were occasional golf partners, an association that began in Kennedy's Hollywood days but continued, by one reliable account, until 1961.

That the Kennedy boys would target their father's old cronies in their search for national prominence caused tension within the family, tension that boiled over in a confrontation in Hyannis Port. Bobby arrived for Christmas in 1956 exhilarated at the progress of his initial inquiries into labor racketeering, but found his father angered by his enthusiasm. Joe Kennedy "thought the inquiry into labor racketeering a terrible idea," Jean Kennedy Smith recalled later. The father was "deeply, emotionally opposed, and father and son had an unprecedentedly furious argument." Politics was a factor, but there was fear as well. "The old man saw this as dangerous, not the sort of thing or the sort of people to mess around with," said Kennedy family intimate Lem Billings, who witnessed the confrontation. Kennedy Sr. did not let the matter drop—he appealed to Justice William O. Douglas to try and persuade Bobby to drop the inquiry, and Douglas obliged, but to no avail.

As a freshman senator from Massachusetts, Jack Kennedy followed his brother's lead in the assault on the mob. Once the McClellan Committee hearings got under way, he expressed wholehearted support for the campaign. "We have only one rule around here," he told a staff investigator. "If they're crooks, we don't wound 'em, we kill 'em." Jack had not yet distinguished himself politically beyond the aura of dash and sophistication that his war record and heavily ghosted publishing career had generated—the platform of crusading crime fighter would lend substance to his national ambitions.

Neither Kennedy had any illusion as to the stakes for which they were playing. "If the investigation flops it will hurt Jack in 1958 and 1960, too," Bobby told his close advisor, P. Kenneth O'Donnell. "A lot of people think he's the Kennedy running the investigation, not me. As far as the public is concerned, one Kennedy is the same as another Kennedy." Of course, the obverse was also true—a successful investigation could bring an enormous political payoff for both. Jimmy Hoffa realized that when he raged to Pierre Salinger, "You tell Bobby Kennedy for me that he's not going to make his brother President over Hoffa's dead body."

Upon Kennedy's election to the White House in 1960, and the appointment soon after of his brother Robert to the post of attorney general, the new administration made it clear the attack on the mob would continue. "Organized crime," Bobby declared in his first speech as attorney general, "has become big business." Noted William Shannon in his book on Robert Kennedy, "His zeal to break up the syndicates was reminiscent of a sixteenth-century Jesuit on the hunt for heresy."

That zeal revitalized the Department of Justice's Organized Crime and Racketeering Division, which Kennedy pumped up from fifteen to sixty attorneys. The results were immediate: days in court by criminal division attorneys nearly tripled, from 283 in 1960 to 809 in 1961. Convictions of racketeers followed—19 in 1960, 96 in 1961, 101 in 1962, 373 in 1963. Pressured to keep pace, J. Edgar Hoover suddenly expanded the bugging of mob operations, including the leasing in 1961 of twenty-five telephone lines in Las Vegas to eavesdrop on conversations at the Desert Inn and several other casinos.

To the public, and to many inside the mob, the arrival of the Kennedy brothers at the White House meant that criminals were on the run, that the underworld conspiracy revealed by Estes Kefauver and targeted again by the McClellan Committee, was being smothered by relentless squads of G-men. Jimmy Hoffa, of course, worked vigorously against the Kennedy candidacy, and Carlos Marcello of New Orleans feared Kennedy's victory enough to contribute $500,000 in cash to the Nixon campaign.

But in certain select circles, in the command-level echelon of the Chicago Outfit and in casino lounges around Tahoe and Las Vegas, some of the very gangsters targeted in the war on crime believed at first that it was a sham, and then that they could handle it through surreptitious "diplomacy." Sam Giancana and John Rosselli, along with several of their confederates, were the last to realize that the Kennedy campaign against them was for real. Almost to the end, they believed they could strike a deal.

Giancana and Rosselli were not naïve, nor were they seduced by an inflated estimate of their political influence. The fact is that they understood the Kennedys, Joseph Sr. and Jack in particular, knew them better than the public and the press and even many of their closest advisors knew them at the time. For in his climb to power, in the darkest hours of John Kennedy's campaign for President, when his candidacy seemed to be hanging by a thread, Joe Kennedy did indeed make a deal with the mob.

The rough outline of the deal was laid out in an FBI memo dispatched to J. Edgar Hoover from the Tampa field office in August 1962, and summarizing information developed from "numerous" unnamed sources. The memo reported:

> Before the last presidential election, Joseph P. Kennedy (the father of President John Kennedy) had been visited by many gangsters with gambling interests and a deal was made which resulted in Peter Lawford, Frank Sinatra, Dean Martin and others obtaining a lucrative gambling establishment, the Cal-Neva Hotel, at Lake Tahoe. These gangsters reportedly met with Joseph Kennedy at the Cal-Neva, where Kennedy was staying at the time.

The other partner in the Cal-Neva, the Nevada Gaming Commission learned later, was Sam Giancana.

The memo, sections of which were deleted by the Freedom of Information Act processing division at the FBI, did not relate the nature of the "deal" that Joseph Kennedy worked out. But considering the timing of the meeting and the course of subsequent events, it seems apparent that Kennedy was soliciting support for his son's campaign.

Organized crime came to Jack Kennedy's aid twice during his desperately close race for the White House, the first time in May 1960 during the critical West Virginia primary. Kennedy had failed to deliver Hubert Humphrey a knockout blow the month prior in the Wisconsin primary, and his campaign was mired in "a terrible sense of gloom."

The key to politics in West Virginia was, simply, cash, money that couldn't be traced, distributed to county candidate slates in what Arthur Schlesinger, Jr. termed "a quasi-legal cover under which money flowed to local politicians." In some cases the payoffs were more traditional—"anywhere from $2 and a drink of whiskey to $6 and two pints of whiskey for a single vote." The Kennedy campaign came up with the cash from an unlikely source by the name of Paul "Skinny" D'Amato, a mob nightclub operator who served as Sam Giancana's factotum at the Cal-Neva. D'Amato and a New Jersey associate, attorney Angelo Melandra, spent two weeks crisscrossing the state dispensing more than $50,000. Evidence of D'Amato's efforts later turned up on FBI wiretaps.

Hubert Humphrey tried to keep up, but couldn't match the Kennedy spending pace. "Obviously our highest contribution [to the West Virginia pols] was peanuts to what they had received from the Kennedy organization," Humphrey complained later. "I can't afford to run through the state with a little black bag and a checkbook." Humphrey was trounced at the polls by a 60–40 margin and dropped from the race.

The second mob assist to the Kennedy campaign came in November, in the tight race against Vice-President Richard Nixon. Illinois was considered a key state: once again, Kennedy faced a make-or-break proposition, and once again, Sam Giancana was in a position to help. Giancana contributed money, but this time, his influence was more important. Politics, the creation of candidates and votes, the control of elections, was integral to the operation of the Chicago Outfit, and Giancana worked hard to hand his key city wards to the Democratic nominee. When the votes were tabulated, Nixon had carried 93 of the state's 102 counties, but Kennedy won Illinois by 8,858 votes. The difference was the inner-city landslide in Chicago, where the mob wards went for Kennedy by an 80–20 margin. It was enough that Giancana would boast later that he had "elected" Kennedy to the White House.

The Kennedy Character

To THE NATION THAT elected him President in 1960, Jack Kennedy represented all the promise of the post-war era, a man who combined youth and good looks with intelligence and will, who embodied the can-do vigor that had brought America to its position of world leadership. His speeches were forward-looking, filled with references to character and self-sacrifice that came not in admonition, but in confidence and optimism. As Kennedy pronounced in a tract in *Life* magazine: "Our national purpose consists of the combined purposefulness of each of us when we are at our moral best: striving, risking, choosing, making decisions, engaging in a pursuit of happiness that is strenuous, heroic, exciting and exalted."

Kennedy was instantly mythologized, by the medium of television, which played to his strengths, and by the intelligentsia, which lionized him. Eisenhower had always seemed so drab and bureaucratic. But Kennedy expressed in every aspect the righteousness of the world's greatest democracy, a war hero and a crime fighter with touseled hair and an easy smile, a man of elegant taste who, nevertheless, played touch football on the lawn with his brothers.

At least that was the public side, the image that proved so critical to the Kennedy success. But the Kennedy persona was two-sided, and the hypocrisy went deeper than expedient deals in heated electoral campaigns. Behind the high moral tone they publicly espoused, the family winked at the public mores in a libidinous pursuit of "happiness" that seems shocking even today. Again, it was a trait they inherited from their father.

Joseph Kennedy, Sr.'s womanizing was notorious and incessant, to the point that he had his Hollywood paramour, Gloria Swanson, accompany him and Rose on a now-famous cruise across the Atlantic. He made passes at his children's friends, and entertained hookers at the family compound at Hyannis Port. The boys picked up the same ethic: "The male side of the family were all like that," recalled one family friend. "They came by it naturally—from the father, who chased anything in skirts."

The Kennedy womanizing was matched by a fascination with celebrity, an attraction that found expression in the late 1950s in a family romance with the Rat Pack. Frank Sinatra befriended Joe Kennedy, Sr., in the middle 1950s, and Sinatra was frantically active in Jack's 1960 campaign, raising money and cutting a remake of "High Hopes," urging voters to "back Jack."

The bonds between the Rat Pack and the Kennedy clan were cemented in 1954 by the marriage of Patricia Kennedy to Peter Lawford, an English actor and charter member of Sinatra's smart-alecky Hollywood entourage. Lawford was a hedonist verging on a degenerate, a drug abuser and heavy drinker who died of liver disease in 1984. According to police intelligence reports recounted in his FBI file, Lawford patronized whores by the handful and, like Sinatra, was impressed by the steely glamour epitomized by John Rosselli. Jack and Bobby Kennedy both enjoyed parties around the pool at Lawford's beachfront home in Malibu, where the guest list often included high-priced call girls and, on several documented occasions, Marilyn Monroe. The night of Jack Kennedy's inauguration, Lawford arranged a lineup of six Hollywood starlets to entertain the new President. Kennedy chose two. "This ménage à trois brought his first day in office to a resounding close," Lawford said later.

Adultery in politics is commonplace enough—it was not until Gary Hart's antics were exposed in 1988 that a politician's personal "indiscretions" were considered legitimate fodder for the news pages. But the Kennedys' concupiscence carried heavier baggage than moral opprobrium. As famous politicians, as friends of celebrities, they traveled in exclusive circles, the chic nightspots of Hollywood and Miami and Las Vegas. And behind the high-priced veneer of elegance, that world was the domain of the mob.

Once again, it was John Rosselli who stood on that cusp of the culture where the leading lights of legitimate society mingled with their counterparts in the Mafia. He had played a similar role in Hollywood in the late 1930s; now his vantage point as a member of the social elite provided him a window on the personal affairs of a family that, in 1960, looked like an American dynasty. Rosselli knew Joe Kennedy from the golf course, and knew family friends Sinatra and Lawford from show business. But his strongest link to the Kennedy clan was consummated in Jack Kennedy's affair with Judith Campbell Exner.

A socialite who grew up in the role of Hollywood party girl, Judy Campbell started her affair with Jack Kennedy in February 1960, when the senator took a breather from the campaign and attended Sinatra's show at the Sands Hotel in Las Vegas. Afterward, Kennedy joined in a Rat Pack revel. Sources quoted by *Newsweek* magazine in 1975 said that, in the interest of discretion, it was decided to bring in an "outside girl" to entertain the candidate—word went to Giancana, and he made a call to Los Angeles. Giancana would soon enjoy an affair of his own with Judy Campbell, but at that point he had yet to meet her. Almost certainly it was Rosselli who took the call from Giancana, and who produced his friend to meet Kennedy.

Years later, Campbell detailed her ensuing trysts with Kennedy in a book and subsequent magazine articles. She described dozens of meetings at hotel rooms around the country and in the White House. FBI stakeouts and presidential telephone logs showing more than seventy calls from Campbell to the President over a period of eighteen months bolstered her account.

Telling the story in 1988, Exner (remarried in 1975) said her connection to the Mafia was tangential, running first through Sinatra, whom she dated briefly, and then through Kennedy. She denied knowing Rosselli at the time she met Kennedy, and as for gangsters in general, she said, "I was seeing them for [Kennedy]. I wouldn't have been seeing them otherwise." But like a lot of people who once knew John Rosselli, Judy Campbell Exner's memory was selective. Rosselli was a close friend of Campbell's before she met Jack Kennedy or Frank Sinatra, and remained close years after.

"Johnny knew Judy Campbell when she was just a kid," recalled Madeline O'Donnell, Brynie Foy's niece. "Her first husband was Bill Campbell, and Bill Campbell was under contract to Warner Brothers, and they were very young, and they lived in the same neighborhood [as Rosselli]. Bill was a young actor who worked for Brynie, and they all just used to know each other. That's how Johnny met Judy Campbell."

After the Campbells' marriage broke up in 1958, Judy frequented the nightclubs in Los Angeles and Las Vegas, and inevitably ran into Rosselli. She was beautiful, with dark hair and sparkling blue eyes, and according to Patricia Breen, Campbell and Rosselli dated frequently. "I remember John walking in with her one New Year's Eve," Breen recalled. "She was absolutely the most gorgeous thing you've ever laid eyes on. John said that night he was putting her on a plane to Washington." In fact, it was in tailing Rosselli that the FBI first realized that his lady friend was making phone calls to the President.

Another key facet of Judy Campbell's story changed over the years.

She first insisted under oath that she had never revealed to Kennedy her relationships with Rosselli and Sam Giancana. Later, in a sensational *People* magazine cover story, she asserted that she had carried sealed envelopes between both Rosselli and Giancana and the White House, and that she had arranged "about 10 meetings" between Kennedy and Giancana.

No proof has been produced for that claim, and FBI agents who tailed Giancana have rejected the story out of hand, but that should not diminish the significance of the relationship. At a minimum, Rosselli and later Giancana—whose relationship with Exner began in 1961—were well aware of the President's adultery: they were seeing the same woman as the President, and at the same time. Researchers have since speculated that the mobsters might have used the material for blackmail, but there is no evidence that such a plot was ever hatched. More important was that Kennedy's philandering placed him in the same realm as the gangsters. He was not alien to them, a distant power in Washington, but a peer, practically a friend, a man of foibles who was willing to bend the rules, and to enlist them in doing so.

Aside from Exner's own account, there are a number of indications that Rosselli's relationship with the Kennedys went beyond the President's affair with Judy Campbell, suggesting that Rosselli knew Jack Kennedy personally. Again, the medium was women.

Jeanne Carmen was a neighbor and close friend of Marilyn Monroe before the actress's death in 1962. Carmen said she met Rosselli at Monroe's apartment in the late 1950s and saw him there on several occasions. She and other sources say Monroe was a friend of Rosselli's—not surprising considering their social connections—though Carmen said there was no affair between the two. More intriguing, Carmen once happened to ask Monroe how she had come to know Rosselli. "She said she knew Johnny through the Kennedys," Carmen related in an interview.

Los Angeles private investigator Fred Otash reports that Rosselli intervened in a divorce case that threatened to expose yet another Kennedy liaison, this time with an actress named Judy Meredith. Meredith's husband, Peter Fairchild, was planning to block an alimony judgment by presenting in court a list of his wife's lovers, including Dean Martin, Jerry Lewis, Frank Sinatra, and Jack Kennedy.

A former Los Angeles cop, Otash said he already knew Rosselli when he received a call from him in the spring of 1961 requesting a meeting at the Brown Derby restaurant in Beverly Hills. Rosselli came to the point directly, telling Otash that he was there "at the request of the attorney general," and to drop Kennedy from the suit.

"It was one of the hairiest meetings I ever had," Otash recalled. "I'm sitting with a guy I know very well, and he's telling me he's representing the White House. He says, 'Otash, you know, you're going to have some serious problems. If you persist in this, they're going to come down on you like a Mack truck.' " Was Jack Kennedy aware that John Rosselli was running interference for him? "Sure he was," Otash laughed. "He knew who these guys were."

The Leak

BoB MAHEU KNEW NOTHING of John Rosselli's social contacts with the Kennedys when he enlisted Rosselli in the conspiracy against Fidel Castro. That Rosselli was intimate with the President's lover, and at the same time engaged in conspiracies with the President's secret agents, only indicates the rarefied social strata he inhabited.

Yet Rosselli could not have avoided linking the two in his mind. Partying in Las Vegas and plotting in Miami, Rosselli was engaging in his own version of Camelot. He was confident in the Cuba mission, pleased to play the role of patriot, and hopeful that his service to the President might yield benefits down the road.

For the Kennedys, the decision to allow the government's secret collaboration with the Mafia to continue was more delicate. In the light of their own hidden history, their acquiescence made sense, but it must have been grudging, especially in Bobby's case. The true test would come if, somehow, the conspiracy were blown and the Kennedy brothers forced to prove their allegiances. Presumably, they hoped that dilemma would never arise, but it did, and early in the game, the consequence of Sam Giancana's curious conception of love.

Almost from the outset, John Rosselli took the plots against Castro more seriously than Giancana. Rosselli was by nature less cynical than his Chicago boss, and had a more direct role. Moreover, he always felt the operation could succeed. Betsy Duncan recalls Rosselli discussing Castro with George Raft in a Los Angeles bar in 1958, after Raft had returned from a stint at one of the Havana casinos. "George said they were worried about Castro, but John just laughed. He said, 'You give me a couple of guys with machine guns, we could go down there and take over the whole island.' I used to rib him about that later."

Sam Giancana was never so optimistic. Joe Shimon, the Washington, D.C., detective who moonlighted for Maheu, met Giancana in 1960 as the plots were taking shape. "How you gonna kill that guy over there?" Giancana asked Shimon at the time. "He's an assassin. He knows all the tricks." FBI agent Bill Roemer, who tailed Giancana for years, said his eavesdropping on mob conversations convinced him that "John Rosselli had a real and definite and clear ambition to kill Fidel Castro. He would have loved to do whatever could be done. On the other hand, I think Giancana had a little con in his heart and a smile on his face. He was sincere, but only if it was easy—he felt, let's not get in over our heads."

More enticing to Giancana than the plots in Miami was the prospect of having the CIA as a partner. Giancana was always fascinated with the high-tech world of bugging and electronic surveillance, and within a week of meeting with Maheu and the other conspirators at the Fontainebleau, he decided to put the spy agency to work for him on a personal matter. Late in 1960, Giancana had become infatuated with pop singer Phyllis McGuire, who was at the time engaged to comedian Dan Rowan, star of the television hit "Laugh-In." Jealous and unsure where he stood with McGuire, Giancana asked Maheu to have the CIA bug Rowan's hotel room in Las Vegas. Maheu complied, using CIA funds to dispatch Miami private eye Arthur J. Balletti to Las Vegas.

What ensued was later described by Jim O'Connell as a "Keystone Comedy act." Balletti and a second man, unknown to him but assigned to the job by Maheu, wired Rowan's room and telephone at the Riviera Hotel. On October 31, 1960, the surveillance team went out to lunch, leaving their own room strewn with electronic gear. A maid came through to change the beds and reported the suspicious equipment to hotel security, which called the sheriff. Deputies found Balletti when he returned alone to his room and took him off to jail.

Balletti's first call was to Maheu, and his second was to Rosselli's Los Angeles attorney, James Cantillon. Rosselli then arranged for T. W. Richardson, a gambler with interests in several Las Vegas hotels, to put up $1,000 for Balletti's bail.

Upon learning that Balletti was from Miami, the Las Vegas sheriff brought the FBI into the case. The Bureau's interest increased when they came across Maheu's name in the case record. And when the FBI caught up with Maheu in April 1961, the onetime agent offered a surprising explanation—that the illegal bug was placed as part of a top-secret CIA operation "relative to anti-Castro activities," and involved Chicago mobster Sam Giancana. FBI Director J. Edgar Hoover was notified immediately.

Maheu's decision to leak the secret of CIA collaboration with the Mafia drew mixed reactions from his coconspirators. Sam Giancana, never convinced the plots could succeed, laughed out loud when Rosselli informed him that the wiretap had been discovered. "I remember his expression, smoking a cigar, he almost swallowed it laughing about it," Rosselli recalled later. Rosselli himself was deeply disturbed. "It was blowing everything," he testified later, "every kind of cover I had tried to arrange."

From the beginning, Richard Bissell's greatest fear in working with the Mafia to assassinate Fidel Castro was the possibility "of some sort of unfavorable publicity, if by chance it leaked out." As he recalled in testimony to a House committee in 1978, "I knew it was serious. I knew these were Mafia leaders. And I knew they were in a position to make very damaging revelations about the agency. But we thought it was all under control."

Bissell and the other CIA officials involved in the plots were correct to place confidence in the gangsters. Steeped in the code of *omerta*, accustomed to the veiled language of criminal activity, the CIA's Mafia "assets" kept mum on their clandestine project. Where Bissell missed his mark was in his appraisal of the CIA personnel assigned to the project, and in particular, Bob Maheu. As Joe Shimon noted later, "Maheu was the guy who blew the whistle."

In fact, Bob Maheu had already leaked word of the government's plan to murder Fidel Castro. By 1960, Maheu had become a regular employee and valued consultant to billionaire financier Howard Hughes, a relationship Maheu put on hold to pursue the plots in Miami. Annoyed at Maheu's extended absence, Hughes called from Los Angeles to demand that he return to the West Coast. Fearful that he might lose such a well-paying client, Maheu divulged the details of his assignment, including "plans to dispose of Mr. Castro in connection with a pending invasion." The pool of people who knew of the CIA plots was growing dramatically.

J. Edgar Hoover was always a master in the use of damning political material, and he jumped on the Balletti wiretap case. He was furious that his efforts to prosecute two of the nation's leading gangsters had been compromised, and he was "astonished," he said later, "in view of the bad reputation of Maheu and the horrible judgment in using a man of Giancana's background for such a project." Sheffield Edwards confirmed in vague terms that the CIA was indeed working with Maheu and his mob associates, and that the Agency would oppose prosecution of the wiretap case. Determined to learn the full extent of the CIA plot, Hoover demanded an explanation.

On May 3, 1961, Edwards complied. Giancana had been recruited "in connection with the CIA's clandestine efforts against the Castro government." No results had yet been achieved, but "several of the plans are still working and may eventually pay off," Edwards reported. Carefully distancing himself from the plots, Edwards stated that "he had never been furnished with any details of the methods used by Giancana and Maheu because this was 'dirty business' and he could not afford to know the specific actions." Edwards concluded by reporting that Richard Bissell had "told the attorney general that some of the [Bay of Pigs] planning included the use of Giancana and the underworld against Castro."

Edwards's memorandum represented a major break for Hoover, who had been jealous of the CIA's rising power and budget since the Agency was formed in 1947. Moreover, Hoover was battling for prestige in the new administration, and Robert Kennedy was pushing a plan to consolidate federal law enforcement functions under a National Crime Commission, which could weaken Hoover's national prominence. Now, Hoover had evidence that the CIA had overstepped their authority, engaging in possibly illegal plots with major American criminals, and that the attorney general was aware of the mob's involvement. On May 22, 1961, Hoover dispatched a memo to Robert Kennedy detailing Edwards's report.

Hoover was letting Kennedy know, in effect, that the plots were safe, but that he could now include the FBI among those who knew the government's deepest secret. But the memo carried significance beyond the political machinations of the FBI director. It established on the record that the President's brother was aware that the CIA had engaged a top mafioso, one of the very gangsters Kennedy had targeted for aggressive prosecution, in their "dirty business."

This was the breach that Robert Kennedy had feared, and he treated it in gingerly fashion. No inquiries were made to the CIA as to the nature of "dirty business," and no referrals to Kennedy's own organized crime squad. Instead, he apparently assigned the matter to Courtney Evans, the

Justice Department liaison to the FBI, jotting in the margin of the memo, "Courtney, I hope this will be followed up vigorously." (Strangely, Evans later testified he could not recall ever learning of plots involving the Mafia, or discussing the subject with the attorney general.) Over the ensuing months, action on the Balletti case dwindled to a stop, and Robert Kennedy made no further inquiries.

The Cover-up

THE BALLETTI WIRETAP CASE had lit a fuse, but J. Edgar Hoover couldn't be sure of the nature of the dynamite that lay at the other end. He got his first inkling on June 30, 1961, when Bob Maheu admitted during a follow-up interview that he had planned the Dan Rowan bugging with John Rosselli.

The next break in the case came the following November. Wiretaps and surveillance teams in Las Vegas and Los Angeles had revealed that Rosselli was close friends with Judy Campbell, who on occasion used Rosselli's Crescent Heights apartment when he was out of town. Covering all bases, the agents ran a trace on Campbell's own long-distance calls. And to their surprise, several had been placed to the switchboard at the White House.

FBI agents interviewed Judy Campbell for the first time in Palm Springs on November 27, 1961. Campbell revealed little, but became the target of regular surveillance thereafter. The investigation broke in January 1962, when Rosselli was seen in Campbell's company leaving Romanoff's Restaurant in Beverly Hills. What was assumed to be a passing acquaintance was suddenly seen to be a close friendship.

The pace of the FBI investigation into Rosselli picked up immediately. A years-dormant probe into the status of his citizenship was reopened. Installation of new wiretaps and microphones were considered. And on February 7, the CIA director of Security, Colonel Sheffield Edwards, was asked again to state his position on the possible prosecution of those involved in the Balletti wiretap. Toward the end of the month, Hoover exchanged a series of cables with the Los Angeles field office relating to Rosselli, Giancana, and "a friend," and captioned "UR-GENT."

The significance of Campbell's tie to Rosselli and Giancana was not lost on the FBI director. He had already reported to Bobby Kennedy several allegations of presidential infidelity that surfaced in connection with routine field work. And he had already reported on the involvement of the CIA with Mafia figures. But here the President's philandering was placing him in alarming proximity to the very gangsters Hoover knew to be participating in top-secret CIA schemes. Through Judy Campbell, the President himself could be named in connection with the CIA's "dirty business."

On February 27, Hoover apparently felt ready to approach the Kennedys. He issued a terse memo to the attorney general informing him that Campbell was seeing the President, and at the same time was "in contact with" Rosselli and Giancana. On the same date, a memo was sent to P. Kenneth O'Donnell, special assistant to the President, containing the same information but in a more conversational tone. "My dear Mr. O'Donnell," Hoover's memo opened, "I thought you would be interested in learning of the following information which was developed in connection with the investigation of John Rosselli, a West Coast hoodlum."

The reaction of the Kennedy brothers to Hoover's understated warning is unknown. What Jack knew of his girl friend's involvement with the mob is known only to Judy Campbell Exner, and her version has ranged from telling the President nothing, to arranging secret meetings between JFK and Sam Giancana. But reckless as he was, the news that Hoover had stumbled onto Jack Kennedy's dangerous romantic entanglements had to be chilling to the President, and to his brother.

The record shows no movement on either side for the next three weeks. Finally, on March 22, 1962, Hoover had an unusual private lunch at the White House with John F. Kennedy. What transpired there was never revealed, but hours later, White House logs reflected the President's final telephone contact with Judy Campbell.

The end of the President's affair was almost incidental to what happened next. Over the next several weeks, through an extraordinary sequence of meetings and memoranda, the Kennedy brothers, Hoover, and officials at the CIA established an elaborate cover-up, a paper trail that falsely recorded the end of the CIA-Mafia plots and limited the complicity of the White House.

The first step was taken by Hoover the day following his lunch with

JFK, when he dispatched a new memo to Sheffield Edwards requesting a ruling on the Balletti wiretap. As the Church Committee observed later: "This memorandum is peculiar in two respects. First, the CIA had already orally objected to prosecution on two occasions. Second, Hoover was quizzing the CIA on behalf of the Department of Justice, a task that would normally be performed by the department's Criminal Division."

On April 10, Edwards responded in writing that prosecution of Maheu —and presumably his accomplices—"would result in most damaging embarrassment to the U.S. government," but that was not the end of it, because that was not the point. Far more pressing was the record, first established in May 1961, that Robert Kennedy, and probably through him his brother, were aware of the CIA-Mafia plots. In demanding a written response from the CIA, Hoover had effectively cleared himself of any involvement. The Kennedys needed the same protection.

That delicate task fell to Bobby Kennedy, who arranged for a meeting on May 7 with Richard Helms, and later that afternoon with Sheffield Edwards and CIA general counsel Lawrence Houston. Helms later denied that any meeting took place, despite a specific indication on the attorney general's personal calendar. Edwards and Houston, however, confirmed that they briefed Kennedy on the details of the assassination plots, and the involvement of the Mafia leaders. Key to the strategy of the session was that both Houston and Edwards said they informed RFK that the plots had been terminated.

Unlike much of the CIA testimony before the Church Committee, both had a distinct recall of the attorney general's reaction. They said Kennedy was "upset" that the CIA had used Giancana, and ordered that any future involvement with the Mafia would first be cleared through him. Houston offered his most colorful testimony on the point: "If you have seen Mr. Kennedy's eyes get steely and his jaw set and his voice get low and precise, you get a definite feeling of unhappiness."

After the meeting, Edwards got together with Houston to draft a memo for the attorney general's file that would clearly establish his being "informed" of the plots, and that, to Kennedy's knowledge, they had been terminated. As Edwards wrote in the memo, "After the failure of the Cuban invasion word was sent through Maheu to Rosselli to call off the operation." The same day, Edwards held a conference with William Harvey and prepared a second document, an "internal memorandum for the record," asserting that the operation was "terminated."

Similarly, on May 9, Bobby Kennedy met again with J. Edgar Hoover, and together they concocted yet another memo, this one presuming that neither had known of the assassination plots, that the use of Mafia figures had not been cleared with the Justice Department, and that the CIA had been ordered to clear any future contacts with the underworld. It was here that Hoover recorded his "great astonishment" at the use of Maheu and Giancana, a fact he had known for nearly a year.

The big lie in all this record-making is that the CIA had not terminated its contacts with the Mafia or its plots against Fidel Castro. The previous November, Richard Bissell had instructed Harvey to apply Executive Action to the Cuba project. And in April 1962, Richard Helms issued "explicit orders" that Harvey contact Rosselli. Harvey called Edwards on April 14, and the two of them flew to Miami together. The very week of the May meetings with RFK, Edwards's subordinate Jim O'Connell was in Miami meeting with Harvey and Rosselli. As the committee noted delicately, "Edwards's statement that he was not aware of these developments is implausible."

William Harvey testified more bluntly. The Edwards memo "was not true, and Edwards knew it was not true." Asked why the record had been falsified, Harvey commented, "If this ever came up in the future, the file would show that on such and such a date he was advised so and so, and he was no longer chargeable with this." It was, he said, "an attempt to insulate against what I would consider a very definite potential damage to the agency and to the government."

In short, it was a cover-up, one which admitted the past, possibly exposed elements of the Mafia plots, and laid the "deniability" groundwork for future intrigues.

The question then becomes, where did the lie stop? Did the CIA officials lie to Robert Kennedy, or did they conspire with him? Here the record is quite sketchy. Committed to protecting the President, even years after his death, the CIA officials involved testified repeatedly that they pursued the Mafia plots under "the highest authority," but none would admit direct involvement by either Kennedy.

Several facts remain, however, that argue against the theory that the CIA had usurped its authority in its continuing relations with John Rosselli. Both Hoover and Bobby Kennedy had known of the Mafia connection for a year before the May 9 meeting without taking any action, their professed "astonishment" notwithstanding. Moreover, when Edwards was called before an internal CIA inquiry into the matter conducted in 1967, he reported that he had briefed Kennedy "all the way."

Another question mark was raised by Bobby Kennedy himself, in his reaction to the CIA "revelations." As indicated in the record, Kennedy ordered that any future dealings with the Mafia be reported first to him. But he never issued an order to stop either the mob contacts or the assassination plots. That seems a staggering oversight by an attorney general ostensibly furious over being kept in the dark.

A final indication that Bobby Kennedy and Hoover knew of the CIA's ongoing conspiracy came in June 1963, when FBI surveillance picked up a meeting in Washington between Harvey and Rosselli. Hoover received detailed reports on the contact, as did Justice Department liaison Courtney Evans, and the CIA was asked to comment. But no bells went off, no alarms, no angry displays were indulged in by Bobby Kennedy. This from the attorney general who ordered with "steely eyes" that he be appraised of any future contacts.

The complicity of the several parties may never be determined, but the results of the meetings in the spring of 1962 set the stage for what followed. J. Edgar Hoover enjoyed a resurgence in stature as the top law enforcement official in the administration. Robert Kennedy felt sufficiently "insulated" to pursue his war on organized crime, including Rosselli and Giancana, despite the explosive information they possessed. And the CIA felt free to pursue its plans without hazarding the contravention of a direct order from the attorney general. In the summer and fall of 1962, it pressed the Castro assassination with renewed vigor.

Phase II

THE CIA TEMPORARILY FOLDED up its Florida operations after the Bay of Pigs, shuttering its training camps until the Taylor Board could complete its review of the debacle, but John Rosselli stayed in position. In maintaining his bridge to the shattered remnants of the Cuban exile forces, Rosselli hooked up with John V. Martino, a mob-connected gambling technician who helped install security systems in the Havana casinos, and who was jailed by Castro when he first came to power. Together Rosselli and Martino set up shop at a motel in an upscale section of Key

Biscayne, entertaining their Cuban allies at barbecue cookouts. There were speedboats on the crystal waters, and women in abundance, and there were optimistic projections of casino shares and cabinet positions once Fidel Castro was run out of Havana. It was a pep rally more than a wake, with Rosselli providing the cheer while the rebels awaited the next move from Washington.

Rosselli's primary contact among the Cuban exiles remained Tony de Varona. Despite the disastrous results of the U.S.-sponsored invasion, de Varona continued to wage his private war against Castro's revolution, dropping bands of saboteurs on the Cuban coast, and maintaining a network of informants and collaborators on the island.

Arrogant and self-serving, de Varona was an unpredictable ally and a dubious choice for Cuba's future. The mercurial commandant was incensed at the Kennedys for their decision not to lend military support to the Bay of Pigs invasion troops, and for their treatment of the rebel leadership. He quarreled as well with the pro-Batista exile faction in Miami, berating them with violent tirades that earned him the nickname "Tronco de Yucca"—The Blockhead. But with his connections to former President Carlos Prio, he seemed likely to wield power in any post-Castro government, and he retained the favor of the White House, which regarded him as a "liberal" alternative to the Batista cronies. Besides, as he had proven in the past, de Varona was more than willing to do business with the mob.

Rosselli reported these activities on a regular basis to Jim O'Connell, who testified later that he was "in and out of Miami" between the Bay of Pigs and the fall of 1961. But de Varona's efforts notwithstanding, the war against Castro remained at a low ebb until Richard Bissell assigned William Harvey to "apply ZR/RIFLE" to Cuba.

In the interim, Rosselli hustled to attend to the rest of his far-flung responsibilities. The year 1961 found him frequently in flight, shuttling between Las Vegas, Chicago, Washington, and southern Florida. To his friends on the West Coast, Rosselli was incommunicado for weeks at a time, his whereabouts unknown. But he kept close tabs on the mob gambling interests in Las Vegas—according to Betsy Duncan, he left his number with Desert Inn casino manager Ruby Kolod, to reach him in case of a crisis. Several times he stopped in Chicago to brief Sam Giancana on the latest news from the Nevada casinos and from Miami.

Ironically, Rosselli's government assignment confounded the FBI office in Los Angeles, which targeted Rosselli in its effort to learn more about mob interests in Las Vegas gambling. In February 1961, acting on direct orders from J. Edgar Hoover, agents rented an apartment across the street from Rosselli's on Crescent Heights Boulevard in Los Angeles, hoping to mount a campaign of intensive twenty-four-hour surveillance. The lease was allowed to expire in April due to zero results—Rosselli was out of town.

In Washington, Rosselli stayed with Maheu's associate Joe Shimon, and held meetings with Jim O'Connell to brief him on developments in Miami. "He checked in with me every time he was in town," Shimon said in an interview. "He'd tell me he was coming, and I'd call O'Connell." Rosselli also stayed in touch with another Maheu contact, the powerful Washington attorney Edward Morgan, who handled litigation for Hank Greenspun, publisher of the Las Vegas *Sun* newspaper. Even before the Bay of Pigs, Rosselli disclosed to Morgan the nature of his work in Miami. The reasoning was simple—Rosselli's position as the only nongovernment player in a top-secret project was inherently dangerous, and a witness in his corner might come in handy down the road.

Rosselli's holding pattern ended in early 1962, when Richard Helms ordered William Harvey to jumpstart the CIA–Mafia plots against Fidel Castro. Harvey met John Rosselli for the first time at the airport cocktail lounge in Miami. The two men could not have been more incongruous; Rosselli was coiffed and tanned as usual, sporting alligator shoes and a $2,000 watch, while Harvey was physically homely and bereft of fashion. A chronic thyroid condition caused his eyes to bulge from their sockets, and his swelling waistline prompted his CIA colleagues to dub him "The Pear." An Indiana native, trained in the FBI, he dressed in the rumpled brown suit one might expect of the career detective.

Perhaps intimidated by the polish of his mob counterpart, Harvey came on strong, slapping his revolver on the table and announcing that Rosselli would work exclusively for him. Maheu, Giancana, and Trafficante were to be cut off as "untrustworthy." Jim O'Connell attended the meeting, and he recalled the tension of the moment in his testimony before the Church Committee. "Initially Rosselli did not trust Harvey," O'Connell said.

Harvey's elimination of the Mafia dons Trafficante and Giancana from the project was a housekeeping matter, an effort to get a handle on the "ongoing affair" he had been assigned to take over. Rosselli voiced no objections. He had fulfilled his obligations by reporting the operation to his superiors in the Mafia, and neither had taken an active role in the project beyond providing initial introductions and endorsements. For Trafficante in particular, the plots against Castro placed him in a difficult position; while he deeply resented the loss of his gambling casinos, he was maneuvering to keep in place a drug-running network he had developed under Batista. To endanger his island contacts was to threaten a second, and so far surviving, source of income. From the beginning, Trafficante's first concern was to keep his participation in the murder plots secret, even among the Mafia.

A second meeting between O'Connell, Harvey, and Rosselli, in New York on April 8, went more smoothly. The CIA officers suggested another attempt at poisoning Castro, and Rosselli promised to speak with de Varona. A new batch of pills were prepared at the CIA labs, this time improved so they "would work anywhere at any time with anything." O'Connell passed them to Harvey on April 18, and three days later, Harvey met alone with Rosselli in Miami. De Varona was enthusiastic, Rosselli reported: he intended to assassinate Che Guevara and Raoul Castro, as well as Fidel. Harvey liked the idea. He told Rosselli, "Everything is all right, what they want to do."

There was one catch. De Varona wanted another cache of equipment, the sort of material that he couldn't obtain on the black market. Harvey went along, requisitioning from the CIA station in Miami a truckload of explosives, detonators, handguns, rifles, radios, and boat radar. The delivery was arranged with the spy-trade precautions of a John Le Carré novel: Harvey rented a U-Haul under an assumed name, packed its lethal cargo and drove with station chief Ted Shackley to an unlit parking lot. Leaving the locked truck behind, they strolled across the street to where Rosselli and Jim O'Connell stood waiting in the shadows. Harvey and Shackley handed over the keys and departed, leaving Rosselli and O'Connell to pass the hours, keeping watch over the contraband in the still, tropical night. Toward midnight, a courier arrived. Rosselli handed him the keys, and the assassination plot was again under way.

Over the following several weeks, Rosselli relayed to Harvey reports from de Varona that the pills and the guns had been landed in Cuba, that a three-man team had followed them in, and that "the medicine" as they called the poison, "was still safe." But Castro remained healthy and vigorous, and de Varona's communiqués grew increasingly vague. He said the second team was held up because "conditions were not right," and asked for more expense money. By September, Harvey had had enough of the ambitious Cuban. He told Rosselli flatly, "There's not much likelihood that this is going anyplace, or that it should be continued."

At Large in Miami

FRUITLESS AS IT WAS, the collaboration with John Rosselli was a bright spot for William Harvey in Miami. The urgent midnight strategy meetings and Rosselli's cool confidence provided a refreshing break to what was fast becoming a dreary administrative routine. As the head of Operation Mongoose, Harvey soon found himself deluged in paperwork. General Lansdale, an aide to Helms recalled later, would "bombard Harvey with a million goddamn papers all the time."

By mid-1962, Task Force W, under the operational code name JM/WAVE, had mushroomed to become the largest CIA station in the world, with 400 agents, several thousand local contacts, an assortment of airplanes, and enough ships to equip a small navy. Paramilitary units ran dozens of missions into Cuba, bombing economic targets and harassing Castro's rural patrols. Yet the signals issued from Bobby Kennedy's Special Group in Washington were decidedly mixed. Hungry for "results" but leery of a second Bay of Pigs, "policymakers not only shied away from the military intervention aspect but were generally apprehensive of sabotage proposals." As the secretary of the Special Group conceded later, "Nobody knew exactly what they wanted to do." The constant vacillation left Harvey exasperated. "What's the matter with those bastards?" he complained. "Why don't they get off their duffs and do something?"

Never comfortable with his Ivy League colleagues in the CIA, Harvey saw Task Force W as his chance to make his mark on the bureaucracy. But the constant interference from the Special Group, and from Bobby Kennedy in particular, left him stymied and angry. In private, he came to refer to RFK as "that fucker."

★

Frustrated with the government, longing for the sense of danger and intrigue he had known on the streets of besieged West Berlin, Harvey drew close to John Rosselli. At least Rosselli knew what it was to live by his wits, to play for keeps, to respect the authority of a snub-nosed revolver. Like Harvey, Rosselli was a firm anti-communist, untarnished by the drawing-room sophistication of post-McCarthy liberalism that dominated the thinking of the CIA leadership. And Rosselli was always sympathetic to Harvey's tirades against stultifying bureaucrats. The pen-pushers in Washington could wrangle over their organizational charts—in Miami, Harvey and Rosselli were grappling with the enemy.

Convinced that assassination was the key to the entire operation, Harvey decided to turn Rosselli loose to run his own commando teams into Cuba, independent of de Varona and the other Cuban exiles. As a cover story, Rosselli was issued the papers and false background of an Army colonel, a rank that lent him full access to the JM/WAVE headquarters in Coral Gables, south of Miami. David Morales, El Indio, the CIA's consummate hit man, was assigned to work with Rosselli on a daily basis.

Rosselli had two bases of operation in southern Florida during this period. One was a roadside motel called The Mariner, located on U.S. 1 near the JM/WAVE headquarters. The second was a safe house established by the CIA on the end of Point Mary, a small strip of sand reaching southwest from Key Largo. Rosselli had his pick of Cuban-exile fighters trained by Army specialists in survival, explosives, and small-team tactics, and usually selected the best marksmen to staff his missions. For transportation, he was supplied with overpowered, steep-hulled V-20 speedboats, commercial craft retrofitted with steel reinforcements and machine-gun mounts, capable of speeds as high as fifty miles per hour on quiet water.

Having jettisoned de Varona, Rosselli also abandoned hopes of a quiet, inside "hit" on Fidel Castro, settling for a more conventional plot to position snipers within telescopic range of the Premier at one of his public appearances. He secured rifles suitable for the job from Mafia sources, but was countermanded by Harvey, whose Executive Action blueprint called for weapons and ammunition that could not be traced to American agents. Accordingly, Harvey secured Belgian FAL assault rifles of the type used by the Cuban Army.

By day, Rosselli frequented the JM/WAVE headquarters compound, sometimes attending the staff briefings but more often engaging demolitions expert Ed Roderick in rounds of cribbage, or heading off with Dave Morales for drinking bouts at the local watering holes. At night, on at least half a dozen occasions by his own account, Rosselli joined with the proliferating groups of Cuban exiles in dodging Castro's patrols on midnight dashes across the Windward Passage.

Like the other rebel commanders running teams into Cuba, Rosselli's men were sometimes captured. "They'd go in, and nothing, never heard from again," said Joe Shimon, whom Rosselli later regaled with tales of the action in Florida. And like the others who tested the skill of Fidel Castro's coastal patrols, Rosselli had boats shot out from under him, at least twice and perhaps more often, according to stories he told his friends. "He went into detail about one incident," said Tom Wadden, an attorney who represented Rosselli in his appearances before the Church Committee. "He said his boat sunk right under him, and he had to swim the equivalent of about eight lengths of a pool to reach a second boat and get out of there."

When his V-20 was sunk a second time, Rosselli scrambled aboard a small dinghy and drifted, alone and exposed to the elements, for several days. An American patrol finally located him and returned him to his men, who had given him up for dead.

None of Rosselli's activity during this accelerated stage of operations was reported to the Church Committee in 1975. But Rosselli himself related some of the material to his attorneys in Washington, and to journalists Jack Anderson and Les Whitten. In addition, there are the revelations of Bradley Earl Ayers, a U.S. Army captain assigned to work with the CIA in training the Cuban exile commandos. In his book *The War That Never Was*, (1976), one of the few insider accounts of Operation Mongoose, Ayers refers to Rosselli briefly as "Colonel" Rosselli, "one of the few Americans authorized to actually go on commando missions into Cuba." In interviews for this book, Ayers expanded on that account for the first time.

Ayers was struck in particular by Rosselli's close relationship with El Indio—"Dave Morales was the kind of guy who accepted those around him on a very selective basis, and it was obvious to me that they were intimates"—and by Rosselli's easy access at JM/WAVE. "Any suggestion that Rosselli's activities were less than legitimized by the establishment is total bullshit," Ayers said. "He wasn't operating as a rogue entity, on some fringe of the CIA. For Chrissakes, he had virtual carte-blanche into the highest levels of the station. He didn't have the credentials to back it up, but it was clear that somebody had said, you know, give this guy whatever he needs.

"When I learned later what Rosselli's true identity was, that he was some kind of mafioso, I thought the implications of that were extraordinary. Here we're talking about an operation that was by its nature very top secret and highly confidential, and you've got this underworld figure who could practically write his own goddamn ticket. It's an absolutely bizarre story. But there was a quality to Rosselli that came off as the patriotic, true blue, one hundred percent American. I could see the spark of patriotism there, and I guess that made it all palatable. We were all trying to get the same job done, although we were coming from entirely different places."

Rosselli's work on the Castro assassination under the direction of Morales and Harvey continued until February 1963. Disappointed with the repeated capture of the commando teams, Harvey had developed a new contact, a Cuban diplomat with access to Castro, and decided to suspend the Mafia plots. He flew to Los Angeles to confer with Rosselli and over drinks, Harvey with his beloved martinis and Rosselli sipping Smirnoff on the rocks, the project was closed, though it was agreed to let stand the $150,000 bounty on Castro's head. The two friends held a second, final meeting on June 20, this time more social than business, at Tino's Continental Restaurant in Washington's fashionable Northwest District. Harvey's wife went along.

Harvey, O'Connell, and Morales were Rosselli's primary contacts with the CIA, but they weren't the only ones. Ayers reported that Rosselli befriended another agent in Florida, a CIA commando named William "Rip" Robertson—the two shared a close friendship and an occasional drinking binge. Another Agency connection may have been E. Howard Hunt, the CIA political officer at the Bay of Pigs who later turned up in connection with the Watergate scandal. Hunt has denied ever meeting Rosselli, but that seems unlikely, considering that both worked closely with Tony de Varona. More important, a well-qualified source has published an account that identifies Rosselli and Hunt as coconspirators in the assassination of Rafael Trujillo.

The Dominican dictator was murdered in an ambush on May 30, 1961, and the Church Committee established that the CIA had supplied his attackers with weapons in an effort to bring about Trujillo's demise. The principal in the plot, according to the committee, was Henry Dearborn, the deputy chief of Mission at the American Embassy. Unauthorized weapons were almost impossible to obtain in Trujillo's island domain, and Dominican dissidents made repeated requests to Dearborn for a variety of small arms.

That record was augmented in 1976 with the publication in Paris of

Cygne, a picaresque but factual autobiography by L. Gonzalez-Mata, who served briefly as Trujillo's chief of security in 1960. According to Gonzalez-Mata, John Rosselli and Howard Hunt arrived in the Dominican Republic in March 1961, there to assist in the plots against Trujillo.

Gonzalez-Mata identified Rosselli as "a friend of Batista" who was operating "on the orders of William Harvey, the liaison between the CIA and the Mafia." Hunt was termed "a specialist." According to Gonzalez-Mata, who was relating "the truth of the history of the assassination of Trujillo, the dictator, as I know it in its details," Rosselli and Hunt met with Dearborn and a Dominican dissident leader named Lorenzo D. Berry, operator of a successful retail market. Berry proposed a plan to force Trujillo into exile, but Hunt was adamant that an ambush was the only reliable course of action. Berry finally agreed when Hunt promised that the CIA would provide the weapons. *Time* magazine correspondent Bernard Diederich later corroborated Gonzalez-Mata's version to the extent of identifying Berry as a key player in the conspiracy to oust Trujillo.

Following Trujillo's assassination, Bobby Kennedy dictated for his personal record his impressions of the killing, and his reaction. Most disturbing to him was not the American role, but the dearth of quality intelligence following the event. "The great problem now is that we don't know what to do because we don't know what the situation is and this shouldn't be true, particularly when we have known that this situation was pending for some period of time." Subsequent internal CIA documents termed the Dominican project a "success."

The picture that emerges from the various accounts of Rosselli's work for the CIA differs substantially from that painted by the testimony taken by the Church Committee. Rather than an isolated and ineffectual plot, removed at great distance from the White House and dismissed by Richard Helms with the offhand comment, "I do not recall ever having been convinced that any attempt was really made on Castro's life," the CIA conspiracy was a vigorous and ongoing project involving several of the Agency's top covert operators, costing the lives of several members of Rosselli's commando teams and very nearly his own. The plots were generated by the White House and reported back in detail, including the role of the Mafia. As the point man in Miami, Rosselli served as a sort of CIA killer-at-large, fully credentialed and in constant touch with his superiors. Rosselli was given the rank of "colonel" by his associates within the government, and gave orders as well as taking them.

The Mafia plots were not the only efforts launched to assassinate Fidel

Castro, but they were the primary ones, a fact that was galling to the Cuban exiles in whose name the murder was to take place. "It was ridiculous for them to use the Mafia," said Felix Rodriguez, an anti-Castro paramilitary activist who later surfaced as a field agent for Ollie North in the secret war against Nicaragua. "The CIA had connections to the decent community in Miami, and we were working on our own assassination projects. Working with the Mafia was absolutely unnecessary."

On the face of things, Rodriguez was right. For the CIA to ally with the Mafia seems absurd and ill-contrived, but that conclusion fails to account for the Agency's intermittent relationship with the underworld, a relationship embodied in Rosselli's friendships with Bob Maheu, David Morales, and Bill Harvey. And it may have gone farther than simply using the mob as an international blackjack, the business end of Executive Action; the CIA may have seen the Mafia as a lever to exercise control over Cuba after Castro's ouster. They encouraged de Varona's collaboration with the mob, and certainly the gangsters would provide a more forceful hammer than the State Department once the Tronco de Yucca took power.

Rodriguez also failed to account for the uniquely American fascination with the Mafia that helped guide the deliberations of the leadership clique at the CIA. The pipe-smoking plotter Allen Dulles, the brilliant Yale-educated Richard Bissell, and later the dissembling Richard Helms were seeking to commit the darkest of deeds. Almost inevitably, they turned out to be the most evil institution America had produced. It was a pathological act, an historic expression of a culture that honored ends beyond means.

11
THE END OF IT ALL

Pressure from the Top

From the moment Jack Kennedy took his inaugural oath, the activities of the first family became a constant factor in the affairs of John Rosselli. He was working for the Kennedy brothers in the assassination plots. He was tracking JFK's social life through the gossip he exchanged with Judy Campbell and Frank Sinatra. He intervened to protect the President in the Judy Meredith affair. And all the while, he and his Mafia cohorts were grappling with an unprecedented war on crime.

In 1961, Robert Kennedy's crime campaign reached its ultimate expression with the deportation of New Orleans Mafia don Carlos Marcello. A Sicilian who arrived in New Orleans in 1910 at the age of 4, Marcello had been ordered deported in 1953, a decision prompted by the Kefauver Committee investigations. His attorneys then engaged in a protracted stalling action, succeeding in blocking enforcement of the order despite evidence that Marcello had forged a Guatemalan birth certificate. When

229

the McClellan Committee subpoenaed Marcello to appear in 1957, his citizenship was the focus of intensive questioning by the Senate panel.

Bobby Kennedy took up the matter of Marcello's deportation immediately upon taking office. He pressed the Immigration and Naturalization Service (INS) to seek an entry permit from Guatemala, and when one was obtained in March, he ordered deportation of the stocky gangster posthaste. On April 4, 1961, accompanied by his attorney, Marcello checked in for his routine quarterly visit with the INS, a procedure required while his appeals meandered through the courts. Without warning, two agents appeared from a side door, placed handcuffs on Marcello's wrists, hustled him to a waiting car, and drove him directly to the airport. Denying him the courtesy of a call to his wife, ignoring the protests of Marcello and his attorney, they placed him on a large INS passenger plane, its engines already running. Within hours, the Mafia don was deposited in the care of an Army colonel on the tarmac in Guatemala City.

On June 5, Marcello's attorneys filed suit in Washington, contending the deportation was illegal and "contrary to the Constitution." The same day, Bobby Kennedy gloated at a press conference that he was "very happy that Carlos Marcello was no longer with us." Marcello soon slipped back into the United States, but he always remembered the deportation as a personal insult. Years later, in testimony before a congressional committee, the memory of the incident still left him spluttering in anger. "They just snatched me," he stammered, "that is it, actually kidnapped me."

John Rosselli also felt the sting of the vigorous anticrime campaign, but it never touched off the personal rage it did in Marcello. He was the target of intensive surveillance, by both telephone wiretaps and microphones, and by teams of FBI agents who tailed him around Los Angeles and Las Vegas, but lost track of him on his frequent trips out of town. He took the intrusion in stride; once, after meeting with an attorney friend, he said "Watch this," then jumped in his car and sped twice around the block, laughing and pointing back at the government car dodging the traffic to keep up with him.

On another occasion, in March of 1963, he bumped into FBI agent Dean Elson in the lobby of the Desert Inn. Rather than ignore him or lambaste him, Rosselli joined in a kidding conversation that Elson then recounted in his field report. "Rosselli jokingly related that he had just recently looked at a new apartment to rent and the rent was $450 a month, which he thought was excessive. He told the manager he should receive a discount since the FBI, the Los Angeles police, and the Los

Angeles Sheriff's Office would immediately begin living in the neighborhood and thus would give the apartment house protection from burglaries." The anecdote was forwarded to J. Edgar Hoover's personal attention.

More troubling to Rosselli was the heavy tax review applied to all the top mobsters at the time. In one conversation picked up by FBI microphones, Rosselli declared that the IRS investigation was "murder" to deal with. Later, an informant reported that Rosselli had "expressed disgust at all the trouble that the IRS had been causing him." But despite the sustained scrutiny, Rosselli managed to keep clear of the tax authorities. He established enough income through finder's fees collected off various hotel and casino financing deals, and from his ice-machine concession, to cover his reportable expenses, and paid for most of his dinners and air travel in cash, leaving little evidence for the tax agents to collect.

Rosselli accepted the official harassment as a natural condition of his occupation. "Johnny always took everything light," said Susan Woods, a friend from Los Angeles. "He never complained, never knocked anybody. He didn't let things get to him." But that equanimity was unusual in a lifelong mafioso, and even Rosselli grew fierce when it came to business. Moreover, he resented what he perceived as the government's double standard—the pressure was increasing at the same time he was risking his life doing Uncle Sam's dirty work in the Florida Keys.

During a plane trip to Washington in 1962, Rosselli voiced his frustration to Las Vegas associate Michael Hellerman. Rosselli did not divulge the details of the assassination plots, but he fumed at the "screwing" he was getting from Bobby Kennedy. " 'Here I am,' " Hellerman quoted Rosselli, " 'helping the government, helping the country, and that little son of a bitch is breaking my balls.' "

★

Most of the mobsters tended, like Carlos Marcello, to regard the attacks of the law enforcement agencies as a personal affront, a violation of their dignity, never considering that they might have earned whatever miseries the government might be able to apply. But none took the harassment so hard as Sam Giancana.

When a subpoena was issued to order his appearance before the McClellan Committee, Giancana evaded the FBI for more than a year, before agents finally caught up with him in Las Vegas and served the papers on him. Described by a Chicago police official as "a snarling, sarcastic, ill-tempered, sadistic psychopath," he indulged in ranting at the agents who tailed him to the point that, in 1962, Tony Accardo felt compelled to talk Giancana down. "You can't go giving these [FBI] guys abuse," he told his onetime enforcer. "You got to talk to them."

Giancana's frustrations were rooted in more than just personal pique. His local operations in Chicago were thrown into chaos by the beefed-up FBI task force there, forcing him to shut down protection rackets and nightclub gambling. "Tell everyone that everything is off," he told a mob conference one night in early 1962. "This is it because of the G. We ain't spending another nickel. Everyone is on his own, they got to make it any way they can."

Similar results were being produced in Las Vegas. In December 1961, J. Edgar Hoover reported in a congratulatory memo to Bobby Kennedy that "information has been received that persons connected with gambling activities in Las Vegas are becoming increasingly apprehensive concerning the intensity of investigations into gambling." Giancana was overheard telling a partner in a Las Vegas casino that he could not pay the interest he owed due to government pressure there. The cash that was the lifeblood of the Chicago Outfit was running dry.

Feeling personally hunted and professionally injured, Giancana determined to play his trump card. He asked John Rosselli to see if he could bring Frank Sinatra's influence to bear on the Kennedys. Rosselli reported back in a conversation taped by FBI microphones in that December of 1961, following Giancana's return from a trip to Europe. The transcript affords rare insight into Rosselli's character, and Giancana's, and their veiled manner of discourse, as well as their deepening resentment toward the Kennedys.

ROSSELLI   Did you go to Luciano's home?

GIANCANA   No.

ROSSELLI   Oh, that's a hell of a place. A real nice home. He's a real nice guy.

GIANCANA   I couldn't get out of that country fast enough.

ROSSELLI   How do you feel, buddy? Did you have a nice time? Did you get a lot of heat over there?

GIANCANA   What kind of heat?

ROSSELLI   Over there.

GIANCANA   Naw.

ROSSELLI   Nobody tailed you? Well, Skinny (D'Amato) called me, and he said get ahold of the guy, he wants to see you. I says right away, so I call him back. I went to Vegas after I come back from . . .

GIANCANA   Who was . . .

ROSSELLI   Frank (Sinatra). You know. So the first week I didn't see him. (Then) I saw him, hello, how are you, and that's all. After his wife left, he sent for me. . . . Now I said, Frank, I don't want to be in your way. I don't want to bother you. He said, I want you to bunk with me . . . will you do that, he says, bunk with me? I says, all right. So he says, when are you going home? I says, today. So he says, cancel out, I want you to come to my home. I says, that'll be fine with me.

So he was real nice to me and offered me some money. I threw it back at him. I had a chance to quiz him. I said Frankie, can I ask you one question? He says, (answer deleted) . . . I took Sam's name and wrote it down and told Bobby Kennedy, this is my buddy. This is what I want you to know, Bob.

That had to be a charged moment. Frank Sinatra, the most important entertainer of his time, a force in Hollywood and a major contributor to the 1960 presidential campaign, quietly scribbling the name of a notorious gangster on a scrap of paper and pushing it across a table top to the hard-charging attorney general. Rosselli did not relate Bobby Kennedy's reaction—he may have frowned, he may have shrugged, he may have seen it simply as Sinatra showing off. But it seems unlikely that Bobby realized the grave implications of Sinatra's approach. A message from a gangster, even a cryptic one, and especially coming from a Mafia don, is a loaded instrument, at once an entreaty and a threat. Young and brash, disdainful of the gangsters despite his own family history, Bobby Kennedy dismissed it out of hand.

Continuing his discourse, Rosselli revealed that Sinatra's next move was to call on the family patriarch:

ROSSELLI   Between you and me, Frank saw Joe Kennedy three different times. Joe Kennedy, the father—He called him three
times.

GIANCANA   Called who?

ROSSELLI   Called Frank (Sinatra). So maybe he's starting to see the
light . . . you're friends. He's got it in his head that
they're not faithful to him. That's what I'm trying to get
in his head.

GIANCANA   In other words, the (campaign) donation that was
made . . .

ROSSELLI   That's what I was talking about.

GIANCANA   He had to pay for it, regardless.

ROSSELLI   That's what made the issue with him. Nothing deliberate,
take it back. . . . He says he's got an idea that you're
mad at him. I says: That, I wouldn't know.

GIANCANA   He must have a guilty conscience. I never said nothing.
. . . Well I don't know who the fuck he's (Frank's) talking to . . . after all, if I'm taking somebody's money, I'm
gonna make sure that this money is gonna do something,
like, do you want it or don't you want it? If the money is
accepted, maybe one of these days the guy will do me a
favor.

ROSSELLI   That's right. He (Frank) says he wrote your name down.

GIANCANA   Well, one minute he tells me this and then he tells me
that and then the last time I talked to him was at the
hotel down in Florida a month before he left, and he said,
Don't worry about it, if I can't talk to the old man (Joseph
Kennedy), I'm gonna talk to the man (President Kennedy). One minute he says he's talked to Robert, and the
next minute he says he hasn't talked to him. So he never
did talk to him. It's a lot of shit. Why lie to me? I haven't
got that coming.

ROSSELLI   I can imagine. . . . If he can't deliver, I want him to tell
me, John, the load's too heavy.

GIANCANA   That's all right. At least then, you know how to work. You
won't let your guard down, know what I mean?

The conversation had gotten sidetracked on Giancana's frustration
with his messenger. Rosselli shortly brought it back into focus, portraying

Sinatra as a tool being used by the Kennedys, and urging Giancana to let the Kennedys taste the other edge of the Mafia sword they had been toying with.

ROSSELLI   He's got big ideas, Frank does, about being ambassador or something. You know Pierre Salinger and them guys, they don't want him. They treat him like a whore. You fuck them, you pay them, and then they're through. You got the right idea, Moe [one of Giancana's nicknames], go the other way. Fuck everybody. We'll use them every fucking way we can. They only know one way. Now let them see the other side of you.

Pressure from Below

THE PRESSURE ONLY INCREASED. Bobby Kennedy was enjoying his notoriety as a crimebuster, and put little stock in any sense of debt his family might owe the mob. New York socialite Kay Lepercq was struck by the irony when she met RFK at a Washington dinner party given by Arthur Schlesinger. "Bobby kept talking about how as attorney general he laid down the law and so forth," Mrs. Lepercq said later. "It wasn't very charming, particularly as I suspected that President Kennedy owed his election in large measure to the intervention of the Mafia."

There were occasional warning signals that the mob expected the Kennedys to honor their underworld associations, but Bobby refused to be compromised. When J. Edgar Hoover's field agents reported back on Sinatra's apparent effort to intervene on Giancana's behalf, Hoover relayed the news to the attorney general, who in turn passed it to his brother. The result was a breach—Jack Kennedy canceled a planned visit to Frank Sinatra's Palm Springs home in March, telling Peter Lawford, "I can't stay there while Bobby's handling [the Giancana] investigation."

Similarly, faced with Hoover's knowledge of Judy Campbell's Mafia friends, Jack Kennedy ended the affair. And when Bobby was confronted with Sam Giancana's role in the Castro assassination plots, he stepped up his investigation. After backstopping his position in the meetings with the CIA on May 7, 1962, he approved a new, more intensive surveillance program against Giancana. Dubbed "Operation Lockstep," it called for round-the-clock surveillance by a team of nine FBI agents, who trailed Giancana into restaurants, on walks around his neighborhood, even onto the golf course, where they played a foursome behind Giancana's party. "How I loved to bang my tee shot into Giancana as he was waiting to hit his second shot," one of the agents recalled.

Giancana responded in surprising fashion, filing a civil rights suit in federal court seeking an injunction against FBI "harassment." It was a risky maneuver. In presenting his case, Giancana would open himself up to cross-examination by government attorneys who could resurrect his past record, his underworld affiliations, and all the unproven allegations of his illegal activity. But Giancana had a trump card—his inside knowledge of the Kennedys and the CIA assassination plots. Taking the stand in June 1963, Giancana was asked if he had ever broken any laws that would merit FBI surveillance, and calmly answered, "No." When the witness was turned over to the U.S. attorney, he waived his rights to cross-examination, citing the attorney general's position that the suit had no standing. William Hundley, chief of the organized crime task force at Justice, told the New York *Times* that "Bobby pushed to get Giancana at any cost." But it was Kennedy who blinked in the staring match in federal court in Chicago.

Giancana won his suit: a victory for the mob in their battle against Bobby, but a minor one. Across the country, Mafia leaders were fuming at the continuing assault by the Justice Department. Dozens of gangsters were being sent to prison. Jimmy Hoffa's Teamsters had begun restricting access to the rich coffers of the union pension funds, and wiretaps exposed even the best-hidden rackets. Buffalo Mafia chief Stefano Magaddino fumed, "They know everything under the sun. They know who's back of it, they know *amichi* [the made mafiosi], they know *capodecina* [family captains], they know there is a commission [the board of the national syndicate]. We got to watch right now, this thing, where it goes and stay as quiet as possible."

In addition, the FBI wiretaps were picking up a new and ominous theme, the frustrated declarations of killers backed against the wall. In Philadelphia, mob lieutenant Willie Weisberg swore, "With Kennedy, a guy should take a knife . . . and stab and kill that fucker, I mean it. This is true. Honest to God. Right in the White House. Somebody's got to get rid of that fucker." And in Buffalo, Magaddino declared, "They should kill the whole family, the mother and father too."

Aggressive law enforcement was never regarded by the Mafia as cause for assassination. They battled with the police, they conspired to thwart federal agents, but while intimidation and murder were tools of their trade, they considered the agents of the government to be off limits. There had been a number of effective gangbusters over the years—Eliot Ness, Thomas E. Dewey, Virgil Peterson in Chicago, Warren Olney III in California—each cost the mob millions in lost revenue and years in prison, but none lost their lives in ambush or bomb blast.

It was different with the Kennedys, because they had crossed the line dividing the underworld and legitimate society. They had accepted favors from the mob, had cavorted with their women, had employed their services in intrigues at the highest level of government. Bobby Kennedy's war on crime was more than an assault, it was a betrayal, a double-cross that violated the core of the Mafia ethic. *Onore* required vengeance. Having enjoyed the beneficence of the mob, the Kennedys then spurned them. The mob's reaction was inevitable. As Rosselli exhorted Sam Giancana, "Now let them see the other side of you."

Indeed, Jack Kennedy himself had shown them the way. Publicly, he denounced "terror, assassination, false promises . . ." But privately, in their obsessive drive to destroy Fidel Castro, Jack and Bobby had banished all scruples. They would murder him, and use the Mafia as their agents. To his coconspirators, Jack Kennedy sent a clear message: he played by their rules.

And so, in their burning frustration, the gangsters thought the unthinkable. Outside the range of the FBI microphones, actual plots were taking shape. In September 1962, Jimmy Hoffa discussed with Louisiana Teamsters leader Edward Partin plans to level Bobby Kennedy's Virginia home with plastic explosives, and to enlist a sniper to assassinate the President. Partin, a government informer, related the conversation to the FBI.

The same month, Carlos Marcello described a more detailed plan in the privacy of a farmhouse on his sprawling country estate outside New Orleans. Ed Becker, a private investigator and free-lance businessman, was meeting with Marcello and his longtime associates Carlo Roppolo and Jack Liberto when their boss pulled out a bottle and poured a generous round of Scotch. The conversation wandered until Becker made an offhand remark about Bobby Kennedy and Marcello's deportation. The reference struck a nerve, and Carlos jumped to his feet, exclaiming the Sicilian oath, *"Livarsi na pietra di la scarpa!* (Take the stone out of my shoe!)"

Reverting to English, Marcello shouted, "Don't worry about that Bobby son-of-a-bitch. He's going to be taken care of." Emboldened by the Scotch, Becker interrupted. "You can't go after Bobby Kennedy. You'll get into a hell of a lot of trouble." In answer, Marcello invoked an old Italian proverb: "If you want to kill a dog, you don't cut off the tail, you cut off the head." Bobby was the tail, an adjunct, an appendage. If the President were killed then Bobby would lose his bite. Marcello added that he had a plan, to use "a nut" to take the fall for the murder, "like they do in Sicily." Seated again, Marcello abruptly changed the subject, and the Kennedys were not mentioned again.

Marcello's closest associate in the national leadership of the Mafia was Santo Trafficante, and during the same month that Marcello swore retribution against the Kennedys, Trafficante made a similar declaration in Florida. The occasion was a meeting with Cuban exile Jose Aleman, Jr., who was seeking assistance in obtaining $1.5 million in development financing from the Teamsters Union through Trafficante's close friend, Jimmy Hoffa.

Two other men were present, Trafficante's Cuban contact, Rafael "Macho" Gener, and another exile leader, George Nobregas, but the pair drifted away when Trafficante began a discourse on the political situation in the United States. "He spoke almost poetically about democracy and civil liberties," Aleman recalled later. Trafficante then focused on the subject of Jack Kennedy, denouncing him as a dishonest politician who accepted graft and did not keep a bargain. "Have you seen how his brother is hitting on Hoffa, a man who is a worker, who is not a millionaire, a friend of the blue collars? He doesn't know that this kind of encounter is very delicate. Mark my words, this man Kennedy is in trouble, and he will get what is coming to him."

Unaware of Trafficante's implication, Aleman disagreed, arguing that Kennedy would be reelected. Trafficante replied by making his point explicit. "No, Jose, you don't understand me. Kennedy's not going to make it to the election. He is going to be hit."

Aleman took the Mafia don at his word, reporting the threat to the FBI. Yet, perhaps aware of the failure of the efforts to kill Fidel Castro, Aleman was unconvinced that the Mafia could pull off the assassination of the American President. He placed a wager with Nobregas, betting that Kennedy would survive his term in office. He lost.

Dallas

AMERICANS LIKE TO REMEMBER the murder of President John F. Kennedy by thinking back to the moment. Where were they when they heard the news? Midday, Friday, November 22, 1963. Grabbing lunch at a corner tavern. Folding laundry in front of the television. Called in to the school auditorium, surprised to find teachers and principal teary-eyed. Ordinary scenes from daily life are preserved in indelible memory, like the residents of Pompeii, frozen in shock by the sudden lava flow.

History as snap shot. It's easier to comprehend that way, and less disturbing. Oswald shot the President. He was a lunatic, a loner, a random bullet seeking a target. Kennedy's murder was a tragedy, a horror. But it passed, the nation moved on. Lyndon Johnson replaced him in office ninety-nine minutes after Kennedy was pronounced dead. Our constitutional government had survived, and so would we.

At least, that was how the government responded to the deep crisis of the assassination. The concern, and the response, were expressed with startling clarity in a memo from Deputy Attorney General Nicholas Katzenbach to presidential assistant Bill Moyers, written three days after the shooting:

> It is important that all of the facts surrounding President Kennedy's assassination be made public in a way which will satisfy the people in the United States and abroad that all the facts have been told and that a statement to this effect be made now.
>
> 1. The public must be satisfied that Oswald was the assassin; that he did not have confederates who are still at large; and that the evidence was such that he would have been convicted at trial.
>
> 2. Speculation about Oswald's motivation ought to be cut off, and we should have some basis for rebutting thought that this was a com-

munist conspiracy or (as the iron curtain press is saying) a right-wing conspiracy to blame it on the communists.

J. Edgar Hoover, whose agency would lead the government investigation, expressed the same position in a conversation two days after the shooting with White House aide Walter Jenkins. "The thing I am most concerned about, and so is Mr. Katzenbach, is having something issued so we can convince the public that Oswald is the real assassin."

Its purpose firmly enunciated, the government strove mightily to achieve consensus. President Johnson appointed the Warren Commission, and ten months later, the commission returned its report, hefty and gray, with twenty-six volumes of testimony, and one tidy conclusion. The press weighed in, Walter Cronkite and the rest, plowing through the Warren Commission documentation and pronouncing the verdict final and correct.

For a time, it worked. Pollster Lou Harris found near-universal support for the commission and its accord. It should come as no surprise. Jack Kennedy represented the ideal that America wanted to see in itself. His sudden demise left that ideal shaken, but the lone-assassin scenario was comforting in a way. Each of us is mortal, after all. We could share in the tragedy. But if it were a cabal, if his enemies had conspired to snuff out the President, the implications were far more unsettling—that beneath the hope and promise that had swept Kennedy into office, dark forces were at work.

The consensus didn't hold. In 1966, Mark Lane published *Rush to Judgment*, his bestselling critique of the Warren Commission report, and there followed an avalanche of criticism, analysis, and speculation on the cause of the assassination and its perpetrators. The close frame that had been hammered into place around the events in Dealey Plaza began to splinter, and then fall away.

The project assigned the Warren Commission was doomed from the start, betrayed on national television, shattered in the clap of a single gunshot. The Kennedy assassination could never be reduced to a single, terrible moment because it involved more than one murder. Lee Harvey Oswald could never stand alone in history because always, in the same breath, on the same TV screen, there would be Jack Ruby, a fedora clamped on his head, a .38-caliber revolver clutched in his fist.

Lee Harvey Oswald was an enigma but Jack Ruby was a beacon, a well-lit street sign pointing to broad avenues for investigation. Jack Ruby was a gangster.

★

Born Jack Rubenstein in a poor neighborhood of Chicago in 1911, Ruby came of age running with a street gang that used "to run innocuous errands" for Al Capone. He graduated to become a top union slugger under Paul Dorfman, and was arrested and questioned by police in connection with the 1939 murder of Leon Cooke, founder of Local 20467 of the Scrap Iron and Junk Handler's Union. Dorfman promptly assumed control, with Ruby as an underling, transforming the local into what the AFL-CIO termed "largely a shakedown operation." After a turn in the Army Air Force, Ruby fell out of favor; he later told a friend he had been "exiled from Chicago" by the mob, and "was directed" to move to Dallas.

From 1947 to 1963, Jack Ruby operated a string of sleazy nightclubs and comported himself in a fashion befitting an exiled Chicago gangster. He was arrested nine times in sixteen years, but developed connections to the Dallas police strong enough that he never faced a trial. He was constantly in the company of known hoodlums and occasionally carried a gun. Ruby was active in gambling, prostitution, and drug trafficking, and when the mob started running guns to Fidel Castro in 1958, Ruby was eager to lend a hand.

From the minute Lee Harvey Oswald shot John F. Kennedy, Jack Ruby was in constant motion, circling the President's assassin until he was finally able to gun him down. He began by witnessing the shooting from the vantage point of the Dallas Morning News Building, which overlooked Dealey Plaza. In the commotion that followed, Ruby drove directly to Dallas's Parkland Hospital, learning for certain the President was dead. That evening, he arrived at the police station where Oswald was being interrogated, and when a press conference was held at midnight, Ruby was still there, a loaded revolver in his right-hand pocket.

The next day, Saturday, Ruby made phone calls to contacts in the press and police to get the latest information on Oswald's status—in particular, when he might be moved from the police station to the jail. That afternoon, Ruby was seen again hanging around the police station, long enough to be sure that Oswald would not be transferred until the next morning. On Sunday he was back, and when Oswald emerged in the basement of the station at 11:15 that morning, Ruby surged forward from a throng of more than 120 press and police personnel, and delivered the shot that silenced Oswald. How Ruby gained access to the restricted area was never determined, but he had excellent relations with the police, including Sergeant Patrick T. Dean, the officer in charge of basement security that morning.

The Mafia may not have been the only party to the assassination in Dallas. Exhaustive analysis by a generation of researchers has raised a series of questions about Lee Harvey Oswald himself—his several contacts with intelligence officers in the weeks before the shooting, and his curious role as a *provocateur* in the Cuban exile community in New Orleans, where he distributed pro-Castro literature but associated with CIA-backed, anti-Castro organizations located in a warren of offices at 544 Camp Street. Oswald also had contacts with the mob, primarily through his uncle, Charles "Dutz" Murret, a bookmaker in Carlos Marcello's New Orleans organization, but also through David Ferrie, a strange character with ties both to intelligence and the mob.

★

These are imponderables, trails of intrigue that have been erased by the passage of time. What is certain is that Oswald himself intimated a conspiracy in his one brief public appearance before his own killing, when he shouted into the crush of reporters and television cameras in the hallway of the Dallas police station, "I'm just a patsy." Before anyone could ask who had used him or why, Oswald was dead.

The precise shape of the conspiracy may never be determined, but the murder of Oswald by Mafia "button" Jack Ruby demonstrated in the most graphic terms a Mafia hand in the assassination. G. Robert Blakey, onetime federal prosecutor and chief counsel to the House Assassinations Committee, reached that conclusion in 1978 based largely on an examination of the threats uttered by Marcello and Trafficante and on Ruby's activities, but also on investigation into every aspect of the case. "I am now firmly of the opinion that the mob did it," Blakey declared. "It is a historical truth."

Indeed, Kennedy's death gave the mob what it wanted: the immobilization of his gangbusting brother. Robert Kennedy received the news of his brother's murder while conducting a two-day "roundup" with his department's Organized Crime and Racketeering section. As one staff attorney recalled, Kennedy immediately adjourned the session. "He never met the section again, and we had been meeting regularly for two-and-a-half years."

The failure of the Warren Commission to find Mafia links to the assassination was, in part, a measure of its commitment to its mission. Thus the commission could report that "the evidence does not establish a significant link between Ruby and organized crime." But the problem went farther than the initial directive from the White House. The commission relied largely on the FBI and the CIA for investigative material, and each agency had something to hide.

J. Edgar Hoover was notorious for his fear of exposing his agency to public ridicule, and in its handling of the Kennedy assassination the Bureau had, by Hoover's own estimation, failed miserably. FBI field agents had repeated contacts with both Ruby and Oswald over the years, and had direct knowledge of Jack Kennedy's dangerous associations with mob hangers-on Judy Campbell and Frank Sinatra, all of which might have placed the Bureau in a position to anticipate an attempt on Kennedy's life. Within weeks of the assassination, Hoover disciplined seventeen FBI personnel for "deficiencies" in connection with the case, but he hid these "internal" matters from the Warren Commission. Moreover, Hoover himself was aware of the CIA collaboration with the mob in Miami, but he kept that secret as well, and worked vigorously to steer the panel away from any presumption of conspiracy, especially one involving organized crime.

The CIA found itself in a similarly embarrassing position. As a one-time defector who had lived in the Soviet Union, Oswald should have come to CIA attention sooner. Later, the CIA had tailed Oswald during his trip to Mexico City in September 1963. And like the FBI, the CIA was quite aware of the Castro plots and Kennedy's liaison with Judy Campbell. But much of this material, especially the Castro plots, was adroitly withheld from the Warren Commission by one of its own members, former Director of Central Intelligence Allen Dulles. The commission was effectively blindered, leaving the complex task of sorting through Ruby's mob connections, and Oswald's possible intelligence background, to congressional investigators a decade later.

★

The Mafia hand in the murder of the President brought the Kennedy story full circle. The image that Jack Kennedy projected epitomized what the American public wanted to believe of itself. But the Kennedy persona was more than the image. It encompassed the full scope of the American post-war ethic, the hunger for power as well as its dexterous manipulation, the connection to the mob as well as to the chic elite of the arts and entertainment. Once arrived in power, Kennedy sought to sever the façade from its roots, but the ties were too strong.

For the American public, the assassination came as a debilitating shock, the beginning of the end of the moral certitude that characterized its post-war outlook. The decade that followed would be marked by confusion and unceasing change, which would make the patriotic posturing of the late 1950s seem naïve and a little absurd. But for John Rosselli, the effect was the opposite. The death of the President only served to reinforce the rigid system of beliefs that had served to guide Rosselli's life. *Onore* was more than a moral code, it was a description of how the world worked. Loyalty and honor were the measure of the man, and to fall short, as Kennedy had, was to open oneself to the terrible hazards of betrayal. In Rosselli's world, people died the way they lived, and Jack Kennedy was no different.

The Tangled Web

BY THE MIDDLE 1960s, John Rosselli had emerged as the Mafia's most effective and most trustworthy covert operator. He was instrumental in building the hidden network of mob interests in the Las Vegas casinos, which remained the primary source of cash in the underworld. And he had deftly handled the delicate position of double-agent in Miami, promoting mob interests while befriending top-level government spies and coordinating contacts with the volatile Cuban exiles. Rosselli was therefore a natural candidate for the mob's next crucial assignment—the continuing cover-up of Kennedy's murder.

Combining the skills of a diplomat and spy, Rosselli came to serve as director of intelligence for the mob. It was the most difficult work he had ever undertaken, and the least rewarding. Like his counterparts in the intelligence community, he was cut off from close friends, and had to trust in dangerous strangers. He had to forfeit the financial rewards of Las Vegas and the Caribbean, and to suffer opprobrium in silence. Yet he gave himself over to his assignment with the single-minded dedication that had become his hallmark. It came to dominate Rosselli's final years, and in the end, cost him his life.

Rosselli revealed the nature of his task four years after the events in Dallas, when he made the startling claim that he had inside knowledge of the assassination. Over the following decade he juggled his knowledge of the assassination with his other great secret, the CIA-Mafia plots, paying out snippets of information to attorneys, to federal investigators, and to journalist Jack Anderson. Yet there was never any sense of confession. Rosselli's revelations were always incremental, and always for a purpose.

Some observers have dismissed Rosselli's claim to knowledge of the Kennedy assassination as simple bravado. But a close examination of the record places Rosselli in the nexus of the tangled web of events leading up to Kennedy's assassination.

The strongest indication that John Rosselli had a hand in the pre-assassination planning is a report of a direct contact between Rosselli and Jack Ruby in early October 1963. There were two meetings, both taking place in small motels near Miami, and both observed by the FBI. One of the federal investigators probing Rosselli's murder thirteen years later came across an FBI report on the meetings and relayed its contents, on a confidential basis, to Washington, D.C., reporter William Scott Malone. An accomplished investigator himself, Malone said in an interview he was confident of the integrity of his source, and said the FBI had determined the actual site of the Miami meetings.

Equally important, Malone's report of direct contact between Rosselli and Ruby fits the circumstances. Beginning in May 1963, Jack Ruby made a series of extraordinary telephone calls and plane flights around the nation that researchers believe lay the groundwork for his role in the plot against the President. Almost all of Ruby's correspondents were individuals involved in the national crime syndicate, and several were people who worked closely with John Rosselli in his capacities as arbiter of mob interests in Las Vegas, and in the effort against Fidel Castro.

Ruby's most frequent contact during this period was Lewis J. McWillie, a prominent Dallas gambling figure who managed Meyer Lansky's Tropicana Hotel in Havana from 1958 to early 1960, and then worked briefly for Santo Trafficante at the Capri. Ruby visited McWillie in Cuba in 1959, and shipped four Cobra handguns to him around the same time.

Ruby said he "idolized" McWillie, a man his own age who dressed like a banker in dark suits that set off his gray hair, but whose reputation as a killer made him an asset in any mob gaming room. Forced out of Cuba in

January 1961, he made his way to Nevada, landing positions at Sam Giancana's Cal-Neva Lodge before finally hooking up with the Thunderbird Hotel in Las Vegas, a relatively small casino controlled by Meyer Lansky. McWillie denied knowing Rosselli when queried by congressional staff in 1976, but that seems unlikely—at every stop after leaving Dallas, McWillie was working Rosselli's turf. Moreover, anti-Castro activist Gerry Hemming named McWillie as one of the underworld gambling contacts Rosselli used in the early plots against Fidel Castro.

On May 10, 1963, Ruby shipped to McWillie in Las Vegas a .38-caliber Smith and Wesson revolver, which McWillie later said he had asked for, but which he never picked up from the post office; a second gun, mailed later, reached its destination. Thereafter, Ruby made "at least ten" calls to McWillie, often just before or just after contacting mob figures in New York, Chicago, and New Orleans.

Another telling communication was a twelve-minute phone call Ruby made on October 26 to Irwin Weiner, a Chicago insurance and investments consultant who served as a close advisor to Jimmy Hoffa. As head of the Chicago office of an Ohio insurance firm, Weiner underwrote half the bonds issued by Teamsters pension funds, and in 1973, the FBI learned that "Weiner was handling all the skimmed money from Las Vegas for Chicago's organized crime community." In 1964, the Chicago *Daily News* termed Weiner, simply, "the mob's favored front man."

The Chicago connection places Weiner close to Rosselli, and his role in handling the Las Vegas skim clinches the matter—Rosselli had to know Weiner, and could easily have been privy to whatever plans were being laid. Also, like McWillie, Ruby, and Rosselli, Weiner had a stake in pre-Castro Havana, holding shares in the Deauville Casino and the Capri. When describing his lost Cuban interests to a friend in 1962, Weiner broke down in tears. A ranking Chicago gangster concerned about his holdings in Havana might have been expected to keep tabs on them through Rosselli.

Subpoenaed before the Warren Commission, Weiner refused to discuss Ruby's phone call, and said he could not recall his whereabouts at the time of the Kennedy assassination. But he did remember making a trip to Miami at about that time, where he conferred with Santo Trafficante.

Also in the fall of 1963, Ruby made a number of phone calls to the West Coast. Twice, following a call to McWillie in Las Vegas, Ruby spoke with William Miller, a Los Angeles booking agent and casino investor who had long toiled in Rosselli's shadow. A friend of McWillie's who once worked as entertainment director at the Sahara Hotel in Las Vegas, Miller was later implicated in helping siphon $1.7 million from a Teamsters pension fund.

Ruby's final mob contact was also a West Coast figure, a small-time felon named Alexander Gruber, who ran a card room in Los Angeles. Gruber's associates included mob contacts and Los Angeles Teamsters officials, and he had once roomed with Ruby in Chicago. Gruber called Ruby November 17, and the following week, drove cross-country to meet with Ruby in Dallas. In 1978, pressed to explain that journey, Gruber contradicted an earlier account, and then shrugged. "I don't know why I went there really." He gave an equally vague explanation for the last word he received from Ruby, a three-minute phone call two hours after the Kennedy assassination.

Another account of a Ruby-Rosselli connection alleges that Ruby met with Rosselli during a trip he made to Las Vegas November 17. That seems impossible, as the FBI reported Rosselli in Phoenix from November 16 to 19. The fact remains, however, that Ruby's contacts throughout the summer and fall of 1963, with Rosselli's associates and with Rosselli himself, placed him at the center of what appears an evolving conspiracy. John Rosselli's primary business at that stage in his life was to know exactly what was going on around him. For Rosselli to remain unwitting of Ruby's escalating pattern of activity seems highly improbable.

John Rosselli's circumstantial ties to the Kennedy assassination extended beyond his various connections to Jack Ruby. He worked closely with Santo Trafficante, who made the firm prediction of Kennedy's impending death to Jose Aleman. And Rosselli's collaboration with the Cuban exiles placed him in close proximity to some of Oswald's associates in New Orleans, including ex-FBI agent Guy Banister.

A fervent right-winger who retired from the Bureau in 1957, Banister opened a private detective agency at 544 Camp Street, where he helped organize the Cuban Revolutionary Democratic Front and the Friends of a Democratic Cuba. When Anthony de Varona's Cuban Revolutionary Council (CRC) opened a chapter in New Orleans, it was located in the same building. And when Lee Harvey Oswald began his questionable pro-Castro agitation in the summer of 1963, he signed on with Banister as an "agent."

The apparent thread, from Rosselli to de Varona to the CRC to Banister, is buttressed by Banister's personal secretary, Delphine Roberts. In 1978, Roberts told author Anthony Summers that Rosselli visited the offices at 544 Camp Street. Rosselli's early work with Standard Fruit in Guatemala may have yielded another connection to anti-Castro activists in New Orleans—the Information Council on the Americas, which was staffed by several Standard Fruit employees, was instrumental in "exposing" Oswald as a closet communist on a local television broadcast.

There are even accounts that place Rosselli at the scene of the assassination. Jimmy Starr, the Hollywood gossip columnist and a friend of Rosselli's, raised the prospect in passing during an interview with one of the authors. "What I heard about the Kennedy assassination was that Johnny was the guy who got the team together to do the hit." Starr said the scenario was "fairly well-known" in the underworld, but was reluctant to go into detail. "I don't remember where I got that—I think it was from a couple of mob guys back East. I wasn't back there, so I had no reason to follow it up."

A similar but more detailed version was put forward by Robert L. Russell, a convicted felon who detailed his allegations in *pro per* filings in federal court. Russell's story rambles over thirty-seven pages and seems to draw heavily on the volumes of available assassination research. But what seems to be the crux of his discourse is a chance meeting with a woman named "Cindy," not further identified, who said she worked for Jack Ruby and had assisted in the Kennedy shooting.

"Cindy" told Russell that the day of the assassination, she had driven John Rosselli and a second man, a sharpshooter from Miami, to the grassy knoll at the far end of Dealey Plaza. When the President's motorcade approached, the sniper fired two shots, handed his rifle to Rosselli, and walked down the slope to lose himself in the crowd. Cindy then drove Rosselli and the rifle away from the scene. It seems auspicious that Russell would place Rosselli in Dallas on November 22; the FBI surveillance of Rosselli loses his trail on the West Coast between November 19 and November 27.

These reports are fragmentary and inconclusive, falling short of any standard of proof that John Rosselli played a part in the Kennedy assassination. But taken together, they lend weight to Rosselli's later contention that he knew what had happened in Dallas. Together with his direct experience in the CIA plots against Castro, Rosselli held the key to secrets that would haunt the nation, guilty knowledge that would betray America's faith in itself.

12

KEEPING THE FAITH

Life in the Clear

There was one final detail in the immediate aftermath of the assassination that John Rosselli attended to personally. While the nation commiserated with the public grief of the Kennedy clan, John Rosselli was coping with the private suffering of the late President's secret lover.

Perhaps anticipating the events to come, Rosselli had installed Judy Campbell in a suite of rooms at the Beverly Crest Hotel in Los Angeles two days before the assassination, and called her repeatedly in the immediate aftermath. She refused to answer her phone, and after five days had passed, Rosselli showed up in person, persuading the management to open the locked door to her room.

Rosselli found Campbell gaunt and disheveled, having passed the week in a stupor of sleep, alcohol, and grief. The persistent harassment of the FBI agents who tailed her and the end of her relationship with Kennedy had driven her to the point of breakdown, and the horror of his murder left her distraught. Campbell asked Rosselli to leave but he refused, and gently, patiently, he persuaded her to join him for dinner. It was her first meal in a week.

The next day Rosselli drove Campbell to Palm Springs, where they were joined by Dorothy Towne, an interior designer and a girl friend of Rosselli's. They spent a week in the pale winter sun, Rosselli and Towne watching attentively as Campbell regained some degree of equilibrium. At dinner one night they encountered her erstwhile lover, Frank Sinatra, but he ignored her. She was cut off from her past, with only Rosselli to keep her grounded.

On December 6, Rosselli drove Campbell back to Los Angeles, and toward the end of the month he returned, taking her with him to Las Vegas for New Year's Eve, where they passed the holiday at the Desert Inn with hotel president Moe Dalitz. Rosselli's attentions were therapeutic for Campbell, but they may have been for Rosselli as well, helping to close a discordant chapter on a note of relative harmony.

★

The assassination of John F. Kennedy brought a hiatus in the frantic pace John Rosselli had maintained since his assignment to Las Vegas in 1957. The schemes against Castro were finished, and Robert Kennedy's withering drive against organized crime was quietly folded up. Returning to the familiar cityscape of Los Angeles and Beverly Hills, Rosselli adopted a life of pattern and routine, indulging in the comforts of semiretirement.

At the urging of Dorothy Towne, Rosselli moved in March 1964 from his poolside apartment on Crescent Heights to a spacious suite of rooms on the eighth floor of Glen Towers on Beverly Glen Boulevard in West Los Angeles, which advertised "some of the most beautiful and luxurious apartments in the nation." His oversized living-room windows overlooked the UCLA campus, and to the east, the cool green fairways of the exclusive Los Angeles Country Club. Rosselli's new residence placed him within a short stroll of the home of his close friend and attorney, Jimmy Cantillon, and down Wilshire Boulevard, the business district of Beverly Hills.

Rosselli became a regular patron of the Friars Club, an exclusive, men-only social club in Beverly Hills, where the doorman spoke Italian and treated him with deference. The Friars Club drew its glamour from the Hollywood–Las Vegas entertainment axis that Rosselli had helped create —its roster included Frank Sinatra and Dean Martin, who had sponsored

Rosselli for membership, and Las Vegas regulars Milton Berle and George Burns. Rosselli made the club a second home, spending languorous hours in the sauna, letting the heat ease the ache of his chronic arthritis, and chatting with the film personalities and business executives, mostly Jewish, who played illegal, high-stakes gin games behind locked doors on the third floor of the club's windowless, mustard-yellow building.

In the evenings, he frequented elegant, expensive restaurants, places where the chefs knew him and the maître d's greeted him as an old friend. Chasen's was a regular stop, and Perino's. La Dolce Vita became an immediate favorite when it opened in 1966 across the street from the Friars Club. Rosselli had earned owner Jimmy Ullo's lasting affection two years prior when Ullo was a waiter at another popular Italian restaurant. Rosselli had entered one night to find the waiter drunk and, inquiring of the staff, learned that Ullo was celebrating the birth of a son. Later that night, as Ullo was leaving, Rosselli thrust a $100 bill in his hand, and muttered in gruff humor, "Buy the kid a silver cup."

When Ullo opened his own place, with brick walls, leather booths, and subdued lantern lighting, he adopted the practice of engraving the names of his more famous customers on brass plaques and hanging them above their regular booths. Frank Sinatra was one, and George Raft—and John Rosselli, the celebrity's celebrity. Rosselli would arrive from the Friars Club around 6:30 or 7 P.M. and head directly into the kitchen, where Ullo kept for him a special stock of extra-virgin olive oil and skinned, seeded tomatoes.

Rosselli usually headed home soon after dinner, leading the FBI men who maintained a twenty-four-hour surveillance to speculate that he was lonely. But he never lacked for companionship. Rosselli kept up with a small group of close friends, including Maury Friedman, an obese but shrewd businessman with substantial interest in the Frontier Hotel and other Las Vegas properties. He renewed his friendship with Bryan Foy and Allen Smiley from his Hollywood days. And he maintained a special relationship with Robert Maheu, who despite his indiscretions in the Balletti wiretap case, had become a very important man to know.

As right-hand man to Howard Hughes, Maheu handled virtually all of the billionaire's personal and political affairs, making him one of the most powerful men in the nation. Maheu in turn relished his relationship with a top mafioso, and when faced with a heavy tax liability in 1964, intimated to a business partner that he could turn to Rosselli for a quick infusion of cash. Rosselli often dropped by Maheu's business offices in Westwood, and built a relationship with his family. He spent the Christmas holiday with Maheu in 1964.

Women were also important to Rosselli's social makeup, but he kept them at a distance, preserving his reputation as a ladies' man by escorting a succession of beautiful young women. For intimacy he enjoyed the occasional affections of several long-term lovers—a figure skater in Los Angeles, a newspaper publisher from the Midwest who wintered in Palm Springs, a daughter of an old friend in Washington, D.C.—and thereby avoided the compromises of a full-time mate.

His independence was threatened once by Judy Campbell, still reeling from the collapse of her personal life, the continuing harassment by the FBI, and the terror that Jack Kennedy's killers would come for her next. Campbell became pregnant in late 1964, and announced to Rosselli that the child was his. That was too close for Rosselli—he turned her away, and Campbell finally put the baby, a boy, up for adoption. Still, Rosselli was never harsh with her, and he remained a mainstay in her life for years afterward.

Rosselli and Campbell were seeing each other as late as 1968, when the two entertained Rosselli's half-sister Mona Cardillo at the La Costa Country Club in San Diego. Once during their stay, when Rosselli was busy elsewhere, the two women took Cardillo's children for a visit to Disneyland. Cardillo said later that Campbell took the opportunity to express her lasting "love and admiration" for Rosselli.

Rosselli was coming to terms with society, and with himself, in the insulated, cloistered world he created. He traded in his dark suits for more relaxed, more colorful Palm Springs fashions. He donated to charities sponsored by the Friars Club. And, perhaps as an act of atonement, he entered into negotiations to make a religious film, based on the life of a Bishop James Healy, America's first black bishop, who presided over the diocese of Portland, Maine, from 1875 to 1900. Rosselli secured $300,000 in financing, and proposed the project to friends in the Catholic Church. The film was never made, but Rosselli's interest in religious subjects was genuine. Years earlier, he had purchased from Joe Breen, Jr. the rights to the story of a nun who lived a pioneer's life in the American Southwest. He tried but failed to drum up studio interest in the project.

Rosselli was frustrated by the fact that he could not escape the gangster tag that had dogged him since the Bioff-Browne conviction—when the 1963 book *Green Felt Jungle* portrayed him as the Mafia don of Las Vegas, he raged against the authors. But he had learned to live with the

John Rosselli in his
prime. (WIDE WORLD PHOTOS.)

Booked for grand larceny,
concealed weapon, 1925.
(COURTESY USC SPECIAL
COLLECTIONS.)

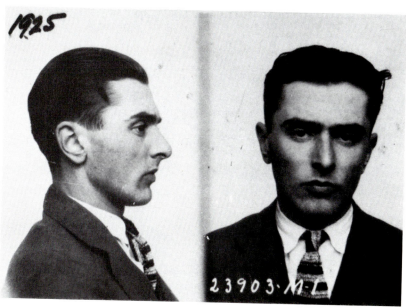

1925

23903·M·L

Maria Antoinette DiPascuale
Sacco. (COURTESY DAVID NISSEN.)

Vincenzo Sacco.
(COURTESY DAVID NISSEN.)

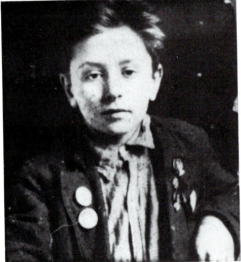

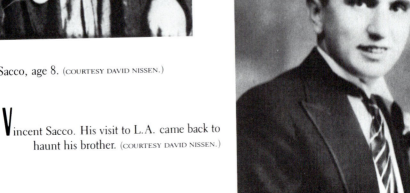

Filippo Sacco, age 8. (COURTESY DAVID NISSEN.)

Vincent Sacco. His visit to L.A. came back to
haunt his brother. (COURTESY DAVID NISSEN.)

Tony Cornero (*right*) and friend on deck.

Crowds await transport to gambling ships.

Jack Dragna (*left*), "The Al Capone of Los Angeles," shares a laugh with Jimmy Cantillon.

Willie Bioff. Before…
(WIDE WORLD PHOTOS.)

…and after his murder in
Phoenix. (WIDE WORLD PHOTOS.)

Sam Giancana.

Paul "The Waiter" Ricca (*left*) and Louis "Little New York" Campagna.

Ann Corcoran. (COURTESY ACADEMY OF
MOTION PICTURE ARTS AND SCIENCES.)

June Lang. (COURTESY ACADEMY OF MOTION
PICTURE ARTS AND SCIENCES.)

Judy Campbell in 1960.
(WIDE WORLD PHOTOS.)

Bob Maheu on the Strip. (WIDE WORLD PHOTOS.)

Santo Trafficante, Jr.
(WIDE WORLD PHOTOS.)

The Silver Fox.
(WIDE WORLD PHOTOS.)

Busted, 1966. (COURTESY DAVID NISSEN.)

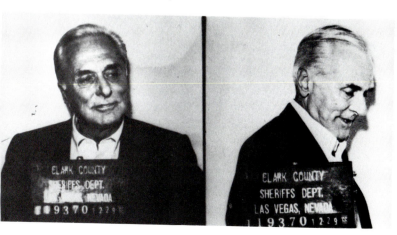

JFK awards Richard Bissell, Jr., the Medal of Freedom, 1962. (WIDE WORLD PHOTOS.)

New Orleans District Attorney Jim Garrison. (WIDE WORLD PHOTOS).

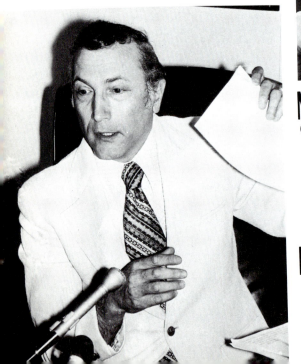

Richard Schweiker: "I have to believe Rosselli's hidden agenda had something to do with his killing." (WIDE WORLD PHOTOS.)

indignity of his reputation, and even to find humor in his lifelong secret identity.

On a trip to Chicago in 1963, Rosselli spent the noon hour downing rounds of martinis with Sam Giancana and Judy Campbell, and that afternoon an aimless drive brought them to the Queen of Heaven Cemetery. As Campbell recalled it in her book:

> Johnny and Sam started running around looking for the name Rosselli on tombstones. Every time they saw one Johnny would say, "Ah, I remember him well," and go into a long story about this uncle or that aunt, or niece or nephew, and it was a riot to see them having so much fun. "Ah, poor uncle Giuseppe," Johnny said, waving his hand toward a large tombstone. "Died of lead poisoning. What a prince among men he was, my Uncle Giuseppe. Very rich, big man in olive oil and machine guns, wanted to put me through college, embalming college, but I preferred the other end of the business." That had them both going hysterical. I had no idea Johnny's real name was Filippo Sacco.

Even with strangers, Rosselli was not so secretive as he had been in the past. When he was introduced to a friend of Jimmy Cantillon's, a Hollywood talent agent who soon became a regular golf partner, the man asked Rosselli where he had gone to college. "Atlanta," Rosselli replied. "But the only thing there is a federal prison," his new acquaintance observed. Rosselli lifted his eyebrows in answer.

The talent agent had retained Cantillon in an effort to obtain visiting rights to his two children, who were living with his estranged wife in Grand Rapids, Michigan. Soon after they met, Rosselli asked his new friend how the case was going. Worse than he expected, the man explained. His ex-wife wouldn't allow the children to meet with their grandparents, after nine years of separation. Rosselli seized on the problem, eager, perhaps, to show a positive aspect to his powers. "Where is she," Rosselli demanded. "There's nothing you can do, John," his friend said. Rosselli insisted, and the talent agent gave his wife's name and address.

A week later, he received a call from his wife, their first communication since their divorce. If his parents wanted to visit their grandchildren, that was all right. When could they make the trip to Michigan? The talent agent was dumbfounded, and sought Rosselli out to thank him. "He just smiled and said, 'Remember, if you ever have a problem, whatever it is, just ask.'"

Like most men approaching their sixtieth year, John Rosselli was slowing down. If he wasn't at the Friars Club, he liked to spend afternoons playing golf, usually on public courses around Los Angeles where his police record wouldn't embarrass his friends. Or he would laze around his apartment, watching westerns on television. He had long conversations with Father Joe Clark, a good friend and confidant.

But if Rosselli was finding more time for himself, if he was pausing, even, for introspection, it was not a process of reappraisal. He never closed out the criminal side of his life. Rehabilitation was never a serious option. The mob didn't work that way—membership in the secret society was a lifetime affair. If he was no longer the CEO in charge of the primary enterprises of the national syndicate, he remained a consultant, a level-headed veteran who could draw on forty years of hard-won experience. Older and wiser, he had learned to sit back and let the action come to him.

Part-Time Crime

JOHN ROSSELLI'S NEW STYLE found expression in his friendship with Maury Friedman. Bulbous and oafish, socially awkward but enormously rich for his forty-five years, Friedman fawned over Rosselli, whose power seemed to derive from sheer personal charisma. Friedman had arranged an introduction to Rosselli in the 1950s through Beverly Hills barber Harry Drucker, whose high-line shop both men frequented. Drucker obliged him, but warned Rosselli that Friedman would try to "screw him." Rosselli figured he could manage it, and besides, Friedman was a casino owner and operator in Las Vegas. He might come in handy.

Friedman took the lead in the relationship, picking up all the tabs when the pair went out for drinks or dinner, and looking for chances to ingratiate himself with his new Mafia pal. Such an opportunity presented itself at the Friars Club, where Friedman was a regular in the gin games on the third floor.

Rosselli rarely played cards himself, but he enjoyed the banter at the illegal games, and he frequently dropped in on the afternoon sessions. The crowd had a distinct Hollywood tinge: the players included comedians Phil Silvers and Zeppo Marx, singer Tony Martin, theatrical agent Kurt Frings, and Harry Karl, a shoe-store tycoon and husband of Debbie Reynolds. All were successful men with high social standing, and all relished the atmosphere of greed and ego that they found at the felt card tables.

Along with the Hollywood set, the Friars had enrolled several of the leading gamblers on the West Coast, presumably to jack up the tension on the heavily carpeted third floor. These men were better known to Rosselli than to his fellow Friars—hustlers like Manuel "Ricky" Jacobs, a gambler with a gift for numbers who owned a Santa Monica card club; Albert "Slick" Snyder, a veteran of Mickey Cohen's gambling rackets whose rap sheet tallied more than fifty arrests; and T. W. Richardson, who had bailed Balletti out in Las Vegas. The most colorful of the crew was Al Mathes, a onetime bookmaker under Jack Dragna who liked to drive a gleaming white Rolls-Royce. Mathes was partners with Lana Turner's ex-husband Steve Crane in several swank Los Angeles restaurants; to name one, they made an acronym of their names and came up with the appropriate sobriquet SCAM. The presence of the gamblers on the membership list cast the Friars Club in a shady hue, one that founding "abbot" George Jessel did nothing to dispel. That was the edge that set the Friars apart.

The games were always termed "friendly," the pots occasionally running into the thousands of dollars. But beginning in 1962, Friedman increased the stakes dramatically, taking on all comers in a series of marathon games, often twelve hours at a stretch and some running all night. As the games accelerated, the other Friars would fold up their hands and gather at a discreet distance to watch the losses and the tension mount. Occasionally Friedman would take on a partner, Mathes or Jacobs or Snyder, or they would pair off for four-handed games, but almost always, Friedman's side of the table won.

The losses were staggering, but the pigeons, as the card sharps called them, kept coming back for more. They couldn't believe their lousy "luck," and their egos wouldn't let them leave the table. Over the course of an evening, more than $40,000 might change hands. Over the next five years, Harry Karl alone lost hundreds of thousands of dollars, wiping him out financially and destroying his personal life. Once he paid off his losses in a single $10,000 bill, another time, from a shopping bag full of fives and tens.

Rumors began to circulate that the games were rigged, that Friedman and his associates were cheating. Rosselli went to the source, and with a schoolboy's enthusiasm, Friedman described a scheme more intricate than even his pigeons might imagine. Peepholes had been drilled in the ceiling of the Friars Club, and a man posted in the rafters was reading the cards of the well-heeled Friars. Signals were conveyed to the hustlers via a tiny radio transmitter strapped to the card cheat's midsection. If the game involved two-man teams, the hustler with the receiver would relay information through an elaborate voice code. A word or phrase beginning with the letter A meant to hold kings, B meant queens, C, jacks, and so on. They couldn't lose.

Rosselli's response was characteristic. He wanted nothing to do with the cheating; in fact, he agreed to stay away from the tables to allay suspicion. But he expected a full share of the winnings. After all, the card cheating was taking place on his turf. Soon thereafter, Friedman informed his conspirators that they had a new partner.

Rosselli's partnership in the Friars Club scam soon translated into outside endeavors as well. When he learned that Ricky Jacobs, aside from his aptitude for cards, liked to deal in stolen and counterfeit securities, Rosselli quietly began assisting him, providing him with contraband paper and with Mafia contacts in Miami and elsewhere that could supply him more. At the same time, Rosselli helped him develop outlets in Europe and Latin America where Jacobs could get top dollar for his wares. All Rosselli asked was a piece of the action.

Maury Friedman capitalized on his friendship with Rosselli in early 1964, when he asked him to help find investors for a new Las Vegas casino, tentatively named the International. The object wasn't money so much as power—Mafia backing would give Friedman an edge over the other potential investors, with first draw on the legitimate casino earnings and, presumably, a piece of the skim. It was the sort of deal Rosselli thrived on, allowing him to cement his position as the arbiter of mob interests in Nevada on the strength of a few phone calls.

Rosselli quickly swung into gear, arranging a March 10 meeting in Palm Springs between Friedman and two leaders of the Detroit Mafia, Anthony Joseph Zerilli and Michael Santo Polizzi, who had missed the early rounds of mob investment in Las Vegas and were hungry to get in on the action. Rosselli vouched for Friedman, and the Detroit gangsters agreed to foot roughly half the bill for construction of the new property.

Rosselli's next move was to contact Teamsters president Jimmy Hoffa, whose interest was similar to that of the Detroit gangsters. The Teamsters had invested heavily in Las Vegas, but always as second or third party in interest, either refinancing existing hotels or financing their expansion. With the International Hotel, Hoffa and the Teamsters, for once, would have a ground-floor position.

The details were worked out at a meeting in Chicago on April 12: Zerilli and Polizzi represented Detroit, Hoffa spoke for the union, and Friedman and Rosselli presented the project. The makeup of the meeting was remarkable, but the timing was moreso, a testament to the Teamsters president's singular arrogance. One month prior, Hoffa had been sentenced to eight years in prison on charges of jury tampering in Tennessee. A second trial, this time for defrauding the Central States Pension Fund of more than $20 million, was slated to begin two weeks later. Cocksure that he could beat both cases, Hoffa agreed to put $6 million into the International. But the deal collapsed three months later, when Hoffa's legal problems finally drove him to cover.

Undaunted, Friedman continued to court the leaders of the Detroit Mafia, using Rosselli as his conduit. He offered Zerilli and Polizzi a $500,000 stake in the Silver Slipper casino, but they declined "because the deal was not big enough." He then proposed another new venture, the Frontier, with construction costs projected at $20 million. This time they jumped, even attempting to get their own names listed on the casino gambling license. They were turned down by the Nevada Gaming Control Board in March 1966, but invested anyway, their interests secured by Friedman, fellow Friars Club conspirator T. W. Richardson, and several others. Rosselli also induced Anthony Giardano, the Mafia boss in St. Louis, to join as a hidden investor.

There was one small catch, when at a second licensing hearing in June 1967, the members of the state gaming board queried Friedman on his relationship with Rosselli. Friedman answered carefully: "Well, he's considered in this community with the law enforcement agencies I'd say as a persona non grata, having been convicted of a felony in the past. . . . In California, I don't think it applies because he travels in the highest of social circles with the highest people in all walks of life." Friedman didn't renounce Rosselli, conceding that "I think I'd be hypocritical if I said if I got a license I'll never talk to the man again," but denied any business association. That was enough for the board, and the Frontier was certified to open.

★

As he did with Friedman in Las Vegas, Rosselli remained active in the affairs of the Chicago mob, but only on a limited basis, as an advisor to Sam Giancana, who in the middle sixties was struggling to keep his position as leader of the national crime syndicate. Within the Chicago Outfit itself, Giancana faced constant agitation from ambitious hoodlums looking to move up, and weakening support from the old leadership clique of Accardo, Humphreys, and Ricca, who felt that Giancana's well-publicized affair with Phyllis McGuire had left him with too high a public profile. At the national level, Giancana was feuding with Brooklyn don Joe Bonanno, who had staked out territory in Arizona and was pressing for access to Las Vegas.

Moreover, despite his legal victory over the FBI surveillance teams, the government campaign against Giancana was taking its toll. Bobby Kennedy's fierce personal interest in the organized-crime drive had waned, but the machinery he had put in place remained in motion, Giancana remained at the top of the target list.

Desperate for information on the plans and tactics of his ubiquitous enemies, Giancana called on Rosselli, who in turn enlisted the services of Joe Shimon, the Washington detective who had served Bob Maheu as a wiretap expert. Together, Shimon and Rosselli established what amounted to a private intelligence service, with Shimon providing the latest electronic technology—the microphones and wiretap equipment then in use by the FBI and CIA—and Rosselli naming targets and analyzing the results.

In one instance, hoping to learn of a possible mutiny among his lieutenants, Giancana had microphones installed in his own headquarters, the Armory Lounge, a bar and steak house located in Forest Park, a suburb west of Chicago. The Armory had been wired previously by the FBI, and with the two sets of microphones operating on different radio frequencies, both systems were reduced to scratchy static.

Rosselli and Shimon made frequent trips to Chicago, flying in from their respective homes on opposite sides of the country, registering under false names in a nondescript motel, and meeting with Giancana to evaluate the results of their electronic eavesdropping. "I would get a call, and Johnny would say Sam wants to see us," Shimon recalled in an interview. "They [Giancana and Rosselli] might be interested in how the cops were thinking. They might be interested in court procedures. Maybe they'd want to check on someone.

"Johnny was the strategist," Shimon continued. "That was on his [business] card, and that's what he was. Strategy. Protection. Security. How to stay alive. There were a lot of things to deal with. Because remember, if the mob is going to hit you, they're going to do it through your family, or somebody very close to you. So Sam had a lot to think about."

Giancana's "intelligence" team may have helped him see it coming, but there was little he could do to block U.S. Attorney Edward Hanrahan in June 1965, when he subpoenaed more than fifty witnesses before a federal grand jury in an all-out attack on Giancana. After laying an extensive foundation, Giancana himself was ordered to testify under a grant of immunity, which effectively stripped him of the protections of the Fifth Amendment. His attorney, Ed Bennett Williams's associate Tom Wadden, advised him to cooperate, but Giancana realized that he would inevitably perjure himself. When the hearing opened, he gave his name and address, but then invoked the Fifth. He was taken directly to jail.

The implications for Rosselli of Giancana's imprisonment were dramatic and immediate. His stature in the Chicago mob was rendered ambiguous, as his standing was linked directly to Giancana's. By the same token, his footing in Las Vegas was now unsure. Equally unsettling was the fact of the government's sudden success in wounding the nation's most powerful gangster. If they could score on the boss of the Chicago Outfit, his top lieutenants would be vulnerable as well.

The Cops Catch Up

LIKE A LOT OF the Italian gangsters, Salvatore Piscopo had a knack for making money, but had trouble managing it once it came in. A longtime mafioso with a fat bankroll, Piscopo spent every day of the racing season at Hollywood Park and Santa Anita, plying the lucrative trade of layoff bets, picking up the heavy wagers that the retail bookmakers couldn't handle. The profits were steady, but Piscopo never once filed an income tax return, making him a perfect candidate for discrete assistance by the FBI.

Racetrack security staff caught wind of Piscopo's financial vulnerability in late 1963 and relayed it to Clarence Newton, a bull-necked, crew-cut

FBI agent. Newton sensed immediately that Piscopo could be a valuable asset—operating under the alias Louie Merli, nicknamed "Dago Louie," Piscopo's underworld activities dated back to the middle 1930s, when he was a slugger in Jack Dragna's crime family. Only later did Newton realize the degree of his good fortune—that Piscopo would lead him directly to John Rosselli, the top hoodlum on J. Edgar Hoover's West Coast hit list.

Newton took a cautious approach, helping Piscopo square his accounts with the IRS and letting him know he could reciprocate with information on the Los Angeles Mafia. Piscopo was amenable. *Omerta* barred any contacts with law enforcement, but he figured he could gain a lot of protection by parceling out a little harmless information. Within weeks, Newton and Piscopo were meeting on a regular basis in a "safe" apartment in Westwood. In addition, unbeknownst to Piscopo, Newton had his new friend placed under surveillance.

In December 1963, Newton caught Piscopo in a lie. He said he would be spending the day at Hollywood Park but instead went to the airport, where he met a man carrying an overnight bag, embraced him like a brother, and drove him back to his apartment. FBI agents photographed the meeting, traced the traveler's plane ticket, and determined him to be a janitor who lived with his mother and sister in a Boston suburb, a man with no criminal record, named Albert Sacco.

The next morning at the safe house, Newton confronted Piscopo with the photograph and Sacco's background, and demanded an explanation. Piscopo turned pale, was silent for a moment, and then the whole story came tumbling out. Albert Sacco was the brother of John Rosselli.

For at least the past twenty-five years, Piscopo had served as Rosselli's personal courier. Once a year and sometimes more often, at Rosselli's instruction, Piscopo would fly to Boston with a package of cash to deliver to Rosselli's mother, Maria Sacco. Piscopo had befriended the Sacco family, and that year, Al Sacco had suggested a switch in the routine. He'd never seen Los Angeles, it was cold in Boston; why couldn't he fly West this time?

There was more. Piscopo had known Rosselli more than thirty years, and knew his entire story. He knew about the immigration from Italy. The narcotics arrest in Boston. The apprenticeship to Capone.

Clarence Newton was stunned. By the slightest coincidence, his surveillance of a mid-level informant had turned into the biggest case of his career. Once again, he moved carefully. He realized that Piscopo was in serious danger, and cut back his contacts to a minimum. J. Edgar Hoover was notified, and he ordered the Boston office to assemble a dossier on Filippo Sacco. Agents-in-charge were notified in Las Vegas, Chicago, and New York, but warned to take no action unless directed. The entire matter was classified top secret.

Law enforcement officials had long suspected that Rosselli was not who he claimed to be. The Immigration and Naturalization Service had determined as early as 1950 that his Chicago birth certificate was a fraud, but an investigation in 1954 had failed to turn up any indication of his true nationality or identity. Similar material was presented to a U.S. attorney in 1961 in hopes Rosselli could be prosecuted as an illegal alien, but it was rejected as a difficult case to try. Now, however, the FBI had a name. It took two years to pull together a complete file, including the Chicago forgery, INS documentation of his entry into New York in 1911, school records from East Boston, and court records from Boston and Cambridge, documenting arrests on narcotics and burglary charges, and his disappearance after posting bond.

When it was ready, Hoover decided to try another tack. Certainly Rosselli's knowledge of the operations of organized crime was unparalleled. Perhaps he could be forced to turn.

The Bureau made its move on a bright, cool morning in the first part of May 1966. Rosselli had stopped in at Drucker's for a haircut, and was strolling up Brighton Way toward Rodeo Drive, when he was approached by Harold Dodge, a sharp young agent who had for years been the lead officer on the Rosselli case. As Rosselli moved to step around him, Dodge uttered two words: "Filippo Sacco."

Rosselli paused, shot Dodge a glance, and moved past him. A few steps later a second man appeared, a crew-cut agent named Wayne Hill. He was playing the role of good cop in the two-handed routine. "This has nothing to do with you personally, John," Hill said, offering Rosselli an unmarked manilla envelope. "We got nothing against you."

Rosselli replied sharply without breaking stride. "Go see my attorney. I don't know what you're talking about." Flanking Rosselli on either shoulder, Dodge and Hill kept pace. "We're the only ones who know about this," Dodge offered. "We want to talk to you personally," Hill said. "We can meet up in Ventura. Nobody will know." Hill then dropped his voice to a conspiratorial tone. "It's a matter of national security."

Rosselli repeated his answer, "Go see my attorney," and kept walking, staring straight ahead, and the agents left. Later, when Rosselli returned to his apartment, he found the envelope. He left it lying on the doorstep and called Jimmy Cantillon. They opened it together.

Inside the envelope were two yellowed photographs, one of a young woman, square-jawed and unsmiling, and the second of a child, a little boy about four years of age. Cantillon looked at the pictures, and then looked at Rosselli. "That's my mother," Rosselli said evenly. "And that's me."

Rosselli's secret identity was gone. The implications were unsettling, but more on a psychic level than a practical one. The crimes he had committed as Filippo Sacco were too old to pose much of a threat. But the veil, the cloak of mystery that had become the unbroken thread of Rosselli's life, had been torn. Always before, that secret had provided for Rosselli a sort of inner sanctum, a final door within the fortress of layered identities he had erected, to which he alone had the key. Now it had been violated, trespassed by the enemy. It was a portent, vague but dark, an augur of vulnerability.

More troubling in the short term was Wayne Hill's parting whisper. What could his dealings with the FBI have to do with national security? Rosselli had never been told that the Bureau knew of his work with the CIA, and he feared that the plots against Castro had been discovered. If that were the case, his handlers at the intelligence agency should know immediately they had been compromised. Secrecy was something Rosselli understood and respected, whether it was a mob operation that needed protection, or the government's.

The following morning Rosselli booked a flight to New York with Jimmy Cantillon, and then flew alone by shuttle to Washington, where he stayed with his friend Joe Shimon. Arriving the morning of May 12, he placed a call to Sheffield Edwards, the former director of security at the CIA.

Rosselli met with Edwards at 5 P.M. in the deserted cocktail lounge of the Lawyers Club in downtown Washington. Sipping his customary vodka over ice, Rosselli detailed the encounter in Beverly Hills. He was concerned, he said, because this was a highly unorthodox approach, and inquiries by his attorney had failed to turn up any new information. Edwards observed that Rosselli seemed shaken by the FBI's new information, and "somewhat distraught." Yet Rosselli made it clear that he would not consider violating his pact with the CIA. He told Edwards that "if he did talk to the FBI, he was not going to tell them anything about national security."

Rosselli made two other stops in Washington, the first a personal visit to his old comrade in arms, William Harvey, whose CIA career had been destroyed by his feud with Bobby Kennedy. After a brief term as head of the Agency mission in Rome, Harvey had left the intelligence business for good to start his own law firm in the capital. Possessed of a law degree but with little practical experience, business for Harvey was slow.

Rosselli's next stop was pure business. Cantillon flew in from New York to join him, and together with Joe Shimon, they went to the law offices of Edward Morgan. A former chief inspector with the FBI, Morgan advised Rosselli to cooperate with the agents who had accosted him. Shimon objected, but Morgan said he'd handled similar cases in the past, including Longy Zwillman, Rosselli's old contact in New Jersey. "Oh that's a swell example," Shimon shot back. "They hung that stool pigeon."

Rosselli cut the conversation short. He had no interest in negotiating with the FBI. What he wanted from Morgan was a name—the name of the informer who had leaked his personal story. Morgan said he'd see what he could do.

Rosselli returned to Los Angeles, and after several conferences with Cantillon, decided to meet with the agents and find out the terms they were offering. A rendezvous was set for the third week in May at Dupar's Restaurant, a blue-plate eatery in Thousand Oaks, forty miles north of the city. Agent Harold Dodge did most of the talking. It was a straight pitch, an offer of leniency in return for Rosselli's cooperation.

Dodge said his office had known for years that Rosselli had been born in Italy and never acquired citizenship. He knew the Chicago birth certificate was false, and offered some detail on the background of Rosselli's family. The next step would be to open a formal investigation into the background of Filippo Sacco, possibly involving a federal grand jury. Dodge then stated that he wanted to "help" Rosselli, but could only do so if Rosselli cooperated—specifically, supplying information on gambling operations in the State of Nevada. He gave Rosselli twenty-four hours to make up his mind, and a phone number to call with his decision.

The following day Dodge received a call from Jimmy Cantillon. He'd held a long meeting with Rosselli, and they had decided there would be no cooperation with the Bureau. "So we'll be seeing you, I guess," Cantillon concluded.

For Rosselli, the key to the meeting was Dodge's failure to mention "national security" or the plots against Castro. Despite the agents' initial enigmatic approach, this was simply an effort to turn him. Immediately after the meeting, Rosselli again called Sheffield Edwards in Washington, but Edwards was not in. He then called Bob Maheu, who was in Washington at the time, and asked him to relay a message to Edwards. Maheu didn't tell Rosselli, but Edwards was meeting with Maheu at that very moment, on an "unrelated" matter. Rosselli's message was brief: he had met with the FBI, their interest in him had nothing to do with the CIA, and Edwards could "forget the whole matter."

Rumblings from New Orleans

THE FBI THRUST AGAINST Rosselli in 1966 was disturbing, but it did not represent a serious threat. The worst crime they had uncovered was failure to register as an alien, which was a misdemeanor. If they could make that stick, Rosselli might face deportation proceedings, but again, the threat that he would actually be forced from the country was minimal. After all, the government had stripped Paul Ricca of his citizenship in 1957, and nine years later he was still in the country, still active as a gray eminence in the Chicago organization. Even Carlos Marcello, deported to Guatemala in 1961, had returned to Louisiana with seeming immunity.

The revelation of Rosselli's true identity was a personal matter, a nuisance, a diversion from his duties as a consulting intelligence analyst for the national crime syndicate. He demonstrated his priorities when he immediately alerted Sheffield Edwards to the possible breach of security in the CIA plots against Castro. But toward the end of 1966, Rosselli was faced with the potential exposure of the second of the great secrets he harbored. The story would not break publicly for another several months, but there were clear signals from New Orleans of an ambitious and far-reaching new inquiry into the Kennedy assassination.

★

Jim Garrison was a lanky, wisecracking attorney, a former FBI agent and veteran of both World War II and Korea, when he was elected district attorney of New Orleans in 1961 by bucking the local Democratic machine. He followed his upset victory by clamping down on some of the more blatant vice in the famed French Quarter, courted reporters and established a reputation as a law enforcement maverick, once likening the judges of the local bench to "the sacred cows of India." He was elected handily to a second term in 1965, and turned his attention to a crime more intriguing than the excesses of Bourbon Street. For years, New Orleans had reverberated with rumors of various entanglements in the Kennedy assassination. In the summer of 1966, Garrison decided to reopen the investigation.

At the start, the focus of Garrison's probe was David Ferrie, a former pilot for Eastern Airlines who had befriended Lee Harvey Oswald in New Orleans in the summer of 1963. Ferrie had been questioned by the FBI, the Secret Service, the New Orleans police, and one of Garrison's own investigators in the days following the assassination, but despite a series of vague and contradictory responses, Ferrie was never called before the Warren Commission nor mentioned in its report. Three years later, Garrison figured an intensive look at Ferrie would yield new leads, if not a whole new body of evidence.

An amateur scientist with an active interest in the occult, a right-wing militant routinely arrested on morals charges, Ferrie was the single most bizarre individual in the strange coterie that surfaced in connection with the plot against Kennedy. Even his appearance was strange—all his hair had fallen out, a condition for which he compensated by wearing ill-fitting hairpieces and painted half-moon eyebrows. Yet as Garrison discovered, Ferrie served to link all the different players that came together in Dallas. He was seen repeatedly by half a dozen witnesses accompanying Oswald around New Orleans. He was a private investigator for Guy Banister, the ex-FBI agent who collaborated with the anti-Castro Cubans out of his offices at 544 Camp Street. Ferrie worked with Sergio Arcacha Smith and other Cuban exiles, who affectionately dubbed him "the Master of Intrigue." And he was a close aide and sometime confidant of New Orleans mafioso Carlos Marcello, serving on the defense team in the Justice Department's effort to deport Marcello, and working as an investigator for Marcello attorney G. Wray Gill.

Garrison's interest in Ferrie became an open secret in New Orleans in the fall of 1966, a rumor he confirmed on December 15, when he had Ferrie brought in for questioning. The session centered on a sudden trip Ferrie had made the evening of the assassination, when he drove the 350 miles from New Orleans to Houston with two friends, Layton Martens and Alvin Beauboeuf, the trio arriving at a motel owned by Marcello at four the next morning. After placing a call to Marcello's headquarters at the Town & Country Motel in New Orleans, Ferrie headed to Galveston and Hammond, Louisiana, before returning to New Orleans November 25. By that time, law enforcement authorities were searching the city for Ferrie: his library card had been found in Oswald's wallet in Dallas.

Garrison's interrogation in 1966 convinced him that Ferrie was lying about the reasons for his trip, and that he was covering up for the perpetrators of the assassination. That conviction pointed down two paths—in the years following, Garrison became convinced that the CIA had engineered Kennedy's murder, with Ferrie and Banister instrumental in setting up Oswald as a pro-Castro communist and, ultimately, as "the patsy." But initially, Ferrie's close ties to Carlos Marcello led Garrison to suspect that organized crime, and Marcello in particular, had pulled off the shooting in Dallas.

Both the CIA and the Mafia angles provided ample leads for Garrison to follow, and were later picked up by a succession of private investigators and congressional committees. But Garrison himself self-destructed. In the welter of national press attention that followed the announcement of his inquiry, Garrison was shown to have induced testimony by bribery and hypnosis, and threatened recalcitrant witnesses with jail. Several members of his staff quit in protest of his methods.

Perhaps most damaging, Garrison was reported to be under the sway of Carlos Marcello. As evidence, *Look* magazine reported in 1969 that Garrison had bought his spacious two-story home at a discount from a contractor considered to operate as a front for Marcello. During the middle 1960s, Garrison dismissed more than eighty cases brought by police against men in Marcello's organization, most involving illegal gambling. In 1972, Garrison was indicted for taking bribes to protect gambling interests. Aaron Kohn, head of the New Orleans Crime Commission, was a persistent critic of Garrison's contention that Marcello was "a respectable businessman."

Still, while Garrison mirrored J. Edgar Hoover's skepticism of the existence of the Mafia, it was an oversight, not a collaboration with Marcello. Garrison was willing, in late 1966, to follow the trail that Ferrie was blazing. His focus on Ferrie himself had to be disturbing to Marcello, as was Garrison's subsequent interrogations of Ferrie companions Martens and Beauboeuf, who refused comment until they could confer with Jack Wasserman, a Washington, D.C., attorney who represented Marcello.

Santo Trafficante also had reason to sweat. Casting a wide net, Garrison had come across the story of Melba Christine Marcades, a narcotics addict and a stripper who worked for Jack Ruby under the stage name Rose Cheramie. On November 20, 1963, Cheramie was discovered lying by the side of the road in the town of Eunice, Louisiana, having been hit by a car. Not seriously injured, she was transported to East Louisiana State Hospital by Francis Fruge, a lieutenant with the state police. She was quickly released, and Fruge put her in a jail cell to sober up. When she began to experience severe pains from heroin withdrawal, Fruge drove her two hours to the state hospital in Jackson.

During the ride, Cheramie related a remarkable story. She had been driving from Florida to Dallas with two men whom she presumed to be Italians, when they got into an argument at a roadside bar and she was thrown out. She suffered her accident while hitchhiking. Fruge then asked Cheramie what she was planning to do in Dallas. As he recalled it later, "She said she was going to, number one, pick up some money, pick up her baby, and to kill Kennedy." Cheramie repeated to a doctor at the hospital that Kennedy would be killed.

Fruge had dismissed Cheramie's allegation as drug-induced rantings, but he changed his mind when he heard the news two days later that Kennedy had been assassinated, immediately calling the hospital and asking them to hold Cheramie until he could speak with her. Cheramie repeated her account, telling Fruge that the two men traveling with her from Miami were going to Dallas to kill the President. Fruge reported his findings to the Dallas police, but was flatly ignored, and filed his report with the district attorney in New Orleans. Cheramie died in 1965, but Garrison pulled the file the following year.

Soon after, Garrison dispatched investigators to track down another Miami lead, a former Cuban Congressman named Eladio del Valle. A friend of Ferrie's who had helped finance some of his work against Castro, del Valle was also linked to Trafficante. Garrison hoped del Valle might be able to shed some light on the connections between Miami and New Orleans.

Santo Trafficante never offered any public reaction to Garrison's probe into his territory, but in September 1966, as the investigation was heating up, he attended a high-level Mafia conference in New York with Carlos Marcello. And three weeks later, on October 12, he traveled to Las Vegas. There is no record of a meeting, but it seems unlikely that he would come so far without checking in with his friend and coconspirator in the CIA plots, the man who knew Las Vegas best, John Rosselli.

Gambit

THE COLLAPSE OF THE Garrison investigation in New Orleans proved a devastating blow to the cadre of official and amateur researchers investigating the Kennedy assassination. It was the broadest and best-financed inquiry to be launched since the Warren Commission, and it had ended in disgrace and ridicule. Yet in its early stages, before his public embarrassment, Garrison seemed to hold all the cards. He said he knew the identity of the President's killers, and that all he needed was proof.

As the minister of information for the mob, as their man with the best ties to Washington and the intelligence community, it fell to John Rosselli to limit the potential damage of the Garrison investigation. Taking his cue from the skilled craftsmen at the CIA, and possibly with their complicity, Rosselli launched a sophisticated and surprisingly effective disinformation project. He planted a false lead, designed to throw Garrison and the other assassination investigators off the scent.

The plant came late in 1966, near the date of Garrison's interrogation of David Ferrie. The conduit was Edward P. Morgan, the Washington attorney to whom Rosselli had confided his role in the Castro plots even before the Bay of Pigs, and who worked closely with Robert Maheu and Howard Hughes. Morgan was enormously powerful in Washington, with strong ties to the Republican Party and the FBI. He would know just how to handle Rosselli's communiqué.

As Rosselli explained it in a meeting with Morgan, the last of the sniper teams dispatched to assassinate Fidel Castro in 1963 was captured in Havana. The commandos were tortured until they divulged the details of the operation, and their sponsorship by the CIA. At that point, Rosselli claimed, Castro was heard to utter, "If that was the way President Kennedy wanted it, he too could engage in the same tactics." Castro thereafter assembled teams of marksmen who were infiltrated into the United States to carry out the assassination of Kennedy. Rosselli himself knew of two such men—they were in hiding in the State of New Jersey.

This wasn't the first time that one of the Mafia collaborators in the

CIA effort against Cuba had suggested that Castro had killed Kennedy. Soon after the assassination, John Martino, Rosselli's onetime associate in the Florida Keys, sought out an investigator for the Warren Commission and related the same story, citing a source "high in the Cuban government." Martino was referred to the FBI, which elected not to follow the lead.

The Castro-retaliation theory was a classic piece of disinformation. Its veracity was grounded in the revelation of a true story—the CIA plots against Castro, until then a closely held secret. And the twist at the end, the assertion that Castro had engineered the shooting in Dallas, covered a number of key bases. It explained the ubiquitous presence of Cubans in the Kennedy plots, it dovetailed with Oswald's public identity as a pro-Castro sympathizer, and it anticipated the possibility that Garrison or another investigator would trace a hit team back to Trafficante's Miami— where else would Castro's sharpshooters make their U.S. beachhead? Moreover, there was a sort of moral justice in the tale. The President's own iniquitous plots had come back to haunt him.

In subsequent years, in a series of conferences with journalist Jack Anderson, Rosselli expanded on his story. The hit team had not just been captured and tortured, but they had been brainwashed, a la *The Manchurian Candidate,* and sent back themselves to murder the President. More important, Rosselli told Anderson the original hit team was composed of members of the "Trafficante mob." Once again, he was constructing a perfect cover in the event that Trafficante was ever linked to the Kennedy assassination.

As Rosselli intended, and as he may have instructed Morgan, word of his "revelations" about the CIA and Castro traveled fast. Morgan's first call was to Jack Anderson, a close personal friend who had helped Morgan establish his lucrative connection to Las Vegas newspaper publisher Hank Greenspun in the 1950s. In an interview with the authors, Anderson recalled that it took months to extract Rosselli's story from Morgan, but the sequence of events shows a more speedy pace.

By late January, within a month of Rosselli's "disclosures," Anderson arranged for his boss, Drew Pearson, to meet with Morgan at Pearson's home. Morgan knew that Pearson was friendly with Earl Warren, and suggested that Warren would know how to handle the explosive new information that Castro had staged the Kennedy assassination. Pearson took the bait, and within a week, met with Warren. Pearson asked Warren to meet with Morgan, but at the time, Warren was distancing himself from the investigative quagmire of the assassination, and insisted on referring the matter to federal authorities. Aware that the FBI was loath to reopen the case, Pearson suggested the Secret Service.

On January 31, 1967, Warren informed Secret Service Director James Rowley of the dramatic new information. "He wanted to get it off his hands," Rowley said later. But despite Pearson's strategy, Rowley simply referred the matter to the FBI, and sure enough, top officials at the Bureau determined that no investigation should be conducted. This was not the sort of exposure that Rosselli and his collaborators were seeking— Garrison's investigation was proceeding, with no telling where it might turn.

Jim Garrison increased the pressure February 17, when he announced his investigation publicly. David Ferrie dismissed the inquest as "a big joke," but worried that his life was in danger, and was taken into protective custody. Four days later, Garrison released him to house arrest at his New Orleans apartment. The move forced the hand of Ferrie's coconspirators. The next morning, February 22, Ferrie was found dead. The coroner ruled that Ferrie had died of a cerebral hemorrhage brought on by stress, but the circumstances were exceedingly strange. Ferrie had left two unsigned, typewritten suicide notes—it seems highly unlikely that Ferrie might have anticipated his demise in time to type the letters, or had actually induced his own aneurysm.

In Miami, where Garrison's investigators were actively searching for Eladio del Valle, Ferrie's Cuban accomplice met a more certain end. On February 23, twelve hours after Ferrie's body was discovered, del Valle was found murdered in a shopping-center parking lot. He'd been tortured, his head split with an axe, and then shot in the heart at point-blank range. The murder bore the hallmark of Santo Trafficante, whose killers were known for their enthusiasm. Ferrie's trail was growing cold fast.

Still, Garrison remained committed to his investigation, buoyed by increasing public skepticism of the Warren Commission. Thwarted by J. Edgar Hoover, Rosselli and his collaborators went directly to the public, through the offices of the "Washington Merry-Go-Round," the nationally syndicated column published by Drew Pearson and Jack Anderson. If Castro could be positioned as the new, best suspect in the assassination, the pressure could be conveniently deflected.

Rosselli's story finally saw light on March 3, in a column published under Anderson's by-line. "President Johnson is sitting on a political H-bomb," Anderson wrote, "an unconfirmed report that Sen. Robert Kennedy may have approved an assassination plot which then possibly backfired against his late brother." The assassination plot was the Mafia scheme to kill Castro; it backfired when Castro learned that the CIA was behind it. "With characteristic fury, he is reported to have cooked up a counterplot against President Kennedy." Lest his readers miss the point of the column, Anderson spelled it out in a trenchant fifth paragraph: "This report may have started New Orleans' flamboyant District Attorney Jim Garrison on his investigation of the Kennedy assassination, but insiders believe he is following the wrong trails."

Not mentioned in the column was the simple, powerful argument against Cuban sponsorship of the Kennedy assassination—the profound risk Castro would run if a plot against the American President was discovered. As the Church Committee noted, such a blunder would have "exposed Cuba to invasion and destruction." Later, it was learned that Castro had opened new channels of diplomacy at the time of the shooting in Dallas, showing himself, in the words of one diplomat, "anxious to establish communications with the United States." Finally, with the benefit of hindsight, Rosselli's story of CIA marksmen being "turned" seems highly implausible, a product of Korean War recruiting films.

Nor did Anderson note his own close relationship to his source; that Morgan had no evidence, beyond Rosselli's statements, to back up the Castro retaliation theory; nor that Rosselli may have been pursuing his own, independent agenda. As Anderson himself conceded in an interview years later, "I may have been a card in the hand he was playing."

Anderson's column sent tremors through official Washington. Not only did it accuse Castro of plotting against Kennedy, but it revealed for the first time, albeit sketchily, the CIA plots against Castro. President Lyndon Johnson reacted swiftly. He demanded that the CIA prepare a full report on the allegations, and that the FBI thoroughly investigate the source of the report. Senator Bobby Kennedy reacted as well, but in his own fashion. He made no public response, but quietly had his secretary request from J. Edgar Hoover a copy of the May 7, 1962 memorandum backstopping his involvement in the Castro assassination plots. If called upon, he could thereby prove he had moved to stop them.

Rosselli's maneuver had worked perfectly. Rather than renew their investigation into the Kennedy assassination, and the likely scenario of mob involvement, the chief intelligence agencies of the federal government were, instead, turned inward. The CIA had been ordered by the President to report on its own complicity in the plots against Castro, and the FBI was busy tracking Morgan's allegation that Castro had retaliated against Kennedy.

Not content with the success of his ploy, Rosselli continued to keep a close watch on Garrison's progress. According to a CIA report declassified in 1979, Rosselli met with Garrison himself in Las Vegas in March 1967, the week after the Anderson column was published. Garrison has emphatically denied the report—"I have never even seen John Rosselli in my life, nor have I ever had a 'secret meeting' with any racketeer anywhere"—but he did travel to Las Vegas that March, where he was interviewed by journalist James Phelan. Tellingly, Garrison conceded later that year that his expenses in Las Vegas were paid by Mario Marino, a Marcello flunky then working in the casino at the Sands. "I may be naïve," Garrison said of the $5,000 in gambling credits he accepted, "but I don't see what's wrong with it." The House Assassinations Committee was more concerned by Garrison's meet with Rosselli, which it termed "particularly disturbing."

A Stand-up Guy

PLANTING THE CASTRO STORY was a brilliant move on Rosselli's part, but a risky one. What if the FBI had latched onto the fact that a high-ranking member of the Mafia was claiming inside knowledge of the Kennedy assassination? Until that point, Hoover had avoided a thorough investigation of the mob connections of Oswald and especially Jack Ruby, but a wrong move might finally awaken him to the promising leads that had been ignored.

Even more dangerous to Rosselli was the possible reaction of his brethren in the Mafia. Even assuming that Trafficante and Marcello were the men behind the Kennedy assassination, the rest of the national commission, and of organized crime, knew nothing of the plot. If they were to learn through Rosselli that a faction of the mob had plotted such a crime, Rosselli himself would be a marked man. More simply, by speaking with Morgan, and through him to the federal government, Rosselli had violated his oath of secrecy. *Omerta* had never been updated to encompass the subtleties of disinformation.

Over the years, observers have been struck by the bold nature of Rosselli's gambit, and speculated as to its cause. The consensus was that Rosselli was seeking leverage over the government in his tangle with the FBI over possible deportation. The House Assassinations Committee reported in 1979 that "John Rosselli manipulated the facts of the plots into the retaliation theory in efforts to force the CIA to intervene favorably into his legal affairs. . . ." As evidence, the committee cited Rosselli's contacts with Harvey and Sheffield Edwards. Author John Davis went further, writing in 1989, "Why would a mafia don of John Rosselli's visibility risk certain extermination by running off at the mouth this way? Rosselli was in a lot of trouble at the time he made the allegation."

In fact, Rosselli was not in trouble at the time of his conference with Morgan. The FBI had made their pitch to turn him, but when he rejected their advance, the matter lay dormant. The worst Rosselli could anticipate was prosecution for a misdemeanor, and possible court proceedings over deportation. Besides, the blackmail scenario contradicts Rosselli's entire relationship with the CIA. As William Harvey observed later, there was "a very real possibility of this government being blackmailed by . . . figures in organized crime for their own self-protection or aggrandizement, which, as it turned out, did not happen."

Morgan himself defused the "manipulation" theory when he was questioned by the House Assassinations Committee in 1978. "Morgan did not know anything about Rosselli's deportation case at the time," the committee interviewers reported. Morgan knew of the approach by the FBI agents to Rosselli in Beverly Hills, but at that point, no prosecution had been initiated. As for Rosselli's contact with Sheffield Edwards, once the question of "national security" was cleared up, and well before the Anderson column was published, Rosselli had called Edwards with the express instructions to "forget the whole matter."

Ironically, there was one collaborator in the Castro plots who did use his inside information to blackmail the government, but it wasn't John Rosselli. In 1966, Missouri Senator Edward Long was conducting a broad inquiry into illegal wiretapping, and planned to call Robert Maheu to testify on suspicious activities unearthed by U.S. Attorney Robert Morgenthau in New York. Working again through Ed Morgan, Maheu contacted CIA general counsel Lawrence Houston, who persuaded Long to drop his demand that Maheu testify. As in the Balletti wiretap case, it was

Maheu, the government man, and not Rosselli, the gangster, who dodged a federal inquiry by threatening to expose the Castro plots.

More important, the crux of Rosselli's revelation to Morgan was not the plots against Castro, but Castro's alleged role in the Kennedy assassination. There is no indication that posing Castro as Kennedy's killer would have weakened the government's resolve to prosecute Rosselli. Indeed, in the months that followed, it increased.

The answer to the question of why Rosselli named Castro as a plotter against Kennedy lies in the act itself. Clearly, in floating the story through the offices of Ed Morgan and then in the press, Rosselli was seeking to influence the course of the Kennedy investigation. Short of sparking an American invasion of Cuba, there was no other benefit to be obtained. Rosselli's multiple connections to the apparent players in the assassination make him a likely conduit for such a ploy, and the results proved the strategy worthy.

More intriguing than Rosselli's motive is the question of who actually sponsored the bogus lead that Castro killed Kennedy. In light of the del Valle murder, and his trip to Las Vegas in the fall of 1966, Santo Trafficante seems the most likely party. But Garrison's investigation also, and later exclusively, raised questions about the CIA connections to Oswald and the anti-Castro Cubans he associated with in New Orleans. Significantly, ranking CIA staff officer Victor Marchetti has reported that Garrison's progress was the subject of repeated discussion at Richard Helms's morning staff meetings in Langley in 1967.

Might the CIA have floated the Castro theory, again to deflect the Garrison investigation? If the CIA were actually involved in the Kennedy assassination, as some leading researchers believe, the scenario would fit. Considering his intimate association with the Agency, Rosselli would have accepted their directive as well as Trafficante's. And Ed Morgan himself had close ties to the Agency, both through Maheu and from a prior stint as counsel to the Senate Foreign Relations Committee.

Morgan might even have launched the Castro retaliation theory himself, using Rosselli initially as an unwitting foil. Joe Shimon, who attended one of Rosselli's early meetings with Morgan, said later that Rosselli had described the CIA-Mafia plots to the attorney, but had never mentioned the Kennedy assassination. And Robert Maheu, in an unguarded moment during a taped interview with one of the authors, commented that, in relation to the Kennedy assassination, "They were putting words in Johnny's mouth, and I was very, very peeved at Ed [Morgan] about that. He never checked that out with me or anyone." Asked several weeks later to elaborate, Maheu said he could not recall the statement or what he might have meant by it.

Either way, if Rosselli launched the story on orders from Trafficante and Marcello, or if it was Morgan, using Rosselli at the behest of a faction within the government, the result was the same. Rosselli stood by Morgan, expanding on his tale in subsequent discussions with Jack Anderson, and diverting investigators from the true sponsors of the Kennedy assassination. At that point, Rosselli was accepting directives from both the mob and the CIA. For both, as he had been all his life, Rosselli was a stand-up guy.

13

FINAL SCORES

Bamboozling a Billionaire

By the fall of 1966, the pattern of John Rosselli's life had shifted from the day-to-day responsibilities of active project management to more occasional attention to resolution of high-pressure, high-level crises. Rosselli stirred himself from his comfortable routine only when forced to, either by law enforcement, or by the course of major events. Floating the Castro story was one such event, but another occurred around the same time, and closer to Rosselli's normal arena. In late November, arriving via private rail car under cover of night, Howard Hughes came to Las Vegas.

In a town that existed almost solely on the coinage it could siphon off free-spending visitors, the arrival of the world's richest man was sensational news. But Hughes' impact on Las Vegas would be far greater than a boost in the daily gambling volume. Hughes was restless, having recently abandoned his longtime base of operations in California for a temporary

277

layover in Boston, from which he contemplated moves to Montreal, Miami, the Bahamas, and finally, Nevada. And he was flush with cash, having ended his battle for control of Trans World Airlines by selling out, leaving him holding a windfall of $546 million. As the denizens of the Las Vegas strip would learn in the months to come, Howard Hughes was in a spending mood.

None of this was lost on John Rosselli, who knew Hughes personally from his days in the film industry, when he was the youngest of the moguls and frequented Hollywood's café society. More recently, Rosselli had kept a close eye on Hughes through his friendship with Bob Maheu, whose political savvy and intelligence connections had earned him a position as Hughes's closest advisor, more influential than the corporate officers who administered Hughes Tool Company, Hughes Aircraft, and TWA, and more trusted than the clique of Mormon aides who attended to the details of Hughes' bizarre personal life—the washing of food containers, the obsessive sanitation routines. Maheu never met Hughes in person, but they communicated hourly by telephone and handwritten memo, their relationship cemented by Maheu's annual salary, astronomical for its time, of $520,000. By comparison, Hughes' longtime executive aide Noah Dietrich received a paltry salary of $75,000.

Hughes had decided as early as June 1966 that he would make Las Vegas his new base of operations, but more important, that he would make substantial investments there, buying into gambling casinos where his profits could not be contested by rival shareholders, and where the cash revenues would prove difficult for the IRS to trace. Hughes realized that dealing in Las Vegas would require dealing with gangsters, but that did not faze him. In 1952, he had negotiated the sale of RKO Studios to a business syndicate that included Ray Ryan, once a partner with Frank Costello in a Texas oil deal. The deal collapsed only after the *Wall Street Journal* ran an exposé on the buyers' mob connections. Besides, Hughes figured he could rely on a key connection in Las Vegas. He had asked Maheu to locate, as Maheu put it later, "a person who had connections with certain people of perhaps unsavory background," and was pleased when Maheu suggested Rosselli's name. Without going into detail, Hughes confided to Maheu that he had known Rosselli "for many years."

When the decision was finally taken in Boston to make the move to Nevada, Maheu contacted Rosselli to help with the arrangements. Maheu handled the transportation details, hiring a secret train and posting security guards armed with submachine guns along the route. In Las Vegas,

Rosselli secured through Moe Dalitz' partner Ruby Kolod the ninth-floor penthouse suite at the Desert Inn Hotel for Hughes, and all of another floor for his entourage. Rooms were in short supply, but Kolod assured Dalitz that Hughes would be out by Christmas, freeing up space for heavy gamblers during the peak holiday week.

At 4 A.M. on Sunday, November 27, Hughes' train pulled to a stop at a crossing just north of Las Vegas, to be met by Rosselli, his friend Joe Breen, Jr., and a small motorcade. Hughes was removed from the train on a stretcher, a mask of gauze covering his face. Maheu later denied vehemently that Rosselli was there that night, but Rosselli and Breen both recounted the occasion to friends. Patricia Breen recalled the story in detail; that Hughes was awake, and when he recognized Joe Breen, Jr.'s voice, had asked after the health of his father, the film censor.

Hughes arrived at a time of great turbulence for the hidden mob interests in the Las Vegas casinos. In July, investigative reporter Sandy Smith had written an explosive exposé on skimming operations, naming the gangsters behind Caesars Palace and the Dunes Hotel, and naming couriers who transported the funds to mob outposts from Chicago to New England. The report was followed by a state gaming commission inquiry into skimming, and then by a federal grand jury investigation, which got under way two days before Hughes pulled into town.

At the same time, the leadership of the various mob families Rosselli represented were in chaotic transition. In Chicago, Giancana was jailed and, upon his release in May 1966, went into self-imposed exile in Cuernavaca, Mexico. His absence prompted the return of Tony "Joe Batters" Accardo, never a close ally of Rosselli's. In New York, the five Mafia families were engaged in a vicious and deadly battle for power, initiated when Booklyn's Joseph Bonanno moved to take over sole control. Teamsters president Jimmy Hoffa was losing the appeals to his convictions and would soon be confined to a federal prison cell. The delicate machine Rosselli had helped create to acquire and distribute illicit gambling profits was being threatened from without and within.

Hughes himself added to the turmoil when he announced to Dalitz that he would be staying on at the Desert Inn through the holidays and beyond. Dalitz was incensed, and threatened to have the billionaire evicted. Maheu gained a temporary stay only by eliciting a phone call to Dalitz from Jimmy Hoffa, who gruffly persuaded Dalitz to cooperate. Tempers simmered, and the question of who really ran Las Vegas was left hanging.

The confusion was underscored on December 29, when Sheriff Ralph Lamb arrested John Rosselli for the misdemeanor charge of failure to register as a convicted felon. The roust was not serious—Rosselli was released that night and continued to live in the city unmolested—but it was demeaning, an insult, and Rosselli registered his shock in the bemused expression captured in his police booking photo. Lamb was well acquainted with Rosselli but never before bothered to challenge Rosselli's presence on the Strip. Clearly, the arrest was a signal, from Maheu, from Dalitz, or perhaps from one of the new dons emerging in the power struggles back East, that a new era was dawning in Las Vegas.

Rosselli was shaken by the arrest, but he did not retreat, and he did not seek retribution. He had business to attend to, negotiations that would resolve Dalitz' conflict with Hughes and, on a larger plane, restore the security of the mob skim operations in Las Vegas. Rosselli knew that Hughes was looking to buy gambling properties, and he knew that the casino owners were seeking a new front organization that would shield them from the skimming investigations. It was a simple matter of putting people together.

Even before Moe Dalitz' eviction notice, Rosselli broached with Kolod the possibility of selling to Hughes. By mid-December, the talks had progressed to the point that Rosselli introduced Kolod to Maheu. As the manager of the Desert Inn casino, and as a direct representative of the Chicago mob, Kolod was a partner with Dalitz, but was also a rival. Dalitz had always chafed under Chicago's influence, and he was furious when he learned Kolod had opened sales talks without consulting him. That anger might have prompted a directive to Lamb to make the Rosselli arrest, but Dalitz' frustration cooled when he learned the terms that Rosselli was working out.

Hughes would buy the rights to operate the 450-room hotel, but would leave the title to the building and its grounds in the hands of the Dalitz group, leasing the property until the year 2022. The license for the casino would be transferred to Hughes, but the casino operation, and the all-important skim, would remain in the hands of Kolod and his fellow gangsters. Dalitz would be kept on as a consultant; the only change would come in the executive suites at the Desert Inn, where Rosselli's pal Bob Maheu could be trusted not to meddle. Recovered from his pique, Dalitz decided to go for the deal, and casting about for a sharp attorney to represent his end of the bargaining, he asked Las Vegas *Sun* publisher Hank Greenspun for a referral. Greenspun named the powerhouse Washington attorney who had represented him so capably in Las Vegas—Edward P. Morgan.

Hughes also was seeking advice. He left Maheu in charge of his Las Vegas team, but asked his friend, developer, casino operator, and former New York Yankess co-owner Del Webb, to suggest someone to analyze the operating figures submitted by the Desert Inn group. Webb responded with the name of E. Parry Thomas, the chief executive officer of the Bank of Las Vegas and a director of Webb's Nevada resort company. It was a prudent move on Hughes' part, but also demonstrated the dangers of trying to buy into so close-knit a fraternity as the world of Las Vegas gambling. Known in some circles as "the hoodlum banker," Thomas had served as the chief financial conduit for the Teamsters pension-fund investments in Nevada.

In January 1967, the sales negotiations began in earnest. The Desert Inn team included Dalitz and Ed Morgan. Hughes was represented by Bob Maheu, Morgan's client and close friend, and Parry Thomas. John Rosselli was not at the table, but he was the thread that connected all five parties. Not surprisingly, his interests were the ones that prevailed.

The bargaining went on for three months. Hughes quibbled over every clause, driving Maheu to the point of a threatened resignation. But in the end, he agreed to the basic terms that Dalitz was pushing for. Hughes would buy the lease to the hotel and casino for $6.2 million and assume $7 million in liabilities. In addition, Hughes would pay $1.1 million a year to the Dalitz group until 1981, and $940,000 each year thereafter. All operating expenses were to be paid by Hughes.

Operation of the Desert Inn changed hands on midnight, March 31, and on April Fool's Day, 1967, Howard Hughes took control. Dalitz grumbled later that he had received a "low price" for the sale, but paid Morgan a "finders fee" of $150,000. Morgan, in turn, split the fee, paying $25,000 to Greenspun for bringing him into the deal, and $50,000 to Rosselli. But once again, as in so many prior enterprises, the money wasn't the important thing to Rosselli. The key was that, with Hughes on the gambling license and Maheu at the helm, the skim from the Desert Inn casino could continue under a veneer of respectability. Hughes would discover, as did the Hollywood producers when they enlisted Rosselli in controlling the studio unions, that a partnership with the mob is always a chancy affair.

Company Town

THE ANNOUNCEMENT OF THE Desert Inn deal heralded a new era in the life of Bob Maheu. The former gumshoe was now a tycoon, a free-wheeling business executive with an expense account and authority limited only by the autocratic but ill-informed Howard Hughes. Maheu's position afforded him the opportunity to create his own private empire in the desert, and he seized it.

Maheu's first step was to establish a front, the Hughes Nevada Operation (HNO), through which he ran the billionaire's Nevada concerns free from interference by other Hughes executives. The HNO was not a formal legal entity and had no authority to enter into contracts, but its name convinced both the public and Hughes' own employees that Maheu wielded unlimited authority from Hughes himself.

HNO was run along the lines of Maheu's RAMA outfit in Washington: Richard Ellis, Maheu's accountant at the time, recalled that secrecy was a primary directive. "One individual never particularly knew what another individual was doing." Maheu then established a string of subsidiary companies—Radiarc, Xenotec, Kyle Canyon Utilities, Cuyama Land and Cattle Company, M. F. Timber and Industries Inc.—staffed by Hughes employees, and which frequently were subcontracted to do Hughes work, billing their services at 25 to 50 percent over cost. At Mount Charleston, thirty-five miles west of Las Vegas, Maheu developed a $2 million ski resort.

Maheu was not stingy with his new prosperity. He staffed the HNO with friends, former classmates, and relatives, paying handsome salaries, sometimes from HNO but sometimes directly from the payroll accounts of Hughes' own properties. And he enriched the key players in the Desert Inn deal, inviting their participation in a continuing string of hotel and casino acquisitions by Hughes—the Desert Inn was followed by the Sands, the Castaways, the Frontier, the Landmark, and the Silver Slipper. Ed Morgan and Parry Thomas participated in most of them, collecting fees as advisors to either buyer or seller. By the end of 1967, Morgan was receiving a $100,000 annual retainer from Hughes on top of whatever fees he could land.

Hank Greenspun was a special case. A personal friend of Morgan's, publisher of a newspaper and owner of a television station who utilized his public relations background to promote his opinions and his influence, Greenspun became a confidant of Maheu, a position that he profited by. In the summer of 1967, Maheu approved the advance purchase by Hughes of $500,000 in advertising space in Greenspun's Las Vegas *Sun*, space that was never used. In September, Greenspun obtained a $4 million personal loan from Hughes Tool at 3 percent interest, roughly half the going rate. Later, he sold Hughes his television station for $3.6 million, and his weedy Paradise Valley Country Club for $2.6 million more. Greenspun reciprocated to Maheu, lending him $150,000 at zero interest and with no due date, but he never fully trusted him. Around his home, Greenspun and his family referred to Maheu as "Mister D"—the D stood for devious.

Politicians also benefited. Drawing from the cashier's cage at the Silver Slipper, Maheu and his aide, attorney Thomas Bell, distributed hundreds of thousands of dollars to scores of candidates for offices high and low throughout Nevada. Hughes continued his practice of making large donations to prominent candidates for national office, but the emphasis on local politics was new for him, and new for Nevada. The key player here was Governor Paul Laxalt, who developed a strong relationship with Hughes, and became a regular tennis partner with Maheu.

On a personal level, Maheu played his new role as desert raja to the hilt. He built a $640,000 French Colonial mansion abutting the Desert Inn golf course, outfitted for entertaining with a five-stove kitchen and a dining patio that would accommodate fifty. Publicly, Maheu joined the YMCA Century Club, Boy Scouts of America, American Foundation for Ecumenical Studies, Nevada Southern University Land Foundation, and the Las Vegas Symphony Society. He was everywhere, active and eloquent, the earthly embodiment of his increasingly demented, utterly reclusive sponsor.

Always, behind the scenes, conferring quietly with Maheu and orchestrating the casino acquisitions, there was John Rosselli. Just as he had prompted the Desert Inn talks, it was Rosselli who initiated the $14.6 million sale of the Sands, by instructing Sands shareholder Bryant Burton to get in touch with Ed Morgan. Again, Rosselli collected a finder's fee from Morgan, this time in the amount of $45,000. He played a similar role when Hughes bought the Frontier from Maury Friedman for $23 million, but his payoff took a different form. Meeting with Friedman the night of the Hughes purchase, Rosselli signed a long-term lease for the gift shop, a valuable concession that sold jewelry and overpriced knickknacks to the high rollers. His friend Joe Breen, Jr. ran the shop in return for one-third interest; Rosselli's end paid him roughly $60,000 a year for the rest of his life.

Howard Hughes, with Maheu as his chief executive, was the front Rosselli had always dreamed of, a respectable owner with limitless resources. Gone were the nettlesome licensing hearings, the frustrating scramble to find compliant owners. No longer would Sheriff Lamb have to embarrass himself with dissembling statements like, "As far as I know, everyone in the gambling business out here has always been a gentleman." As Paul Laxalt described it to the press, Hughes "has added a degree of credibility to the state that it would have taken years of advertising to secure. Let's face it, Nevada has an image problem—the typical feeling is that sin is rampant here. Anything this man does, from the gaming industry all the way down the line, is good for Nevada."

Equally important, Hughes and Maheu had little interest and little expertise in the day-to-day operations of the casinos. The gambling staff, the men who had been running the skim from the early days, remained intact. "There were very few changes in personnel," recalled Sands casino manager Harry Goodhart, himself a forty-year veteran in the business. Retired Air Force Major General Ed Nigro, a college classmate of Maheu's, was appointed the HNO deputy in charge of gambling, but admitted he was ill-equipped to monitor the action at the tables. "These guys who have been in gambling for twenty years have a sixth sense," he explained. "We haven't got enough time in our lives to learn what they know." Still, they might have tried harder. Hughes' own internal auditors were barred from the casino counting rooms, and when they appealed to the HNO directors for authority to run surprise audits, Maheu turned them down.

Improbably, the Hughes casino holdings began to lose money. Even the best of them, the Desert Inn and the Sands, lost their luster; their combined profits for 1967 and 1968 totaled under $5 million, less than what the Sands alone formerly earned in a single year. The gamblers were still coming to Vegas, and the veteran gaming crews were still intact—only the money was missing. An IRS audit in 1971 determined that somewhere on the order of $50 million had been drained from the Hughes casino coffers under the Maheu regime. The skim was continuing, on an even larger scale than before: the question the IRS couldn't answer was where the money had gone.

"We investigated three possibilities," said Andy Baruffi, former IRS intelligence chief in Las Vegas. "That Maheu was stealing money, that Hughes himself was stealing it, or that organized crime was doing it either with one or the other or on its own. We knew the mob was somehow involved because the same mob people who ran the casinos before Hughes bought them ran them after, and these people would not have run a skim of that magnitude without orders from the top. And we knew that the money had disappeared."

The bubble burst in 1970 when Hughes, urged on by aides jealous of Maheu's power and his autonomy, abruptly departed his penthouse headquarters, slipping out on Thanksgiving eve, his stretcher carried aloft down a rear fire escape by a squad of Mormon guards. By the next morning, he was safely hidden in another ninth-floor penthouse suite, but this time in the Bahamas. Maheu, the security expert, didn't learn of Hughes' escape for a week, and by then, he'd been stripped of his corporate authority.

Two years later, Hughes declared the reasons for the breach with Maheu in a news conference: "Because he's a no-good dishonest son-of-a-bitch, and he stole me blind. I don't suppose I ought to be saying that at a news conference, but I just don't know any other way to answer it. You wouldn't think it could be possible, with modern methods of bookkeeping and accounting and so forth, for a thing like the Maheu theft to have occurred, but believe me, it did, because the money's gone and he's got it." Maheu's close relationship with Rosselli and the Mafia may have added to Hughes' wrath. Bob Bennett, a Washington, D.C., influence broker on Hughes' payroll, told Nixon attorney John Dean that "the Hughes people had been forced to fire Maheu after discovering his involvement with notorious gangsters."

Actually, it seems unlikely that Maheu got much of the money Hughes lost in Nevada. A free spender, Maheu was frequently short of funds, even when collecting Hughes' high salary, to the point that his wife tearfully told a friend, "We can't even pay the grocery bill." Hughes apparently never considered asking his old friend John Rosselli what had become of the missing millions.

Running the Fox to Ground

ROPING HUGHES INTO FRONTING for the mob at the casinos in Las Vegas was Rosselli's greatest caper, a crowning achievement that drew on all his past experience in Hollywood, in espionage, and as a criminal strategist. It would also be his last. A new man had taken over as chief of the criminal division at the U.S. Attorney's office in Los Angeles, a punctilious, tireless young attorney named David Nissen, who made organized crime his top priority. Meeting with the FBI soon after his appointment, Nissen decided to revive the Rosselli immigration case, and prepared to call witnesses before a grand jury.

Then in early 1967, the FBI got another break when an agent on the surveillance team in L.A. that shadowed Rosselli on his daily rounds noticed a man in overalls emerging from a skylight on the roof of the Friars Club.

Investigation soon revealed the basic outlines of the card-cheating ring, but as in the Rosselli immigration case, the U.S. Attorney was initially unimpressed. "Rich people cheating other rich people at an exclusive club is not the sort of thing that a prosecutor gets excited about," recalled Gerald Uelmen, then an assistant prosecutor in the Los Angeles office.

A lead from an unexpected quarter revived the attorneys' interest. Beldon Katleman, Rosselli's old associate at the El Rancho Vegas, had become involved with the Friars Club conspirators, inviting them to drill peekholes in the ceiling of the den in his mansion near Bel-Air. A man of many vices, Katleman was at the same time meeting on a regular basis with George Bland, a veteran FBI agent who specialized in developing confidential informants.

Relaxing in Katleman's kitchen one morning, Bland mentioned the curious case that had turned up at the Friars Club. To Bland's surprise, Katleman began to talk. The two began to compare notes—the methodology of the peek, the players involved—and then Katleman introduced a new name to the scenario. "When he mentioned Rosselli, I became very, very interested," Bland said later.

Katleman's information convinced the FBI brass in Los Angeles to resubmit both the immigration and the Friars cases to the U.S. Attorney. This time, Nissen was sold. Neither case was ready to take to court, but he felt that aggressive use of the grand jury system, where attorneys were barred from the proceedings and witnesses who were not defendants could be compelled to testify, would yield enough facts to prosecute. On Friday, July 20, 1967, a squad of six FBI agents raided the Friars Club and seized the electronic paraphernalia hidden in the third-floor rafters. Later the same day, more than a dozen Friars were subpoenaed to appear before a federal grand jury that convened the following week.

Five weeks later, on August 25, John Rosselli was called to testify. He arrived at the courthouse wearing a light suit and sunglasses, accompanied by attorney Jimmy Cantillon and his old friend Allen Smiley, who was questioned but never charged in the case. Beset by dual investigations, Rosselli stonewalled. Five minutes after his arrival at the closed-door proceedings of the grand jury, he was ordered to appear in open court before U.S. Judge William P. Gray. A transcript of the jury's questioning was read.

"Are you a person who uses the name John Rosselli?"

The transcript registered no response.

"Do you refuse to answer true or false as to whether that is your name?"

Still no answer.

"Would you like to talk to your attorney outside?"

Rosselli replied with a blanket statement: "I stated from the beginning that I will not answer any questions because they might tend to incriminate me."

Judge Gray then conferred with Cantillon. The question of Rosselli's name was loaded, the attorney explained, an effort to build the government's immigration case. The judge agreed, and ordered Rosselli back to the grand jury to discuss the Friars, with the question of his name left hanging. Gerald Uelmen was impressed. "I still use this as an example when I teach criminal procedure, because there is a principle as to when you can invoke the Fifth," Uelmen said years later. "Rosselli was the only case I ever saw where he actually walked into the room, was asked what's your name, and took the Fifth Amendment. And it was a legitimate invocation of the Fifth."

The ruling was a landmark of legal trivia, but for Rosselli, significant only in pointing up his vulnerability. Even his name might be used against him, and under Dave Nissen, the government was pulling out all the stops. Toward the end of August, subpoenas went out to eight members of the Sacco family, including Rosselli's brother Albert, and his sisters Concetta and Edith, calling them before grand juries in Florida and Massachusetts, and then ordering them to appear before a second grand jury in Los Angeles September 8. A week later, several of Rosselli's friends in Los Angeles were called—Barbara Crosby, 34, the wife of Bing Crosby's son Gary; Carol Laffan, 19, a blond reservations clerk; Nancy Czarr, 23, a former ice skater then working in television; and a barber, Jimmy Capone (no relation to the Chicago mob leader). Czarr typified the reaction of the witnesses when she declared flippantly to the press, "He must have three million friends. I wonder if they're going to call them all."

But Nissen was making progress. Rosselli's family denied ever seeing their elder brother after his flight from Boston, yet Nissen managed to establish the identity of Vincent, the Sacco brother who died in 1936, and that Rosselli had been visited by the same man in Los Angeles, introducing him around as "Jimmy Rosselli." On October 21, 1976, Rosselli was indicted on six counts of failure to register as an alien. He was booked immediately and released on $5,000 bond. Two months later, in the Friars Club case, Rosselli and five others were indicted on charges of conspiracy and interstate commerce in aid of racketeering.

Neither case came close to penetrating the core of Rosselli's criminal activities, nor did they carry the threat of substantial jail terms. The petty nature of the charges made them all the more galling. Rosselli was being persecuted, he felt, and his family harassed, by a government that had unblinkingly solicited his services in the war on communism. Betrayal was all around him. The government had turned on him, as had his longtime accomplice, the gangster Salvatore Piscopo. Backed against the wall, Rosselli lashed out in classic mob fashion.

Rosselli had demanded from Ed Morgan the identity of the informant who had revealed his true identity, and Morgan, apparently unconcerned at complicity in a possible murder, had drawn upon his FBI sources to produce Piscopo's name. Rosselli then went through the mob's protocol of death—he contacted Giancana and won his endorsement for a hit on Piscopo, and had Giancana call DeSimone in Los Angeles to give the order. But Rosselli's disdain for the weakened Los Angeles crime family, evident since the transfer of his official affiliation back to Chicago in 1957, worked against him. DeSimone was jealous of Rosselli's prestige in the underworld, and let Giancana's order lie.

The hit on Piscopo was a matter of revenge more than strategy, and Rosselli did not pursue the matter. More threatening was the continued good health of George Seach, an electronics expert who helped rig the Friars Club cheating aparatus. A small-time burglar who won a transfer from a California state prison in 1964 on grounds of chronic psychosis, Seach was nonetheless the government's chief witness in the Friars case. As Nissen put it, "Without Seach's testimony, there was really no way we could make a case against Rosselli."

This was a crucial job, and this time, Rosselli dispensed with the formalities. Meeting with his longtime button man, Jimmy Fratianno, in the security of Jimmy Cantillon's Los Angeles law office in January 1968, Rosselli assigned Fratianno and Frank Bompensiero to murder George Seach. Maury Friedman advanced $2,000 in expense money, which Rosselli passed in an unmarked envelope. Fratianno was at the time facing trial on criminal conspiracy charges in connection with a trucking operation, but The Weasel was always ready for a hit.

Fratianno headed directly for Las Vegas, and the night he pulled into town, spotted George Seach at one of the card tables in the Sands casino. Bompensiero arrived three days later, but the opportunity was gone. The government had caught word of the contract Rosselli had placed on Seach, perhaps through Bompensiero, who was then feeding information to the FBI. Seach had abandoned his home in Las Vegas and entered the federal witness protection program.

Frustrated in a frontal assault, Rosselli turned to the back rooms, working through his contacts in Washington to undermine official support for the prosecution in Los Angeles. A memo from Hoover assistant J. H. Gale to the FBI's White House liaison, Cartha DeLoach, noted in early 1968 "that certain efforts are being made to hamper the government's investigation into Rosselli." In Los Angeles, Dave Nissen heard reports of "unnamed people in the circles in Washington saying that John was a patriotic citizen who deserved some form of consideration." The effort raised hackles on the field agents working the case: "A couple of the working agents were a bit put out that there seemed to be people taking up for Rosselli in the middle of a criminal case and maybe somebody was bought or something," Nissen reported. But again, the tactic was ineffective. "Nobody said anything to me directly," Nissen recalled, "and it wouldn't make any difference to me."

Still, Rosselli refrained from playing his trump card, the threat to reveal his secret work as an agent of the CIA. He maintained his contact with William Harvey, visiting him in Washington in November, 1967 and again in March, 1968, on the eve of his immigration trial. But there was no mention of blackmail, no hint that Rosselli would turn on the government that had turned on him. Ironically, Harvey was reporting to the FBI on his contacts with Rosselli, compounding the betrayal of his friend and coconspirator. "Subject gave a fill-in on pleadings in the case," Harvey reported to the FBI after the meeting in Washington. "Rosselli did not ask for any assistance. He did not appear to be deeply concerned with his situation, but obviously is irritated."

There was another element in Rosselli's reaction to Nissen's tightening net, one that revealed soul more than strategy. As he had when faced with the collapse of the film labor racket in 1940, Rosselli sought refuge in romance. The object of his affections this time was Helen Greco, widow of the band leader Spike Jones, a pretty, petite singer, soft-spoken, "sheltered and very naïve" despite her show business background. Rosselli had dated Greco in the past, but now his intentions grew serious, and he presented her with an engagement ring, a large sapphire encircled by diamonds.

For a time, it seemed that Rosselli would marry once again. "He was really nuts about her," said singer Betsy Duncan, a friend to both. The couple announced their engagement, and Greco showed off the ring to friends. "She was going to go ahead," Duncan recalled. But Rosselli's legal troubles pursued him, with Nissen's progress reported closely in the press, and Greco's parents vetoed her betrothal. "All of a sudden it was cancelled, and somebody said it was her family," Duncan said. "They were very strict, and they weren't going to let something like that happen." This time, Rosselli would face the burden of his prosecution alone.

With his own unique version of pretrial maneuverings exhausted, Rosselli resigned himself to a long and virtually hopeless legal struggle. His immigration trial opened before U.S. District Court Judge Pierson Hall on April 23, when the government presented reams of material documenting Rosselli's true birth and immigration, and the false representations he made in arrests dating back to 1924, when he claimed his place of birth variously as New Jersey, New York, and Chicago. The trial was interrupted on May 2 to allow, over defense objections, the interrogation of Rosselli's mother, who was stricken with cancer and unable to travel. On May 24, after the jury convened for just ninety minutes, Rosselli was convicted of willful failure to register as an alien.

The Friars Club trial got under way three weeks later, and the complex case would not be submitted to the jury until the following December. Jimmy Cantillon raised a range of issues—the poor reputation of star prosecution witness George Seach; the thin evidence tying Rosselli into the conspiracy; a tape recording of Al Mathes telling coconspirator Ben Teitelbaum, "I never gave Rosselli a nickel in my life." In addition, the defense had a hidden edge, transcripts of Seach's grand jury testimony obtained illegally from a court reporter. But Nissen scored early and often, describing the intricate nature of the card cheating and eliciting a limited confession from Friedman on the witness stand. The clincher against Rosselli was a single check, $10,000 won by Friedman off banker Richard Corenson, which Friedman's secretary cashed in Las Vegas, and then turned over to Rosselli.

Throughout the summer and fall of 1968, Rosselli arrived at court each day via limousine, dark suited and carefully coiffed, his expression implacable. "I never saw him smile, not once during six months in court," Nissen said. "Rosselli was a tough guy," added the attorney for one of the other Friars defendants. "That was the most important thing to him, to be tough and to be quiet. Another guy in his position might have been sitting in the corner complaining about how these guys were taking him down with them, but not Rosselli. He played the big boy all the way through."

Rosselli let his guard down only once, in the courthouse corridor, venting his frustration to FBI agent George Bland. "Y'know," Rosselli argued, "I'm a patriotic citizen. Just check the file, you'll see what I'm talking about." Bland was a poor choice as a potential source of compassion. He cultivated underworld sources with an air of sympathy and understanding, but always maintained his reserve. He was a hunter, and criminals were never more than prey. Bland had learned of Rosselli's CIA work in preparing for the Friars Club trial, and gave no ground to Rosselli's entreaty. "I know all about that," he sneered. "You took the CIA money and did nothing." Bland walked off, leaving Rosselli fuming.

On December 2, 1968, after twenty hours of deliberation, the jury returned guilty verdicts against five defendants, Rosselli included. There was another round of legal motions before sentencing, with Cantillon arguing that the case against Rosselli was tainted by years of illegal electronic surveillance by the FBI, but U.S. District Court Judge William P. Gray ruled that the wiretaps had not contributed to the government case. Cantillon then presented his last line of defense, a packet of references, letters commending Rosselli's character from old film industry allies Lou

Greenspan and George Burrows, from Catholic priest Joseph Clark; even from Friars Club founder George Jessel, who, despite card-cheating scandal, termed Rosselli "sincere, honest, and one of the best Friars, believe me." Demanding a stiff jail sentence, Nissen countered by hammering on Rosselli's reputation as a gangster. "He is a member of the organized criminal element with a long record," Nissen declared. "His involvement in street crime declines as he advances in supervising the organization."

Judge Gray took Nissen at his word, handing down prison terms for four Friars defendants on February 4, 1969. Friedman drew the toughest penalty, six years and $100,000 in fines, but while Gray conceded that Rosselli had "stayed in the background," he placed a close second; $55,000 and five years in a federal penitentiary, plus a six-month term for the immigration violation tacked on to run concurrently. Cantillon filed an appeal, but it was *pro forma*. At 64 years of age, twenty-one years after his release from Terre Haute, Rosselli was headed back to jail.

Settling Accounts

FOR ROSSELLI, THE MOST painful moment in the government's successful drive to capture and imprison him came early on, at the conclusion of the immigration trial, when Cantillon petitioned Judge Hall to release Rosselli on bond pending an appeal of the conviction. Hall knew of Rosselli only from trial proceedings, where Rosselli himself had declined to testify, and from sentencing memos filed by the prosecution. Still, Hall figured he had a pretty good fix on Rosselli, a lifelong hoodlum, a "genuine menace to society," in Nissen's words, the black sheep of a good Italian family.

Judge Hall consented to Rosselli's release, but with one condition. Condescending, chastising, Hall told Rosselli: "I am not going to remand you to custody at this time and one of the reasons is because I saw the three photographs of your dying mother that were introduced into evidence. This case has shown me that you have led a very selfish life and that you are a very selfish man. I am going to let you remain at liberty under bond . . . if you will promise me that you will go back to Boston and visit your dying mother." The lecture was humiliating, and seemed grossly unfair. Hall never realized, as the facts had not been presented at trial, that it was actually Rosselli's loyalty, his annual cash tribute to *la famiglia*, that had led to his undoing. But Rosselli maintained his composure, stoically promising the judge that yes, he would make a journey back to Boston.

In the hiatus between the immigration trial and the Friars Club case, Rosselli made good on his pledge. Renewing bonds with a family he had not seen for forty years intimidated even him, though, and he elected to bring a friend. Joe Shimon, the ex-Washington detective who befriended Rosselli during the plots against Castro, accompanied him on the trip north.

Maria Sacco was gravely ill when her eldest son arrived at her bedside. Bleeding inside, cheeks sunken, her weight down to just eighty-four pounds, she spoke hardly a word. But she was awake and aware, and gazed intently at Rosselli, as if her shining eyes could bridge the chasm of a lifetime apart. He had changed; his hair was silver, his face taut, his voice low and deep; but his smile was still winning, and his eyes still that pale, stratospheric blue. "It was strange with Mother," her daughter Connie said later. "She was overcome. She just stared and stared."

The homecoming lasted three days. "Oh, what a reunion," Joe Shimon laughed in recollection. "There were three sisters and the brother and their families and we start eating this Italian dinner at eight o'clock and don't stop until one. They were all kids when he left home, and they'd hardly seen him since. Oh, what a party." In the days following, Rosselli showed Shimon around his East Boston, the old neighborhood where he still had relatives, the schoolyards and the church, and the home he had attempted to burn down. Everywhere, he was greeted fondly and with deference. *La famiglia* proved enduring, after all.

Rosselli's interregnum was broken on June 5 by dramatic news from Los Angeles. In the midst of a frantic, late-entry campaign for the Democratic nomination for President, Bobby Kennedy had been shot and mortally wounded. The saga of the destruction of a political dynasty had become a recurrent national nightmare, but this time around, Rosselli had no role to play. He was immersed in the currents of his own personal travails, and continued his East Coast sojourn with a stop in Miami, where Rosselli's sister Edith had married and raised a family with Joseph Daigle, a NASA engineer.

Rosselli never contacted the Daigles during the months of his clandestine work for the CIA, but with his secret identity now a matter of record, he took the opportunity to meet his nieces JoAnn and Eloise, and their spouses, for the first time. Rosselli would return to Boston once more, in the summer of 1969, but there was no celebration. On August 1, at the age of 83, Maria Sacco died of cancer. She was buried in Malden, in the same cemetery as her husband, Vincenzo, and Rosselli joined his family for the funeral. In the absence of the matriarch, there were hard feelings for the years of absence. Quarrels erupted, and Rosselli returned to Los Angeles alone and discouraged. The criminal conviction had made his continued presence in Las Vegas untenable, and the court proceedings had exhausted his funds. Rosselli approached the Hughes Nevada Operation for a $50,000 loan to assist in his legal battle, but they turned him away. He finally managed to swing the same amount from Frank Sennes, Dalitz' longtime entertainment manager who remained active with HNO under Maheu. Rosselli got the money, but it was difficult, and it was never enough.

Rosselli relied on his attorney and close friend, Jimmy Cantillon, to press his appeals, but Cantillon himself was reeling in the face of personal and professional disaster. His father, an accomplished attorney who served as a life model for the son, had died just before the Friars case went to court. Cantillon's grief was compounded when he was charged with criminal violations for accepting copies of the stolen grand jury transcripts. Formerly regarded as one of the top legal minds in Los Angeles, Cantillon began to drink heavily, a vice that led to his death.

With his appeals and his jail sentence pending, Rosselli was called before yet another federal tribunal, one more dangerous than any he had faced since 1942. In exchange for a reduction in sentence, Maury Friedman had made a deal: he was cooperating with a government investigation into hidden mob interests in Las Vegas. Dave Nissen was again leading the inquiry, and while Friedman had told the story of the Detroit Mafia investments in the Frontier, Nissen was convinced that Rosselli could deliver much, much more. Rosselli was already down—Nissen felt that if he could apply enough pressure, Rosselli would crack.

Rosselli appeared before the federal grand jury in Los Angeles on May 1, 1970, and the arduous process of examination began again. He claimed the privilege of the Fifth Amendment, and was promptly taken before a judge and granted immunity from prosecution. Recalled that afternoon, he was questioned about his connections to organized crime, including Chicago mob and gambling figures Tony Accardo, Paul Ricca, and Lou

Lederer. As he had before the Kefauver Committee twenty years before, Rosselli managed to walk the fine line between compliance with court orders and outright cooperation. "Rosselli would respond," Nissen said later. "He'd say oh, yeah, I know so and so, but when it came down to whether they ever did anything together or said anything together that was about a crime, it was no, no, not them."

On May 12, Rosselli was returned to the grand jury chambers and grilled on his influence in Las Vegas. On May 14, he was questioned about Frank Bompensiero, Jimmy Fratianno, Moe Dalitz, and Giancana lieutenant Frank LaPorte. Rosselli conceded that he had met with LaPorte in Cantillon's office, but when asked who else had attended the meeting, and what was discussed, he angrily balked, asserting that he was being "set up for a perjury charge." On May 19, he was quizzed on the sale of the Desert Inn to Howard Hughes, but still yielded no new information.

Frustrated, Nissen moved to turn up the heat. A month later, on June 17, Rosselli was questioned on his personal financial involvement in Las Vegas, and then again on Bompensiero. This time, Nissen had called Bompensiero as well, and Rosselli's regular hit man was sitting outside the hearing room. With his "recollection" exhausted, Rosselli was asked to step outside and identify Bompensiero, a request he refused. He was then ordered into the waiting room, where he and The Bomp sat together in tense silence.

Rosselli never let on, but the pressure of the investigation was literally eating him up inside. He suffered repeated, excruciating bouts of diverticulitis, and in July, underwent surgery at the Sansum Clinic for removal of fourteen inches of his colon. Besides easing the pain in his bowels, the operation provided him some respite from Nissen's onslaught, but the reprieve did not last.

In August, Nissen turned again to the tactic of setting Rosselli up before his peers in the mob. Rosselli was subpoenaed to appear on the same day Anthony Zerilli was brought in from Detroit to testify. Once again, Rosselli confirmed that he knew Zerilli and that he had met with him and Maury Friedman, but said he could not recall any conversations. And once again, Rosselli exchanged grim glances with his fellow gangster outside the grand jury hearing room.

Rosselli was aware of the danger he was facing. In a note to Cantillon, he worried, "They're trying to make it look like I'm talking when they know I'm not." But in the end, Nissen relented, realizing that continued interrogation was pointless. "I don't think John ever threw any crumbs of any kind to anybody," Nissen said in grudging admiration.

Rosselli's ordeal before the grand jury was over, but his time at liberty was running out. His Friars Club and immigration convictions had been affirmed by the Ninth Circuit Court of Appeal on June 19, 1970, and a petition for hearing before the Supreme Court was dismissed on November 9. Disappointed with Jimmy Cantillon, Rosselli turned to Ed Morgan, who referred him to Tom Wadden—a former partner of Ed Bennett Williams—who had extensive experience defending Las Vegas gambling operators.

Wadden learned the details of Rosselli's dealings with the government from Morgan, and decided that Rosselli's only avenue was to threaten the CIA. Word went out from Wadden to Morgan, to Maheu, to Jim O'Connell, and finally to Director of Central Intelligence Richard Helms, that if the CIA did not intervene on Rosselli's behalf, he would spill the entire story of his work for the Agency. Helms was fully aware of the explosive nature of the material, but he was shortsighted enough to believe that the damage would be limited to the reputations of the men involved at the time, and not the Agency per se. On November 18, Helms decided the CIA would make no move to assist John Rosselli. Bob Maheu was notified of the decision, and advised that he was in "complete agreement."

In early January 1971, Rosselli made good on his threat. Divulging his secret violated deeply held precepts, but the government had been hounding him without a break for three full years. They had broken the rules of conduct, and finally, he would too. Still, Rosselli moved haltingly, only at the prodding of his attorney, and his reluctance was reflected in the method he chose to employ. He would discuss the matter only with his attorney, but he invited the press to eavesdrop.

The conduit was Jack Anderson, the columnist who had served Rosselli so well in publishing the Castro plant. Anderson and his assistant, Les Whitten, met on January 11 with Rosselli and Joe Shimon at Tom Wadden's home in Washington. The journalists posed their questions to Wadden, who then queried his client; the answers took the same route, from Rosselli to Wadden, with Anderson and Whitten listening in. "It was a peculiar arrangement, as if there were a translator," Anderson recalled in an interview. "Johnny never acknowledged us. He acted as if we weren't there."

Thus the story came out, the meetings with Maheu, the sniper squads slipped into Cuba, the sinking of Rosselli's speedboat. Trafficante's name was never mentioned, nor Giancana's; nor was the tale that Castro had captured and "turned" one of Rosselli's hit teams. Rosselli was telling his own story, one of government service and government betrayal.

Jack Anderson broke the blockbuster story nationwide in his column on January 18. "Locked in the darkest recesses of the Central Intelligence Agency is the story of six attempts against Cuba's Fidel Castro," the syndicated column began. It was the first time the tale had been told, and Anderson told it in detail, naming Rosselli, Maheu, O'Connell, and Harvey. John McCone, the CIA director when "Phase II" was under way, denied the story emphatically. "It could not have happened," he told Anderson.

Anderson covered for Rosselli in the column, ascribing him "a flat no comment," but the CIA knew full well the source of the story. Tight-lipped, they awaited the fallout; their only official response was a secret request that the INS "flag" them on any progress in the deportation case. Ironically, the only step taken to stall deportation came from David Nissen, who asked that Rosselli be allowed to remain in the country long enough to serve his full prison term.

Surprisingly, perhaps, no reporters contacted Rosselli for comment or reaction on the Anderson column. For the moment, history had passed Rosselli by. The war on communism had shifted from the Caribbean to Southeast Asia, where the Khmer Rouge was laying siege to Phnom Penh. Jimmy Hoffa was attempting to stage a comeback from a federal prison cell. And in Los Angeles, the crime beat was dominated by Charlie Manson, then being tried for murder.

Formerly at the center of events, John Rosselli now fought his battles on a more personal plane. He had taken the opportunity to revive his dormant relations with his family, and he had repaid the government's duplicity with a betrayal of his own. He had played out his hand, he had balanced his books, and he was ready to do his time. On January 25, 1971, a cool, hazy Monday morning in Los Angeles, Rosselli turned himself in to the county sheriff.

A Modicum of Mercy

FOR A MAXIMUM-SECURITY jail, McNeil Island Federal Penitentiary had a reputation as relatively low-key. Isolated off the forested coast of Steilacoom, Washington, it could be reached only by ferry. Escape was unlikely, and as a result, security restrictions on a prisoner's day-to-day activities were light. Cellblock violence rates were low, and supervision was lax enough that inmates once built and operated a small still inside the prison walls.

Yet for John Rosselli, his assignment to McNeil Island represented a mortal threat. The cold, wet ocean wind aggravated his feeble lungs, once weakened by tuberculosis and now ravaged by emphysema. He was already ill with a cold when he arrived on February 25, 1971, after a month in the custody of the L.A. sheriff, and his condition soon took on aspects of pneumonia. In addition, whether brought on by his own frustration with his sentence or by his reputation as a high-level gangster, Rosselli received rough treatment at the hands of the prison guards. Depressed by the betrayal that had landed him on that desolate outpost, his horizons limited to the gray wash of the sea and the slate winter skies, Rosselli began to fear that he would end his days in jail.

It was then, in his moment of isolation and despair, that the pendulum of Rosselli's fate finally reached the end of its arc, and began to swing back in his favor. The first sign came from Washington, where Jack Anderson and Les Whitten decided to publish another column on Rosselli's service to the government. Rosselli had impressed the two journalists as a rare character whose story held enough pathos to bear a second look. "I remember saying to Jack when [Rosselli] left, Jesus, what a buccaneer," Whitten said in an interview. "He was sort of your modern-day pirate in a way. I had respect for the guy's guts, to tell you the truth."

The day of Rosselli's arrival at McNeil Island, Jack Anderson's syndicated column was released under the headline, "Mystery Man CIA Chose to Assassinate Castro Lies in Jail; Risked Neck, At Own Expense, Making Trips to Cuban Coast." Anderson's previous columns had focused on the plots against Castro; this time he focused on Rosselli, touching on his background as a bootlegger and gambling executive, and describing his efforts, "James Bond fashion," to eliminate Castro. "Rosselli's reward," Anderson concluded, was prosecution on what William Harvey described in the column as a "bum rap." Harvey had declined to discuss the details of Rosselli's CIA work, but he went on record with Anderson to assert, "The Friars Club indictment is phony. Rosselli had no more to do with that than I had."

Anderson's column produced no immediate results, but perhaps that was for the best. On February 26, 1971, Tony Zerilli, Michael Polizzi, and four others were indicted on federal racketeering and conspiracy counts in connection with their hidden interests in the Frontier Hotel casino. Maury Friedman was named an unindicted coconspirator, and served as the lead prosecution witness during two weeks on the witness stand. The trial concluded two months later with multiple convictions and extended jail time for the leaders of the Detroit and St. Louis Mafia, the first time that out-of-state gangsters had been convicted of skimming operations in Las Vegas. Despite his tight-lipped performance before the grand jury, and despite the fact that he was not among the forty-seven witnesses called in the case, Rosselli was fortunate to have been removed from the proceedings by 800 miles and the bars of his prison cell.

Rosselli's next break came in July, the fruit of the labors of Washington attorney Tom Wadden. Pursuant to a writ of habeas corpus, Rosselli was granted a hearing on reduction of his jail term. Once again, as in the confrontation with the CIA, Wadden planned to invoke Rosselli's service to his country. And once again, Rosselli was deeply reluctant to endorse Wadden's strategy.

Wadden arranged for Rosselli to meet with Adrian Marshall, a client attorney on the West Coast, to help prepare for the judicial hearing. But when Marshall showed up at the visiting section of the federal penitentiary at Terminal Island in Los Angeles, Rosselli was tight-lipped and angry, refusing to discuss his case, and raged at the prison guards who brought him in for the interview. Years later, Rosselli told journalist Jimmy Breslin that he still considered Wadden's plea "a breach of security." "The lawyer should not have used that [the CIA story] to try to get me out," he said flatly.

Knowing that Judge William P. Gray was a veteran of Army Intelligence, convinced that appealing to his patriotic sympathy was Rosselli's best chance for an early release, Wadden and Marshall continued to build their case without their client's participation. For documentation, they turned to Jack Anderson and Les Whitten, who agreed to submit affidavits swearing to the veracity of their published stories. The journalists took that unusual step, Whitten said later, out of a sense of fairness: "They were letting the goddamn guy go down the drain. Rosselli was the one everybody was turning disloyal against. And everybody said there was never a Mafia guy more loyal than Johnny Rosselli. You could talk to anyone in the mob, and they'd say Johnny Rosselli is a real gentleman. Well, that means something different in their terms than it might in yours and mine. But it's odd, isn't it, that everyone turned on Rosselli who had a reputation for probity, you know, in that world."

On July 6, 1971, Marshall presented his argument: that Rosselli deserved some recognition in his sentence for risking his life in service to his country. Judge Gray professed to be little impressed:

"I sentenced Mr. Rosselli on the basis of his prior record, and coupled with the offenses of which he was found guilty in this case, and I am not going to consider in sentencing Mr. Rosselli a speculation about what he may or may not have done in other respects.

"Also I have to tell you, Mr. Marshall," Gray declared, "that I am just not able to conclude that Mr. Rosselli is entitled to brownie points for having tried to assassinate Fidel Castro, if that is the fact. . . . If so, in the court's judgment, it would be a catastrophic occurrence. I am not going to conclude that a court should give credit to a person who attempts the assassination of anybody."

The only reporter to cover the hearing, Gene Blake of the Los Angeles *Times,* treated the appeal skeptically, especially after managing to contact Bob Maheu in Las Vegas. Asked if he would confirm Rosselli's account of the plots against Castro, Maheu once again gave Rosselli short shrift. "I will not dignify such a story by even commenting on it," Maheu intoned.

For his own part, Rosselli escaped the indignities of Gray's chiding and Maheu's published rejection, electing to remain in his jail cell rather than attend the sentencing hearing. Soon after, he was returned to the grim confines of McNeil Island.

Despite Judge Gray's terse response, Adrian Marshall's appeal apparently had an impact. It may be that, in the privacy of his own chambers, the judge reflected on his own experience in the military, and on the affidavits detailing the risks Rosselli had run. Or it could be that Gray took notice of the fact that Friedman, the primary architect of the Friars Club scheme, was already free, having turned state's witness in the Frontier case. Whatever the reason, Judge Gray relented, and in October, issued an order reducing Rosselli's jail term to four years.

Rosselli got a second break in December, this time via a less conventional intercession. Political fixer Fred Black, who was himself convicted of tax evasion in 1964 but saw the case thrown out by the Supreme Court due to illegal bugging by the FBI, managed to arrange for Rosselli's transfer from McNeil Island to the more hospitable climes of a minimum-security federal prison camp in Safford, Arizona. Black learned of Rosselli's predicament from their mutual friend Allen Smiley during a chance meeting at Drucker's Barber Shop in Beverly Hills. "I happened to run into Smiley there and I asked after Rosselli, and he told me he was dying up there at McNeil Island," Black recalled in an interview. "He asked if I would help, and I made a call to Washington [D.C.], and a week later he was moved to Arizona." Black said he could not recall who it was he had contacted, but his influence in Congress and the Washington bureaucracy at the time was legendary.

Rosselli also took comfort from the continuing interest of a powerful sponsor who had little influence over the prison system, but might prove an important ally in the years to come. Santo Trafficante, the Mafia leader who worked with Rosselli in the beginning of the Castro plots, went out of his way to inquire after his old friend's welfare, and to offer assistance to Rosselli's family. Rosselli had introduced Trafficante to the Daigles over dinner at the Fontainebleau Hotel in 1970, and Trafficante took a proprietary interest in the family's fortunes thereafter.

The transfer south took the sting out of the remainder of Rosselli's jail term. At Safford, and then at the federal prison camp in Lompoc, California, Rosselli received the sort of treatment an elderly, gray-haired inmate might expect. He "got everything he wanted," he told a friend later, and twice, when his intestines acted up, he received specialized treatment at the national medical center for federal prisoners in Springfield, Missouri. In turn, Rosselli played the part of model prisoner, respectful of authority and friendly toward his fellow inmates. He worked in the landscape department and was placed in charge of the tool room. "John has been a significant constructive influence among the other men assigned to the crew," a progress report noted, "always emphasizing the propriety of following the rules of the camp and performing work satisfactorily. His behavior has been excellent."

Rosselli was released on parole on October 5, 1973. He had served just two years and nine months in prison; most of the first year was hard time, but the balance was relatively easy. The day he got out, Rosselli took a room at the Beverly Hilton Hotel, slipped into the cool waters of the pool, and then strolled down Wilshire Boulevard to enjoy a gourmet dinner at La Dolce Vita.

The government had taken its best shot, Rosselli had done his time, and now all that was behind him. Stopping to turn into the familiar dusk of the restaurant, Rosselli didn't even have to glance over his shoulder. After three decades of surveillance, the FBI had dropped its tail.

14

THE WHEEL OF HISTORY

Watergate

Lifelong gangsters rarely grow old. They die of the hazards that mark their trade, by gunshot or garrote, or by the fast life that goes with it, from alcoholism or early heart attack. But for those who do manage to live past their prime, for Mafia chiefs like Tony Accardo and Meyer Lansky, old age frequently brings peace and relaxation, free from government interference and the daily headaches of the crime syndicate.

John Rosselli found no such respite. His conspiracies had reached beyond the myriad but essentially routine scams that separated men from their money. In his intrigues with the CIA, and later by intimating inside knowledge of the assassination of John F. Kennedy, Rosselli had entangled himself in the affairs of the nation, epochal events that would continue to rumble, restless and unsettling, in the corridors of the American consciousness. History had passed Rosselli by, but his name was etched in its

303

transcript, and when the wheel turned, it would find him again, drawing him inexorably back into the vortex of great events, of unfinished business.

Rosselli's first weeks of freedom in 1973 followed the pattern of his early probation in 1947. Checking out of the Beverly Hilton, he headed up the coast to Santa Barbara, where he spent a week undergoing tests and close examination at the Sansum Clinic. Returning to Los Angeles October 16, he moved in with his old friend, film producer Bryan Foy, at Foy's rambling Spanish-style estate in the Santa Monica Mountains, overlooking Beverly Hills. The pair took up where they had left off almost twenty years before, spending afternoons at the racetrack and evenings at show biz hangouts like the Bistro and Chasen's in Beverly Hills.

Rosselli was pleased to find that his cachet at the dinner clubs had survived his latest jail term. Attorney Leslie Scherr observed the unspoken authority at Rosselli's command during a visit to Los Angeles just after Rosselli's release from prison. "We went out to a very fancy Italian restaurant, Allen Smiley and myself, and John brought up the rear. The place was jammed, I mean people everywhere, waiting, just jammed. And the maître d' asks my name and I say Scherr, and he says do you have a reservation, and I said no, and he looks at me with this very patronizing smile. By then John had come up, and he looks at John and says, 'Oh, Mr. Rosselli, of course we have your table.' It was just stunning. I saw this crew come running out and set up this extra table, in an alcove, they had to move another over, just to make room. I've never seen anything like it in my life. Johnny never said a thing. And I know we didn't have a reservation."

Rosselli's revel was interrupted the afternoon of October 22, when he and Foy attended the races at Santa Anita. While Rosselli made a trip to the betting window, track security agent John Hansen collared Foy and told him a patron of the exclusive Turf Club had spotted Rosselli in the crowd, and had taken offense at the presence of the ex-con in their midst. Foy was informed that convicted felons were barred under track rules, and Rosselli would be ejected. Foy responded angrily, "I could point out a dozen guys out here who fit that description," and that Rosselli had permission from his parole officer to attend the races. Unimpressed, Hansen waited for Rosselli to return, and then curtly explained that he was being ejected and barred from the track.

Around the same time, Rosselli found he was being tailed again, not by the FBI but by the Intelligence Division of the Los Angeles police. Clearly, he was attracting too much attention in his old home town. Yet

Rosselli knew he could not return to the familiar cityscape of Las Vegas. His conviction and jail term had effectively put him out of circulation there, and his lifelong mentor, Paul Ricca, had died in his sleep while Rosselli was in prison, further eroding his ties to the old Capone Outfit.

In his final act as don of the gambling capital, Rosselli helped to ensure an orderly transition of power by meeting in Palm Springs with Tony Accardo and Tony "The Ant" Spilotro, a vicious gambling and narcotics operator who stepped in as Chicago's representative in the desert. In place of charm and tact, Spilotro relied on strong-arm intimidation, terrifying his minions until his own murder in 1986, and leaving them nostalgic for Rosselli's more civil era.

On November 13, Rosselli abandoned the West Coast, flying to Florida to visit his sister. He told his probation officer that, if it could be arranged, he hoped to move there permanently. Plantation, Florida, was a quiet, upscale suburban neighborhood twenty minutes from Miami, laced by freshwater canals and boasting half a dozen golf courses. Edith and Joe Daigle lived on the eastern edge of town in a nondescript, white brick tract home with an extra bedroom and a small backyard pool. Perhaps here, in the bosom of his long-lost family, Rosselli would find his peace. The Daigles accepted him warmly, even vacating the master bedroom in recognition of his age and his prestige. Ignoring the niceties of his fictional identity, they called him Phil around the house. On December 7, Rosselli requested and was granted permission to reside in Plantation. For the first time in more than fifty years, he spent Christmas with his family.

In Miami, Santo Trafficante's solicitude continued. He offered to set Rosselli up as an executive in charge of one of his quasi-legal front businesses. But Rosselli knew the dangers of joining a partnership with a hair-trigger killer like Trafficante, and chose to maintain a discreet distance, consorting socially with the Florida don at his home, and in the evenings at restaurants and nightclubs, but avoiding deeper entanglements.

For a man accustomed to living off the occasional windfall, Rosselli's income had dwindled to the sums he collected from Social Security and the Frontier gift shop, but he kept his expenses minimal, living rent-free in Plantation and staying with friends on his travels. Rather than begin a chancy effort to get back into business, he kept busy plotting strategy in his court battle with the INS, which had resumed deportation proceedings upon Rosselli's release from prison. To assist in his defense, Rosselli hired David Walters, a leading Miami attorney and a specialist in immigration matters. Walters once served as the American ambassador to the Vatican, and listed among his clients such prominent international figures as Carlos Prio, former Venezuelan President Marco Perez-Jimenez, and, perhaps not incongruously, Santo Trafficante. The initial hearing in Rosselli's deportation case was held in Los Angeles on January 4, 1974; thereafter the case was transferred to Miami.

It was in February 1974 that history first crooked a beckoning finger toward Rosselli, when he was subpoenaed to appear in secret session before the special prosecution force investigating the Watergate break-in. Senator Sam Ervin's nationally televised hearings in 1973 had focused on the role of the Nixon administration in covering up its connection to the burglary of the Democratic Party National Headquarters, but had never pinpointed the reasons for the "third-rate burglary" that precipitated Nixon's demise. Separately, however, Special Prosecutor Leon Jaworski and his staff were tracking that very question, an effort that led them to Rosselli.

The investigation hinged on Richard Nixon's successful effort in June 1972 to have the CIA intervene and block the FBI's inquiry into the Watergate break-in. As was later revealed in the release of the White House tapes, Nixon had forced the spy agency's hand by warning CIA Director Richard Helms that "this entire affair may be connected to the Bay of Pigs, and if it opens up, the Bay of Pigs may be blown." The implications knocked the cool-headed spy chief out of character. "Richard Helms yelled like a scalded cat," John Ehrlichman described the scene later. CIA involvement in the Bay of Pigs had already received extensive public attention, of course, but what remained an official secret was their collaboration with the Mafia.

Rosselli had tried the same ploy against the CIA when he sought their assistance in his battle with the Justice Department, but Helms refused to go along, presuming the press would ignore the story of a convicted felon. In his later confrontation with the Agency, Nixon had more success.

What intrigued the Watergate prosecutors was the possibility that Nixon himself had something to hide in the "Bay of Pigs thing," and that he had ordered the Watergate break-in, as well as E. Howard Hunt's aborted burglary of Hank Greenspun's safe in Las Vegas, to determine whether the secret had leaked. The presumed source of the leak was Bob Maheu, friend to both Greenspun and Democratic National Committee chairman Larry O'Brien. And the explosive secret Nixon feared might come out was his own direct involvement in the initial assassination plots against Fidel Castro. Significantly, E. Howard Hunt's "exposé" book on the Bay of Pigs *Give Us This Day,* which cited Nixon's support for assassination but said the tactic was rejected by the CIA leadership, was published in 1973, soon after Hunt accepted tens of thousands of dollars in hush payments from the Nixon White House.

Another possible target in the break-ins was information on illegal loans made by Hughes to Nixon through Bebe Rebozo, material that, again, could have been leaked by Maheu. But Frank Sturgis, Hunt's team leader at the Watergate, gave ammunition to the Bay of Pigs angle in an interview with journalist Andrew St. George. "One of the things we were looking for in the Democratic National Committee's files, and in some other Washington file cabinets, too, was a thick secret memorandum from the Castro government addressed confidentially to the Democrats' platform committee," Sturgis alleged. "The Cubans were providing an itemized list of all the [CIA] abuses. The complaints were especially bitter about various attempts to assassinate the Castro brothers."

Hoping to get to the bottom of the Nixon administration burglaries, the Watergate prosecutors turned to John Rosselli. Leslie Scherr, the Washington, D.C., attorney who appeared with Rosselli at the closed hearing, recalled, "It was so convoluted, you really had to be John Le Carré to follow it." But judging from the questions posed to Rosselli, Scherr said, the prosecutors felt that "the reason why the break-in occurred at the Democratic Party headquarters was because Nixon or somebody in the Republican Party suspected that the Democrats had information as to Nixon's involvement with the CIA's original contact with Rosselli. [The Republicans] felt that a document existed showing Nixon was involved with or knew what was going on with the CIA and the assassination of Castro and Rosselli's involvement, et cetera. It's for that reason that they wanted to try to get this information that Nixon suspected they were going to use against him. That was the theory, and they asked John to come in and testify."

Scherr said he could not recall the details of Rosselli's testimony, but said his client offered nothing that would confirm Nixon's involvement in the CIA plots, or shed any light on the motivations of the Watergate burglars. The testimony was concluded in a single session, and no word of his participation was made public. On February 25, Rosselli returned home to Plantation.

Rosselli made it through his first appearance before Washington investigators without incident, but the Watergate hearings ushered in an unprecedented period of inquiry and examination in the capital. Moved by the revelations of conspiracy and criminal activity in the White House, suspicious after the systematic deception that attended the prosecution of the war in Vietnam, the Congress and the press initiated a series of probes into every facet of government activity, focusing with special intensity on the clandestine activities of the intelligence community, and eventually encompassing the assassination of John F. Kennedy. It was a powerful movement, a national catharsis rooted in the shock of discovery and a sense of betrayal, and John Rosselli emerged as a central figure in the drama.

The Committee

GERALD R. FORD TOOK TWO important steps to cool the fever of investigation that had seized Washington when he became President after Nixon's resignation. The first was to issue a blanket pardon to his predecessor, effectively heading off any further probing into Watergate.

Ford's second move came less than a year later with the appointment, on January 4, 1975, of the Rockefeller Commission, a blue-ribbon panel formed to address allegations of domestic spying by the CIA, but this time the ruse didn't hold. Comprised of such establishment stalwarts as Vice-President Nelson Rockefeller, General Lymon Lemnitzer, Council on Foreign Relations member John T. Connor, and Governor Ronald Reagan, the commission came under immediate attack, and its final report largely exonerating the CIA was dismissed immediately upon its release in July 1975.

Not to be usurped, the Senate went ahead with the creation of its own Select Committee on Intelligence Activities, chaired by Senator Frank Church and charged with a broad mandate to probe both the CIA and the FBI. Even while the Senate team was getting under way, leaks from the Rockefeller Commission staff provided the press with a steady supply of stunning new allegations—that the CIA had approved the assassination of Che Guevara and the Castro brothers, and, separately, that Bobby Kennedy had known of the plots, and of the collaboration with the Mafia.

Almost from the beginning, the Church Committee made the assassination plots a top priority, in part because they represented, in Church's words, "the most infamous and extreme action taken by the CIA," but also due to the sheer shock registered by the revelations. "The assassination inquiry went beyond our wildest expectations," staff director Bill Miller recalled. The initial committee proceedings took place in secret, but the public got inklings of its subject matter from the media. On February 28, Daniel Schorr reported on the "CBS Evening News" that the committee had received material on assassination plots. And on May 21, after he emerged from a three-hour briefing by CIA Director William Colby, a visibly shaken Frank Church told reporters, "It is simply intolerable that any agency of the government of the United States may engage in murder."

With CIA assassinations at the top of the agenda, the spotlight of inquiry began to swing inexorably to the mobsters involved in the plots, to Rosselli, Santo Trafficante, and Sam Giancana. The onetime conspirators watched the proceedings closely. "Everybody was concerned how much exposure there was going to be," recalled Joe Shimon, confidant of both Giancana and Rosselli. "We had no idea which way Church was going to go." They got their answer on June 13, following the testimony of former CIA Director Richard Helms, when committee investigators were directed to bring all three gangsters in to testify.

Each reacted in his own fashion. Trafficante, the only one whose name had not yet surfaced publicly in connection with the CIA, made himself scarce, departing Florida for an estate he kept in Costa Rica, well beyond the reach of congressional process servers. In Chicago, Sam Giancana was indignant. Gravely ill and recuperating from abdominal surgery, he had already been called before a federal grand jury in Chicago, and had little taste for a grilling by a congressional committee. "He called me up when he got the subpoena," said Shimon. "He said he didn't mind coming in, but that he had nothing to tell them. He didn't see the point. Sam never had much to do with that whole [assassination] thing, and that's what he was going to say."

Rosselli, of course, was deeply involved in the plots, but he was more willing to testify. His only qualm, he told Shimon, was his obligation to the CIA. "John said, 'I'll do whatever the CIA says. It's their decision.' So he checked with Jim O'Connell, and he said to go ahead, that it was all coming out anyway," Shimon recalled. "There wasn't any problem with the organization [the Mafia], because he wasn't talking about anything connected with them. There was no problem."

But there was a problem. On June 19, a week before his scheduled appearance in Washington, Giancana enjoyed a casual dinner with his daughter Francine and her husband, Jerome DePalma, and trusted henchmen Chuckie English and Butch Blasi. Giancana said good-bye to his guests around 10 P.M., and retired to his basement den, a personal fortress with double-lock steel doors, where he set about cooking an after-dinner snack of sausage and escarole. Sometime before midnight, unbeknownst to a housekeeper upstairs, Giancana was joined by a friend. And as the former Chicago don busied himself at the stove, the friend quietly pulled out a silenced .22-caliber target pistol, stepped up behind his host, leveled the barrel at the base of his head, and pulled the trigger. When Giancana slumped to the floor, already dead, the killer rolled the body over and carefully fired six more shots, one into his mouth and five in a semicircle under his chin. In the Mafia's argot of death, the message was clear: Giancana had been silenced. Permanently.

John Rosselli received word of Giancana's murder at 6 A.M. the following morning. He was staying at Fred Black's apartment at the Watergate Hotel, preparing to meet that day for a preliminary session with Church Committee staff investigator David Bushong. Attorney Leslie Scherr heard news of the slaying on the radio, and called Rosselli immediately. "He was startled, he seemed as surprised as we were," Scherr recalled. But there was no break in Rosselli's manner, no discernible lapse into emotion or fear. Rosselli had received phone calls like this before. "He wasn't shocked, I remember that. He was strangely unaffected. He didn't say 'Oh my God' or anything like that. He reflected for a moment on the phone, and then he put himself together in a hurry, and said come on down and we'll talk about it."

Spurred by the dire news from Chicago, Tom Wadden hurried over to the Watergate, expecting to make a hasty exit to some more secure location. But arriving at Rosselli's suite, he found him relaxed, almost expansive. "I come busting into the apartment and he's got his finest smoking robe and his silk pajamas on and part of the breakfast he'd ordered was there and part of it was still coming up," Wadden remembered. "I said, 'Get your goddamn clothes on and let's get outta here,' and Johnny said, 'They're not going to do anything to me. If they want to kill me they're going to kill me, but they're not going to scare me. Let's just sit down and have some breakfast.' So we did. I don't think Johnny was ever afraid of anything."

If Rosselli was untroubled, David Bushong and the staff of the Church

Committee were decidedly shaken. Though the authorities in Chicago were satisfied that Giancana's killing stemmed from internal bickering within the local underworld, the investigators in Washington were convinced that the imminent CIA hearings had precipitated the act, and that Santo Trafficante had commissioned it. "Everybody knew when he was going to be served [with a Church Committee subpoena], and they killed him contemporaneous with that service," Bushong observed years later. "I mean, we weren't knocking at the door when they were shooting at him, but basically it was almost that close. And the guy who had the most to lose was Trafficante. He had the muscle to kill [Giancana], and he had the motive and the rationale in that time frame to kill him. He ran the risk of the full force and attention of the American political institutions focusing their attention on him, and then he had to worry about other people worrying about what he would say the way he was worrying about what Giancana would say. What Trafficante stood to lose was his life."

Convinced that Rosselli faced the same danger, fearful that he might lose his only remaining witness from the underworld side of the CIA assassination plots, Bushong decided to forfeit the initial deposition and proceed directly to a hearing before the full committee. "It was clear to me [after the Giancana murder] that here was the only live witness left," Bushong said. "I wanted him on the record, and I wanted him quick." Rosselli was scheduled to appear on Tuesday, June 24.

The Hearings

INTENSELY AWARE THAT IT was delving into the most delicate clandestine activities of the American government, the Church Committee appropriated for its proceedings the most secure area available, a remote hearing room located high by the Capitol dome, a windowless chamber with a single access and enclosed within a bug-proof, five-foot casing of concrete, formerly the domain of the Joint Atomic Energy Commission. "They were planning not to be surveilled under any circumstances," said Church Committee staff attorney Frederick Baron.

The day of his appearance, Rosselli and attorney Leslie Scherr slipped into the Capitol building through a back entrance, their movements attended by a detail of Capitol police. Guided down a long, echoing corridor into the pale, subdued light of the hearing room, they were directed to a witness table facing a raised horseshoe bench. Sitting behind, arrayed by party and seniority, were eleven of the nation's preeminent politicians, each powerful and famous in his own right, including Democrats Frank Church, Walter Mondale, and Gary Hart, and Republicans Barry Goldwater, John Tower, Howard Baker, and Richard Schweiker. "It was a full house," Baron recalled. "Johnny Rosselli's testimony was a highlight of the secret investigation. All the senators on the committee were both disturbed and fascinated by Rosselli's involvement in the CIA plot, and determined to understand where it all led."

Dressed in a finely cut black suit, a tailored shirt, and conservative tie, his face lined and a little drawn but still tanned and sharply defined, Rosselli impressed the senators with his easy charm and his relaxed manner. "His nonchalance really surprised me," Gary Hart recalled. "I expected a typical hood, I guess, but he was more of a George Raft type of character, avuncular, almost humorous. He seemed rather proud of having been involved."

The questioning got under way at a deliberate pace, with the senators pressing for every detail—how did the plots get under way, who were the CIA people involved, who were the Cuban contacts; dates, times, locations, weapons—and Rosselli laid it out in a low, throaty narrative. "John gave a fully detailed description," Scherr recounted. "Everything that had gone on in '61 and '62, everything from that era, and every one of those guys were mesmerized by John. He was hypnotic. The guy would have been a wonderful lawyer."

As the story unfolded, the tension in the room ratcheted higher. The sense of discovery was electrifying. Helms and Colby had summarized the broad outlines of the CIA plots, but here was one of the actual conspirators, the subject of hushed rumor and secret inquiry, describing in fine detail the meetings and methods, the weapons and poisons deployed in a reckless scheme that seemed implausible even for fiction. Moreover, there was the big-as-life apparition before the senators of a bona fide mafioso, a gangster who ran with the fabled Al Capone. "I was especially intrigued by the fact that we actually had a member of the Mafia in before us," Richard Schweiker recalled. "It certainly brought reality into the witness room."

Rosselli was real, all right, but his panache, his cool confidence, and his offhand recital of diabolical facts lent the hearing an almost dreamlike cast. Forty minutes into the presentation, Barry Goldwater broke into the narrative with an observation. "Mr. Rosselli, we've had CIA agents, we've had FBI agents, we've had other members of the government here, and all of them came in with their notes and files, and they referred to them in answering our questions, and it's remarkable to me how your testimony dovetails with theirs. Tell me, Mr. Rosselli, during the time that all this was going on, were you taking notes?"

Rosselli looked back at him, deadpan, silent for a moment, and then replied. "Senator, in my business, we don't take notes." That broke the spell. "Everybody was on the floor, laughing at this spontaneous statement," Scherr said, smiling at the memory. "It's a moment I'll never forget. And that really made everything a lot easier. Everybody was chatting with him and he was very, very funny and he really captivated them."

Rosselli's testimony represented a crucial element in helping the Church Committee reconstruct the basic events and connections that comprised the most sordid and secret chapter in the annals of the CIA. Agency officials had conceded their participation in assassination plots, but the committee members had learned to distrust the official line, and looked to Rosselli for confirmation. With the murder of Giancana and the flight of Trafficante, Rosselli was the only man outside the Agency who could tell the tale. "There was a sense of wanting to get the story first-hand, unfiltered," Gary Hart recalled.

Yet while Rosselli cooperated with the committee, he never volunteered more than he was asked. He never mentioned his close association with David Morales, the CIA control agent in Miami, because the committee never inquired. He provided few details about Phase II, the period of his most intense activity, only supplementing the sketchy account offered by William Harvey. And he was careful to minimize his references to Santo Trafficante, the man who stood the most to lose by exposure of his role in the plots against Castro.

Rosselli appeared before the committee a second time on September 22, as the inquiry into the assassination plots was wrapping up. Scrutiny of the memos and logs submitted to the committee by the FBI had turned up evidence of Jack Kennedy's relationship with Judy Campbell Exner, and of her close friendship with the CIA's primary contacts in the Mafia. Concerned as it was with the extent of the Kennedy brothers' involvement and knowledge of assassinations, the committee considered Exner's liaisons dangerous indeed. Exner was subpoenaed to testify, and Rosselli was recalled, but both denied that she had known of or played any role in the conspiracy. Exner was treated cautiously in the committee's public report, her relationships described discreetly but her name and gender withheld.

By the winter of 1976 the committee had concluded its work on the CIA and moved on to the domestic activities of the FBI—COINTEL-PRO, the infiltration and destruction of dissident political groups, the attempted blackmail of Martin Luther King, Jr. The committee and the press had shifted their focus away from the CIA revelations, and it looked like the Agency and their Mafia collaborators could breathe easy.

But the inquiry was not through yet. During the course of the hearings, Senators Schweiker and Hart became increasingly disturbed over the failure of the CIA and the FBI to cooperate fully with the Warren Commission, especially their decision to withhold information on the plots against Castro, and the FBI's later, perfunctory handling of Rosselli's Castro-retaliation story in 1967. The committee was leery of attempting to replicate the work of the Warren Commission, but did pursue a limited probe into the Kennedy assassination and its aftermath, and on April 23, 1976, called Rosselli for a third time.

This session was even more closely guarded than Rosselli's two prior appearances. It was conducted by Senator Schweiker and his staff in the old Carroll Arms Hotel, a retired hostelry a block from the Senate Office Building that was used as an annex for congressional staff offices. Rosselli flew in from Miami for the one-day session and returned that night—he didn't even inform Joe Shimon that he was in town.

Schweiker was hoping to expand on Rosselli's revelations to Ed Morgan and Jack Anderson; his questions pressed for details on the grounds for Rosselli's charges against Castro. In addition, the senator was intrigued by the possibility that the Mafia had planned the Kennedy assassination, and he queried Rosselli on his knowledge of Santo Trafficante and Jack Ruby. But while Rosselli remained cordial, his interest in promoting the Castro angle had apparently lapsed. He conceded that he had told several people he believed that Castro had engineered Kennedy's shooting, but said he had "no facts" to back his opinion. Curiously, Rosselli denied discussing the matter with attorney Morgan. He was equally circumspect with regard to Ruby and Trafficante. Realizing he had reached a dead end, Schweiker released Rosselli for the last time.

★

John Rosselli believed his reckoning with history was over. He returned to Plantation, to the sanctuary of his sister's home, and began to plan a gradual reentry into an active life. But the great events he had helped foment, plots and assassinations that altered the course of the nation, could not be dispensed with so easily. On July 28, three months after meeting with Schweiker at the Carroll Arms, Rosselli was kidnapped, murdered, dismembered, and sunk in his rusting steel coffin.

The discovery of Rosselli's remains three weeks later, combined with the auspicious timing of Giancana's death, raised the same question posed by Rosselli's meetings with Ed Morgan in late 1966: why did he agree to testify at all? Rosselli's own attorney, Les Scherr, commented flatly, "He made no effort to get out of testifying." That surprising posture made an impression on the committee. "I don't recall that Rosselli was reluctant," said staff attorney Fred Baron. "I remember that we had to subpoena Giancana, but I think that when Rosselli was contacted, he was prepared to come forward." Added Richard Schweiker in an interview, "It has always puzzled me why he came in, and why he was so forthcoming."

The standard explanation runs along the same lines as the argument put forward in connection with the Castro-retaliation theory—that Rosselli testified in hopes that his cooperation would be of some assistance in his legal battle to avoid deportation. "Rosselli was in great fear of going to jail, and he was in fear of going to Sicily," said David Bushong, who helped secure Rosselli's cooperation for the Church Committee. Rosselli's murder only seemed to confirm the notion that he had testified out of fear, in violation of the Mafia oath, and been killed in retaliation. "Mafia Reported to Have Murdered Rosselli Because He Testified Without Its Approval," a New York *Times* headline concluded.

But once again, the facts in the case give little indication that Rosselli was under duress at the time of his appearance before the Senate committee. The people close to Rosselli report that he seemed comfortable with his role as federal witness, and had little to fear from the INS. Washington attorney Les Scherr contends that Rosselli never once mentioned a possible link between his committee appearances and his deportation. Moreover, Miami deportation specialist David Walters asserted that the INS had little hope of securing Rosselli's ouster. "They were miles away," Walters declared. "If Rosselli had exhausted every appeal, he would never have seen Italy."

An alternate view is that he attended the committee hearings not to divulge information, but to gather it. Tracking the course of the investigation and deflecting it when it focused too closely on the Mafia in general, and on Santo Trafficante in particular, would have been an assignment more in keeping with Rosselli's character and circumstances. Having lived his life in strict accord with the code of *omerta,* it seems unlikely that he would abandon core beliefs at the behest of a congressional committee.

Significantly, Rosselli was in close contact with Trafficante throughout the months of his testimony before the Church Committee. Rosselli's family in Miami reported seeing the two men together repeatedly; they specifically mentioned two occasions in January 1976—once when Trafficante and Rosselli stopped in for coffee, and another time for dinner, at the restaurant run by Jose Quintana, the husband of one of Rosselli's nieces. At that point in time, Rosselli had already appeared twice in Washington, and would return for the third, crucial session devoted to the Kennedy assassination: his friendly relations with the ruthless don hardly fit the pattern of a man testifying in bold defiance of his boss.

In addition, Rosselli's attorneys told authorities soon after his murder that he had arranged to conceal Trafficante's identity in his testimony, despite the fact that CIA personnel had already placed Trafficante's name in the record. David Bushong, who conducted intensive interviews with Rosselli separate from the committee hearings, contends that "no deal" was ever accepted in taking Rosselli's testimony. But Les Scherr was quite specific, and had no reason to deceive: Rosselli would not use Santo Trafficante's name, but would refer to him in testimony only as "Mr. X."

Was Rosselli once more assuming the role of mole, of intelligence operative for the mob? David Bushong conceded: "I didn't get anything from him that I didn't have corroborated or didn't have in existence before I talked with him. I'm positive that he didn't give me anything new about the plots, and he didn't give me anything new about Trafficante." Moreover, the House Assassinations Committee, reviewing the work of the Church Committee three years later, found, "The 1975 and 1978 testimony of Rosselli and Trafficante corroborate each other, but remain contrary to how the principals reported the facts in 1967." In other words, the House committee reported, Rosselli collaborated with Trafficante in an effort "to downplay his role." Yet, when interviewed in 1990, Bushong rejected the idea that Rosselli might have been playing a double game. "It was not reconnaissance by Rosselli. They [the Mafia] don't deal in subtleties like that. You're talking about dinosaurs here."

On one point, at least, Bushong was simply wrong. Subtleties were

Rosselli's stock in trade. Information, intelligence, electronic eavesdropping on a par with the most sophisticated government intelligence operations—they were Rosselli's primary occupation in the last years of his life. Unlike Bushong, Richard Schweiker maintained a healthy respect for the dark forces the committee had disturbed in its investigation, and never wholly accepted Rosselli's performance. "There was very likely a hidden agenda in Rosselli coming to the committee, and I have to believe that had something to do with his killing."

The End

THE CONCLUSION OF HIS testimony before the Church Committee left Rosselli in limbo, an ambassador without portfolio, cut off from the new leadership in Chicago and hesitant to sign on with the Trafficante organization in Florida. However it may have beckoned initially, he found retirement in Plantation unfulfilling. Restless, he began traveling aimlessly, and initiated a series of talks on ways to get back into business.

Rosselli spent two weeks in April with his half-sister Mona (Camilla) and her family in New Jersey, and then returned to Plantation, where he entertained girl friends on weekends when the Daigles were away. Later he turned up in Belize City, the capital of British Honduras, where he bumped into Bryan Foy, who was there seeking to retrieve a stolen boat. The two exchanged surprised greetings and hurried on, each too busy to stop and chat. In Miami, Rosselli met with Fred Black to discuss forming a liquor distributorship in Florida, but eventually passed on the proposal.

Rosselli even considered getting back into the movie business. He talked with Brynie Foy about joining in a film production company, but again to no avail. Foy was considering making a spin-off of the hit movie *The Exorcist,* this version featuring a nun possessed by the devil, but Rosselli rejected it as sacrilegious. Rosselli countered by suggesting a treatment of the CIA plots against Castro; Foy liked the idea and said he would see about raising funds.

The days in Miami slid by slowly, hot and sultry. Rosselli occupied himself reading magazines by the pool, with afternoon rounds of golf, and with evening drinks on the powerboat that doubled as a home to his niece Eloise and her husband, Eugene McKnight. Rosselli operated with the caution of his trade, sticking close to home, and, when he did go out, having his sister telephone ahead and place reservations in her name. His one regular contact from the rackets was Santo Trafficante, who became something of a family friend, several times taking his wife to dinner with Rosselli and the Daigles at posh restaurants like the Golden Spike, or to the Fontainebleau Hotel. Money was a problem; Rosselli approached Fred Black, Joe Breen, and other friends for small loans. Still, he could rely on Social Security checks and the Frontier gift shop concession, and when pinched, he called on Lou Lederer, his old Chicago gambling colleague, to deliver a briefcase stuffed with cash.

Rosselli was stymied, but did not seem deeply frustrated. One girl friend who visited with him in Plantation, a woman named Carol Ann Hoover, said later that Rosselli was "in high spirits" in the early summer of 1976, and "not worried about anything." Hoover said Rosselli's sister Edith commented to her that "he had been more relaxed" since his senate testimony, "as though he had a big weight lifted from his shoulders."

In late May, Rosselli made a trip back to Los Angeles. He met with his attorney, and then joined his old friends Allen Smiley and Jimmy Fratianno for dinner at the Sea Lion Restaurant in Malibu, where they reminisced to the soothing churn of the Pacific surf. Rosselli spent the following week at the clinic in Santa Barbara, and then returned to his suite at the Beverly Hilton in Los Angeles. He met for dinner at the Trader Vic's, next door to the hotel, with Fratianno and Mike Rizzitello, a newly inducted slugger in the local Mafia family. The conversation was light and friendly, sports and movies and women, but Fratianno was distant, preoccupied, and waited for an opportunity to speak to Rosselli alone.

He got his chance in the restaurant lobby, as the dinner confab was breaking up. Fratianno had heard from John "Peanuts" Tranalone, a Cleveland mobster with strong ties to Florida, that a contract had been put out on Rosselli's life. Fratianno was not ready to expose himself by relating the details, but he wanted to warn his loyal old friend. "Johnny . . . be careful, will you. This thing of ours is treacherous. You never know when you're going to make the hit list," Fratianno pleaded. "Don't let Trafficante or [Accardo aide Jackie] Cerone set you up."

Rosselli shrugged off Fratianno's concern. "Will you stop worrying? I'm all right. Everything's under control."

Rosselli fretted about his health and chafed at his financial straits but never once indicated that trouble might be brewing. "I would go down to Florida, and if I didn't, John called me once a week, just to check in," Les Scherr recalled, "and there was never the slightest hint that something was going on." More important, Rosselli continued to deal with Trafficante as a friend and collaborator, a trusted connection at the top of the Mafia ladder.

Rosselli broke his pattern of serene confidence only once, in late June, when he made a second trip West, this time in the company of Joe Daigle. They attended a testimonial dinner in Palms Springs hosted by Frank Sinatra, and then both checked in to the Sansum Clinic. Later, Rosselli stopped by to see Father Joseph Clark, his longtime friend, then aged and infirm. They visited and talked of old times, but they also conducted some business. For the first time since childhood, Rosselli got down on his knees and made confession. It may be that Fratianno's warning had made a deeper impression than he had let on, or it could be, as Rosselli told Joe Breen, that he didn't want to see the old priest go to his grave without knowing that Rosselli had squared himself with the church. But whatever the source of the impulse, Rosselli's uncanny knack for setting his affairs in order had once again asserted itself.

John Rosselli returned to Plantation in early July. He was getting tired of the muggy Florida heat, tired of his distance from the action and excitement of the rackets. He asked Joe Breen to find him an apartment in Las Vegas, but seemed in no particular hurry to move.

On July 16, Rosselli enjoyed a leisurely, waterside dinner with Santo Trafficante; his wife Josie; Edith Daigle; and Rosselli's namesake, his nephew Phillip, visiting from New Jersey. Again, no sign of friction, or even of business dealings. When his mother asked if there was anything said at the restaurant, Phillip described the meeting as "definitely a social outing only." Separately, Edith Daigle said "there was no business discussed."

Eleven days later, the night of July 27, Rosselli received a second warning. He was sitting in the kitchen in Plantation, keeping Edith Daigle company as she cooked dinner, when the phone rang. It was Fred Black, the businessman and lobbyist, calling from Los Angeles. Their contacts had always been casual, but now there was an urgency in his voice. "Get out of Miami," Black implored Rosselli. "You're in serious danger. The Cubans are after you." Once again, Rosselli scoffed at the advice of a friend. Black pleaded. "Come to Los Angeles. I've got a room reserved for you." Rosselli declined the invitation.

Interviewed after his release from prison on tax evasion charges in 1990, Fred Black denied making any warning call to Rosselli in the final week of his life. But he recounted the conversation to his friend Joe Shimon soon after the discovery of Rosselli's body. And separately, Edith Daigle told homicide investigators that the call Rosselli had taken in the kitchen had come from Fred Black. Moreover, though Black said in the interview that he was staying in Las Vegas the day of Rosselli's disappearance, records from the Beverly Hilton Hotel showed that he was in fact registered in Los Angeles, and had in fact placed a call to Plantation on July 27.

On Thursday, July 28, 1976, Rosselli stuck to his customary, relaxed routine. He arose late, perused the paper while sitting out by the pool, and shared a late brunch with his sister. At 12:50 P.M., without mentioning a destination, Rosselli headed off in the Daigles' silver Impala, clad only in blue pants and a pink Qiana shirt, his golf clubs in the trunk of the car. Edith Daigle never saw her brother again.

There is only one published account of what happened next, related by an anonymous Mafia source to New York *Times* reporter Nicholas Gage several months after the murder. According to Gage's source, Rosselli drove to a marina where he joined an unidentified old friend and a third man, a killer dispatched from Chicago, for an afternoon ocean cruise. The boat put out from shore, and while Rosselli was sipping a drink, the stranger stepped up behind him, grabbed him in a bear hug, and wrapped a hand across his mouth and nose. Frail and elderly, his lungs chronically weak, Rosselli hardly struggled. Within minutes, he was dead.

Gage's source said the hit team immediately committed the grisly dismemberment and entombment of Rosselli in the rusting oil drum, and then hoisted the drum over the side and dumped it in the Intracoastal Waterway that same afternoon.

That seems unlikely, however, and raises questions with the veracity of the entire story. The killers probably would not have bothered with the messy business of cutting off Rosselli's limbs unless rigor mortis had rendered his corpse rigid, meaning several hours would have passed between the killing and the disposal of the body. Otherwise, it would have been easier simply to fold Rosselli's remains into the drum. And the heavy equipment required to carry out the job, the winch, lengths of chain, and the acetylene torch and fuel tanks, would seem out of place on a pleasure cruiser.

More probable was that, however Rosselli was killed, he was then transported to a private garage or wrecking yard, one with a floor drain to wash away the blood, where the mutilation and concealment of the body took place. Mafia "sources" dispensing tips on the true nature of an execution are dubious enough, but when contradicted by the facts of the case, they only underscore the question of a possible false plant.

Still, Rosselli was gone, a man of abiding loyalty betrayed in the end by someone he trusted. Edith Daigle became concerned that evening, as Rosselli had planned to return the car in time for her to drive to a dinner engagement. At 3 A.M., Edith called Joe Daigle, who was on assignment at Cape Kennedy, and told him she feared the worst. Daigle returned the following morning, and spent the day calling Rosselli's friends around the country, asking if they had seen or heard from him. All responses were negative, and Daigle thought back to a joking comment Rosselli had once made to him: "If I'm ever missing, check the airports, because that's where they usually leave the car."

On Saturday morning, accompanied by Eugene McKnight, Joe Daigle set out on a grim expedition. He stopped first at Fort Lauderdale International Airport, spent half an hour circling the parking lot, and found nothing. Proceeding to Miami International, he began the same routine, and to his dismay, came across his wife's Impala on the third floor of the parking garage. Daigle opened the trunk, took note of his brother-in-law's golf clubs, and then headed home to share the bad news with his wife.

They waited for a week, speaking frequently with Scherr, Wadden, and Joe Shimon in Washington, and with Joe Breen in Las Vegas, and finally, on August 7, they got a call from the Dade County authorities that Rosselli's body had been found. The police would not speculate on the identity of his killer, but one man did. The morning of August 8, immediately after the news of Rosselli's murder was released, Fred Black placed three calls, one to the Daigles in Miami, one to Rosselli's half-sister Mona Cardillo in New Jersey, and one to Joe Shimon in Washington. Each time, Black's message was the same: Santo Trafficante had ordered Rosselli's execution.

Conscience in the Capital

THE DADE COUNTY MEDICAL Examiner released the remains of Rosselli's body at 11 A.M. on Tuesday, August 10. Three days of inspection
had yielded little new information, and it was time to let the family take
over. Albert Sacco had flown down from New England, and arranged for a
quick and private service at the Lithgow Funeral Home in Miami. Crema-
tion was frowned upon by the Catholic Church, but in Rosselli's case, the
body was already mutilated to the point that there was little choice. The
incineration took place at noon, and services were conducted an hour
later.

There were no trappings of power at the funeral, none of the bouquets
and Cadillacs and sleek-suited men that mark the classic mob send-off,
none of the starlets and gamblers and power brokers who had peopled
Rosselli's world. Inside the marbled cool of the mortuary were just a handful of mourners, Rosselli's sisters Connie, Mona, and Edith; his brother
Al; three nieces; and a collection of husbands and wives, there to pay last
respects to a man they hardly knew.

It was only outside, in the muggy Miami heat, that the ceremony
reflected the life Rosselli had lived—from a pair of boxy, unmarked Fords,
Dade County detectives snapped photographs of the funeral party and
their license plates in a vain effort to develop leads on the murder. For the
past thirty years, Rosselli had been subject to almost constant scrutiny,
with bugs and wiretaps and surveillance teams fielded by half a dozen
police agencies, and they maintained their presence to the bitter end.

By 3 P.M. it was all over. Rosselli was finally at rest, and the family,
fearful and awkward even among themselves at the grotesque cruelty that
had destroyed their eldest brother, made hasty arrangements to return to
homes scattered along the eastern seaboard. They couldn't even gather at
Joe and Edith Daigle's white home in Plantation—the pair had vacated
the house for fear of further violence. "It was awful," Rosselli's sister
Connie recalled. "What could we say to each other?" Finding little from
his life that might redeem him, Rosselli's survivors were left to search for

grace in the motive for his murder. "Deep down, in a way, I probably hope it was connected with [the Castro plots]," mused Peter Cardillo, Rosselli's brother-in-law. "At least then Johnny, he would have died for a cause."

That element of intrigue provided solace to Rosselli's family in Miami, but provoked continuing debate in Washington over the safety of congressional witnesses and, ultimately, over the integrity of the government. After all, the crimes Rosselli discussed before the Church Committee were not those of the criminal underworld but of the government, national security officials and the CIA, and even the President. Rosselli had served as living proof that the government would employ any means, even murder, to achieve its objectives, and now he was dead.

★

The Church Committee had been disbanded weeks before Rosselli's murder, succeeded by the permanent Senate Select Committee on Intelligence. But Senators Howard Baker and Daniel Inouye, the ranking members of the new panel, were determined to assert the integrity of congressional process. They voiced their concern in a letter to Attorney General Edward Levi, insisting that the Justice Department enter the Rosselli murder investigation. The senators cited a law protecting congressional witnesses and asked for a determination on the possible link between Rosselli's testimony and his death.

With Levi out of town, FBI Director Clarence Kelley responded the next day, calling a press conference August 11 to assert that the FBI had no business entering the case. Following in the tradition of official caution that had long characterized the Agency's approach to organized crime, Kelley commented, "We have no jurisdiction over a murder which is committed in a state without the ramifications which would bring us into it."

The Washington *Post* weighed into the debate the following day with a lead editorial asserting that the Rosselli murder was rife with ramifications. "Is it really, as the sophisticated wisdom goes, 'paranoid' on our part to brood about the suggestive and possibly monstrous interconnections" leading from Rosselli and Sam Giancana, to Judith Campbell Exner, Jack Kennedy, and Fidel Castro, the *Post* asked. "If we know anything, we know that the mafia operations in which Messers. Giancana and Rosselli figured had become intertwined with the operations of the United States government," the editorial observed. Noting that Giancana's murder had been dismissed as a typical mob killing, the *Post* added: "The plain fact is that, given the provocative and suggestive history of the two men, it is not possible for either the Congress or the Executive Branch to look the other way or to complaisantly accept the earmarks-of-a-gangland-slaying bromide."

The combination of press and Congress proved too potent for the Department of Justice to ignore, and on the afternoon of Friday, August 13, Attorney General Levi reluctantly moved to override Clarence Kelley and ordered the FBI to enter the case. In a terse announcement, a department spokesman explained that the FBI would "investigate whether the Rosselli homicide was the result of his testimony before the [Church] committee." Still, Levi said Dade County law enforcement would retain "principal responsibility" in the case.

The growing pressure even penetrated the hermetic environs of the CIA headquarters in Langley, Virginia, where Rosselli's disclosures had led to unprecedented congressional scrutiny and a devastating loss of public trust. Disturbed by speculation that the CIA might have killed Rosselli to silence him, former Director William E. Colby felt compelled to issue a categorical denial. "I can guarantee you that the CIA had nothing to do with [Rosselli's] death," he declared in a televised interview.

The Washington figure who took the most active interest in the case was Gary Hart, the Colorado Democrat who formerly sat on the Church Committee. What prodded him to action was not so much the apparent connection between Rosselli's testimony and his killing, but Hart's visceral reaction to the photographs of the murder scene dispatched from Dade County to the Senate Intelligence Committee. "The pictures of John Rosselli as he was found were the most unpleasant I'd ever seen," Hart recalled later. Moreover, Hart had taken a deep personal interest in the government skulduggery that Rosselli had revealed in his testimony. Then serving his first term in the Senate after gaining prominence as chairman of George McGovern's 1972 presidential campaign, Hart had come to Washington as a skeptical outsider, but said it was still a shocking experience "to find that your government has hired the Mafia to assassinate a foreign leader."

Hart canvassed the former members of the Church Committee and found a consensus that the Senate should assist the Dade County detectives in any way possible. After recruiting an investigator and two attorneys from the committee staff, Hart booked plane tickets under an assumed name for Friday August 20, and flew to Miami.

Meeting for more than six hours with Lieutenant Gary Minium and detectives Ojeda and Zatrepalek, Hart detailed Rosselli's contacts with the Cuban exile community in Miami and reviewed his appearances before the Church Committee. The session did little to solve the murder, but it served to underscore the crucial nature of Rosselli's testimony in confirming the details of the conspiracy against Fidel Castro. And it emphasized the unique position that Rosselli occupied in the nation's capital. Never before had the murder of a hoodlum generated a crisis of conscience in Washington.

Who Killed John Rosselli?

LAUNCHING A FULL INVESTIGATION of the crime, Dade County detectives Julio Ojeda and Charles Zatrepalek traveled to Washington, Chicago, Las Vegas, Los Angeles, and San Diego, tracking down leads and piecing together the fragments of Rosselli's far-flung life. They spoke to gangsters, gamblers, entertainers, and businessmen, to police and attorneys and federal agents.

It seemed apparent early on that Rosselli's murder had indeed been ordered and sanctioned by the Mafia, and in keeping with the territorial code of the crime organization, had been carried out under the auspices of Florida don Santo Trafficante, Rosselli's ostensible friend and benefactor. The primary sources for the detectives were underworld informants in Florida, and Frank Bompensiero in San Diego, who had overheard discussions of the murder by the leaders of the national crime syndicate, including Joseph Aiuppa's comment in Cicero, Illinois, that Trafficante had botched the job.

Within several weeks, information surfaced pointing to a primary suspect, a dangerous thug in Trafficante's Tampa organization named Sam Cagnina, whose association with the mob leader began as a friendship between the two men's fathers. Known to the DEA as a smuggler of large quantities of cocaine, Cagnina had an extensive police record, including indictments for armed robbery, assault with intent to kill, and conspiracy to injure a witness. In addition, he had a solid reputation as "fully capable of execution-type murders," one contact told a police investigator. More important, Cagnina had bragged to two separate sources, including a dealer in his drug organization, that he had participated in the Rosselli murder.

The investigation even turned up the likely site where Rosselli's body was dumped into the canal, evidence that further eroded the New York *Times's* Mafia "source." Bloodhounds given a scrap of Rosselli's clothing tracked the scent to a small clump of trees, fifty yards from the water and just upstream from where the steel drum was located.

But while the detectives felt they were nearing a fix on the actual killing, they were farther than ever from determining the motive, from learning who had ordered the hit. In their quandary, they failed to make a single arrest in the investigation, of Cagnina or any other suspect. The problem was not a lack of information, but a flood of it—operating at the highest levels of organized crime, Rosselli had made enemies as well as friends, and his cooperation with the government toward the end of his life had incurred mistrust and resentment.

A leading theory was that Rosselli's secret testimony before the federal grand jury in Los Angeles had led to convictions in the Frontier Hotel case; the detectives speculated that Rosselli's killing may have been a simple act of revenge. Another possibility was that Rosselli's West Coast meetings in May and June might have signaled an attempt to muscle in on his old territory, and that he was killed in a power struggle.

But the continuing investigation failed to develop evidence for these theories, and Rosselli's history argued against them. In the Frontier case, the most damaging witness, who unlike Rosselli had testified for weeks in open court, was Maury Friedman, and the mob had made no move to retaliate against him. As for the West Coast meetings, if any business was discussed, which Fratianno later denied, then it was probably an effort to bring Rosselli in, not to bar him: Rosselli was always welcome in a Mafia enterprise, because he always made money. For more than half a century Rosselli had brokered deals for Mafia families across the country, always building on a reputation as a man of honor and respect.

What stood out in the events leading up to Rosselli's murder was not his ongoing mob activities and associations, but the glaring break with past practice—his testimony before the Senate. There again the obvious conclusion was that Rosselli had broken the code of silence, and was murdered in retribution. But again, the facts did not fit. If the killing was designed to assert the Mafia code, the murder would be public, to send a message, *à la* Giancana—not secret, as Rosselli's death was intended to remain. Moreover, Rosselli had never broken contact with Santo Trafficante during the months of his testimony, apparently believing his appearances had syndicate sanction.

More likely than the standard mob-rivalry or retribution motive was that Rosselli was indeed killed in connection with his Senate testimony— that the "monstrous interconnections" invoked by the Washington *Post* were in fact at issue. In close collaboration with Trafficante, Rosselli had served over the years as the key man in the effort to keep those interconnections hidden, first by floating the Castro-retaliation theory in 1967, and then by keeping tabs on the Church Committee. Significantly, it was only after his testimony, in Washington, and not before, that Rosselli's coconspirators decided he was expendable.

Still, close friends of Rosselli's, both in and out of the mob, reject the notion that Trafficante would have turned on his friend. The party that suffered the most from Rosselli's revelations, and could yet sustain further damage, was the government. Rosselli's testimony before the Church Committee was only part of the story. The rest, his work with David Morales, and possibly ties between Cuban exiles or their CIA handlers and the Kennedy assassination, was the most critical, and the most dangerous chapter in his saga.

The CIA certainly had the contacts in Cuban Miami to pull off Rosselli's execution, and as it had demonstrated by enlisting him in the first place, it had the will. Even the evidence pointing to Trafficante did not rule out collaboration by the spy agency. Beginning around 1968, Trafficante had gained control of the opium pipeline from Southeast Asia, an enterprise that required ongoing cooperation from CIA officers in the region.

Lacking a corroborated confession from the actual killer, the question of who killed Rosselli becomes one of motive and wherewithal, and two candidates emerge: his colleagues in the Mafia, and his old allies in the CIA. But in the end, in the Rosselli murder as well as the Kennedy assassination, the work of determining which of those two was the culprit becomes moot. In southern Florida, beginning at least in 1960 and continuing well into the 1970s, the Mafia and the CIA were one and the same, indistinguishable in their objectives, in their personnel, in their methods.

Inundated by leads, the trail growing colder as the weeks slipped by, the Dade County detectives began to acknowledge that Rosselli's killers

had succeeded in eluding them. Their work took on an element of pride—
they would pursue every avenue of inquiry, even if the possibility of an
eventual conviction was a longshot. A month after Rosselli's body turned
up, Julio Ojeda told a reporter, "Maybe ten years from now, I want someone to look at my file and say, 'Hey, he talked to everybody.' And maybe
he'll hear something and bang, that's the arrest." A decade later, no such
coincidence had occurred.

★

A sensational murder, wreathed in mystery and fraught with ominous
implications—it was a fitting end for John Rosselli, a man who lived his
life in the shadows, trading on resources of charm and power to earn the
role of broker at the highest echelons of American life. Always operating
behind the scenes, Rosselli was the wild card in the deck, the whiff of
menace in the smoke-filled room, the glint in the eye of the intelligence
planner.

Rosselli's life was marked by contradiction, and by savage irony. A
poor immigrant who rose to wealth and stature, he embodied the American ideal, but his path was marked by intimidation, violence, and death.
In Hollywood he was courted by moguls whose films preached that crime
never paid. Convicted of a multimillion-dollar extortion scheme, Rosselli
moved on to preside over the mob's greatest cash bonanza since Prohibition. In the same year that Attorney General Bobby Kennedy designated
Rosselli a top public enemy, Rosselli was recruited by the government to
help assassinate Fidel Castro. And when word of those plots sparked a
Senate investigation, it was John Rosselli, the consummate mobster, who
furnished the American public with the details of the government's
darkest secret.

The paradox of Rosselli's life persisted even in death. Suffocated, mutilated, and anchored in a steel drum, Rosselli was meant to disappear,
silently, without a ripple. But nature and perhaps fate intervened, and
Rosselli's steel coffin drifted quietly to the surface, where its discovery set
off a paroxysm of conscience in Washington and across the country. The
story of John Rosselli, his life and times, his relationships and his connections, is perhaps the ultimate account of the dark side of the American
dream.

NOTES

Abbreviations

John Rosselli was the subject of a series of major trials and investigations through the course of his life, and they form the documentary backbone of the research for this book.

The descriptions of the crime scene and official investigation of Rosselli's murder are drawn from internal reports of the homicide division of the Dade County Public Safety Department, obtained by the authors from a confidential source in Miami, referred to as Dade file.

Rosselli's citizenship was contested and his family history examined in a federal trial in 1967, *U.S. v. Filippo Sacco, aka John Rosselli*, Federal District Court, Central California, Criminal Case 68-1175; referred to as *U.S. v. Sacco*. A probation report filed in connection with the case and detailing his criminal history is referred to as *U.S. v. Sacco*, PR. Further details were laid out in the government's answer to Rosselli's appeal of his conviction in that case (Ninth Circuit Court of Appeals, Case #24,220), referred to as *U.S. v. Sacco* (A).

The mob infiltration of the Hollywood labor scene was exposed in the trial of Rosselli and six other defendants, *U.S. v. Louis Campagna et al;* Federal District Court, Southern New York, Criminal Case #114-101; referred to as *U.S. v.*

Campagna. Page numbers refer to a transcript of the proceedings supplied to the authors by prosecutor Boris Kostelanetz.

Some of Rosselli's activities in Las Vegas were revealed in depositions and testimony arising from Robert Maheu's protracted legal battle with Howard Hughes. The case was tried at federal district court in Los Angeles, and the court files reviewed there by the authors: Civil Case #72-305, referred to as *Maheu v. Hughes.*

FBI files were obtained under the Freedom of Information Act. Documents are identified as memos, field reports (FR), or intelligence summaries (IS), and where possible are referenced by date and FBI document number (#). Where the document was not coded (usually supplied by sources), or the code not recorded by the authors (at the FBI reading room in Washington), the date is included. Records were also obtained from the Immigration and Naturalization Service (INS), and the Bureau of Prisons (BOP).

Separately, the authors obtained through a confidential source a summary of the Rosselli file maintained by the Federal Parole and Probation Commission (#34205-136). That document will be referred to, without page numbers, as FPPC.

A private investigative file on Rosselli was maintained by the Thoroughbred Racing Protective Bureau (TRPB), a security agency that polices tracks across the nation. Rosselli's TRPB file was obtained through a confidential source; its contents are referenced by the initials of the agency and listed by date.

In October 1950, Rosselli testified at some length before the U.S. Senate Special Committee to Investigate Organized Crime in Interstate Commerce, chaired by Estes Kefauver. His testimony can be found in the published proceedings, Volume V, pages 373–407. Referred to as IOC.

Two congressional committees investigated Rosselli's involvement in the plots to assassinate Fidel Castro and the assassination of President John F. Kennedy. The Senate Select Committee on Intelligence Activities, chaired by Frank Church, produced two relevant documents: an Interim Report titled *Alleged Assassination Plots Involving Foreign Leaders* (1975, SR 94-465), referred to as CC.IR; and a *Final Report,* including Book Five, *The Investigation of the Assassination of President John F. Kennedy: Performance of the Intelligence Agencies* (1976, SR 94–755), referred to as CC.V. The House Select Committee on Assassinations likewise produced two relevant volumes: the *Hearings* (1978, Vols. 1–5), referred to as HAH; and the *Final Report* (1979, HR 95-1828, part 2), referred to as HAR.

1. The Eldest Son

1)   What Blundell saw: Dade file.
4)   The case would be "awesome": Washington *Post*, 9/12/76.
5)   "These guys went to": Ibid., 8/9/76.

5)   "It was four or five days": Miami *Herald*, 8/9/76.

5)   Charles Zatrepalek and Julio Ojeda: Washington *Post*, 9/12/76.

7)   "Dancing and delightful": Interview with Harold Fitzgerald, Los Angeles, December 1989.

7)   "That made you feel like": Interview with Susan Woods, Palm Springs, September 1989.

7)   Rosselli's attorney proposed a joke: Interview with Leslie Scherr, Washington, D.C., June 1990.

7)   To Fratianno, Rosselli had been: Interview with Jimmy Fratianno, confidential location, November 1987.

7)   Bryan Foy learned of Rosselli's demise: Interview with Madeline Foy O'Donnell, Los Angeles, February 1990.

8)   Aiuppa had been there: Allegation made by mafioso Frank Bompensiero, Dade file.

8)   "Trafficante had the job": Ibid.

8)   "You remember that guy": Ovid Demaris, *The Last Mafioso: The Treacherous World of Jimmy Fratianno* (Bantam, 1981), 396.

9)   Wadden called Morgan: Statement of Edward P. Morgan, Dade file.

9)   Morgan called Senator Howard Baker: Ibid.

9)   Baker equates Rosselli, Giancana: Miami *Herald*, 8/9/76.

9)   Baker called Clarence Kelley: Ibid., 8/12/76.

9)   Rosselli's sister Connie learned: Interview with Concetta Sacco, Boston, October 1989.

2. *The Old and the New*

11)   John Rosselli was born: Birth certificate recorded at Esperia, Frosinone Province, Italy.

12)   The Saccos and the DiPascuales: Civil Register, Frosinone Province, Italy.

12)   Vincenzo had departed: *U.S. v. Sacco*, PR.

12)   The *Mezzogiorno:* James Ianni, *A Family Business* (Russell Sage Foundation, 1972), 15. See also, Richard Gambino, *Blood of My Blood: The Dilemma of the Italian-Americans* (Doubleday, 1974), 3; Richard de Marco, *Boston's Italian North End* (UMI Research Press, 1980), 1.

13)   "There were so many rebels": General Della Roca, from his memoirs, quoted in John Davis, *Conflict and Control* (MacMillan Education, 1988), 173.

13)   "Delinquency is the war": General Pallavicini, quoted in Ibid., 180.

13)   "It was not": Carlo Levi from *Christ Stopped at Eboli*, quoted in Gambino, *Blood of My Blood*, 8.

13)   The individual without family: Rudolph Bell, *Fate, Honor, Family and Village* (University of Chicago, 1979) 1.

14)   "Even today tales": Gambino, *Blood of My Blood,* 52.

15)   "In such numbers": Adolfo Rossi, interviewed by Gino Speranza, *Charities,* Vol. 12, 1904, 467–70.

16)   "Permanent": INS questionnaire, 1911.

16)   The S.S. *Cretic:* Saccos on the ship: INS forms, 1911. Ship history: Eugene Smith, *Trans-Atlantic Passenger Ships: Past and Present* (George H. Dean Co., 1947), 75.

17)   1911 migration: INS *Annual Report,* 1986, 1.

17)   "It was the smell": Traveler quoted in Barbara Benton, *Ellis Island* (Facts on File, 1985), 126.

18)   Vincenzo's flat: *U.S. v. Sacco* (A).

18)   Filippo Sacco entered the first grade: Ibid.

18)   "I stopped talking Italian": Rosselli autobiography quoted at length in Miami *Herald,* 8/23/76.

19)   "Mama would get angry": Interview with Concetta Sacco, Boston, October 1989.

19)   "By the time I reached": Miami *Herald,* 8/23/76.

20)   "Senile dementia": Certificate of Death, State Vital Statistics, Massachusetts.

20)   Move to Somerville: *U.S. v. Sacco* (A).

20)   The influenza epidemic: Somerville *Journal,* 10/18/18.

20)   On October 5: Certificate of Death, City of Somerville.

21)   Maria returned: *U.S. v. Sacco* (A).

21)   "Everybody knew her": Concetta Sacco interview.

22)   Driving a milk wagon: *U.S. v. Sacco,* PR.

22)   "It was getting crowded": Miami *Herald,* 8/23/76.

22)   Turf boundaries: Interview with East Boston native Andy Blake, Boston, October 1989.

22)   Throngs of ragged teen-agers: William Foote Whyte, "Race Conflicts in the North End of Boston," *New England Quarterly,* Vol. XII (December 1939), 623.

22)   "When I was a kid . . .": Quoted in Noel Behn, *Big Stick-Up at Brinks!* (Putnam's, 1977), 60.

23)   Cianciulli: *U.S. v. Sacco* (A).

23)   "The family life": *U.S. v. Sacco,* PR.

23)   "Because of the way": Maria Sacco, statement to FBI, 4/30/68. From court files, *U.S. v. Sacco.*

23)   Federal officials considered: Interview with Dennis Condon, Massachusetts State Department of Public Safety, Boston, October 1989.

23)   Drug sale observed: *U.S. v. Sacco,* PR.

23)   Filippo was arrested again: Criminal court records, Middlesex County Courthouse, Cambridge, Massachusetts.

24)   "The government narcotics informant": *U.S. v. Sacco,* PR.

24)   "I followed the instructions": Miami *Herald,* 8/23/76.

25)   Criminal gangs dominated: Frederic D. Homer, *Guns and Garlic:*

Myths and Realities of Organized Crime (Purdue University Press, 1974), 32. See also, Stephen Fox, *Blood and Power: Organized Crime in Twentieth Century America* (Morrow, 1989), passim.

25) New York's street gangs: Howard Abadinsky, *The Mafia in America* (Praeger, 1941), 3.

25) Whyos price list: John Kobler, *Capone: The Life and World of Al Capone* (Putnam's, 1971), 31.

26) "The most vicious": Fuchs quoted in Fox, *Blood and Power*, 35.

27) Al Capone: Material in this section on Capone, Torrio, and Colosimo is drawn from Kobler, *Capone;* George Murray, *The Legacy of Al Capone: Portraits and Annals of Chicago's Public Enemies* (Putnam's, 1975); and Carl Sifakis, *The Mafia Encyclopedia* (Facts on File, 1987). Also, telephone interview with Carl Sifakis, New York, February 1990.

28) "Chicago is unique": Merriam in Kobler, *Capone*, 64.

29) Capone induction ceremony: Sifakis, *Mafia Encyclopedia*, 60.

30) Criminal informants: Interview with former FBI agent George Bland, Aptos, California, January 1988.

30) Frank Hronek, an investigator: Confidential memo, Los Angeles District Attorney's office, Intelligence Division, July 1963.

30) "He was very close": Interview with Jimmy Fratianno, confidential location, November 1987.

30) As he retold the story: Miami *Herald*, 8/23/76.

31) Jack McGurn: Sifakis, *Mafia Encyclopedia*, 203.

32) Ricca at Diamond Joe's: Louis Sidran in *The Chicago Crime Book*, ed. Albert Halper (World Publishing, 1967), 428.

33) Rosselli at Diamond Joe's: IOC.V.377.

33) A doctor discerned: Fratianno interview.

3. City of Angels

35) Los Angeles in the middle 1920s: Bruce Henstell, *Sunshine and Wealth: Los Angeles in the Twenties and Thirties* (Chronicle Books, 1984); Carey McWilliams, *Southern California: An Island on the Land* (Peregrine Smith, 1973).

36) Hanging around the back lots: IOC.V.375.

37) Rosselli and D'Acunto: 1958 FBI interview of Frances Louise Broszmer; FBI.IS 2/14/63, #92-3267-426.

37) The Italians: Gloria Ricci Lothrop, "The Italians of Los Angeles," *The Californians: The Journal of the California Historical Society*, May/June 1987, 28.

37) Ghetto life was dominated: *Gangland Killings: Los Angeles Area, 1900–1951*, a report published by the Los Angeles Police Department, 1952.

38) "When Christ died on the cross": Interview with Patricia Breen, Las Vegas, May 1989.

39) Rosselli's arrest record, or rap sheet, was reproduced in numerous court filings and government memoranda.

39) "I was a young fellow": IOC.V.378.

39) "I got into a few": Ibid., 384.

39) Anthony Cornero Stralla: Ed Reid, *The Grim Reapers: The Anatomy of Organized Crime in America* (Bantam, 1970), 172–73; Stephen Fox, *Blood and Power: Organized Crime in Twentieth Century America* (Morrow, 1989), 36–37.

40) Cornero's gang roster: Los Angeles *Times*, 5/6/26.

40) Cornero's false tip: Los Angeles *Examiner*, 8/5/25.

40) Cornero's war with Page: Los Angeles *Times*, 8/5 and 8/6/25.

40) Walter Hesketh murder: Los Angeles *Daily News*, 3/30/26.

41) Cornero arrest: Ibid., 4/4/26.

41) Rosselli arrested with Cornero: Los Angeles *Times*, 5/6/26; Los Angeles *Examiner*, 5/6/26.

41) Charges against Rosselli: Rosselli rap sheet.

41) Rosselli moved: FBI.IS 3/62, #92-3267-146 probably gleaned from LAPD files.

42) "The secret is not": Confidential interview.

42) He liked to tell the story: Confidential interview.

42) Rosselli's last job for Cornero: Hank Messick, *The Beauties and the Beasts: The Mob in Show Business* (David McKay Co., 1973), 99. Lamentably, Messick never used footnotes or went into detail on his sources in his many works on crime and mobsters, but is viewed by other journalists and law enforcement as one of the foremost authorities in the field. Messick had excellent sources at the IRS, an agency whose records are exempt from the provisions of the Freedom of Information Act.

43) He checked into a sanitarium: *U.S. v. Sacco*, PR.

43) "The Greatest Show": New York *Times*, 9/22/27.

43) The party began: IOC.V.376.

43) "In the Loop": New York *Times*, 9/22/27.

44) "I'm wetter than": John Kobler, *Capone: The Life and World of Al Capone* (Putnam's, 1971), 204.

44) Capone-Aiello war: Ibid., 209–10.

44) Rosselli's momentous Thursday: IOC.V.376.

44) "Governors and mayors": New York *Times*, 9/22/27.

44) "There must have been": IOC.V.376.

45) Rosselli visited: Ibid., 378.

45) Capone in L.A.: Los Angeles *Daily News*, 12/12/27; Los Angeles *Examiner*, 12/13/27.

45) Rosselli offered his home: Los Angeles *Times*, 12/14/27.

45) Suggested by Capone: Interview with Jimmy Fratianno, confidential

location, November 1987; interview with George Bland, Aptos, California, January 1988.

46) Dragna as unofficial mayor: Interview with Billy Dick Unland, formerly of LAPD Organized Crime Intelligence Division, Irvine, California, November 1989.

46) "Strictly a muscle outfit": *Gangland Killings*, 16.

46) Most of the city's vice: Charles Stoker, *Thicker'n Thieves* (Sidereal Company, 1951), 2–13; William G. Bonelli, *Billion Dollar Blackjack: The Story of Corruption and the Los Angeles Times* (Civic Research Press, 1954), 54–55.

47) McAfee as "The Whistler": FBI.FR 9/10/38, #88-147.

47) "With the advent of Prohibition": *Gangland Killings*, 5.

47) Mayor John Porter: Henstell, *Sunshine*, 51.

47) "Reliable sources relate": *U.S. v. Sacco*, PR.

48) "John had a career": Interview with David Nissen, Santa Ana, California, August 1989.

48) "Johnny did a lot of work": Fratianno interview.

48) "The Italians, led by Jack Dragna": *Gangland Killings*, 2.

49) The story of Dragna's and Rosselli's move against the owners of the *Monfalcone* is related in anecdotal form in TRPB, 6/21/51.

49) *Monfalcone* described: Los Angeles *Examiner*, 11/24/28; Los Angeles *Times*, 11/25/28.

50) A high-speed chase: Los Angeles *Daily News*, 7/30/30. See also, IOC.II.217.

50) "These ships made so much money": IOC.II.217.

51) "Dougherty, Rosselli, and three other men": Rosselli's raid on the *Monfalcone* was related to journalist John Babcock by Dragna associate Bobby Garcia; Babcock shared it with the authors in an interview, Los Angeles, June 1989. Garcia's story was augmented by stories in the Los Angeles *Express*, 5/22/30, and Marina Del Rey *Argonaut*, 1/29/76.

51) Back in business: Los Angeles *Examiner*, 5/10/31; also, IOC.V.404.

52) "Gambling war": Los Angeles *Examiner*, 7/24/32.

52) "Gang Warfare Seen": Ibid., 7/23/32.

53) "Unemployment is a crime": Adamic quoted in McWilliams, *Southern California*, 292.

53) "Everybody knew him": Interview with Johnny Lange, aka Johnny Longo, Los Angeles, May 1990.

53) "John was very observant": Patricia Breen interview.

54) In 1927, the film industry: Ranking by E. B. Smith & Co., bankers, New York, cited in Los Angeles *Examiner*, 4/26/27.

54) Box-office volume: Warren Beck and David Williams, *California: A History of the Golden State* (Doubleday, 1972), 377.

54) The holding company that owned Warner Brothers: Robert Stanley, *The Celluloid Empire: A History of the American Motion Picture Industry* (Hastings House, 1978), 57.

54) Keystone Studios: Andy Edmonds, *Hot Toddy: The True Story of Hollywood's Most Sensational Murder* (Morrow, 1988), 82–83.

54) "After work the studio heads": Telephone interview with Budd Schulberg, Long Island, February 1989.

54) "The huge barroom was loaded": Wellman quoted in Neal Gabler, *An Empire of Their Own: How the Jews Invented Hollywood* (Anchor Books, 1988), 261.

55) "Whose best friends were card sharks": Samuel Marx, *A Gaudy Spree: Literary Hollywood When the West Was Fun* (Franklin Watts, 1987), 171.

4. Stars and Scoundrels

57) Cohn idolized Mussolini: Robert Thomas, *King Cohn: The Life and Times of Harry Cohn* (Putnam's, 1967), 102.

57) Indulged in small-time crime: Neal Gabler, *An Empire of Their Own: How the Jews Invented Hollywood* (Anchor Books, 1988), 158; also, Thomas, *King Cohn*, 8–9.

58) Marx recalled: Telephone interview with Samuel Marx, Los Angeles, February 1989.

58) When Cohn separated: Testimony of Harry Cohn in *U.S. v. Campagna*, 1991, 2021.

58) "I get that much": Thomas, *King Cohn*, 197. (In his book, Thomas gave Rosselli the pseudonym "Charlie Lombard.")

58) One FBI summary: FBI.FR 6/17/39, #62-43639.

58) Local police described: Undated confidential internal report by a reporter for the Los Angeles *Examiner*, prepared for his editor based on police department sources.

59) Became betting partners: Cohn in *U.S. v. Campagna*, 1994.

59) On another occasion: Ibid., 1989.

59) Cohn's greatest debt to Rosselli: This is a story that has been told several times in different ways, but on balance it seems incontrovertible that Harry Cohn did turn to racketeers to raise money at this crucial juncture, and that Rosselli served as his agent. The most detailed source is Hank Messick, who states flatly in *Beauties and Beasts: The Mob in Show Business* (David McKay Co., 1973) that Rosselli obtained the funds for Cohn via Longy Zwillman in New Jersey. In Eugene Rosow, *Born to Lose: The Gangster Film in America* (Oxford University Press, 1978), 151, the same story is told, naming Rosselli as the conduit for Cohn's cash, but attributing Rosselli's source of the funds as, simply, "gangsters." Bob Thomas gives a similar account in *King Cohn*, but suggests that Cohn's source was a "betting advisor" named "Buzzy Appleton." Asked in an interview whether Buzzy Ap-

pleton were yet another pseudonym for Rosselli, Thomas said, "I don't think so," but could offer no further information on "Buzzy." Still another version appears in Mark A. Stuart, *Gangster #2: The Man Who Invented Organized Crime* (Lyle Stuart, 1985), a biography of Longy Zwillman, but while he asserts that Cohn got his money from Zwillman, he cites as the intermediary Cohn's unnamed bookie (p. 88). These published sources were augmented by an interview in Los Angeles in August 1988 with Richard Olsen, a writer and former employee of Pat Casey and the Producers Association. Olsen said Rosselli's intervention on Cohn's behalf was common knowledge in the film industry. "It was part of the folklore," Olsen said.

60)   Every studio had: Interview with Budd Schulberg, Long Island, February 1989.

60)   Orsatti was Mayer's: Gabler, *Their Own,* 260, 390.

60)   "In former years L. B. Mayer": FBI.FR 6/17/39, #62-43639.

61)   "You're a damn Baptist": Bosley Crowther, *Hollywood Raja: The Life and Times of Louis B. Mayer* (Henry Holt, 1960), 260.

61)   Warner and Annenberg: Telegram to express condolences upon Annenberg's death, Warner Studio archives, Special Collections, University of Southern California.

61)   Hellinger "worked closely with": Jim Bishop, *The Mark Hellinger Story* (Appleton/Century/Crofts, 1952), 284.

61)   Warner and Siegel: Jeffrey Feinman, *Hollywood Confidential* (Playboy Press, 1976), 80.

61)   Schenck greets Hays. Philip French, *The Movie Moguls: An Informal History of the Hollywood Tycoons* (Penguin, 1971), 99.

61)   An introduction to Rothstein: Messick, *Beauties and Beasts,* 12.

62)   Schenck on Agua Caliente board: Los Angeles *Examiner,* 5/26/32.

62)   Schenck and Caress: Ibid., 10/6/33.

62)   Schenck's entourage: Gabler, *Their Own,* 260.

62)   Schenck and Rosselli: Interview with James Bacon, journalist, Los Angeles, November 1988.

62)   Drucker's Barber Shop: Interview with Harry Drucker, Los Angeles, May 1990.

63)   "Correct standards": French, *Movie Moguls,* 105.

64)   50 percent cuts: *Daily Variety,* 3/14 and 3/21/33.

64)   Pat Casey: Olsen interview.

65)   "They had a strike": IOC.V.396.

65)   The strike was short: *Daily Variety,* 8/1/33.

65)   "The major companies": Ibid., 10/3/33.

65)   Rosselli on Casey's payroll: IOC.V.396; *U.S. v. Campagna,* Closing Arguments, 10393, 10396, 10411.

65)   "The girls at the office": Interview with Ralph Clare, retired Teamsters official, Van Nuys, California, February 1988.

66)   Rosselli at Garden of Allah: FBI.IS 3/62, #92-3267-146. Also, IOC.V.396.

66)   "Nothing interrupted": Los Angeles *Examiner*, 8/16/59.

66)   "I think I'll get out": Ibid.

66)   Club New Yorker: Confidential Los Angeles *Examiner* report. Also, IOC.V.406.

66)   Rosselli and Harlow: Messick, *Beauties and Beasts*, 60–61; Stuart, *Gangster #2*, 87–89.

67)   The mob takeover of the IATSE has been recounted in anecdotal detail in a number of books. The best are former IRS intelligence officer Elmer Irey, *The Tax Dodgers* (Greenberg Publishers, 1948), 271–88, and Malcolm Johnson, "In Hollywood," in Nicholas Gage, ed., *Mafia U.S.A.* (Playboy Press, 1972), 317–30. Underpinning these and other accounts was testimony presented at trial, *U.S. v. Campagna*.

67)   A national convention: *U.S. v. Campagna*, 146.

67)   Riverside meetings: Testimony of Willie Bioff in *U.S. v. Campagna*, 141–44.

68)   Rosselli made a trip: Confidential interview, Chicago source. Also, Andy Edmonds, *Hot Toddy: The True Story of Hollywood's Most Sensational Murder* (Morrow, 1988), 162.

68)   Browne, Bioff, and Dean in New York: Bioff in *U.S. v. Campagna*, 152.

69)   Browne meets Rosselli: *Daily Variety*, 10/27/43.

70)   Paramount strike: Los Angeles *Times*, 7/5/87.

70)   An emergency meeting: Bioff in *U.S. v. Campagna*, 205–11; Testimony of George Browne, 1070.

70)   IATSE in Miami: Bioff in *U.S. v. Campagna*, 210–13; Browne, 1084–85.

71)   A pleasure cruise: Bioff in *U.S. v. Campagna*, 244.

71)   "Bioff walked into": Interview with George Dunne, Loyola Marymount College, July 1988.

71)   "I want you to know": Testimony of Nicholas Schenck in *U.S. v. Campagna*, 1340.

72)   Asking for wage increases: *U.S. v. Campagna*, 935.

72)   "It was very costly": Ibid., 653.

72)   IATSE declining wages: Chicago *Daily Tribune*, 3/18/43.

72)   "We have had less": Stephen Fox, *Blood and Power: Organized Crime in Twentieth Century America* (Morrow, 1989), 214.

72)   "Count it": Bioff in *U.S. v. Campagna*, 217; Schenck, 1349.

73)   "I had Hollywood": Florabel Muir, "All Right, Gentlemen, Do We Get the Money: The Astonishing Success of Bad Boy Willie Bioff in Movieland," *Saturday Evening Post*, 1/27/40.

73)   "The bloodiest": Gaeton Fonzi, *Annenberg: A Biography in Power* (Weybright, 1970), 60.

73) Annenberg's sluggers: Carl Sifakis, *The Mafia Encyclopedia* (Facts on File, 1987), 271.

74) Paid Capone $100,000: Fonzi, *Annenberg*, 76.

74) Capone invited Annenberg: Sifakis, *Mafia Encyclopedia*, 15.

74) "That's how the Annenberg": Martin A. Gosch and Richard Hammer, *The Last Testament of Lucky Luciano* (Little, Brown, 1970), 107.

74) 15,000 clients: Sifakis, *Mafia Encyclopedia*, 15.

74) "I would see books": IOC.V.384.

75) "The corner pocket": Dwight McKinney and Fred Allhoff, "Bombing the Lid Off Los Angeles," *Liberty*, 9/25/39.

75) "Frank Shaw was the figurehead": Grant Cooper, interviewed for TV show, "The Hollywood Strike," part of *The L.A. History Project* series on KCET-TV, Los Angeles.

75) "Joe Shaw is": FBI.IS 9/10/38, #95-521-15.

75) "Right now": Confidential Los Angeles *Examiner* report.

75) Rosselli as a Shaw "gunman": FPPC.

75) Kynette's operation: McKinney and Allhoff in *Liberty*.

76) Joe Shaw and the old syndicate: Charles Stoker, *Thicker'n Thieves* (Sidereal Company, 1951), 12–13.

76) Rosselli and funeral bill: Los Angeles *Times*, 3/20/43.

76) "Capone gang execution": San Francisco *Chronicle*, 5/22/32.

76) "Our people": Bioff in *U.S. v. Campagna*, 807.

77) "The closest man": Confidential Los Angeles *Examiner* report.

77) "Inseparable companions": FBI memo, 9/26/38, #95-521-19.

77) "Glaringly incompetent": Guy W. Finney, *Angel City in Turmoil* (Amer Press, 1945), 24.

78) "He has a habit": Confidential Los Angeles *Examiner* report.

78) "You see, Johnny wasn't": Interview with Vincent Barbi, Los Angeles, March 1990.

79) Vincent in L.A.: *U.S. v. Sacco* (A).

79) "I don't want to go": Interview with Concetta Sacco, Boston, October 1989.

79) He stopped off in Chicago: *U.S. v. Sacco* (A).

5. The Fall

81) Siegel background: Virgil W. Peterson, *The Mob: 200 Years of Organized Crime in New York* (Green Hill, 1983), 157 (Big Seven), 178 (Masseria murder).

82) National committee formed: Ed Reid, *The Grim Reapers: The Anatomy of Organized Crime in America* (Bantam, 1970), 11, 171.

82) Lansky called Dragna: Confidential interview.

82) Rosselli and Siegel: Confidential Los Angeles *Examiner* report.

82)   Harlow and Siegel: John Babcock, "These Mean Streets: Mobsters, Moguls and Crooked Cops," *L.A. Style,* June 1986.

82)   Rosselli and Caliente: IOC.V.392. Siegel and Caliente: Dean Jennings, *We Only Kill Each Other: The Life and Bad Times of Bugsy Siegel* (Prentice-Hall, 1967), 141.

82)   Caliente reopening: Los Angeles *Daily News,* 7/21/37.

83)   Cohen holdup: Mickey Cohen with John Peer Nugent, *In My Own Words* (Prentice-Hall, 1975), 36–38.

83)   "Naturally, he knows": Ibid., 39.

83)   Siegel controls extras: Jeffrey Feinman, *Hollywood Confidential* (Playboy Press, 1976), 79–80.

84)   Bruneman defies Siegel: Reid, *Grim Reapers,* 171.

84)   Bruneman shot: Los Angeles *Daily News,* 7/21/37.

84)   Rosselli named: Ibid., 10/27/37.

84)   "It's like the old": Ibid., 7/21/37.

85)   Bruneman shot again: Los Angeles *Times,* 10/26/37.

85)   "All anybody": Los Angeles *Daily News,* 10/27/37.

85)   Dragna and Rosselli: FBI memo, 9/26/38, #95-521-19.

85)   Fratianno names The Bomp: Ovid Demaris, *The Last Mafioso: The Treacherous World of Jimmy Fratianno* (Bantam, 1981), 37–38.

85)   Webb blasted Shaw: Los Angeles *Daily News,* 7/30/37.

85)   IRS and FBI: Ibid., 7/26/37.

86)   "The Eastern Gun Gang": Ibid., 7/27/37.

86)   "A thorough investigation": Ibid., 8/5/37.

86)   Clinton findings: Grand jury minority report, Clifford Clinton papers, Department of Special Collections, UCLA.

86)   "The same bunch": Los Angeles *Daily News,* 10/30/37.

89)   Thugs get gun permits: Florabel Muir, "All Right, Gentlemen, Do We Get the Money: The Astonishing Success of Bad Boy Willie Bioff in Movieland," *Saturday Evening Post,* 1/27/40.

89)   "There were roving goons": Herb Sorrell, Oral History interview, Department of Special Collections, UCLA, p. 25.

89)   "It was a bitter war": Muir in *Saturday Evening Post.*

89)   "We were living on": Telephone interview with Jean La Vell, Los Angeles, March 1990.

89)   Bioff to Chicago: Bioff in *U.S. v. Campagna,* 250, 665.

90)   Holmden described: Testimony of Harlan Holmden in *U.S. v. Campagna,* 1894.

90)   "Misleading and misinforming": Los Angeles *Examiner,* 5/22/37.

90)   Bioff meets Schenck: Bioff in *U.S. v. Campagna,* 662.

90)   "We had organized": Sorrell, Oral History, 27.

90)   Rosselli celebrates: Testimony of George Simko in *U.S. v. Campagna,* 2095.

91)   McWilliams investigation: Letter from Carey McWilliams to West-

brook Pegler, 1/9/40, from Westbrook Pegler papers, Herbert Hoover Presidential Library.

91) Cohn calls Mayer: Cohn in *U.S. v. Campagna*, 1980–2000.

92) "I just called you up.": IOC.V.395.

92) "The strike is off.": Bioff in *U.S. v. Campagna*, 280.

93) "Conditions bordering on racketeering": Los Angeles *Daily News*, 11/9/37.

93) "It has been alleged": Los Angeles *Times*, 11/19/37.

93) A subsequent investigation: Los Angeles *Times*, 7/5/87.

93) IATSE dissidents' leaflet: Handbill in Hollywood labor collection, Southern California Library for Social Studies and Research, Los Angeles.

93) Kent approaches Bioff: Bioff in *U.S. v. Campagna*, 694.

94) Skelton owned the Wilshire Palms: Interview with Johnny Maschio, Hollywood agent, Los Angeles, July 1990.

94) "A real gentleman": Telephone interview with Leon Schwab, Los Angeles, September 1989.

95) Phillip Dare: Los Angeles *Examiner*, 10/12/39.

95) "Rosselli was impressed": Interview with Vincent Barbi, Los Angeles, March 1990.

95) "I can let you have": Testimony of William R. Wilkerson in *U.S. v. Campagna*, 2677.

96) "You'd find all": Telephone interview with Jimmy Starr, Phoenix, Arizona, September 1988.

96) "Rosselli had a big, open swing": Confidential interview.

96) "If there were ten girls": Telephone interview with Jonie Taps, Friars Club, Los Angeles, November 1989.

96) Rosselli and Turner: Interview with James Bacon, journalist, Los Angeles, November 1988.

96) Rosselli and Reed: Interview with Patricia Breen, Las Vegas, May 1989.

96) Biographical information on June Lang is collected in David Ragan, *Who's Who in Hollywood 1900–1976* (Arlington House, 1976), 241.

97) "One of Hollywood's": Los Angeles *Examiner*, 4/2/40.

97) "Rosselli, although well-known": Ibid.

97) Lang plans a ranch home: Ibid., 4/14/40.

97) Jealous of her time: Ibid., 2/21/42.

97) Loud fights: June Lang divorce suit, Los Angeles Superior Court.

98) Lang told Louella Parsons: Undated column, June Lang biography file, Margaret Herrick Library, Academy of Motion Picture Arts and Sciences, Los Angeles.

98) "The most stupid thing": Ragan, *Who's Who*, 241.

98) Schenck's prosecutors knew: Elmer Irey, *The Tax Dodgers* (Greenberg Publishers, 1948), 285.

98) "Everybody is talking": Bioff in *U.S. v. Campagna*, 335.

99)   Burrows met Rosselli: Testimony of George Burrows in ibid., 2635.
99)   Rosselli and Talk-A-Vision: Ibid.
99)   Rosselli hired by Spitzel: FBI.FR 9/27/47, #58-2000-156X2. Also, written Rosselli statement to induction authorities, U.S. Army, undated.
99)   Spitzel specialized: Confidential interview.
99)   Wilkerson insurance: Wilkerson in *U.S. v. Campagna*, 2678.
100)   Spitzel's office a mob hangout: TRPB report, 6/21/51.
100)   Annenberg's deal: Carl Sifakis, *The Mafia Encyclopedia* (Facts on File, 1987), 16.
100)   Ragen's struggle for control of the wire service is summarized in *Gambling and Organized Crime: Report of the Senate Committee on Government Operations*, U.S. Senate Report #1310, 3/8/62, 3.
100)   The efforts of the Dragna-Siegel combine to take over West Coast wire operations was summarized in the *Final Report*, Special Crime Study Commission on Organized Crime, California State Attorney General's office, 1950, 23.
100)   Dragna's meetings with Brophy: George Redston with Kendall F. Crossen, *The Conspiracy of Death* (Bobbs-Merrill, 1965), 71.
101)   "We tore that": IOC.V.397; Commission on Organized Crime, *Final Report*, 23; Redston, *Conspiracy of Death*, 20, 71; Jennings, *We Only Kill*, 80; Cohen and Nugent, *My Own Words*, 61–62. Cohen asserts that Rosselli tried to block the Brophy beating, and that the raid represented a challenge by Siegel to Dragna's authority. Cohen is contradicted, however, by the other accounts cited here, including Redston, who was working for Brophy.
101)   Rosselli meets Bioff: Bioff in *U.S. v. Campagna*, 337.
101)   Bioff meets Korshak: Ibid., 347.
102)   Campagna visits Bioff: Irey, *Tax Dodgers*, 285.
102)   Rosselli and Frank: IOC.V.375.
102)   Rosselli and Hutton: Los Angeles *Examiner*, 4/24/42.
102)   Kostelanetz grilled Zevin: Chicago *Daily News*, 3/19/43.
103)   Rosselli's attempts to enlist: Report of Physical Examination and Induction, U.S. Army, 6/13 and 6/18/42.
103)   The Sicas enlist: Cohen and Nugent, *My Own Words*, 64.
104)   Rosselli as bit player: Rosselli Selective Service Record.
104)   Wilkerson correspondence: Wilkerson in *U.S. v. Campagna*, 2679.
104)   Rosselli bronchitis: Army Clinical Record.
104)   The 81st Armored Regiment: Mary Lee Stubbs and Stanley Russell Connor, *Armor-Cavalry* (Army Lineage Series, Office of the Chief of Military History, U.S. Army, 1969), 459–60.
105)   Correa wrote the War Department: Letter from Correa to Office of Adjutant General, War Department, 2/1/43.
105)   Correa's perjury accusation: New York *Times*, 3/20/43.
105)   Rosselli in uniform: Los Angeles *Examiner*, 3/20/43.

106)   Hoover rejects IATSE investigation: U.S. House Committee on Expenditures in the Executive Departments, "Investigation as to the Manner in which the United States Board of Parole Is Operating and as to Whether There Is a Necessity for a Change in Either the Procedure or Basic Law," *Final Report*, 6/19/48, 7.

107)   Schenck investigation: Irey, *Tax Dodgers*, 284.

107)   "He never agreed": Telephone interview with Boris Kostelanetz, New York, March 1990.

107)   Carey murder scene: John Bartlow Martin, "Who killed Estelle Carey?," *Harper's*, June 1944.

107)   "As soon as she was killed": Kostelanetz interview.

108)   "We sit around in jail": Irey, *Tax Dodgers*, 287.

108)   "Total demolition": Chicago *Herald American*, 3/20/43.

108)   Mobsters post $500,000: The FBI field reports relating to bail for the Chicago mob leaders span several months of 1947: #58-2000-223–35.

109)   Bioff wisecracks: Bioff in *U.S. v. Campagna*, passim.

110)   "The monies were extracted": *Estate of Frank Nitti v. IRS,*13 T.C. #111 (1949), Finding of Fact, Judge John Kern.

6. Life as a Convict

111)   The "old Bastilles": Telephone interview with Lloyd Hooker, Bureau of Prisons, Washington, D.C., November 1990.

111)   "Infested with vermin": FBI.FR 10/2/47, #58-2000-274.

112)   "When the subjects entered": Ibid., 10/7/47, #58-2000-373.

112)   Sanford went to D'Andrea's cell: Ibid., 347.

112)   "He said that with the guards": Confidential interview.

112)   Sanford report on Campagna, Ricca: FBI.FR 9/26/47, #58-2000-130.

113)   Rosselli prison activities: BOP Admission Summary, 4/27/44.

113)   Rosselli correspondence: FBI.FR 10/8/47, #58-200-334.

113)   Compared to Atlanta: Hooker interview.

113)   "Exceptionally obedient": BOP Progress Report, 10/23/46.

114)   "Beneath the surface": Ibid.

114)   Various theories on the release of the Chicago mob leaders surfaced in the Chicago press throughout the fall of 1947. The same theories were taken up in public hearing by the House Committee on Expenditures and discussed in its *Final Report*.

115)   "While the hearings have disclosed": Ibid., 1.

116)   "Most of the additional work": Memo from M. E. Gurnea to Clyde Tolson, 10/23/47, #58-2000-518.

116)   "I agree": Memo from Clyde Tolson to J. E. Hoover, 10/16/47; note added 10/28/47, #58-2000-87.

116) "I'm not bragging": Pendergast quoted in Stephen Fox, *Blood and Power: Organized Crime in Twentieth Century America* (Morrow, 1989), 246.

116) "Tom [Pendergast] asked me": House Committee on Expenditures, *Final Report*, 170.

116) About the same time: Ibid.

116) Columnist Drew Pearson reported: Memo from Edward Tamm to J. E. Hoover, 9/27/47, #58-2000-111X5.

117) Dillon put the word out: FBI.FR 10/8/47, #58-2000-296.

117) Dillon subsequently admitted: House Committee on Expenditures, *Final Report*, 173.

117) "Tom Clark would like": Memo from Guy Hottel, Washington Field Office, to J. E. Hoover, 9/27/47, #58-2000-155X7.

117) Rogers said later: FBI interview of Rogers, 9/20/47, #58-2000-32.

118) He was greeted: FBI.FR 10/3/47, #58-2000-363.

118) James Steinberg: Ibid., 10/8/47, #58-2000-334.

118) And Joe Schenck: Confidential interview, former Eagle Lion employee.

118) Rosselli checked himself in: FBI.FR 10/3/47, #58-2000-363.

119) "This is a town": Telephone interview with Gloria Romanoff, Los Angeles, June 1990.

119) Rosselli and Schenck: Interview with James Bacon, journalist, Los Angeles, November 1988; Romanoff interview.

119) Damon Runyon profile: Los Angeles *Examiner*, 11/25/41.

120) "Brynie was always close": Confidential interview.

120) "Bryan Foy has a reputation": FBI.FR 9/27/47, #58-2000-156X2.

120) What the audiences didn't realize: Petition for Writ of Habeas Corpus, *U.S.A. ex rel. John Rosselli v. Robert E. Clark, Marshal*, Civil Case 8483-Y, Federal District Court, Southern California, July 1948. Also, IOC.V.374.

120) John Higgins said: Telephone interview with John Higgins, Los Angeles, March 1988.

121) Court documents reflected: Writ of Habeas Corpus, *U.S.A. ex rel. John Rosselli v. Robert E. Clark, Marshal*.

121) "John Rosselli recently obtained": TRPB report, 6/21/51.

121) Rosselli IRS report: Ibid.

121) "It was very important": Interview with Betsy Duncan Hammes, Palm Springs, May 1990.

121) "He drove a beat-up old Ford": Interview with Patricia Breen, Las Vegas, May 1989.

121) "Johnny said, 'I won't drive' ": Confidential interview.

121) Father Joe Thompson: FBI.FR 9/27/47, #58-2000-156X2.

122) Rosselli's influential Hollywood friends: FPPC.

122) DeSimone at dinner: FBI.FR 9/27/47, #58-2000-156X2.

123) Subsequent dinner meetings: Ibid., 12/23/57, #92-3267-4.

123) Siegel's death warrant: Carl Sifakis, *The Mafia Encyclopedia* (Facts on File, 1987), 303.

123) Sinatra flew in: Nicholas Gage, *The Mafia Is Not an Equal Opportunity Employer* (Dell, 1972), 113; also, Kitty Kelley, *His Way: The Unauthorized Biography of Frank Sinatra* (Bantam, 1986), 132–34.

123) "It was a clean": Los Angeles *Herald Examiner*, 1/15/88.

124) Before engaging: Ovid Demaris, *The Last Mafioso: The Treacherous World of Jimmy Fratianno* (Bantam, 1981), 1.

124) On the evening of August 18: Ibid., 34.

125) "That Mickey Cohen": Confidential interview.

125) "Twice a week": Interview with Jimmy Fratianno, confidential location, November 1987.

126) "We knew who Rosselli was": Interview with Marion Phillips, Eagle Rock, California, March 1988.

126) "We knew him from": Interview with Billy Dick Unland, formerly of LAPD Organized Crime Intelligence Division, Irvine, California, November 1989.

126) A brief memo: FBI memo, 12/6/47, #58-2000-366.

126) "A figure in the": Los Angeles *Times*, 7/28/48.

126) He was called to testify: FBI memo, 12/6/47, #58-2000-366.

127) Foy helped lay the groundwork and the hearing itself: IOC.V.378.

129) In a press conference: Los Angeles *Times*, 10/8/50.

129) "This professional blackmailer": State Commission on Organized Crime, *Report on Organized Crime*, 1953, 22.

130) Another frequent companion: Hammes interview; Collins, McKay, and Giesler also named in FPPC.

130) Rosselli cast about: FPPC.

130) He called on Harry Cohn: Robert Thomas, *King Cohn: The Life and Times of Harry Cohn* (Putnam's, 1967), 205–6.

131) Rosselli at Hollywood Park: TRPB report, 6/21/51.

131) Tom Thumb venture: FPPC.

131) Burrows bailed Rosselli: Ibid.

131) The Diburro Film Company: Assignment of Chattel Mortgage, recorded at Los Angeles County, 6/23/52.

132) The Hollywood Kid: FBI.IS 8/9/60, #92-3267-77.

132) Sinatra was dogged: Gage, *The Mafia Is Not*, 112; Tony Sciacca, *Sinatra* (Pinnacle Books, 1976), 46. Sciacca cites Justice Department sources for the story.

132) Dorsey gave the story credence: Kelley, *His Way*, 69.

133) Kelley scenario: Ibid., 212–13.

133) "He was asked to intercede": Sciacca, *Sinatra*, 155.

133) Author Katz suggests: Leonard Katz, *Uncle Frank: The Biography of Frank Costello* (Drake, 1973), 249–50.

133) "The Maggio role": Interview with Joe Seide, Los Angeles, February 1989.

7. Back in Action

135)   "Johnny called it": Interview with Patricia Breen, Las Vegas, May 1989.

136)   Charlie "Babe" Baron was: Ovid Demaris, *Captive City: Chicago in Chains* (Lyle Stuart, 1969), 230.

136)   Lederer and Bally: Ovid Demaris, *The Last Mafioso: The Treacherous World of Jimmy Fratianno* (Bantam, 1981), 213.

136)   Fratianno assaults Sedway, Stacher: Ibid., 82–84.

136)   Dragna "made very few": Ed Reid, *The Grim Reapers: The Anatomy of Organized Crime in America* (Bantam, 1970), 176.

137)   "John Rosselli was the chief": FBI.IS 9/26/60, #92-3267-81.

137)   Rosselli in Reno: Telephone interview with Frank McCulloch, journalist, San Francisco, June 1990. McCulloch said he ran across Rosselli while working in Reno in 1948.

137)   According to Armstrong: Telephone interview with Bryn Armstrong, Reno, Nevada, September 1990.

137)   McKay and Graham's backers: Armstrong interview; see also, Demaris, *Last Mafioso,* 56–57.

138)   Casino openings: Ed Reid and Ovid Demaris, *The Green Felt Jungle* (Pocket Books, 1963), 36, 53–64.

138)   Cornero at the Stardust: Los Angeles *Examiner,* 7/8/55. And, Cornero dies: Los Angeles *Herald,* 8/5/55.

138)   Rosselli's Vegas "interests": TRPB report, 6/21/51.

138)   "Airport Squad": Report from TRPB to Nevada Gaming Control Board, 1/18/57.

139)   The case of "Russian Louis": Interview with Jimmy Fratianno, confidential location, November 1987. See also, Demaris, *Last Mafioso,* 80–82.

140)   An "in" joke: Reid and Demaris, *Green Felt Jungle,* 179.

140)   Bioff and Goldwater: Ibid., 42–43.

140–41) Rosselli "hadn't seen Bioff": Los Angeles *Examiner,* 11/5/55.

141)   "They're going to be on my back": Patricia Breen interview.

142)   "Miami was pretty wide open": In an effort to corroborate this source, the authors reviewed Rosselli's FBI file and found a reference (FBI Correlation Summary, 10/30/70, #92-3267-1037) to a specific report titled "Criminal Influence in Miami Hotels, Motels and Nightclubs," which apparently included reference to Rosselli. Despite specific requests for the file, despite an FOIA request dating back more than four years, the FBI still had not released that file by the time of publication.

143)   "This guy had ties": Confidential interview.

144)   Lansky history: Hank Messick, *Lansky* (Putnam's, 1971) 103, 123, 194.

145)   "A guy who always": Luciano quoted in Henrik Kruger, *The Great Heroin Coup* (South End Press, 1980), 141.

145)   FBI on Rosselli in Havana: FBI memo to Director, 8/23/76, #72-2382-81. Most of the message was deleted, but this sentence was released: "Source advised Rosselli associated in gambling casinos in pre-revolutionary Cuba with [deleted] and associates continued into Castro action group in Miami area."

145)   A friend to Batista: Telephone interview with Nancy Bretzfield, Los Angeles, November 1990. See also L. Gonzalez-Mata, *Cygne* (Grasset, Paris, 1976), 94.

145)   Rosselli accompanied her father: Antoinette Giancana and Thomas C. Renner, *Mafia Princess: Growing Up in Sam Giancana's Family* (Avon Books, 1985), 242.

146)   Rosselli "had a management role": G. Robert Blakey and Richard N. Billings, *The Plot to Kill the President* (Times Books, 1981), 230.

146)   "About fifteen years": Testimony of Santo Trafficante, HAH.V.357.

146)   "It was as if": Interview with Refugio Cruz, Miami, August 1990.

146)   Morales as El Indio: Telephone interview with Bradley Earl Ayers, Woodbury, Minnesota, September 1990. Also, interview with Robert Dorff, Los Angeles, September 1990.

146)   "He was outrageous": Ayers interview.

147)   1953 Morales listing: Department of State, *Biographic Register*, 1959.

147)   Morales in Guatemala: David Atlee Phillips, *The Night Watch* (Atheneum, 1977), 49.

147)   Morales from 1958–1960: Department of State, *Foreign Service List*, January, April, October, 1960. Also, Department of State, *Biographic Register*, 1968.

147)   Morales and Fischetti: Confidential report relayed by Bob Dorff.

147)   "Rosselli was the only man": Ayers interview.

148)   Armas "in way over his head": Stephen Schlesinger and Stephen Kinzer, *Bitter Fruit: The Untold Story of the American Coup in Guatemala* (Anchor Books, 1982), 122.

148)   Armas faced Army faction: David Wise and Thomas Ross, *The Invisible Government* (Random House, 1964), 181–82.

148)   "They took over": Interview with Alfred Barrett, Chapel Hill, North Carolina, June 1990.

149)   Most contemporary observers: Barrett interview; telephone interview with Frank McNeil, former political officer at U.S. Embassy in Guatemala, Maryland, August 1990.

149)   Lewin and gambling ships: Los Angeles *Times*, 7/5/39.

149)   Lewin in association with Rosselli: Ibid., 9/20/68.

149)   Lewin, Marcos, and CIA: Sterling Seagrave, *The Marcos Dynasty* (Harper and Row, 1988), 161–64, 329–30, 334. See also, Joseph Burkholder Smith, *Portrait of a Cold Warrior* (Putnam, 1976), 284–86.

149)   "We thought it was": Barrett interview.

149)   Castillo Armas "a man of great probity": McNeil interview.

149)   Lewin jailed: Los Angeles *Times*, 7/24/57. Lewin's widow, Dorothy,
         said in a telephone interview (Los Angeles, January 1991) that Lewin
         was arrested *after* the assassination, and that Castillo Armas had sup-
         ported the casino operation. Gus Nichols (telephone interview, Las
         Vegas, January 1991) supported that version of events. But the record
         clearly reflects that Lewin was arrested several days *before* the shooting
         occurred, and Barrett was emphatic about Armas's opposition.

149)   Lewin partner Nichols: Nichols interview.

150)   "Direct intervention": New York *Times*, 5/15/59.

151)   Vaccaro was indicted: Ibid., 7/24/40.

151)   *Wall Street Journal* exposé: Stanley Penn, "On the Waterfront," in
         Nicholas Gage, ed., Mafia U.S.A. (Playboy Press, 1972), 313–16.

151)   Weiss and Standard Fruit: Peter Dale Scott, *Crime and Cover-up: The
         CIA, the Mafia, and the Dallas-Watergate Connection* (Westworks,
         1977), 16.

151)   Weiss convicted in 1940: New York *Times*, 11/23/40.

151)   Weiss "to run New Orleans": Messick, *Lansky*, 84.

152)   "Throughout Latin America": McNeil interview.

153)   The CIA and Luciano: Rodney Campbell, *The Luciano Project*
         (McGraw-Hill, 1977), passim.

153)   INCA was founded: *VICTORY: The Official Publication of the Infor-
         mation Council of the Americas*, Preview Edition, 12/11/63 (supplied
         to the authors by Paul Hoch, San Francisco).

154)   Dr. Alton Ochsner: Scott, *Crime and Cover-up*, 14–16.

154)   CIA agent William Gaudet: Thomas McCann, *An American Com-
         pany: The Tragedy of United Fruit* (Crown, 1976), 49.

154)   Standard Fruit was represented: Scott, *Crime and Cover-up*, 16. See
         also, *VICTORY:* Monaghan is listed as a member and Gil as the editor
         of the newsletter; in a later edition (3/3/65), Deutsch is named as the
         group's attorney and Weiss as a charter member. Gil's connection to
         the CRC is recorded in Bernard Fensterwald, Jr., and Michael Ewing,
         Assassination of JFK: Coincidence or Conspiracy? (Zebra Books,
         1977), 496.

154)   United Fruit and Panama: San Francisco *Chronicle*, 6/5/74.

154)   Standard Fruit payoffs: Ibid., 11/26/75.

154)   Oliva a "liaison": Susan Jonas et al., *Guatemala: "And So Victory Is
         Born Even in the Bitterest Hours"* (North American Congress on
         Latin America, 1974), 81.

155)   McCann said: Telephone interview with Thomas McCann, Boston,
         August 1990.

155)   And scattered press accounts: New York *Times*, 10/4/59; 10/24/59.

155)   Unnamed "North Americans": Ibid., 10/24/59.

156)   The other residents: Interview with the manager of the apartment
         complex, who requested anonymity.

156)   Boys from a Catholic orphanage: Interview with Harold Fitzgerald, Los Angeles, December 1989.

156)   Rosselli and Clark: Letter from Rev. Joseph P. Clark to federal probation authorities, 5/8/68.

156)   Winchell and Rosselli: Letter from Sansum Clinic staff physician C. A. Domz to federal probation authorities, 6/11/68.

157)   "Katleman was awful": Interview with Betsy Duncan Hammes, Palm Springs, May 1990.

157)   "You treat people": Interview with Joaun Cantillon, Los Angeles, April 1990.

157)   Harold Fitzgerald and Rosselli: Fitzgerald interview.

157)   "Brynie happened to be": Interview with Madeline Foy O'Donnell, Los Angeles, February 1990.

158)   "All my children": Maheu interviewed by staff of Barbour/Langley Productions for Jack Anderson television special, "American Exposé: Who Murdered JFK?" aired 11/2/88; raw tapes reviewed by the authors.

158)   Rosselli sent couriers: Interview with George Bland, Aptos, California, January 1988.

8. Life at the Top

161)   Rosselli transfer to Chicago: Ovid Demaris, *The Last Mafioso: The Treacherous World of Jimmy Fratianno* (Bantam, 1981), 123–24.

162)   Giancana and Vegas: William Brashler, *The Don: The Life and Death of Sam Giancana* (Ballantine Books, 1977), 200–2. See also, Antoinette Giancana and Thomas C. Renner, *Mafia Princess: Growing Up in Sam Giancana's Family* (Avon Books, 1985), 242–47.

162)   Caifano in Vegas: Ed Reid and Ovid Demaris, *The Green Felt Jungle* (Pocket Books, 1963), 60–61, 213–17. See also William F. Roemer, Jr., *Roemer: Man Against the Mob* (Donald I. Fine, 1989), 41, 134.

163)   Ricca and Humphreys: Confidential interview.

163)   Giancana assigned Rosselli: There are numerous references in FBI files to Rosselli's relationship with Giancana. The two most explicit were drawn from the authors' review of Giancana's file at the FBI reading room in Washington, D.C.: the flat statement that "Rosselli is the direct representative of Chicago top hoodlum Sam Giancana in the Las Vegas area (7/18/61)"; and Giancana's own statement, relayed by an informant, "Giancana stated he had sent John Rosselli out to Las Vegas (1/10/62)." While Bill Roemer also identifies Rosselli as a Chicago emissary to Las Vegas, he gets the succession backward, proposing that Rosselli was replaced by Caifano in the middle 1950s (*Roemer*, 133). As an FBI field agent in Chicago, Roemer produced some of the

best intelligence ever on mob operations, but the facts in his memoir prove shaky when he ventures outside the Windy City.

163)   Ben Jaffe: Chicago *Daily News*, 5/22/57; also, Reid and Demaris, *Green Felt Jungle*, 71.

163)   Rosselli at Tropicana: FBI interview with John Rosselli at his apartment at the Tropicana, 3/12/58, #92-3267-17. Also, files from the intelligence division of the Los Angeles District Attorney, supplied by a confidential source, reported in July 1963 that "John Rosselli was in charge of the Tropicana until three years ago."

163)   Kastel at Tropicana: Reid and Demaris, *Green Felt Jungle*, 71–73.

163)   Kastel helped engineer Costello's: Leonard Katz, *Uncle Frank: The Biography of Frank Costello* (Drake, 1973), 100–8.

164)   Rosselli, Drucker, and Perino: Interview with Harry Drucker, Los Angeles, May 1990.

164)   Rosselli ran the concessions: FBI interview, 3/12/58; FBI.IS 2/16/62, #92-3267-118; also, Drucker interview.

164)   Rosselli setback: FBI interview, 3/12/58, #92-3267-118.

164)   Costello shooting: Katz, *Uncle Frank*, 203–12.

165)   Tropicana note: Reid and Demaris, *Green Felt Jungle*, 69–71.

165)   "We were always lucky": Interview with Joe Shimon, Washington, D.C., June 1989.

166)   Gus Greenbaum's life and death were recounted in Reid and Demaris, *Green Felt Jungle*, 30–48. Ed Becker was the source of the story in that account, and is the source here as well (see Preface).

167)   "Set up protection": FBI memo, 12/22/58, supplied to authors by a confidential source.

167)   "Of all the people": Michael Hellerman with Thomas C. Renner, *Wall Street Swindler* (Doubleday, 1977), 83.

168)   "Rosselli had incredible vision": Interview with Fred Black, Washington, D.C., September 1990.

169)   Hidden control of Monte Prosser Productions: FBI.IS 9/28/61, #92-3267-112; 3/10/62, #92-3267-146.

169)   "The biggest deal": Hollywood *Reporter*, 4/23/58.

169)   A friend of Prosser's: Interview with Patricia Breen, Las Vegas, May 1989.

169)   Vegas sheriff leak: FBI.IS 1/5/62, #92-3267-116.

170)   Rosselli controlled ice machines: Letter from Franz Breitling, President, Ajax West Corp., to federal parole authorities, 8/7/68.

171)   Robert Sunshine: Don Barlett and James B. Steele, *Empire: The Life, Legend, and Madness of Howard Hughes* (Norton, 1979), 285–86.

172)   "The source stated": FBI.IS 3/10/62, #92-3267-146.

172)   "Rosselli was the 'power' ": FBI.FR 6/15/64, #92-3267-591.

172)   "Icepick Willie": As told to Becker by Israel Alderman.

173)   1963 earnings: Wallace Turner, *Gamblers' Money: The New Force in American Life* (Houghton Mifflin, 1965), 17.

173)   "Everything's nice": Demaris, *Last Mafioso*, 132–33.

9. Castro

176)   "To eradicate this cancer": Richard Nixon, *Six Crises* (Doubleday, 1962), 352.

176)   Castro and Rothman: William Scott Malone, "The Secret Life of Jack Ruby," *New Times*, 1/23/78. Also, George Crile III, "The Mafia, the CIA, and Castro," Washington *Post*, 5/16/76.

177)   Sturgis and Castro: HAR.176.

177)   Hoffa and Castro: Dan E. Moldea, *Hoffa Wars: Teamsters, Rebels, Politicians, and the Mob* (Paddington Press, 1978), 106–7, 122–23.

177)   "We had it pretty good": HAH.V.353.

177)   Rosselli, Giancana, Ruby visit Trafficante: Malone in *New Times*.

177)   Trafficante and Raoul Castro: HAH.V.355.

177)   "I could see": Ibid.

177)   Lansky's $1 million bounty: Malone in *New Times;* John H. Davis, *The Kennedys: Dynasty and Disaster 1848–1984* (McGraw-Hill, 1985), 396; Nicholas Gage, *The Mafia Is Not an Equal Opportunity Employer* (Dell, 1972), 78.

177)   Sturgis's plot: HAR.176.

177)   Giancana boasted: Ibid., 175.

178)   Prio's connections to mob: Ibid., 170–72.

178)   Early plots: CCIR.72.

178)   King's action plan: Ibid., 92.

179)   Nixon had personal roots: Howard Kohn, "The Hughes-Nixon-Lansky Connection: The Secret Alliances of the CIA from World War II to Watergate," *Rolling Stone*, 5/20/76. Also, Hank Messick, *Lansky* (Putnam's, 1971), 188–90.

179)   The 54/12 Group: Henrik Kruger, *The Great Heroin Coup* (South End Press, 1980), 154.

179)   "Early in 1960": Nixon, *Six Crises*, 352.

179)   "The vice-president was": E. Howard Hunt, *Give Us This Day: The Inside Story of the CIA and the Bay of Pigs Invasion* (Arlington House, 1973), 40.

179)   Nixon "The father": Bonsal quoted in Arthur M. Schlesinger, Jr., *Robert Kennedy and His Times* (Ballantine, 1978), 523.

179)   On March 17: Peter Wyden, *Bay of Pigs: The Untold Story* (Touchstone Books, 1979), 19–20.

179–80) Eisenhower discusses "removal": Ibid., 25.

180)   Bissell profiled: Wyden, *Bay of Pigs*, 10–20.

180)   "A capability to eliminate": CC.IR.74.

180)   Bissell turned to Edwards: Ibid.

180)   "[The CIA] may have": HAR.176.

180)   "Bissell attributed": Wyden, *Bay of Pigs*, 42; Wyden interviewed Bissell extensively.

182)   "Jim O'Connell described": CC.IR.74.

182–83) Robert A. Maheu Associates: Jim Hougan, *Spooks: The Haunting of America—The Private Use of Secret Agents* (Morrow, 1978), 273–74, 278–80.

183)   Frank used Maheu offices: Alan A. Block, "Violence, Corruption and Clientelism: The Assassination of Jesus de Galindez, 1956," *Social Justice: A Journal of Crime, Conflict and World Order*, Summer, 1989, 83.

183)   Frank used a RAMA credit card: In 1957, Maheu produced a detailed itinerary of Frank's travels for the FBI. FBI file on Galindez (Washington Field Office file #97-881), section titled Robert A. Maheu, reviewed by the authors at the FBI reading room in Washington, D.C.

183)   Maheu gets Dominican contract, reports to CIA: Ibid.

183)   Maheu at Republican Convention: FBI interview with Maheu, 3/29/57 in FBI file on Galindez.

183)   FBI interview with Maheu: Ibid.

183)   "The Galindez operation": Letter from Morris Ernst to Sydney Baron, in the FBI file on Galindez.

183)   The mob and Galindez: Sandy Smith, "The Mob," two-part series, *Life*, 9/1 and 9/8/67.

183)   "One of the fastest": Washington *Post*, 8/1/71.

184)   "Maheu was always impressed": Telephone interview with Les Whitten, Washington, D.C., May 1990.

184)   Hoffa hired Maheu: Moldea, *Hoffa Wars*, 131.

184)   Maheu met Rosselli "very casually": Maheu interview, Barbour/Langley Production tapes for Jack Anderson TV special, "American Exposé: Who Murdered JFK?," aired 11/2/88.

184)   "It was a busy weekend": Telephone interview with Robert Maheu, Las Vegas, May 1990.

184)   "Maheu claims not": CC.IR.75.

184)   Shimon on Maheu and Rosselli: Interview with Joe Shimon, Washington, D.C., August 1990.

184)   Rosselli on Maheu: During a brief encounter Rosselli allowed he had known Maheu "about five years," then declined further comment. FBI.FR 7/7/61, #92-3267-111.

185)   Maheu's Thanksgiving: Maheu interview, Barbour/Langley tapes.

185)   "I can't tell you that": Telephone interview with Robert Maheu, Las Vegas, September 1990.

185–86) Jim O'Connell's testimony: CC.IR.75–76. In the same passage, the committee noted that Maheu said it was O'Connell who proposed using Rosselli. The committee made no judgment as to which man named Rosselli, but observed that O'Connell first met Rosselli at one of Maheu's clambakes.

186)   "After lunch": Maheu interview, Barbour/Langley tapes.
186)   "High government officials": CC.IR.76.
186)   A second meeting: Ibid.
186–87) Rosselli gained a valuable edge: HAR.176.
187)   "He said it was": Interview with Betsy Duncan Hammes, Palm Springs, May 1990.
187)   "Honor and dedication": CC.IR.82.
187)   "He finally said he felt": CC.IR.76.
187)   "He paid his way": Ibid., 85.
187–88) Rosselli and Maheu in Miami: Ibid., 76.
188)   Edwards met with Bissell: Ibid., 94.
188)   "Edwards deliberately avoided": Ibid., 95.
189)   Rosselli and Gener: HAH.V.357–58.
189)   O'Connell to Miami: CC.IR.76.
189)   "He told me": HAH.V.357.
189–90) Fontainebleau meeting: CC.IR.76–80.
190)   "Did the job": Ibid.
190)   "What's wrong": Warren Hinkle and William Turner, *The Fish Is Red —The Story of the Secret War Against Castro* (Harper & Row, 1981), 38.
191)   "One time, one afternoon": HAR.V.241.
191)   Sinatra's Fontainebleau opening: Kitty Kelley, *His Way: The Unauthorized Biography of Frank Sinatra* (Bantam, 1986), 290.
191)   There was talk: Shimon interview.
191)   Maheu "opened up his briefcase": CC.IR.81. Maheu denied the story, and could not recall being present when poison was passed. He was contradicted by Rosselli and Joe Shimon; Rosselli, however, did not recall Shimon being there. In the end, Rosselli's version seems the most reliable.
192)   "Johnny's going to handle everything": Ibid., 82.
192)   Stage a second attempt: Ibid., 80.
192)   Meetings with de Varona: HAH.V.360–61.
192)   De Varona seeking money, running raids: Hinkle and Turner, *Fish Is Red*, 74–75; Hunt, *Give Us This Day*, 160.
192)   He struck a deal: CC.IR.81.
193)   Rosselli identified Orta: CIA memo to Dade County homicide detectives, Dade file.
193)   Orta Castro's personal secretary: Hinkle and Turner, *Fish Is Red*, 50.
193)   Kennedy's "deep feeling" on Castro: Garry Wills, *The Kennedy Imprisonment* (Pocket Books, 1983), 242.
193)   Endorsing "the non-Batista": Nixon, *Six Crises*, 353–54.
194)   Dulles at Hyannis Port: Wyden, *Bay of Pigs*, 67.

194)   Nixon "exploded" in anger: Ibid.
194)   Second briefing: CC.IR.120.
194)   "Kennedy did not seem surprised": Wyden, *Bay of Pigs*, 68.
194)   "It is quite possible": CC.IR.121.
194)   "Although Bissell testified": Ibid., 117.
195)   Smathers on Kennedy: Ibid., 123–24.
195)   "Grabbing their nuts": Wills, *Imprisonment*, 244.
195)   "The terrors of the earth": Davis, *Kennedys*, 394.
195)   "We were hysterical": CC.IR.142.
196)   Taylor and RFK verdict: Ibid., 135.
196)   "To stir things up": Davis, *Kennedys*, 395.
197)   Bill Harvey profiled in David Martin, *Wilderness of Mirrors* (Harper & Row, 1980), passim.
197)   Harvey assigned to launch: CC.IR.183.
197)   "Staff D": Martin, *Wilderness*, 121.
197)   "Maximum security" and "nonattributability": Ibid., 122.
197)   "The Magic Button": CC.IR.183.
197)   Bissell was "chewed out": Ibid., 141. Discussion of Executive Action from this point to Kennedy's speech on page 200 all from this source.

10. The Kennedys

201)   "If we do not": Robert F. Kennedy, *The Enemy Within* (Popular Library, 1960), 253.
201–2) "He saw civil rights": Arthur M. Schlesinger, Jr., *Robert Kennedy and His Times* (Ballantine, 1978), 307.
202)   Joseph Kennedy's bootlegging: Stephen Fox, *Blood and Power: Organized Crime in Twentieth Century America* (Morrow, 1989), 60. Also, Doris Kearns Goodwin, *The Fitzgeralds and the Kennedys: An American Saga* (Simon and Schuster, 1987), 442.
202)   "Frank said that": John Miller in Leonard Katz, *Uncle Frank: The Biography of Frank Costello* (Drake, 1973), 69.
202)   Kennedy and Tom Cassara: Fox, *Blood and Power*, 315–16.
202)   Rosselli knew Joe Kennedy: Summary report, Dade file; also, interview with Harold Fitzgerald, Los Angeles, December 1989. Fitzgerald said Rosselli made an offhand reference in 1960 to discussing the Kennedy boys' problems with women while golfing with the father. Separately, Church Committee attorney David Bushong said in a telephone interview (June 1990) that Rosselli testified in a sworn deposition that he had played cards with the elder Kennedy. Bushong said he did not pursue the matter, as it did not fall under the committee's purview.
202)   Jean Smith on Joe Kennedy: Schlesinger, *Robert Kennedy*, 153.

202)   "The old man saw": Peter Collier and David Horowitz, *The Kennedys* (Summit, 1984), 220.

203)   "We have only one rule": Pierre Salinger, *With Kennedy* (Doubleday, 1966), 26.

203)   "If the investigation flops": Schlesinger, *Robert Kennedy*, 154–55.

203)   "You tell Bobby Kennedy": Salinger, *With Kennedy*, 22.

203)   "Organized crime": Schlesinger, *Robert Kennedy*, 281.

203)   "His zeal": William Shannon, *The Heir Apparent: Robert Kennedy and the Struggle for Power* (Macmillan, 1967), 66.

203)   Criminal division days in court: Victor Navasky, *Kennedy Justice* (Atheneum, 1971), 49.

203)   Convictions of racketeers: Schlesinger, *Robert Kennedy*, 299.

204)   Marcello donation to Nixon: Dan E. Moldea, *The Hoffa Wars: Teamsters, Rebels, Politicians, and the Mob* (Paddington Press, 1978), 108.

204)   The Kennedy deal: Personal memo to the Attorney General from J. Edgar Hoover, 8/16/62; reviewed by the authors in the Peter Lawford file at the FBI reading room. See also, Kitty Kelley, *His Way: The Unauthorized Biography of Frank Sinatra* (Bantam, 1986), 304; Michael Hellerman with Thomas C. Renner, *Wall Street Swindler* (Doubleday, 1977), 105.

205)   "Terrible sense of gloom": Kennedy campaign official Lawrence F. O'Brien, in Schlesinger, *Robert Kennedy*, 212.

205)   Payoffs "a quasi-legal cover": Ibid., 215.

205)   "Anywhere from $2 and a drink": Charles D. Hylton, editor, *The Logan Banner*, in John H. Davis, *The Kennedys: Dynasty and Disaster 1848–1984* (McGraw-Hill, 1985), 286.

205)   D'Amato and Melandra: Kelley, *His Way*, 581.

205)   D'Amato on FBI wiretaps: Ibid., 295, 581.

205)   "Obviously our highest contribution": Schlesinger, *Robert Kennedy*, 215–16.

205)   Giancana worked hard: William Brashler, *The Don: The Life and Death of Sam Giancana* (Ballantine, 1977), 210–11.

205)   Chicago vote totals: Ovid Demaris, *Captive City: Chicago in Chains* (Lyle Stuart, 1969), 193.

206)   "Our national purpose": *Life*, 8/22/60.

206)   "The male side of the family": Garry Wills, *The Kennedy Imprisonment* (Pocket Books, 1983), 29.

207)   Lawford and whores: From authors' review of the Peter Lawford file at the FBI reading room.

207)   "This menage a trois": C. David Heymann, *A Woman Named Jackie* (Lyle Stuart, 1989), 261.

207)   Rosselli and Lawford: Interview with Fred Otash, detective, Los Angeles, September 1989; Interview with Susan Woods, Palm Springs, September 1989.

208)   Sources quoted by *Newsweek: Newsweek*, 12/29/75.

208)   Presidential telephone logs: CC.IR.129.

208)   "I was seeing them": Kitty Kelley, "The Dark Side of Camelot," *People*, 2/29/88.

208)   "Johnny knew Judy Campbell": Interview with Madeline Foy O'Donnell, Los Angeles, February 1990.

208)   "I remember John": Interview with Patricia Breen, Las Vegas, May 1989.

208)   FBI first realized: CC.IR.129.

209)   She first insisted: *Newsweek*, 12/29/75; New York *Times*, 4/12/76.

209)   Exner's later version: Kelley in *People*.

209)   "She said she knew": Interview with Jeanne Carmen, Newport Beach, California, August 1989.

210)   "It was one of the hairiest": Otash interview.

211)   "George said": Interview with Betsy Duncan Hammes, Palm Springs, May 1990.

211)   "How you gonna kill": Interview with Joe Shimon, Washington, D.C., August 1990.

211)   "John Rosselli had a real . . . ambition": Interview with William F. Roemer, by staff of Barbour/Langley Productions for Jack Anderson TV special, "American Exposé: Who murdered JFK?," aired 11/2/88.

211)   Maheu sends Balletti: CC.IR.77.

211)   "Keystone Comedy act": Ibid.

211)   Balletti phone calls: FBI.FR 6/6/61, #139-1201-45.

211)   Richardson and Balletti: Ibid., 6/12/61, #139-1201-51.

212)   Maheu's explanation: Ibid., 6/6/61, #139-1201-45.

212)   "I remember his expression": CC.IR.79.

212)   "I knew it was serious": HAR.179.

212)   "Maheu was the guy": Shimon interview.

212)   "Plans to dispose of Castro": CC.IR.75.

213)   Hoover "astonished": Ibid., 132.

213)   Edwards complied: Ibid., 126.

213)   Hoover memo to RFK: Ibid., 127.

214)   "Courtney, I hope this": Ibid., 128.

214)   Evans could not recall: Ibid., 331.

214)   Bob Maheu admitted: FBI.FR 6/30/61, #139-1201-62.

214)   Campbell used Rosselli's apartment: FBI.IS 2/16/62, #92-3267-118. Campbell is not mentioned by name in the file, but is referred to as a "close friend"; Los Angeles Police Detective Ed Lutes, a veteran of the organized crime detail, added in an interview that Campbell occasionally made use of Rosselli's apartment.

214)   Campbell's first FBI interview: G. Robert Blakey and Richard N. Billings, *The Plot to Kill the President* (Times Books, 1981), 380.

214)   Rosselli and Campbell at Romanoff's: FBI.IS 2/16/62, #92-3267-118. Here the first reference to Campbell is "an unknown woman." That sighting is followed up in a field report (2/19/62, #92-3267-

123): "Rosselli . . . observed leaving Romanoff's with a girl, believed to be [deleted]. The exact nature of the association between Rosselli [deleted] Giancana [deleted]." The report is followed in the file by J. Edgar Hoover's memo to Ken O'Donnell (see below), which revealed his knowledge of Campbell and her associations. Finally, there is a memo to the attorney general (2/27/62, #92-3267-126): "Information has been developed with the investigation of John Rosselli, one of the second group of forty hoodlums receiving concentrated attention, that he has been in contact with [three lines deleted]. The relationship between [two lines deleted] is not known. Information has also been developed that [deleted] associated with Sam Giancana, a prominent Chicago underworld figure. [line deleted] This information is being made available to Hon. P. Kenneth O'Donnell, Special Assistant to the President."

Taken together, the sequence of field reports and memos seem clearly to be concerned with Judy Campbell, and to demark the seemingly innocuous event, a lunch meeting with Rosselli, that precipitated Hoover's alert.

215)   Allegations of presidential infidelity: Athan Theoharis and John Stuart Cox, *The Boss: J. Edgar Hoover and the Great American Inquisition* (Bantam, 1990), 371–72.

215)   "My dear Mr. O'Donnell": Hoover memo, 2/27/62, #92-3267-125.

215)   An unusual, private lunch: CC.IR.130.

215)   Over the next several weeks: All information on the meetings during this time and the "paper trail" cover-up come from CC.IR.130–34.

218)   Harvey and Rosselli in D.C.: FBI.FR 6/25/63, #92-3267-482.

218)   Rosselli and Martino: Warren Hinkle and William Turner, *The Fish Is Red—The Story of the Secret War Against Castro* (Harper & Row, 1981), 173.

219)   "Tronco de Yucca": E. Howard Hunt, *Give Us This Day: The Inside Story of the CIA and the Bay of Pigs Invasion* (Arlington House, 1973), 78.

219)   "In and out of Miami": CC.IR.83.

220)   FBI apartment rental: FBI.FR 3/28/61, #92-3267-98.

220)   "He checked in": Shimon interview.

220)   Rosselli disclosed to Morgan: Interview with Fred Black, Washington, D.C., September 1990.

220)   Harvey met Rosselli: CC.IR.83.

220)   At the airport cocktail lounge: David Martin, *Wilderness of Mirrors* (Harper & Row, 1980), 138.

220)   Maheu, Giancana, and Trafficante: CC.IR.83; HAR.152.

220)   "Initially Rosselli did not trust": CC.IR.83.

221)   Trafficante's drug-running network: George Crile III, "The Mafia, the CIA, and Castro", Washington *Post*, 5/16/76. Crile and several others (including Joe Shimon and Jack Anderson) believe that Trafficante had

a drug partnership with Castro, and believe that the assassination plots failed because Trafficante was tipping the Cubans off. We reject that position: Rosselli was too smart to fail to sniff out such a connection and thereby jeopardize his own life; Trafficante provided too much concrete assistance to the anti-Castro Cubans to sustain Castro's loyalties; Trafficante was desperately concerned that his role in the plots remain secret; and finally, Trafficante was cut off from much of the actual plotting. In addition, Miami attorney David Walters, who represented Trafficante and knew him well, asserts that the gangster's hatred for Castro was bitter and genuine. Still, by any account, Trafficante remains a treacherous figure.

221)   Trafficante's first concern: Shimon interview.

221)   A second meeting: CC.IR.84. The events resulting from the second meeting are all reported in this congressional probe.

222)   Lansdale would "bombard Harvey": Martin, *Wilderness*, 130.

222)   "Policymakers not only": CC.IR.146.

222)   "Nobody knew exactly": Martin, *Wilderness*, 133.

222)   "What's the matter": Ibid., 134.

222)   RFK "that fucker": Ibid., 136.

223)   Rosselli was issued the papers: Interview with Bradley Earl Ayers, Woodbury, Minnesota, September 1990.

223)   The Mariner: Ibid.

223)   Point Mary safe house: Bradley Earl Ayers, *The War That Never Was: An Insider's Account of CIA Covert Operations Against Cuba* (Bobbs-Merrill, 1976), 38.

223)   Belgian FAL assault rifles: Jack Anderson, "The Washington Merry-Go-Round," 1/18/71.

223–24)   At night, on at least: Interviews with Jack Anderson (Washington, D.C., June 1990), Joe Shimon, Tom Wadden, and Bradley Ayers. In *The Last Mafioso*, Ovid Demaris contradicts these accounts quoting Rosselli as telling Jimmy Fratianno, "This whole thing has been a scam. All these fucking wild schemes the CIA dreamed up never got further than Santo [Trafficante]. He just sat on it, conned everybody into thinking that guys were risking their lives sneaking into Cuba, having boats shot out from under them, all bullshit." That may well be what Rosselli told Fratianno, but there is too much evidence of concerted activity by the CIA and the Mafia, compiled by the Church Committee and augmented in the interviews cited above, to write off the entire episode as a scam. More likely, and consistent with his methods, Rosselli was buttressing his cover in his conversation with Fratianno, ensuring that even within the mob, stories of his collaboration with the CIA would be dismissed as rumor.

224)   "They'd go in and nothing": Shimon interview.

224)   "He went into detail": Wadden interview.

224)   When his V-20 was sunk: Les Whitten, notes from Rosselli interview,

January 1971, Department of Special Collections, Lehigh University. The notes show that Whitten was directed to ask Rosselli about the incident, but that Rosselli declined comment.

224) "Colonel" Rosselli: Ayers, *War That Never Was*, 38.

225) Harvey flew to Los Angeles: CC.IR.84.

225) Final meeting on June 20: FBI.FR 6/21/63, #92-3267-481.

225) Dearborn the principal in the plot: CC.IR.192.

226) "A friend of Batista": L. Gonzales-Mata, *Cygne* (Grasset, Paris, 1976), 92.

226) Diederich on Berry: Bernard Diederich, *Trujillo: The Death of the Goat* (Little, Brown, 1978), 54.

226) RFK on Dominican after Trujillo: CC.IR.215.

226) Subsequent internal CIA documents: Ibid.

226) "I do not recall": Ibid., 152.

227) "It was ridiculous": Telephone interview with Felix Rodriguez, Miami, April, 1990.

11. The End of It All

229) Marcello deportation: John H. Davis, *Mafia Kingfish: Carlos Marcello and the Assassination of John F. Kennedy* (McGraw-Hill, 1989), 90–93.

230) "Watch this": Telephone interview with Sheldon H. Sloan, attorney, Los Angeles, September 1989.

230) "Rosselli jokingly related": FBI.FR 3/12/63, #92-3267-439.

231) IRS was "murder": Ibid., 4/15/63, #92-3267-452.

231) Rosselli had "expressed disgust": Ibid., 11/9/63, #92-3267-530.

231) "Johnny always took everything": Interview with Susan Woods, Palm Springs, September 1989.

231) " 'Here I am' ": Michael Hellerman with Thomas C. Renner, *Wall Street Swindler* (Doubleday, 1977), 86.

232) Accardo on FBI: Antoinette Giancana and Thomas C. Renner, *Mafia Princess: Growing Up in Sam Giancana's Family* (Avon Books, 1985), 333.

232) "Tell everyone that": FBI.FR 2/2/62; Giancana file, FBI reading room.

232) "Information has been received": Memo from J. E. Hoover to Attorney General, 12/11/61; Giancana file, ibid.

232) Giancana was overheard: Memo from J. E. Hoover to Attorney General, 2/12/62; Giancana file, ibid.

232-33) "Did you go to Luciano's": The transcript of this taped conversation was not included in the material released to the authors by the FBI. It was published, however, in Giancana and Renner, *Mafia Princess*,

278–82, and in Kitty Kelley, *His Way: The Unauthorized Biography of Frank Sinatra* (Bantam, 1986), 320–22. The two versions differ in length and slightly in content; this is a composite, taken verbatim.

235) "Bobby kept talking": C. David Heymann, *A Woman Named Jackie*, (Lyle Stuart, 1989), 379.

235) "I can't stay": Kelley, *His Way*, 328.

236) "How I loved": William F. Roemer, Jr., *Roemer: Man Against the Mob* (Donald I. Fine, 1989), 261.

236) "Bobby pushed": John H. Davis, *The Kennedys: Dynasty and Disaster 1848–1984* (McGraw-Hill, 1985), 405.

236) "They know everything": HAR, JFK Exhibit F-629.

236) "With Kennedy": Ibid., Exhibit F-616.

237) "They should kill": Ibid., Exhibit F-630.

237) Jimmy Hoffa discussed: Dan E. Moldea, *The Hoffa Wars: Teamsters, Rebels, Politicians, and the Mob* (Paddington Press, 1978), 148–50.

237) Carlos Marcello described: As told to Ed Becker. The story was first published in Ed Reid and Ovid Demaris, *The Green Felt Jungle* (Pocket Books, 1963). Before the book was published, the FBI attempted to discredit Becker with Reid and to confiscate galley proofs of the book before publication. Becker related his encounter with Marcello to the FBI soon after the meeting, and well before the Kennedy assassination, but no action was taken by the Bureau. Former FBI agent Julian Blodgett, who was familiar with Becker at the time, corroborates Becker's account.

238) Trafficante made a similar declaration: George Crile III, "The Mafia, the CIA, and Castro", Washington *Post*, 5/16/76. See also, HAH.V.301-343, and JFK Exhibit F-603.

239) "It is important": CC.V.23.

240) Hoover and Jenkins: Ibid., 33.

240) Lou Harris found: David E. Scheim, *Contract on America: The Mafia Murder of President John F. Kennedy* (Shapolsky, 1988), 47.

241) Ruby ran errands: Warren Commission, Exhibit 1288.

241) Arrested and questioned: Scheim, *Contract*, 76.

241) "Largely a shakedown": Seth Kantor, *Who Was Jack Ruby?* (Everest House, 1978), 101.

241) "Exiled from Chicago": Ibid., 102.

241) Ruby arrested nine times: Ibid., 109.

241) Dallas Morning News Building: Scheim, *Contract*, 267.

241) Ruby was still there: Bernard Fensterwald, Jr., and Michael Ewing, *Assassination of JFK: Coincidence or Conspiracy?* (Zebra Books, 1977), 66. Fensterwald cites Warren Commission papers to show that Ruby first admitted carrying a gun the night of the assassination, and then recanted.

242) Sgt. Patrick T. Dean: G. Robert Blakey and Richard N. Billings, *The Plot to Kill the President* (Times Books, 1981), 321.

242) "I am now firmly of the opinion": *Newsweek,* 7/30/79.

242) "He never met": Blakey and Billings, *Plot to Kill,* 199.

243) "The evidence does not": Warren Commission, Appendix XVI.

243) Hoover disciplined FBI personnel: CC.V.4.

243) The CIA found itself: Blakey and Billings, *Plot to Kill,* 76–79; Arthur M. Schlesinger, Jr., *Robert Kennedy and His Times* (Ballantine, 1978), 662–63.

245) There were two meetings: William Scott Malone, "The Secret Life of Jack Ruby," in *New Times,* 1/23/78. Also, interview with Malone, Washington, D.C., May 1988. Malone still had the tape of his telephone conversation with the federal investigator, which he played for the authors.

245) Ruby chronology: Scheim, *Contract,* 239.

245) Lewis J. McWillie: Ibid., 101–2.

246) "Weiner was handling": Ibid., 104.

246) "The mob's favored": Kantor, *Who Was Jack Ruby?,* 30.

246) Weiner broke down: Scheim, *Contract,* 104.

247) Miller was implicated: Wallace Turner, *Gamblers' Money: The Force in American Life* (Houghton Mifflin, 1965), 240–42.

247) "I don't know": Scheim, *Contract,* 257.

247) Rosselli in Phoenix: FBI.FR 11/18/63, #92-3267-531.

247) Oswald and Banister: Anthony Summers, *Conspiracy* (McGraw-Hill, 1980), 324.

247–48) Rosselli at Camp Street: Ibid., 579.

248) "What I heard about Kennedy": Interview with Jimmy Starr, Phoenix, Arizona, September 1988.

248) Russell's story: *Robert Russell v. U.S. Department of Justice et al.,* U.S. District Court, Central California, Civil Case #88-03718.

248) FBI loses Rosselli: FBI agents spotted Rosselli in Las Vegas on November 19 (FBI.IS 11/29/63, #92-3267-539); he was next seen in Los Angeles on November 27 (FBI.IS 1/28/64, #92-3267-554). In the interim, Bureau field reports from Las Vegas show no contact; a report in Los Angeles on December 2 notes "no information indicating that Rosselli has been residing at his Los Angeles apartment during the past ten days" (#92-3267-541).

12. Keeping the Faith

249) Rosselli installed Campbell in hotel: Judith Campbell Exner with Ovid Demaris, *My Story* (Grove, 1977), 286.

250) At the urging of Dorothy Towne: Interview with Patricia Breen, Las Vegas, May 1989.

250)   The doorman spoke Italian: Interview with Ralph Manza, actor and Friars doorman, Torrey Pines, California, August 1990.

251)   "Buy the kid a silver cup": Interview with Jimmy Ullo, Los Angeles, November 1989.

251)   Maheu intimated to a business partner: Deposition of William J. Staten, *Maheu v. Hughes.*

251–52) Rosselli often dropped by: Interview with Jack Tobin, journalist, Los Angeles, May 1989.

252)   Christmas holiday with Maheu: Staten deposition, *Maheu v. Hughes.*

252)   Campbell announced to Rosselli: Interview with Betsy Duncan Hammes, Palm Springs, May 1990. LAPD detective Ed Lutes also said in an interview (Pasadena, March 1989) he had been told by a source that Exner's child was by Rosselli.

252)   Campbell and Cardillo at Disneyland: Statement of Mona Cardillo, Dade file.

252)   A religious film: FBI.FR 10/8/63, #92-3267-523.

253)   "Johnny and Sam": Exner and Demaris, *My Story,* 236.

253)   "Atlanta," Rosselli replied: Confidential interview.

254)   Friedman introduction: Statement of Harry Drucker, Dade file.

255)   Friars Club hustlers: John Kobler, "The (Million-Dollar) Sting at the Friars Club," *New York,* 7/21/75.

255)   Karl losses: Debbie Reynolds and David Patrick Columbia, *Debbie: My Life* (Pocket Books, 1988), 316.

256)   Friedman described a scheme: Statement of Maury Friedman, Dade file.

256)   Rosselli expected a share: Testimony of George Seach, *U.S. v. Maury Friedman et al.,* United States District Court, Central California, Criminal Case #67-1432.

256)   Rosselli and Ricky Jacobs: Richard Hammer and Joe Coffey, *The Vatican Connection* (Holt, Rinehart, and Winston, 1982), 98.

256)   Friedman and Rosselli business deals: Los Angeles *Times,* 2/25/72. *Times* story is on the arguments presented by Assistant U.S. Attorney Tom Kotoske.

257)   "Well, he's considered": Testimony of Maurice Friedman, Nevada Gaming Commission, 6/1/67.

258)   Shimon and Rosselli: Interview with Joe Shimon, Washington, D.C., August 1990.

259)   Salvatore Piscopo: The story of Piscopo's recruitment as an FBI informant was related in detail in an interview with George Bland, Aptos, California, January 1988.

261)   Rosselli case rejected: FBI.IS 11/29/63, #92-3267-539.

261)   The Bureau made its move: Ibid., 3/15/67, #92-3267-751. The FBI effort to turn John Rosselli was also detailed by attorney Jimmy Cantillon in a motion for dismissal filed in the Friars Club case. Separately, Rosselli's version of the story was recounted in a memo to J. Edgar

Hoover by CIA Director of Security Howard Osborn (5/18/66; memo released by CIA).

261) "This has nothing": Osborn memo.

261) "Go see my attorney": FBI.IS 3/15/67, #92-3267-751.

261) Flanking Rosselli: Cantillon filing.

262) "That's my mother": Osborn memo.

262) Rosselli met Edwards: Ibid.

262) Visit to Harvey: Ovid Demaris, *The Last Mafioso: The Treacherous World of Jimmy Fratianno* (Bantam, 1981), 233.

263) Rosselli's next stop: Ibid. Also, noted in FBI.IS 3/15/67, #92-3267-751. Also, recalled by Joe Shimon.

263) Dodge said: FBI.IS 3/15/67, #92-3267-751.

263) "So we'll be seeing you": Ibid.

263) Rosselli again called Edwards: Memo from Osborn to J. E. Hoover, 5/27/66 (memo released by CIA).

265) Garrison calls judges "sacred cows": William Turner, "The Garrison Commission on the Assassination of President Kennedy," *Ramparts*, January 1968.

265) Ferrie background: Much has been written about Ferrie. Perhaps the best treatment is John H. Davis, *Mafia Kingfish: Carlos Marcello and the Assassination of John F. Kennedy* (McGraw-Hill, 1989), passim.

265) Garrison's interest in Ferrie: Sandy Hochberg, James T. Valliere, *Garrison's Investigation, 1964–1969* (Pamphlet, Publishers Special Editions, 1969), 30 (on file with the Assassination Archive and Research Center, Washington, D.C.). The precise genesis of Garrison's investigation remains unclear. In his own books, Garrison places the date somewhere in the autumn of 1966. But when questioned by House Assassinations Committee investigator Mike Ewing in 1978, Garrison "gave a very vague answer," and "would not elaborate" (interview from 11/8/78; notes on file at the Assassination Archive).

266) Garrison on Ferrie's crime connections: Garrison interview by Mike Ewing. The notes read as follows: "It was pointed out that some people have noticed that each of Garrison's original key witnesses in his Kennedy probe had . . . been employed by Carlos Marcello at one time. When asked if he had ever noted this common association, Garrison stated that he had. He went on to state that at one point early in his investigation he had considered looking into a possible connection to the President's assassination involving Marcello, noting that Ferrie had been somewhat close to him. Garrison stated however that 'that trail didn't lead anywhere; we could find no leads' to pursue on it, and thus dropped the Marcello possibility."

266) *Look* magazine reported: Warren Rogers, "The Persecution of Clay Shaw," *Look*, 8/26/69.

266) Garrison was indicted: Boston *Herald American*, 9/28/73.

266) Garrison's subsequent interrogations: Rogers in *Life*.

266–67)   Melba Christine Marcades: HAR *Appendix*, Vol. X, 199–201. See also, Anthony Summers, *Conspiracy* (McGraw-Hill, 1980), 576–77.

267)   Garrison dispatched investigators: Bernard Fensterwald, Jr., and Michael Ewing, *Assassination of JFK: Coincidence or Conspiracy* (Zebra Books, 1977), 303–4.

267)   Trafficante to Las Vegas: FBI.FR 10/12/66; reviewed by the authors in the Trafficante file at the Assassination Archives in Washington, D.C.

268)   As Rosselli explained it: Edward Morgan twice described to government authorities his meetings with Rosselli: first to the FBI, on March 20, 1967 (FBI.FR 3/21/67; supplied to the authors by William Scott Malone); and the second time in 1978, in an interview with House Assassinations Committee investigators James Wolf and Michael Ewing (interview conducted 6/22/78, notes supplied to the authors by William Scott Malone).

269)   John Martino allegation: G. Robert Blakey and Richard N. Billings, *The Plot to Kill the President* (Times Books, 1981), 80.

269)   Rosselli and Anderson: Interview with Jack Anderson, Washington, D.C., June 1990.

269)   Pearson and Warren: CC.V.80.

270)   "He wanted to get": Ibid.

270)   No FBI investigation: Ibid., 82.

270)   Ferrie's death: Davis, *Mafia Kingfish*, 332.

270)   Del Valle's death: Fensterwald and Ewing, *Coincidence or Conspiracy*, 304.

270–71)   "Johnson's H-bomb": Jack Anderson, "Washington Merry-Go-Round," 3/3/67.

271)   "Exposed Cuba to invasion": HAR.182.

271)   Castro "anxious to establish": CC.IR.174.

271)   "I may have been a card": Anderson interview.

271)   The CIA report: CC.V.86.

271)   Kennedy reacted: Davis, *Mafia Kingfish*, 325.

272)   Rosselli met with Garrison: CIA Inspector General's report, published in HAH.IV.146. (Full citation: "Note that Garrison met with Rosselli in Las Vegas in March 1967.")

272)   "I have never even seen": Letter from Jim Garrison to Louis Sproesser, 12/30/85 (copy supplied to the authors by William Scott Malone).

272)   "I may be naïve": Sandy Smith, "The Mob," two-part series, *Life*, 9/1 and 9/8/67.

272)   "Particularly disturbing": HAR.191.

273)   "John Rosselli manipulated": Ibid., 182.

273)   "Why would a mafia don": Davis, *Mafia Kingfish*, 329.

273)   "A very real possibility": CC.IR.102.

273)   "Morgan did not know": House Assassinations Committee interview notes.

273) Long planned to call Maheu: Ibid. Several published accounts presume that Long intended to call Maheu and Rosselli in connection with the Dan Rowan wiretap incident, but that is refuted in the Morgan memo, was denied by Maheu in an interview, and was denied in an interview by Bernard Fensterwald, Jr., who served as counsel to Long's committee.

274) Marchetti has reported: Article by Victor Marchetti from *True*, quoted by Garrison, *On the Trail of the Assassins* (Sheridan Square, 1988), 234. See also, Summers, *Conspiracy*, 329.

274) Shimon, who attended: Shimon interview.

274) "They were putting words": Interview with Robert Maheu, Las Vegas, September 1990.

13. Final Scores

278) Rosselli, who knew Hughes personally: Interview with Robert Maheu, Las Vegas, September 1990.

278) Hughes had decided: Maheu testimony, *Maheu v. Hughes.*

278) RKO sale: Don Barlett and James B. Steele, *Empire*, 184–85.

278) "A person who had connections": Warren Hinkle and William Turner, *The Fish Is Red—The Story of the Secret War Against Castro* (Harper & Row, 1981), 28.

278) Hughes knew Rosselli "for many years": Maheu in *Maheu v. Hughes,* quoted in Don Barlett and James B. Steele, *Empire: The Life, Legend, and Madness of Howard Hughes* (Norton, 1979), 285.

278) Maheu contacted Rosselli: Maheu interview.

278) Submachine guns: Omar Garrison, *Howard Hughes in Las Vegas* (Lyle Stuart, New York, 1970), 65.

279) Maheu later denied: Maheu interview.

279) Rosselli and Breen: Interview with Joe Shimon, Washington, D.C., August 1990.

279) Patricia Breen recalled: Interview with Patricia Breen, Las Vegas, May 1989.

279) Call to Dalitz from Hoffa: Barlett and Steele, *Empire*, 286.

280) Before Dalitz' eviction notice: Deposition of Edward P. Morgan in *Maheu v. Hughes.*

280) Rosselli introduced Kolod to Maheu: Deposition of Moe Dalitz in *Maheu v. Hughes.*

280) Hughes would buy the rights: Barlett and Steele, *Empire*, 289.

281) Thomas "the hoodlum banker": Las Vegas *Review-Journal*, 12/31/64.

281) The bargaining went on: Barlett and Steele, *Empire*, 290.

281) Morgan's fee split: Morgan in *Maheu v. Hughes.*

282) The HNO was not: Barlett and Steele, *Empire*, 327.

282)   "One individual never": Testimony of Richard Ellis, in *Maheu v. Hughes*, quoted in Barlett and Steele, *Empire*, 328.

282)   A string of subsidiaries: Deposition of Susan Berry, HNO secretary, in *Maheu v. Hughes*.

282)   Maheu staffed the HNO: Barlett and Steele, *Empire*, 328.

282)   Morgan and Thomas: Ibid., 298.

283)   Greenspun was a special case: Deposition of Herman M. Greenspun in *Maheu v. Hughes*.

283)   "Mister D": Related by Hank Greenspun to Ed Becker.

283)   Bell distributed: Barlett and Steele, *Empire*, 339.

283)   Maheu joined: Garrison, *Hughes in Las Vegas*, 68.

283)   Rosselli and Burton: Morgan in *Maheu v. Hughes*.

284)   Meeting with Friedman: Patricia Breen interview.

284)   "As far as I know": Ed Reid and Ovid Demaris, *The Green Felt Jungle* (Pocket Books, 1963), 5–6.

284)   Laxalt on Hughes: Barlett and Steele, *Empire*, 305.

284)   "There were very few changes": Deposition of Harry Goodhart in *Maheu v. Hughes*.

284)   "These guys who have": Garrison, *Hughes in Las Vegas*, 68.

284)   Hughes' own internal auditors: Deposition of Cecil Bernard Simmons, casino manager, in *Maheu v. Hughes*.

284)   Even the best of them: Barlett and Steele, *Empire*, 367.

284–85) 1971 IRS audit: Michael Drosnin, *Citizen Hughes* (Bantam, 1986), 128.

285)   "We investigated": Ibid., 498–99.

285)   "Because he's a no-good": Barlett and Steele, *Empire*, 472–73. Hughes' bombast elicited a $17.5 million libel and slander suit filed by Maheu in Los Angeles. In 1974, a jury awarded Maheu a $2.8 million judgment, but the case was sent back for retrial on appeal. Hughes Tool Co. counterfiled, and the entire legal tangle remains in the courts.

285)   Bennett on Maheu: John Dean, *Blind Ambition* (Simon & Schuster, 1976), 69.

285)   "We can't even pay": Morgan in *Maheu v. Hughes*.

286)   "Rich people cheating": Interview with Gerald Uelmen, Santa Clara, California, February, 1988.

286)   "When he mentioned Rosselli": Interview with George Bland, Aptos, California, January 1988.

287)   Aggressive use of the grand jury: Interview with David Nissen, Santa Ana, California, August 1989.

287)   "Are you a person": Los Angeles *Times*, 8/26/67.

287)   "I still use this": Uelmen interview.

288)   "He must have": Los Angeles *Times*, 9/16/67.

288)   To produce Piscopo's name: Ovid Demaris, *The Last Mafioso: The Treacherous World of Jimmy Fratianno* (Bantam, 1981), 244.

289)   "Without Seach's testimony": Nissen interview.

289) Rosselli and the Seach hit: Demaris, *Last Mafioso*, 252.
289) Gale to DeLoach: FBI memo 1/30/68, #92-3267-897.
289) "Unnamed people in Washington": Nissen interview.
290) Rosselli visits Harvey in November: FBI memo 12/12/67, #92-3267-878.
290) And again in March: FBI memo 3/20/68, #92-3267-934.
290) "Subject gave a fill-in": Ibid.
290) Greco and Rosselli: Interview with Betsy Duncan Hammes, Palm Springs, May 1990.
291) "I never gave Rosselli": Los Angeles *Times*, 1/21/69.
291) "I never saw him smile": Nissen interview.
291) "Rosselli was a tough guy": Confidential interview.
291) "I'm a patriotic citizen": Bland interview.
291–92) Packet of references: Case file, *U.S. v. John Rosselli*, Federal District Court, Central California, Criminal Case #67-1432.
292) "He is a member": Los Angeles *Times*, 2/4/69.
292) Rosselli "stayed in the background": Ibid.
292) Rosselli a "genuine menace": Ibid.
292) Hall to Rosselli: INS Investigation Report, 5/24/68, INS File #A8-955-250.
293) "It was strange with Mother": Interview with Concetta Sacco, Boston, October 1989.
293) "Oh, what a reunion": Shimon interview.
293) A stop in Miami: Statement of Eloise McKnight, Dade file.
294) Rosselli joined his family: Concetta Sacco interview.
294) Rosselli approached HNO: New York *Times*, 2/25/77.
294) Sennes loan: Deposition of Frank Sennes in *Maheu v. Hughes*.
294) Cantillon was reeling: Interview with Joaun Cantillon, Los Angeles, April 1990.
294) Rosselli at grand jury: A chronology of Rosselli's grand jury appearances was logged in the Dade file.
295) "Rosselli would respond": Nissen interview.
295) Rosselli being "set up": Los Angeles *Times*, 5/15/70.
295) Rosselli surgery: Clinical record, Lompoc Federal Prison Camp, 6/7/73.
295) "They're trying to make": Dade file.
296) "I don't think John ever threw": Nissen interview.
296) Word went out from Wadden: Memo from CIA Security Chief Osborn to Director, CIA, 11/19/70.
296) Maheu in "complete agreement": Ibid.
296) "It was a peculiar arrangement": Interview with Jack Anderson, Washington, D.C., June 1990.
296–97) Trafficante not mentioned: Les Whitten, notes from Rosselli interview, January 1971, Department of Special Collections, Lehigh University.

297) "Locked in the darkest": "Washington Merry-Go-Round," 1/18/71.
297) Only official response: Memo from CIA Security Chief Osborn to CIA Executive Director-Comptroller, 2/15/72.
297) The only step taken: Memo from INS District Director George K. Rosenberg to INS Regional Commissioner, Southwest Region, 1/22/71.
298) Inmates once built a still: Interview with Lloyd Hooker, Bureau of Prisons, Washington, D.C., November 1990.
298) Rosselli began to fear: Shimon interview.
298) "Mystery Man CIA Chose": "Washington Merry-Go-Round," 2/23/71.
299) But when Marshall showed up: Telephone interview with Adrian Marshall, Miami, August 1990.
299) "The lawyer should not": Jimmy Breslin, "No CIA Brownie Points for Rosselli," Washington *Star*, undated clip, Assassination Archive files.
300) "They were letting": Interview with Les Whitten, Washington, D.C., May 1990.
300) "I sentenced": Breslin column, Washington *Star*.
300) "I will not dignify": Los Angeles *Times*, 6/8/71.
301) Judge Gray relented: *U.S. v. Rosselli*, Judgment filed 10/18/71.
301) "I happened to run into Smiley": Interview with Fred Black, Washington, D.C., September 1990.
301) Trafficante went out of his way: Statement of Jose Quintana, husband of Rosselli's niece; Dade file.
301) He "got everything": Hammes interview.
301) "John has been": Memo from Landscape Foreman to Treatment Team, Lompoc Federal Prison Camp, 5/14/73.
302) Rosselli took a room: Statement of Richard Widman, federal parole officer, Dade file.

14. The Wheel of History

304) Rosselli's first weeks: Statement of Richard Widman, federal parole officer, Dade file.
304) "We went out": Interview with Leslie Scherr, Washington, D.C., June 1990.
304) Hansen collared Foy: TRPB report, 12/4/73.
305) Meeting in Palm Springs: Statement, name withheld by authors, Dade file.
305) Rosselli abandoned the West Coast: Widman statement, Dade file.
305) Trafficante's solicitude: Interview with Joe Shimon, Washington, D.C., September, 1990.
305) Consorting with Trafficante: Statement of Edith Daigle, Dade file.

306)   "This entire affair": H. R. Haldeman with Joseph DiMona, *The Ends of Power* (Times Books, 1978), 38.

306)   "Richard Helms yelled": John Erlichman, *Witness to Power: The Nixon Years* (Pocket Books, 1982), 318.

307)   "One of the things": Andrew St. George in Warren Hinkle and William Turner, *The Fish Is Red—The Story of the Secret War Against Castro* (Harper & Row, 1981), 302.

307)   "It was so convoluted": Scherr interview.

308)   The CIA had approved: New York *Times*, 6/19/75.

308)   RFK had known: Ibid., 5/30/75.

309)   "The most infamous": Loch K. Johnson, *A Season of Inquiry: The Senate Intelligence Investigation* (University Press of Kentucky, 1985), 55.

309)   "The assassination inquiry": Ibid.

309)   "It is simply intolerable": Ibid., 46.

309)   "Everybody was concerned": Shimon interview.

310)   "He was startled": Scherr interview.

310)   "I come busting into": Interview with Tom Wadden, staff of Barbour/Langley Productions, for Jack Anderson TV special, "American Exposé: Who Murdered JFK?," aired 11/2/88.

311)   "Everybody knew he would be served": Telephone interview with David Bushong, Washington, D.C., June 1990.

311)   "They were planning": Telephone interview with Frederick Baron, San Francisco, April 1990.

312)   "His nonchalance really surprised me": Telephone interview with Gary Hart, Denver, February 1990.

312)   "I was especially intrigued": Telephone interview with Richard Schweiker, Washington, D.C., March 1990.

313)   "Mr. Rosselli, we've had CIA": Scherr interview.

313)   "There was a sense": Hart interview.

314)   "No facts": New York *Times*, 2/25/77.

314)   Rosselli denied discussing: CC.V.85.

315)   "He made no effort": Scherr interview.

315)   "I don't recall": Baron interview.

315)   "Rosselli was in great fear": Bushong interview.

315)   "Mafia Reported": New York *Times*, 2/25/77.

315)   "They were miles away": Telephone interview with David Walters, Miami, August 1990.

316)   Two Trafficante meetings: Quintana statement, Dade file.

316)   Rosselli's attorneys told authorities: Statement of Leslie Scherr, Dade file.

316)   "I didn't get anything": Bushong interview.

316)   "The 1975 and 1978 testimony": HAR.168.

317)   "There was very likely": Schweiker interview.

317)   Two weeks in April: Statement of Mona Cardillo, Dade file.

317)   Rosselli bumped into Foy: Interview with Madeline Foy O'Donnell, Los Angeles, February 1990.

317)   Met with Fred Black: Dade file. Black said in an interview he could not recall meeting Rosselli in Miami.

317)   Foy's *Exorcist* spin-off: Shimon interview.

317)   A treatment of the CIA plots: Interview with Johnny Lange, aka Johnny Longo, Los Angeles, May 1990.

318)   His one regular contact: Statements of Jose Quintana, Joann Quintana, Mona Cardillo, and Edith Daigle, Dade file.

318)   He called on Lou Lederer: Shimon, Black, and confidential interviews.

318)   Rosselli was "in high spirits": Statement of Carol Ann Hoover, Dade file.

318)   Rosselli L.A. trip: LAPD Intelligence Report, 6/1/76.

318)   "Johnny . . . be careful": Ovid Demaris, *The Last Mafioso: The Treacherous World of Jimmy Fratianno* (Bantam, 1981), 388–92.

318–19) "I would go down": Scherr interview.

319)   Palm Springs testimonial: LAPD Intelligence Report, 9/6/76.

319)   Rosselli made confession: Interview with Patricia Breen, Las Vegas, May 1989.

319)   He asked Joe Breen: New York *Times*, 2/25/77.

319)   "Definitely a social": Mona Cardillo statement, Dade file.

319)   "There was no business": Edith Daigle statement, Dade file.

319)   "Get out of Miami": Statement of Joe Shimon, Dade file.

320)   Beverly Hilton records: Dade file.

320)   According to Gage's source: New York *Times*, 2/25/77.

321)   Edith called Joe Daigle: Edith Daigle statement, Dade file.

321)   "If I'm ever missing": Joe Daigle statement, Dade file.

321)   Black placed three calls: Mona Cardillo, Shimon, Joe Daigle statements, Dade file.

322)   No trappings of power: Miami *Herald*, 8/11/76.

322)   "It was awful": Interview with Concetta Sacco, Boston, October 1989.

323)   "Deep down": Washington *Post*, 9/12/76.

323)   Baker and Inouye letter: Ibid., 8/11/76.

323)   Clarence Kelley responded: Ibid., 8/12/76.

323)   "Is it really": Ibid.

324)   The FBI would "investigate": New York *Times*, 8/13/76.

324)   "I can guarantee": Washington *Post*, 8/15/76.

324)   "The pictures of Rosselli": Hart interview.

325)   Hart detailed Rosselli's contacts: Dade file.

325)   Cagnina: Ibid.

326)   Fratianno later denied: Demaris, *Last Mafioso*, 388–92.

327)   Beginning around 1968: Henrik Kruger, *The Great Heroin Coup* (South End Press, 1980), passim.

328)   "Maybe ten years from now": Washington *Post*, 9/12/76.

INDEX